The Civil War Confiscation Acts

Reconstructing America Series
Paul A. Cimbala, *series editor*

1. Hans L. Trefousse
Impeachment of a President: Andrew Johnson, the Blacks, and Reconstruction.

2. Richard Paul Fuke
Imperfect Equality: African Americans and the Confines of White Ideology in Post-Emancipation Maryland.

3. Ruth Currie-McDaniel
Carpetbagger of Conscience: A Biography of John Emory Bryant.

4. Paul A. Cimbala and Randall M. Miller, eds.
The Freedmen's Bureau and Reconstruction: Reconsiderations.

5. Herman Belz
A New Birth of Freedom: The Republican Party and Freedmen's Rights, 1861 to 1866.

6. Robert Michael Goldman
"A Free Ballot and a Fair Count": The Department of Justice and the Enforcement of Voting Rights in the South, 1877–1893.

7. Ruth Douglas Currie, ed.
Emma Spaulding Bryant: Civil War Bride, Carpetbagger's Wife, Ardent Feminist–Letters, 1860–1900.

8. Robert Francis Engs
Freedom's First Generation: Black Hampton, Virginia, 1861–1890.

9. Robert F. Kaczorowski
The Politics of Judicial Interpretation: The Federal Courts, Department of Justice and Civil Rights, 1866–1876.

The Civil War Confiscation Acts

Failing to Reconstruct the South

John Syrett

Fordham University Press
New York 2005

Reconstructing America Series, no. 10
ISSN 1523-4606

Library of Congress Cataloging-in-Publication Data

Syrett, John, 1942–
The Civil War Confiscation Acts : failing to reconstruct the South / John Syrett.—1st ed.
p. cm.—(Reconstructing America, ISSN 1523-4606 ; no. 10)
Includes bibliographical references and index.
ISBN 0-8232-2489-9 (hardcover)
1. United States—History—Civil War, 1861–1865—Confiscations and contributions. I. Title. II. Reconstructing America (Series) ; no. 10.
E480.S98 2005
973.7′14—dc22 2005001347

Printed in the United States of America
07 06 05 5 4 3 2 1
First edition

To Catherine

Contents

Acknowledgements

This book began as a dissertation over 35 years ago when I was a graduate student at the University of Wisconsin. Professor Stanley I. Kutler suggested the topic and advised me along the way to its completion. Without his interest and advice on how to proceed, it probably would not have been finished. I was not the most persistent student, and his patience with me proved a blessing, both for the dissertation and my teaching thereafter. His extensive and honest criticism of my first chapters also helped me a great deal.

After graduating from Wisconsin, I focused my research on politics in the twentieth century, not constitutional history, and I thought about the confiscation acts only when I happened to read about the Civil War. In the fall of 1997 Professor Paul A. Cimbala of Fordham University wrote to ask if I would be interested in revising my dissertation for publication by Fordham University Press. I agreed, and in the spring of 1998 began my research into the archives that I had not looked at before. Professor Cimbala has been a wonderful supervisor of this project, and I am most grateful for his encouragement. He and Professor Randall M. Miller of St. Joseph's University also asked me to write an essay on the acts for *An Uncommon Time*, a book they edited on the Civil War. That proved a marvelous benefit for me, for I saw my work on the confiscation acts in print.

I would also like to thank the librarians who provided assistance during the two periods in which I worked on the topic. They were all unfailingly cooperative in helping me with the research. I should note that my research trips to Boston were particularly pleasant due to the kindness of my longtime friend Sally Fleschner.

Our sons, Nicholas and Timothy, helped me in numerous ways, and I am very grateful to them. It is a delight to be their father. My greatest debt is to Catherine, my wife, who has endured two bouts with the confiscation acts. In the first round, she helped type the manuscript and, as ever, made my writing more clear and concise. Catherine's contribution to the second round has been, if anything, more important. As before, she read the manuscript with great care and made countless improvements to my writing, most of which I had the wit to accept. And she endured my doubts with grace and humor.

And finally, I wish to thank the editorial staff at Fordham University Press.

—John Syrett

Introduction

In the summer of 1861, as slaves entered Union lines and the North faltered on the battlefield, Congress passed the First Confiscation Act, the text of which can be found in the appendix to this book. Proposed by Republican Senator Lyman Trumbull of Illinois, the first act meant to confiscate property, primarily slaves, used to aid the Confederacy. Although the act freed few if any slaves, in part because the administration did not press the military to enforce it, the measure reflected the frustration of many in the North over how to conduct the war. This concern increased when Lincoln, worried about the allegiance of the border states, rescinded General John C. Frémont's emancipation edict in Missouri in the fall of 1861. Three months later Trumbull introduced the Second Confiscation Act into the Senate. Following lengthy debates that mirrored the increasing division over the administration's war against the South, Congress passed the Second Confiscation Act (see the appendix) in the summer of 1862. It was intended to confiscate all property, including slaves and land, from supporters of the Confederacy. The money realized from the sale of confiscated property was supposed to defray the costs of war. In addition, confiscation's supporters expected that the land taken from the rebels would be distributed to freedmen and poor whites after the fighting ended. Many Republicans in Congress, but not Lincoln, hoped the measure would also destroy the planter class and submit the South to a thorough Reconstruction.

The First and Second Confiscation Acts were not effective, however. They were not well written, and they suffered from a number of significant compromises. As a result, the actual prospect that private property would be taken permanently from rebels did not last much beyond 1862. Lincoln and Attorney General Edward Bates also insured the acts were not vigorously implemented, although the president did use the second act to support his own executive emancipation. Nonetheless, the acts were important. The debates in Congress over their enactment help explain how the North, by the summer of 1862, came to support a harsh war against the South, the abolition of slavery and the arming of the freedmen, all of which seemed unlikely a year earlier. The confiscation acts and their weak enforcement also illuminate the reasons the North did not embrace a radical Reconstruction of the South or provide freed slaves the forty acres and a mule that became part of the mythology surrounding the post-war years. In the end, Congress's discussions of the second act may have been the most radical aspects of the two measures. Some observers, including later historians, mistakenly saw the confiscation acts as part of a plan to punish the South severely and provide the freedmen with land after the war. Others, during and after the war, used the threat of confiscation to raise fears about any possible Reconstruction. Lincoln certainly worried about the consequences of widespread confiscation and prevented the acts from successful implementation. Attorney General Bates therefore discouraged his subordinates from active enforcement of either act and insured that both the military and the Treasury Department were not significant participants in implementation, even though their presence in the South might have resulted in a wider seizure of property.

In the spring of 1864, Republicans tried but failed to repeal an 1862 joint resolution that denied permanent confiscation of property beyond the life of the rebel owner in question. Lincoln had threatened to veto the second act unless Congress agreed to this important limitation. Some historians have seen this as a failure of Republican coordination in 1864, but it actually demonstrated again the lack of support for land redistribution among Republicans that became so evident during Reconstruction. Long before the war ended, the Republican Party had moved away from the second act's slim promise of land for the freedmen to the free labor ideology that dominated Reconstruction and forced former slaves into manual laborers for southern whites after the war.

Ironically, it was Andrew Johnson who initiated the most sustained enforcement of the second act, but only after the fighting ended. Johnson's interest in confiscation did not arise from a wish to reconstruct the South, of course, and ended when he had satisfied his wish to punish the region's elite. He then began pardoning almost every rebel who applied for the privilege. Notwithstanding the efforts by some Freedmen's Bureau agents to distribute land to the freedmen, by 1866, under Johnson's orders, the small amount of property that had been confiscated was being returned to pardoned rebels, and the planter class began to regain its power. Thus, former slaves began their lives as freedmen without the benefit of the land they believed had been promised to them as the basis of their future. Whether the land so promised would have made a significant difference to their fortunes after the war is impossible to determine.

Despite the predictions of Congressmen who opposed confiscation and Lincoln's and Bates's apprehensions over some aspects of the measures, in the years following the war the Supreme Court consistently looked with favor upon the first and second acts. The Court's decisions on both procedural and substantive issues, with some notable exceptions, made it clear that Congress could have enacted far more sweeping confiscation measures. The Court assumed that, as a result of the war, Congress had the power to confiscate whatever property would assist the Union's cause and did not evince much concern about how the property was seized. The Republicans' failure to enact strong and effective confiscation measures demonstrates that the idea of land for freedmen was mostly the wish of a few, men like Trumbull, Thaddeus Stevens, and Charles Sumner. The Republicans dominated Congress throughout the war, yet they failed to write successful confiscation laws, monitor their implementation, or challenge Lincoln to enforce them. Nor did they include land provisions for freedmen in their Reconstruction measures as the war came to a close. In the end, the failure to reconstruct the South, to secure land for freedmen during the war, and to distribute it afterward rests with the Republicans in Congress, who raised the prospect of confiscation in 1861 and 1862 but did not deliver on their promises.

1 The First Confiscation Act

Samuel Gridley Howe and other abolitionists believed that with the firing on Fort Sumter, God had "opened the way" for the emancipation of the slaves and the subjugation of the "Slave power."[1] This, to be sure, was a view only a small minority shared when the Civil War began on April 12, 1861. Most in the North, including President Abraham Lincoln, hoped that the war would soon be over and the Union restored with little pain and suffering. While hundreds of thousands quickly volunteered to fight, few in the North welcomed the war, and probably even fewer predicted that it would end with the abolition of the peculiar institution and the destruction of the Old South.[2]

Many factors contributed to this dramatic transformation of the war. These included the First and Second Confiscation Acts, introduced by Senator Lyman Trumbull of Illinois and passed by Congress in August 1861 and July 1862.[3] The forces that led to their introduction and passage illustrate how the struggle evolved from an effort to restore the Union to the abolition of slavery and the arming of former slaves. Advocates of confiscation wanted to emancipate the slaves, punish those who waged war against the North, and lay the foundation for Reconstruction, whereas opponents argued that the acts were excessive and unconstitutional. The failure of these measures to realize their sponsors' goals also illustrates how confused and moderate Congress was in its efforts to reform the South during the war. Moreover, the interaction of the military, the public, Congress, escaped slaves, and President Lincoln, through the passage of the confiscation acts, demonstrates how difficult it was to win the war, restore the Union, and simultaneously provide a remedy for the American dilemma of race. Even though the confiscation acts helped push Lincoln to embrace emancipation, they did not achieve their intended aims.[4]

After the fall of Fort Sumter, Lincoln emphasized to both North and South that the Union would try to "avoid any devastation, any destruction of, or interference with, property, or any disturbance of peaceful citizens in any part of the country."[5] This conciliatory policy underscored the widespread belief

---

A different version of chapter one appeared as "The Confiscation Acts: The North Strikes Back" in *An Uncommon Time: The Civil War and the Northern Home Front*, ed. Paul A. Cimbala and Randall M. Miller (New York: Fordham University Press, 2002), 280–325.

that most Southerners would not follow the leaders of secession and that support for the Union existed in the South. It was also meant to reassure the border states, particularly Kentucky, that they should remain loyal. Some, however, and not just abolitionists, worried that peace might come before "that arrogance and starch" was "taken out of all traitors," as one constituent wrote Trumbull. On the eve of Fort Sumter, an Ohio man even advocated a "war of Extermination" against "the white population of South Carolina Georgia Alabama and Florida" and demanded that freed slaves be given the confiscated estates of rebels.[6] Such appeals for a wider war than Lincoln contemplated remained in the background, however, as the North prepared for what most assumed would be a relatively swift victory. As Edward Everett, the celebrated Massachusetts orator, reassured a friend in the South, the president "has always professed an intention to respect your rights and your property."[7]

Problems arose, however, when the Union forces encountered slavery in the Confederacy. Fugitive slaves entering federal lines caused the first major dilemma. General Benjamin F. Butler of Massachusetts, a volatile Democratic politician, created a controversy at Fortress Monroe, Virginia, in late May, when, according to Butler, three slaves "delivered themselves up to" his pickets. Rather than return them, Butler kept the "property," put them to work for the Union, and sent a receipt to the owner. Three days later he began employing those "able-bodied persons" who came into Union lines. By the end of May Secretary of War Simon Cameron, and thereby Lincoln, had given approval to this "contraband" policy. It rested on the assumption that such fugitive slaves would otherwise be used to aid the rebellion. As such, it anticipated the First Confiscation Act. While many saw Butler's move as radical, others realized that describing the fugitives as "property" meant the policy was, in fact, consistent with the Supreme Court's decision on *Dred Scott*, which the Republicans had vigorously opposed.[8]

Butler's decisions raised crucial issues. Should the North allow the Confederacy to use slaves to aid the rebellion? If not, how should it handle fugitives? What should the Union forces do when slaves, such as women and children, unable to work for the rebels, entered their lines? What status did they acquire once inside the Union lines? By late July more than nine hundred contrabands had arrived at Fortress Monroe. They also had captured the North's attention.[9] But the administration made no effort to offer a policy despite Cameron's promise to Butler in late May that the "question of their final disposition will be reserved for further determination." In fact, generals were allowed to respond as they saw fit; some turned fugitives away, whereas others returned them to their owners, especially if those owners were loyal. One general, George

McClellan, promised to "crush any attempt at insurrection on their [slaves'] part."[10]

Lincoln's delay in calling Congress into session until July 4 prevented it from responding to the issue that Butler and other generals increasingly confronted. Nor did the president allude to the contraband question in his first message to Congress on that date; he did not even mention slavery. Instead, he saw "much reason to believe that the Union men are the majority in many, if not" all the seceded states. And he believed, "*after* the rebellion had been suppressed," that he "would probably" have "no different understanding" of the federal powers over the states than before Fort Sumter. Reconstruction would doubtless, therefore, be swift and leave slavery intact. On July 9, however, the House passed a nonbinding resolution that Union soldiers did not have to "capture and return fugitives slaves." It also began consideration of Trumbull's first confiscation bill, introduced on July 15.[11]

It is unclear what prompted the Illinois senator to offer his measure, but he was not the first to suggest the idea. Trumbull had been among the few to vote against the Crittenden-Johnson resolutions in late July, which stipulated that Congress would not overthrow or interfere with domestic institutions during the war. Confiscation of loyalist property had occurred in the Revolution, of course, and this may well have been an inspiration, even if the circumstances were different.[12] The Confederate Congress, by late May, had already authorized the confiscation of debts due to Northerners. Doubtless Butler's actions at Fortress Monroe also played a part. As well, Secretary of the Treasury Salmon P. Chase and three members of Congress had proposed confiscation measures. Congress had also received petitions from citizens urging confiscation. In need of money, Chase had proposed that "the property of those engaged in insurrection or in giving aid to insurgents may properly be made to contribute to the expenditures made necessary by their criminal misconduct." Senator Zachariah Chandler of Michigan wanted funds from seizures used to restore the property of Southern Unionists, while Senator Henry Wilson of Massachusetts urged property confiscated from all those who aided the rebellion. Representative Dwight Loomis of Connecticut introduced a bill similar to Chandler's to confiscate the property of Confederate leaders.[13]

Whatever the inspiration, Trumbull introduced his bill on July 15. It contained three parts and was less severe than those offered by Chandler and Loomis. Part one said that if any person permitted his or her "property" to be used "in aiding, abetting, or promoting insurrection" against the United States, "all such property" would "be lawful subject of prize and capture wherever found," and the president was to have it "seized, confiscated and condemned." Importantly, Trumbull referred to the fighting as an insurrection, not a war.

The law, therefore, would exercise the sovereign powers of the government, not the war powers. This meant that all seizures would be in the nature of capture as prize, whether by civil or military officers, regardless where found. Trumbull also spoke of "property," thus excluding slaves, unless one agreed with the South's view of slavery. The bill's second part said that "such prizes and captures" were to be prosecuted in the district or circuit courts where the property was seized. All actions in court would be in rem, not in personam, which meant that the property could be prosecuted without the owner's presence, as was true under revenue laws. The third part said that criminal acts, not the treasonous conduct of the owner, would be the basis for condemnation and sale of property. Whereas the Constitution forbade the forfeiture of property beyond the life of a convicted traitor—in the prohibition against bills of attainder in article three, section three—the property was guilty under the first act and title to it could be transferred indefinitely. It was not clear, however, that the legislators understood these issues clearly in 1861. There certainly was confusion over the same questions when Congress discussed the second act in 1862.[14]

The disaster at Bull Run, seven days after Trumbull introduced his measure, altered his view of confiscation. Reports that some rebels had used slaves to assist them in battle prompted an amendment from Trumbull to include "persons" used to assist the rebellion. His bill now declared that whoever claimed "the service or labor of any other person, under the laws of any State," to further the insurrection would lose the rights to such a person. The Senate accepted the bill as amended. Only those from border states voted against it. The House, however, limited Trumbull's amendment so that only slaves used to aid the Confederate military were liable to seizure. The House then passed the bill 60–48. The Senate concurred with this change; Trumbull, oddly enough, thought the change unimportant. The Senate vote was 24–11. The House discussed the bill a bit more than the Senate, but neither spent much time on the first act, particularly when compared to the lengthy debates over the second act. One Republican Senator opposed it; seven Republicans in the House did so. It passed on August 3, and the president signed it shortly thereafter with some reluctance, according to the *New York Times*, because he realized its potential impact.[15]

Senate conservatives also expressed alarm at the supposed breadth of Trumbull's bill. John Breckinridge, Democrat from Kentucky, thought such a measure would lead "to a general confiscation of all property, and loosing of all bonds." In a superb understatement, James Pearce of Maryland predicted that the law would irritate the South; those directing the South's court system, he warned, would not implement it. To create other courts for its implementation would be unconstitutional, he claimed.[16] In the House, John Crittenden,

Unionist from Kentucky, said Congress could not legislate on the matter. War conferred no new powers upon the government, he argued. In addition, the previous Congress had agreed, in resolutions bearing his name, not to interfere with slavery in the states. Moreover, he claimed the bill violated the Constitution by providing for forfeiture beyond the offender's life, an issue that would plague discussions of the second act too. He predicted the South would see the war, wrongly, as antislavery. Only Thaddeus Stevens of Pennsylvania attempted to refute arguments against the bill. If constitutions contradicted the laws of war, said Stevens, they should be ignored. Nor could Crittenden and others use the Constitution to protect those who had left the Union. "Sir, these rebels, who have disregarded and set at defiance that instrument, are, by every rule of municipal and international law, estopped from pleading it against our action." But, in the end, Stevens cared little how one rationalized the use of confiscation. He wanted results, declaring "if their whole country must be laid waste, and made a desert, in order to save this Union from destruction so let it be." Like supporters of the second act, Stevens saw the first as a military measure, not as a means to abolition. In conclusion, he warned the South that if the war continued, the North would arm their slaves against them.[17]

Compared to the lengthy debates over the second confiscation act, the first act received very little discussion in Congress. Almost no serious consideration occurred in the Senate and the House only gave part of a day to a heated discussion of it. There were several reasons for this limited attention. The challenges facing Congress in the summer of 1861 precluded lengthy discussions on most matters, particularly those, like the first act, that did not address winning the war, the paramount issue for most. The legal issues in the bill were also complex. Moreover, as House Republican Alexander Diven (N.Y.) in the House noted, the bill would be civil law, "to be executed, if executed at all, by civil process." Most members assumed with Diven that only the military could change the South and not until they won on the battlefield. The first act implied action taken against the South after the military began defeating the rebels, which did not seem imminent after Bull Run. Most assumed, as well, that the first act was meant to assist the military.[18]

However brief the discussion of the first act, it did raise concerns that would reappear in consideration of the second act. Representative George Pendleton, an Ohio Democrat, asked the vexing question of what to call the fighting. If a state of war existed, then the rebels were public enemies and must be treated "with the laws of war as prescribed by the law of nations." If, on the other hand, they were still citizens, then they were engaged in rebellion and were subject "to all the penalties which attach to them by the law of treason" along with all the rights. In no case, he argued, should they be treated by a double standard where

Congress confiscated their property under the laws of war and also prosecuted them for treason under the Constitution.[19] When Representative William Kellogg, an Illinois Republican, argued that rebels' slaves could be confiscated, like their horses, as a consequence of treason, Crittenden observed that the confiscated could not then be forfeited beyond the life of the offender; otherwise it would violate the attainder clause of the Constitution.[20] However, these problems did not receive much attention in the brief consideration given to the first act.

The limited reach of the first act also illustrates the caution of Congress in the summer of 1861. Even after the disaster of Bull Run had demonstrated how difficult it would be to crush the rebellion, Congress did not go very far either to punish those loyal to the Confederacy, even in the North, or to strike at slavery. Slaves used in military labor or service in support of the rebellion did not go free under the first act; those claiming their services—the owners—simply forfeited their claim to them. Thus the first act only confiscated slaves if directly employed in the rebellion. The only liberty granted them was not to remain slaves of rebels; Congress did not indicate how this would be carried out. Any property liable to confiscation under the first act had to be proceeded against in the "district or circuit court," which left out almost all property inside the Confederacy.[21] Some outside of Congress realized how narrow the blow made against slavery had been and urged more. As many noted during the first two years of the war, Congress lagged behind the public's wish to strike more directly at the Confederacy, its leaders and slavery. E. F. Bullard, for example, wrote Secretary of War Simon Cameron in late August that "the *People* are far ahead of them [the politicians] and would say amen to the banner of emancipation." He went on to urge that the freed slaves be encouraged to remain in the South. The passage of two measures in August by the Confederate Congress also drew attention in the North. The first measure, the Alien Enemies Act of August 8, demanded that all aliens leave the South and be treated as enemies or become citizens of the Confederacy. The second law, the Sequestration Act of August 30, which chastised the North for "confiscating and destroying the property of people of the Confederate States," called for the confiscation of all property belonging to aliens as of May 21. A day later Trumbull observed that the North "must mete out to secessionists the same measure they deal out to Union men. Then it will be as hazardous for a man to be against as for the Union, & then we will have friends in the South."[22]

"Antislavery men will soon be after you with ballots," John B. Wood scolded Trumbull from Kansas. Why would not Congress "use all of the means which the law of nations" allowed "to cripple" the Confederacy? "Slavery must be abolished if we are to have a permanent peace," he concluded. Thomas G.

Shearman of New York also rebuked Trumbull for the narrow constitutional footing of the bill, noting that secession had reduced the former states to territories "governable by Congress." "I trust the next session will find Congress prepared to take even broader ground" and thus abolish slavery. From Philadelphia M. J. Thomas exploded at moderate Senator John Sherman: "Can it be that *nobody* wishes to abolish Slavery, that great over-shadowing crime of our nation, unless 'forced' so to do?" N. J. Marble, one of hundreds who wrote for an appointment in the military, also urged Senator Ben Wade of Ohio to "present a bill to congress at its next session . . . to abolish slavery in all the states and territories." There were also many in the North who agreed with an anonymous Trumbull correspondent who urged abolition by confiscation but linked it to the colonization of former slaves.[23] This plea for colonization reflected widespread racism in the North among Republicans, not to mention Democrats. Even so, those writing congressmen were alarmed at how timid Congress seemed to be. It is ironic, then, that some antislavery men were much more optimistic. Charles Sumner wrote to Wendell Phillips in early August about the demise of slavery: "Be tranquil. . . . The battle & retreat [of Bull Run] have done much for the slave. . . . I told the Prest. that our defeat was the worst event and the best event . . . the best as it made the extinction of slavery almost inevitable." In late August Thomas Wentworth Higginson was "satisfied that we are gravitating towards a bolder anti-slavery policy. The desideratum is to approach a policy of emancipation by stages so clear & irresistible as to retain for that end an united public sentiment."[24] Only Congress and the president had to catch up with the majority of Republican thinking.

In late August a direct attack upon slavery and for confiscation came from the military in Missouri. On August 30 General John C. Frémont, the Republican presidential nominee in 1856, declared martial law throughout the state, confiscated the property of rebels, and freed their slaves. The reasons for this dramatic move were complex and the aftermath important for the war's course. Missouri was probably the most violently divided state over the Civil War at this time. Guerilla bands operated in some parts and many residents openly sympathized with the Confederacy. Governor Hamilton R. Gamble, for example, announced in early August that no "scheme" or "conduct" that interfered with Missouri slavery would be allowed. At first Frémont had enjoyed the support of Frank Blair Jr., the most powerful Unionist politician in the state, whose brother Montgomery was the postmaster general in Lincoln's cabinet. But military reverses, mismanagement, jealousy, and poor judgment led the Blairs to believe that Frémont should be replaced. Frémont felt considerable pressure in August and even closed down several St. Louis newspapers critical of him, including one that supported the North. Perhaps to bring order from military and political confusion, Frémont, without consulting Lincoln or Cameron, impetuously issued his proclamation. The pivotal part said that the "property, real and personal" of all who took up arms against the United States "is declared to be confiscated to public use, and their slaves . . . are hereby declared freemen."[25] Frémont's proclamation, if implemented, would have gone well beyond the First Confiscation Act and it anticipated the second act, which was not passed until July 1862.

Reactions to this sweeping declaration were revealing. Many Northerners, and not just abolitionists and New Englanders, were delighted. Secretary Cameron, before talking with Lincoln, expressed his approval. Lincoln's friend Senator Orville Browning of Illinois supported Frémont's proclamation, too. Throughout the North, the Republican press applauded the general's proclamation, as did many conservatives. Both the *Missouri Democrat* and *Missouri Republican* endorsed Frémont's freeing of the slaves. Even James G. Bennett's *New York Herald*, often sympathetic to the South, hailed the decision; so too did the frequently Democratic *Philadelphia Ledger*. Abolitionists, naturally, were jubilant. Harriet Beecher Stowe proclaimed, "The hour has come, and the man!" William Lloyd Garrison thought it was "the beginning of the end" while Gerrit Smith wrote a public letter to Lincoln to applaud the general. Even Massachusetts Governor John Andrew broke his self-imposed silence on the slavery question to say that Frémont gave "an impetus of the grandest character to the whole cause" of emancipation. Not surprisingly, the border-states were upset. Secretary Chase of the Treasury received two alarmed reports. From Louisville, Joshua Speed, an old acquaintance of the President from Springfield, said that the Union men opposed the proclamation since it went "beyond the power conferred by the [Confiscation] Act of Congress." He and others had argued all over the state that "this was [not] to be a war upon slavery." He implored Chase to urge a reconsideration of the issue and "for God's sake dont allow us to be turned over to the enemy." From Frankfurt, Garrett Davis, an important Unionist, noted it "caused me despondence for the first time for Ky." Newspapers throughout Kentucky also attacked the proclamation.[26] Lincoln, too, worried about the effect of Frémont's proclamation.

The president wrote a polite letter to the ambitious and mercurial general two days after the proclamation's publication in the East. He asked Frémont to "modify" his proclamation to conform to the First Confiscation Act, a copy of which he included. The threat to confiscate "property" and liberate the "slaves of traitorous owners will alarm our Southern Union friends," Lincoln observed, "and turn them against us—perhaps ruin our rather fair prospect for Kentucky." He closed by noting that he wrote "in a spirit of caution and not censure." A special messenger was dispatched with the letter for speedy delivery to the general. Frémont, however, did not accept the president's advice. His reply admitted that he had acted "without consultation or advice with anyone," relying on "my best judgment to serve the country" and the president. But if Lincoln did not approve of "the liberation of the slaves, I have to ask that you will openly direct me to make a correction." For Frémont to change his proclamation on slavery would "imply that I myself thought it was wrong," which he did not. "I acted with full deliberation, upon the certain conviction that it was a measure right and necessary, and I think so still." Jessie Frémont, a strenuous defender of her husband, delivered the letter in person to Lincoln on September 10, the night she arrived from St. Louis. Their memories differed on what each said, but she was probably correct in believing that the president had already made up his mind.[27]

The next day Lincoln amended Frémont's proclamation to conform to the First Confiscation Act, thereby setting off a howl of protest throughout the North. He began by conceding that Frémont, "upon the ground" in Missouri, was in the best position to determine if martial law was required. However, the "particular clause" relating "to the confiscation of property, and the liberation of slaves, appeared" to Lincoln "objectionable, in its non-conformity" to the first act. So he "cheerfully" accepted Frémont's invitation to modify it. The following day Lincoln informed Jesse Frémont that he had answered her husband's letter but did not divulge the contents. He nonetheless entered his "protest against being understood as acting in any hostility towards him."[28] Most Northerners believed the President's decision was deplorable for reasons of principle. Only Democrats and border state Unionists were pleased.

The protest against Lincoln's letter to Frémont was loud and extreme. For many, Lincoln's decision revealed the central place that slavery now occupied in the battle to defeat the Confederacy. In that light, the Frémont episode certainly assisted the antislavery cause. Frederick Douglass, for example, believed that Lincoln meant to appease the defenders of slavery in the border states by revoking Frémont's order. The controversy made clear that the public, through Congress, would have to play a central role, as would the slaves themselves. As Sumner wisely observed to Wendell Phillips, the *London Times* was "right. We cannot subdue the rebels. But their strength [slavery] will give us the victory at last." To Francis Lieber, soon to write an important work on the rules of war, Sumner wrote that "slavery shall only be touched by Act of Congress & *not through Martial law*. This weakens our armies." Others agreed with Sumner that Congress now had to take the lead, because Lincoln was incapable of seeing the will of the public. A Brooklyn resident wrote to Michigan Senator Zachariah Chandler that "Congress must complete the work it has begun. . . . There has been a great change within sixty days upon that confiscation or more properly stated emancipation act." Senator Wade of Ohio shared the low opinion of Lincoln. Like others, he noted that Lincoln's decision had been "universally condemned and execrated in the north," and he thought this "tenderness to the slave holders of old Kentucky has done more to demoralize us than all things else." Two weeks later Wade despaired of ever "putting down this rebellion through the instrumentality of this Administration."[29]

There were many, particularly in the border states, who thought Lincoln acted properly. And they were right; the time was not ripe for emancipation, at least not through the military without authority from Congress. However, some of Lincoln's closest allies, even in Illinois, remained upset and unable to appreciate his logic. Joseph Medill, the *Chicago Tribune* editor, claimed the reaction in Chicago was more severe than over the news of Bull Run. The penalty for the rebellion of a slaveholder should be "the confiscation and liberation of his slaves: This strikes at the root of the disease." If this revocation was meant to "placate" those in Kentucky, Medill predicted it would have the opposite effect. Men "ask each other, 'what are we fighting for'. . . . Our Democrats are in agony as much as our Republicans," he concluded. More significantly, Senator Browning, a good friend of Lincoln objected. The president replied to his friend at some length, noting that it astonished him that Browning "should object to my adhering to a law [the first act], which you" supported. On the question of principle, had Frémont's proclamation been "within the range of *military* law," and not "*purely political*," Lincoln would have approved. But no such seizure should last beyond the military need; that "must be settled according to law" made by Congress. Indeed, he believed Congress might "pass such a law . . . just such as Frémont proclaimed," one he "might" vote for if he were in Congress. However, he objected to Frémont's request that the president "exercise the permanent legislative functions" of government. As for policy, he realized that Frémont's proclamation was popular "in some quarters" but threatened Kentucky, which was crucial. "I think to lose Kentucky is nearly the same as to lose the whole game." If Kentucky went, he doubted Missouri or Maryland would stay. That would make "the job on our hands . . . too large for us."[30] Lincoln understood that Congress might consider a more vigorous confiscation law and appreciated the growing sentiment for an attack upon slavery, but he doubted the public was ready to accept emancipation. In effect, he challenged the "lawmakers" to act first. It was a wise strategy in the fall of 1861, since most in the military refused to embrace even a vigorous policy on fugitive slaves.[31]

The First Confiscation Act, after all, had been a weak blow against both slavery and the Confederacy by those who now applauded Frémont and attacked Lincoln. The clamor only increased when, in late October, Lincoln relieved "the

Pathfinder" of command in Missouri. Critics eager to link Lincoln's decision in early September with the removal did so, but the connection was tenuous. It overlooked the many problems that informed people, including Trumbull, admitted the general's leadership had tolerated or spawned. Lincoln realized that removing Frémont might create a political martyr and renew criticism of his revocation of the general's proclamation in September, but he had no choice. At the same time, Frémont's removal doubtless led other generals to be more cautious about confiscating property and receiving fugitive slaves. Moreover, Lincoln made no effort to implement the First Confiscation Act then or later.[32]

As the military advanced, it was clear that that most generals felt that they should or could do little under the first act. In part this reflected the confusion over the ambiguous instructions the War Department sent to General Butler just after the act passed. In late July he had asked Secretary Cameron for guidance in handling the nine hundred fugitive slaves inside his lines. Cameron subsequently replied that the first act "discharged" from service those "persons" employed against the United States and that the military should not recognize any claim to their services by disloyal masters. However, the act did not cover "persons escaping from the service of loyal masters." Nonetheless, Butler should receive both class of fugitives "into the service of the United States" and keep "a record" of all slaves who entered his lines. When peace returned, "Congress will doubtless properly provide for all the persons thus received into" the Union's service, from loyal or disloyal masters. The letter closed with an admonition that no troops interfere with the "servants of peaceful citizens," "encourage" them to leave their service, or "prevent" their return "to the service from which" they perhaps escaped. General John E. Wool, Butler's successor in August, interpreted this policy in a generous light, welcoming fugitives into his lines. Many Virginia slaves took advantage of this changed climate to move to Union lines, particularly in Maryland, which greatly troubled slave owners there. Later that fall, however, other generals, such as John A. Dix, William T. Sherman, Don Carlos Buell, and George McClellan, displayed more caution in receiving fugitive slaves.[33]

These generals pursued a more conciliatory policy, which meant more promises of protection for property and the return of fugitive slaves. Dix received command of a department, which included Maryland's Eastern Shore and Virginia, in late July. Confederate sympathy worried him. In mid-November, Dix wrote Lincoln that residents of the area "had got it into their heads that we want to steal and emancipate their negroes; and by giving them the strongest assurances" this was not so, he hoped they would not bend toward the Confederacy. The officer implementing the orders would have "a copy" of the first act, and, Dix added, "I have instructed him to enforce the provisions as far as practicable." Dix's proclamation went further than this, however. It said that Union troops "will invade no rights of person or property" unless attacked. "On the contrary, your laws, your institutions, your usages will be scrupulously respected." Indeed, Dix gave orders "not to permit any such persons [slaves] to come within their lines." The orders were apparently well executed.[34] This was certainly a less aggressive approach than Cameron had authorized or Trumbull had expected in writing the first act, but it reflected Lincoln's wishes.

After the Frémont revocation, generals in Kentucky followed policies that protected the property of all citizens, regardless of past sympathies. Lincoln appointed Brigadier General Robert Anderson, native son and hero of Fort Sumter, who proclaimed in late September that henceforth any residents who did not aid the Confederacy would be protected. When Anderson had to quit after a few weeks, his successor, Brigadier General William T. Sherman, adopted much the same policy. He informed an officer that troops should adhere to Kentucky laws; fugitive slaves therefore would "be delivered up on claim of the owner or agent," without apparent regard to the first act. To another subordinate, Sherman said it was "better to keep the negroes out of your camp altogether, unless you brought them along with the regiment." In November McClellan replaced Sherman with General Don Carlos Buell and instructed him that "we shall most readily suppress this rebellion . . . by religiously respecting the constitutional rights of all." His loathing of abolitionists predisposed Buell to this opinion. McClellan further asserted that the president agreed that "we are fighting only to preserve the integrity of the Union," which meant the "domestic institutions" in Kentucky would "receive at our hands every constitutional protection." General Henry Halleck, whose authority stretched into western Kentucky, also denied entry into Union lines to all fugitive slaves.[35]

It is unlikely that many fugitive slaves knew of these orders. In any case, they came to the Union lines in significant numbers. Most were males and most came to escape slavery. If refused entry, many camped nearby. Some soldiers admitted them despite orders. When masters came to retrieve slaves, the military generally tried to assist their return, as in Kentucky and Florida. But it was a complicated process, particularly if masters claimed to be loyal even as slaves reported that they had been required to labor for the Confederacy. It is impossible to know how many slaves approaching Union lines knew about the first act, but some clearly did; others learned about it once contact had been made. The complexities of the slave issue certainly became more apparent when Union troops advanced beyond the border states.[36]

In November 1861 Union troops occupied islands on the South Carolina coast around Port Royal Sound. Orders from the War Department required them to safeguard property rights and "avoid all interference with" slavery and other "local institutions." The soldiers soon discovered the masters had fled while their slaves, having refused to accompany them, remained. They were, at least for the moment, former slaves. As Union control broadened, troops came into contact with more abandoned slaves whose masters had clearly been sympathetic to the Confederacy. General Thomas W. Sherman had been authorized to employ in service "any persons, whether fugitive labor or not," but he showed no inclination to do so. Others were not so reluctant. At the same time Union officers in Florida accepted owners' claims that they had been loyal and sometimes paid them what fugitives in service to the Union earned. Some even helped owners capture fugitives. As was true in the border states, a patchwork policy toward fugitives emerged in South Carolina and Florida by late 1861.[37]

Attorney General Edward Bates also contributed to the cautious enforcement of the first act. A former Whig from Missouri, who was originally from Virginia, Bates was sixty-eight in 1861. While he thought blacks inferior, he did believe slavery to be wrong. And, like many others, he assumed colonization was the best solution to the problem of race. Once in office Bates persuaded Congress to expand his office and responsibilities. Trumbull introduced his bill, which passed just days before the first act. It authorized the attorney general to supervise and direct all United States and territorial district attorneys and marshals. Whereas in the past they had been under direction of the secretary of the interior, now they would report to Bates and be under his authority. Even so, Bates continued to believe that other departments of the government were trying to interfere with his authority. The bill also allowed Bates to hire badly needed staff. Despite his enlarged powers, however, or perhaps because of the newly elevated status his office now possessed, Bates acted with considerable restraint on confiscation and most other issues. He often, for example, asked district attorneys for advice about how to proceed on legal matters, rather than offer directions himself.[38] Bates's conservative attitude toward confiscation also, of course, reflected Lincoln's view of the first act.

Lincoln apparently had no wish to implement the first act. No record exists that Lincoln spoke to Bates about the measure until January 1863, six months after the second act had been passed, when the president formally authorized Bates to enforce the act of August 6, 1861. Although the greatest amount of confiscable property lay in the South and was only accessible when the military restored federal authority, the first act permitted the seizure of property, real and personal, in the North owned by rebels if it was used to aid the insurrection. A number of prominent Southerners, including John Breckinridge and

John Slidell, owned considerable amounts of property—mostly land in Illinois, Iowa, Kansas, and Nebraska—but proving that it had been used to assist the Confederacy would not have been easy. Moreover, the first act had not been designed as a means to raise revenue. As both Lincoln and Bates realized, the first act was meant to punish rebels and threaten slavery. Vigorous enforcement of the first act would only have antagonized the South at a time when many still hoped that Union sentiment there, particularly in the border states, might shorten the war.[39]

Rather than direct district attorneys and marshals to enforce the first act, Bates did nothing unless asked specific questions about the measure. And even when asked directly Bates often declined to comment. Instead, he directed Assistant Attorney General Titian J. Coffey to inform them of the obvious, that only property used or intended for insurrectionary purposes could be confiscated. Coffey also suggested that marshals consult the relevant district attorneys on confiscation issues. This unwillingness to give directions derived in part from the act itself. It specified that the procedures for confiscation required information available only to someone on the scene. The act said that property used to aid the insurrection was "to be lawful subject of prize or capture wherever" it was found. Such property would be "condemned in a district or circuit court . . . having jurisdiction of the amount, or in admiralty in any district" in which the property was seized, "or into which they may be taken and proceedings first instituted." In other words, only marshals and district attorneys could determine if property was liable to confiscation, and Bates did not believe his office could make such evaluations. The courts would then determine if the seizure had been correct. The act also encouraged informers to tell district attorneys about suspect property, promising to split the proceeds realized from the sale of condemned property with them. The act was silent, however, about procedures to be followed to inform owners that their property had been seized.[40]

Bates's reluctance to answer specific questions about how to enforce the first act meant that no policy was created to direct confiscation. Within fifteen days in September Coffey wrote twelve officials that the attorney general would not comment on the law. To one district attorney from Connecticut, Hiram Willey, for example, Coffey said it was "quite impossible" for Bates to give any instructions on confiscation "in words more explicit than the language of the Act of 6 Aug. 1861." The attorney general "cannot give construction to the Act; that is duty of the court," he observed. He did believe, however, that there would be numerous unlawful confiscation attempts since local officials would wrongly assume the act permitted seizure of property simply because the owners were citizens of seceded states. Yet, Coffey said, Bates also expected that the district attorney would not allow property eligible for confiscation to "escape." The attorney general, said Coffey, urged a strong enforcement of the laws and the maintenance of the government's rights and dignity.[41] In other words, the attorney general would give no directions and, although worried that the law would be improperly applied, nonetheless, wanted it enforced. It was not surprising that local officials were, for the most part, reluctant to implement the first act vigorously.

With no policy from Bates, Secretary of State William H. Seward apparently felt free to offer one of his own. In early September, Seward sent a circular to all district attorneys and marshals to warn against seizure of property simply because it belonged to residents of rebellious states. Even though Seward's directive reiterated Bates's instructions to Coffey that only property used to aid the insurrection was liable to confiscation, the circular clearly upset the attorney general. He immediately wrote Seward to remind him that the attorney general's office had the legal responsibility for directing these officials. Since Bates could find no fault with the instructions themselves, Seward's initiative understandably angered him because it encroached upon his responsibility. Later, to an official who inquired about Seward's directive, Bates wrote that it deserved "all the respect which is due to an opinion of an able and experienced lawyer" but that it had no authority as an "official" instruction. This was, of course, correct, but it ignored his unwillingness to direct the attorneys generals and marshals on the matter. Bates's anxiety over interference from other members of the Cabinet encouraged a narrow view of what the duties of district attorneys and marshals were. In addition to his problems with Seward, Bates also had jurisdictional arguments early in his tenure with Secretary of the Interior Caleb Smith and Secretary of War Cameron.[42]

Bates's conservative administration of the first act also illustrated the problem of proving that property in the North owned by Southerners had been used to aid the insurrection. Even though Assistant Attorney General Coffey admitted that only district attorneys, before a court's judgment, could determine the strength of the evidence necessary to prove unlawful use of property, he insisted that no seizure would be justified unless there was "some" evidence it had been used to aid the Confederacy. Those who ignored this admonition turned the act into a law "for the confiscation of all property of rebels, which it certainly had not been understood to be." But it was not clear how to prove that property in the North had been used to assist the Confederacy.[43] Bates also wanted to avoid filling the courts with cases the government might lose for lack of evidence. Referring to trials for treason, Bates told district attorney Benjamin Smith of Virginia, who wished a broad interpretation of the act, to be sure of his evidence; the government would rather drop a charge than lose a trial.

When given the choice of prosecuting the same man for treason or "a vulgar felony," Bates advised officials to press the latter charge, "as [it is] far easier of conviction & less liable to attract [antiwar] sympathy." This cautious application of the first act reflected both Bates's sympathies and an appreciation of the relative harm that could occur if district attorneys in the North too vigorously enforced a measure that was difficult to implement.[44]

Even when district attorneys did try to confiscate property in the North, they found it difficult to prove that it had aided the insurrection. E. Delafield Smith of the southern district of New York, for example, tried to confiscate stocks owned by a Southerner but could not acquire the proof necessary under the first act. That stocks enriched a rebel sympathizer did not necessarily mean that the property assisted the insurrection. Similar problems beset the efforts in the eastern district of Philadelphia in August and September.[45] While Bates certainly encouraged the strictest adherence to the law, and this doubtless discouraged some from vigorously enforcing the first act, the fact remained that it was not a strong tool with which to punish the South or to discourage the insurrection. Indeed, there is no evidence that any significant amount of property was confiscated, condemned, and sold under the first act. When Congress asked in 1867 for the record of proceeds from confiscation during the Civil War, it asked only to see reports of property confiscated under the second act. No one who has investigated the first act has been able to find any successful cases under the First Confiscation Act, with the exception of those appealed from district courts and discussed later in chapters 10 and 11.[46]

There can be no doubt that Bates, like Lincoln, was apprehensive about both the military as it moved against slavery and the scope of the first act. Ben Butler's treatment of fugitive slaves in Virginia had bothered the attorney general; he doubted that the military could emancipate slaves as if they were prizes of war. Bates thought that Butler was usurping a civil authority that Congress had not yet exercised. Nor did he believe the first act had overturned the Fugitive Slave Act, as some in the military thought. He believed the latter measure was still law and feared that Congress might soon repeal it. Until that occurred, however, he expected fugitive slaves to be arrested. As his biographer concluded, Bates hoped that the president could control the war and prevent eager generals and Republicans in Congress from emancipation.[47] But some within the Cabinet did not share this restricted view of the military's role.

Secretary of War Simon Cameron's report of December 1, 1861, went far beyond what most generals in the field had done with fugitive slaves and suggested the very thing Bates opposed. Without consulting the president, the secretary of war argued that former slaves should be used to fight for the Union and that those "who make war against the Government justly forfeit all rights of property." To leave Confederates "in peaceful and secure possession of slave property" was, said Cameron, "madness." Instead, the North should emancipate rebels' slaves, use them in various ways to help the Union, and arm some of them to fight against their former masters. Before its distribution, Lincoln learned of the recommendation and had it altered, but members of Congress soon learned of the change. Naturally, the border states were angry at Cameron's public proposal and the Kentucky legislature urged that he be dismissed from the Cabinet. Although Cameron's proposals would not be realized until late the following summer, they did reflect sentiment in the North for a more vigorous war policy.[48]

This sentiment was certainly evident in the correspondence to senators in the months following Frémont's proclamation at the end of August and before Congress reconvened in early December. Even though writers had doubts about arming former slaves and others urged compensated emancipation, most wondered if Lincoln and his Cabinet would ever adopt emancipation as a war measure. As L.V. Barney from Akron remarked on the Frémont revocation, "If this Administration is really in earnest" to suppress the rebellion, "they take a curious way of [showing] it." Almost all echoed Orestes Brownson, the reformer, who wrote that it was "impossible to save both the integrity of the Nation & Southern slavery." W. H. Henderson in Illinois believed the "question is—shall the union endure or shall slavery. . . . If this be correct whatever is necessary to save the union let him do—1st abolish slavery." Or as diplomat Rudolph Schleiden said, "abolition is not the object of the war, but simply one of its agencies." It may be that only the converted wrote, but the near unanimity on the need to destroy slavery is striking. When the government sanctioned the return of fugitive slaves, F. D. Parish observed from Sandusky, Ohio, that it seemed eager "to preserve the 'peculiar institution,' unhurt." If so, "I trust God, we will not allow them to succeed." The plural here referred to the public and Congress, who had to lead in destroying slavery. William Kendrick prayed that Congress would pass "new laws to back up our President—compel him to follow after. . . . The people are in advance." Henry Hart from New York inquired if he "and other gentlemen" should begin "a movement to promote" emancipation, although others suggested "that a change in public sentiment was going so rapidly" on the issue that such an effort might "retard & repress" it.[49]

Edward Everett illustrated the shifting Northern attitudes about slavery as the Civil War unfolded. In 1860 he had been the Constitutional Union Party's vice-presidential candidate but became a strong supporter of the Union once the war began. As a former ambassador to England and father-in-law of the current ambassador there, Charles Francis Adams, Everett had a considerable correspondence with foreigners about the war. His major purpose was to prevent British or French diplomatic recognition of the Confederacy, but his letters also showed how a conservative's views on slaves, slavery, and the South evolved as the war lengthened. In November he wrote that he believed the government could not "constitutionally aim at emancipation as the object of the struggle," although he thought the institution would probably die in the border states where "the slaves are already escaping in great numbers." Even if the government could free the slaves, Everett thought at that time it "would probably be disastrous for both races." But in the "immediate theater of military operations, the tenure of slave property is rendered insecure."[50] Everett, no friend to abolitionism in the 1850s, had come to understand the war's power to change what had seemed unimaginable before Fort Sumter, if only in the border states.

Certainly Sumner, Trumbull, and Sherman heard that it was time to strike more boldly at slavery. Virtually all of their correspondents argued the tide was turning. H. Catlin, a newspaperman in Erie, Pennsylvania, saw a trend where "absolute loyalty is antislavery and [tends] to radical action, while the pro-slavery people tend toward compromise and dishonorable peace." Numerous recruiters in Ohio wrote Sherman that it was increasingly difficult to find troops. "I have the flag out and the music in full blast," G. E. Winters reported, "but all this does not seem to stir up the sluggish blood of those who ought to go." If the reports of Frémont's removal were accurate, said John Dalzel from Lima, "it will operate against us in this country for our People swear by Frémont." To Trumbull's suggestion that a more sweeping confiscation proposal be introduced, Senator James Grimes of Iowa expressed strong support in late October. Long an advocate of "a law to confiscate *all* property of rebels," he now wanted the "issue to be fairly + fully made" before Congress. Sumner and Thaddeus Stevens agreed. "All things now tend to an attack on slavery," Sumner wrote in early November. Even a "majority of the cabinet is for this course," he claimed. For his part, Stevens introduced a resolution on December 2, the first day of Congress, to emancipate the slaves.[51] In his annual message to Congress the following day, Lincoln suggested that members eager for sterner measures should put their rhetoric into legislation.

Much of Lincoln's message discussed foreign affairs, the work of various departments, and the country's finances. A third of the way through, he suggested that it was time to recognize Haiti and Liberia, but not without the "approbation" of Congress. His first mention of the First Confiscation Act was to suggest that slaves released from servitude be "deemed free" and then colonized, a project he and others, including Trumbull, supported and would revisit. As for the war itself, he had tried to prevent it from degenerating "into a violent and remorseless revolutionary struggle." These questions "not of vital military importance," he said, had been left "to the more deliberate action of the legislature." As for legislation, he had "adhered" to the first act, and if "a new law upon the same subject shall be proposed, its propriety will be duly considered." He had done nothing to enforce the first act, as we have seen, nor had he tried to prevent its implementation. Here was, in any case, a challenge to legislators with reservations about the administration's policy toward the South and slavery. However, Lincoln believed that nothing had changed the "principles or general purposes," articulated in both his inaugural and July Fourth message to Congress, upon which the North had gone to war. Moreover, his policies had secured Kentucky, Maryland, Missouri, and even western Virginia for the Union. With some success in Virginia, South Carolina, and elsewhere, Lincoln concluded, "These things demonstrate that the cause of the Union is advancing steadily and certainly southward."[52] Lincoln knew that a different conclusion could be drawn from these facts, but he was right to argue that a change in the war's goals could be achieved only if Congress had a clear understanding of its own mind and the public's wishes. Lincoln doubted that they did.

Edward Everett, for one, hoped Lincoln's "temperate and conservative tone" in the message would prevail. At the same time he realized, as did others, that the president faced "considerable opposition from friendly quarters" within his own party. "Such opposition," he speculated, must be "embarrassing" to Lincoln for it arose "from conscientious motives" and involved "a subject intrinsically the most difficult, in all our political relations;—so difficult, that a Patriotic citizen" would find "hard to satisfy himself" as to the best solution.[53] Everett had captured the ambivalence that had surfaced over what to do about slavery as the North's armies advanced into the South. Fugitive slaves, entering Union lines, posed a dilemma that would only increase as the war continued. Yet the administration declined to formulate a policy to guide the generals in the field. Nor had a clamor arisen in the North to have the First Confiscation Act vigorously implemented, although some newspapers began calling for more aggressive confiscation.[54] Although many in the North applauded Frémont's proclamation and attacked Lincoln's reaction, they also hoped that freed slaves would either stay in the South or go to some colony abroad, not move to the North. As the year ended and Congress reconvened, it became obvious to Lincoln and some Republicans that the legislators would have to test the public's opinion on the great question that Everett alluded to: whether the war would fundamentally alter the Union and slavery.[55]

2 The Second Confiscation Act: The Act and Its Opponents

By December 1861 there were several indications in the North that some form of confiscation, mostly related to slavery, had gained public support. In Massachusetts, Amos Lawrence, a merchant and abolitionist, wrote the editor of a Boston newspaper that he supported "the policy of confiscating the property and freeing the slaves" of all rebels. In Philadelphia, Sidney George Fisher confided to his diary that he now saw two parties in the Congress and the North, one for general emancipation and the arming of Negroes and the other for "the confiscation & setting free of the slaves" of rebels. Senator Lyman Trumbull reflected these attitudes and accepted the challenge Lincoln had made in his December first speech to offer legislation if dissatisfied with the war's goals. On December 5, Trumbull introduced the Second Confiscation Act. Several other Republicans followed suit with their own confiscation bills while other members of the party urged caution. Representative John Gurley of Ohio, for example, proposed on December 9 that the slaves of Confederates be confiscated and colonized, but his bill was buried. Senator Timothy Howe of Wisconsin noted an angry exchange the same day in a caucus of Republicans between "timid, hesitating and unresolved" conservatives and "turbulent, passionate and reckless" radicals supporting confiscation.[1]

For the next seven months, Congress debated at length the various issues inherent in confiscation, finally passing a law in July that was significantly limited in order to forestall a presidential veto. Strong opinions on a variety of subjects emerged in the debates over confiscation, including how to define the hostilities, Lincoln's powers, congressional control over the military, colonization, the punishment of rebels, length of property forfeiture, and the basis of the South's restoration. These discussions, with Democrats participating in opposition to almost any form of confiscation, demonstrated that the majority of Republicans were not very radical on the central issues of race and Reconstruction, often agreeing with the president. As well, the debates exposed the confusion and hesitation Congress felt in trying to confiscate property, abolish slavery, punish the South, and plan Reconstruction simultaneously and in the midst of a poorly defined conflict. The result was a badly designed Second Confiscation Act that failed either to realize as much money as many had hoped (or feared) or to restructure the South. The debates and compromises also make clear why freed slaves received no land following the peace and why even the leading rebels suffered only a brief punishment following the war. At the same time, the very nature of the war itself changed during these seven months, in part because of the confiscation debates themselves. Between December 1861 and August 1862 the North altered, in dramatic ways, its goals for the war—and, as a result, the country's future.[2]

The Revolution, of course, provided a precedent of sorts for the confiscation of private property. Tom Paine had urged confiscation of loyalist holdings in *Common Sense*, and the Continental Congress in November 1777 encouraged the colonies to do so. All colonies passed laws to confiscate the property of loyalists, although these laws varied widely in severity. A number of colonies also struggled to define treason just as the Civil War Congress would. New York and South Carolina adopted the most drastic confiscation measures, while those of Maryland, Delaware, New Hampshire, and Georgia were comparatively mild. Except in Georgia, laws were harshest where loyalists were most numerous. If nothing else, confiscation during the Revolution demonstrated that Americans were willing to violate property rights during war and ignore significant civil rights. Some advocated confiscation as a punishment for support of the crown and a means to raise revenue, while others expected that confiscation would reduce property inequality in the colonies. In the end, however, not much property was confiscated, and often the wealthier members of society ended up purchasing it at auction sales, reducing the likelihood that confiscation would lead to greater equality. Several aspects of confiscation in the Revolution were markedly different from the Civil War experience. Loyalists lived among those who confiscated their land and not, like the rebels, in a supposedly separate nation. This may be one reason why colonial legislatures often brushed aside the need to have those liable to confiscation present at the trials. Support for confiscation came from both the colonists and their leaders, whereas there were only scattered pleas for confiscation from the public during the Civil War. Paradoxically, demands for punishing treason came from the colonists, not the crown, which had, like the North in the Civil War, most reason to accuse the revolutionaries of treasonous behavior. And there was relatively little opposition to confiscation, other than from loyalists, during and after the Revolution, while there was significant disagreement in the North over confiscation during the Civil War, both with the idea itself and the premise that it should extend beyond the offender's life. Finally, those who opposed vigorous confiscation during the Civil War relied on the Constitution, which grew out of both the Revolution and those early discussions of treason and confiscation.[3]

Trumbull's original second confiscation bill, introduced on December 5, 1861, was sweeping. It provided "for the absolute and complete forfeiture forever . . . of every species of property, real and personal . . . belonging to persons beyond the jurisdiction of the United States . . . who . . . shall take up arms against the United States, or in any wise aid or abet the rebellion." For Trumbull, confiscation was punishment for assisting the rebellion, not treason, and was primarily directed at those beyond the reach of federal courts, which meant the people inside the Confederacy. Colonization, on foreign soil procured by the president, would be provided for former slaves of rebels or supporters of the rebellion, made free under the act. Proceeds from the act would be "for the benefit of loyal citizens" whose property had been "despoiled" by the "rebellion" and would also help pay for the war itself. Whereas the first act removed from slavery only those slaves used in support of the rebellion, Trumbull's second act potentially freed slaves who might "in anywise aid or abet the rebellion." Unlike the first act, the new bill authorized the military to assist in confiscation proceedings in areas where the courts had ceased to function. Trumbull discarded the word *war* and now referred to the conflict as a "rebellion" or "insurrection." Slaves remained property in descriptions of confiscation but became people in reference to their rights after the fighting, however. The legal proceedings against property continued in rem in the second bill, although the term had not been used in the first act. The owner's presence would therefore not be required for the forfeiture. And finally, the new bill forfeited real and personal property beyond the life of the person judged guilty of aiding the rebellion if that person was beyond the reach of normal judicial process in the Confederacy. Those in the North who aided the rebellion, on the other hand, would be tried for treason, Trumbull explained. If found guilty they would forfeit their real property for life; personal property would be permanently forfeited. Trumbull believed that this distinction satisfied the prohibition against bills of attainder in article three, section three of the Constitution. This article reads, "The Congress shall have power to declare the punishment of treason but no attainder of treason shall work corruption of blood or forfeiture, except during the life of the person attainted."[4] The Senate subsequently referred all the confiscation bills to the Judiciary Committee, chaired by Trumbull. The other four Republican members were Lafayette S. Foster (Conn.), John C. Ten Eyck (N.J.), Ira Harris (N.Y.), and Edgar Cowan (Pa.). The first three were moderates on confiscation; Cowan was conservative.[5]

Congress appeared willing to adopt some form of confiscation. Newly elected Senator James H. Lane (R.-Kan.), in a speech given in Boston in late November, had already advocated the end of slavery and the enlistment of ex-slaves. Republican John Bingham of Ohio, a sponsor of confiscation in the House, observed in December that Congress appeared willing to "liberate all Slaves on the ground that it is necessary to the public defense in this time of

Domestic Rebellion," although he doubted his colleagues would embrace universal abolition. The *New York Times* reported there was a "disposition among Congressmen . . . to pass a law making more certain and stringent the forfeiture of rebel property" beyond the first act. A political observer at the Capitol believed that Congress would enact a law "for confiscating property as broad as the confederate," which was sweeping. Wisconsin Senator Howe believed "the utter extinction of slavery will be watchword and effort of one faction" of the party. As well, both radical and conservative newspapers had urged Congress to enact a stronger confiscation law in the next session.[6]

Trumbull received encouragement for confiscation from many people in different parts of the North but in particular from Illinois, where citizens complained that Lincoln was too timid. W. W. Henderson of Springfield, for example, wondered, "What is Lincoln doing? Does he suppose he can crush—squelch out this huge rebellion . . . [with] pop guns filled with water. . . . The Union must be preserved." From Paris, Illinois, S. Lord thought Lincoln's face was turned "Southward" and urged bold action. "I am in favor of destroying this monstrous system root and branch. If this struggle ends with slavery still in existence, the Battle of Liberty has been only half fought." "I have just read in the telegrams . . . a synopsis of your bill for the Confiscation of Rebel property," D. S. Linegan wrote from Cairo. "I am most pleased with it. . . . I have but the slightest doubt of the power of Congress under the Constitution to Confiscate and make free the slaves of rebels." "It is strange that Seward & Lincoln who long since knew this fact [about the evil of slavery] and uttered it, cannot now act with something like vigor toward the crushing of slavery," observed P. A. Allaire from Aurora. And J. D. Strong from Jacksonville reported that Trumbull's bill "for the Confiscation of rebel's property is just out among our people and meets very general approval. I have not heard a dissenting voice although we have some very bitter sympathizers with reason if they dared to speak out." Almost without exception, those who wrote Trumbull urged confiscation as a means to crush the rebellion, not for the purpose aiding the slaves or reconstructing the South.[7]

In mid-January the committee returned a version of Trumbull's bill that had been modified in significant ways. (For various reasons, the House took longer to begin discussion of its confiscation bills.) Only a bare majority of the Judiciary Committee had allowed it to be reported from the committee in the first place. Absent now was the distinction between real and personal property, and no mention was made of confiscation beyond the traitor's life, although Trumbull insisted that the penalty remained in force. Confiscation resulted from aiding the rebellion, he maintained; it was not a punishment for treason. A provision to allow the return of fugitive slaves to those able to prove loyalty to the Union was added as an apparent sop to loyal slaveholders in the South. However, the military was not allowed to adjudicate this issue, and it was not made clear what happened if master and slave differed on the issue of owner's allegiance. The new bill also gave Lincoln a large role in confiscation. He had the discretion, "as often as in his opinion the military" necessity and the success of "the suppression of the rebellion require," to use civil or military officers for confiscation of property that was "beyond the reach" of "judicial proceedings by reason" of the rebellion. In effect, then, the new bill turned over confiscation in the South to the president to use as he saw fit. The bill also said that "upon commission of the act of forfeiture," all right, title, and claim to any property immediately became vested in the United States, which meant that the government had only to take possession of the property. Had this version passed and been implemented by Lincoln, great amounts of property in the South could have been confiscated and the fee simple transferred to the government.[8]

Advocates of vigorous confiscation later regretted this concession to the president. Furthermore, the bill did not solve the problem of how to describe slaves. It referred to them as property, which left them within the *Dred Scott* decision, until they were freed, when they became people. Nor was it clear how Congress had suddenly received the power to end ownership of slaves. Supporters of abolition argued the war powers gave Congress the right to free slaves, but many doubted this interpretation. Trumbull insisted that the bill was designed to confiscate the property of those beyond the reach of normal legal process; thus the use of in rem proceedings from admiralty and revenue practices, rather than in personam proceedings, which could not occur without the owner. Under the circumstances of the rebellion, Trumbull claimed, in rem proceedings were constitutional. Members of both parties, however, had doubts about the legality of such proceedings and their apparent violation of due process. At the same time, however, Trumbull argued the rebels were enemies without protection from the Constitution. But he also claimed that Congress could treat rebels as both enemies and citizens who could be punished as an enemies and traitors. There was clearly confusion over who could be punished and for what reason. Moreover, since the bill acted upon the property of traitors, Trumbull asserted, it did "not corrupt the blood of the party" and thus was not a bill of attainder. As a result, the forfeitures could extend beyond the life of those found guilty of treason, thus allowing slaves to remain free after their rebel owners had died. Trumbull obviously wanted it both ways, insisting that Congress had the power under both the laws of war and the Constitution. [9] Even many Republicans found this interpretation too broad or contradictory.

Democrats, and even a few Republicans, certainly could not accept such broad aims or wide congressional powers for the conflict. Although most Democrats supported a vigorous military policy to subdue the rebellion, only a few agreed that anything other than restoration of the Union should concern Congress, the military, or the president. As they said repeatedly, the war should preserve "the Constitution as it is and the Union as it was." For Democrats the Constitution's powers did not change or enlarge in time of war, at least in this conflict; confiscation, like other measures related to slavery or Reconstruction, was beyond Congress's powers. If confiscation and abolition were unthinkable in peace, they were no less so during this conflict, which was not even a war, according to Representative William Allen (D.-Ohio). The militia had simply been summoned to suppress an insurrection; the Constitution's war powers could not be invoked on behalf of confiscation. Senator Orville Browning (R.-Ill.) conceded the existence of war, an admission that his friend President Lincoln would not make, but denied that Congress could exercise those "extraordinary powers" called forth by war. To permit congressional interference in the conduct of the war, said Browning, would be tantamount to admitting that it could also "adjudicate a case at law or control the decisions of a court." In the end, only the executive branch could legally supervise the war. Since the Constitution did not admit of secession, said Representative William Holman (D.-Ohio), Congress could not enlarge its powers to end the rebellion. "The Constitution is the same in peace and in war," Holman argued. "If you recognize these States out of the Union, you can pass the laws. If they are in the Union, the Constitution forbids it." Holman, of course, realized that most Republicans would not accept this position. Most Democrats, both in and out of Congress, shared the view of John J. Davis of West Virginia, who hoped for a painless defeat administered to the small minority in the South hostile to the federal government.[10]

Admitting secession's legality was equally treacherous for Democrats. If secession was constitutional, it implied that the Union had power over conquered Confederate states, all but guaranteeing slavery's abolition with restoration. Even so, most Democrats admitted the reality of secession, even if it was illegal. They maintained, though, that only a few Southerners had willingly joined the Confederacy. Many agreed with Senator Willard Saulsbury of Delaware that the de facto governments in the Confederacy forced most rebels to serve; therefore, confiscation would unfairly discriminate if it were pursued during the conflict. Better to punish the disloyal leaders after the war, he said. If the Union wanted to punish rebels during the war, argued Senator Joseph Wright of Indiana, then recognize that the leaders had committed crimes "which may be dealt with in detail under the names of murder, theft, arson" or "comprehended under the name of treason." Traitors deserved the Constitution's protection nonetheless, and that meant due process and no corruption of blood beyond their death. While the "act of secession itself is perfectly harmless," claimed Senator John Henderson of Missouri, taking up arms against the federal government was treason and should be punished. Widespread confiscation should not occur, Democrats concluded, simply because Jefferson Davis and other leaders had committed treason. [11]

Democrats strongly believed that only those who led the South into rebellion deserved punishment. Some Republicans agreed, arguing that a handful of fanatics had deluded the mass of Southerners and led them into a senseless war. As a result, argued Senator Jacob Collamer of Vermont, the overwhelming majority of Southerners had remained loyal during the unconstitutional state secession movements and should continue to receive the privileges and immunities guaranteed other citizens by the Constitution. Senator Edgar Cowan (R.-Pa.) even believed that the majority in the South would end their rebellion once shown the error of their ways. Representative William Dunn (R.-Ill.) believed that once shown the perfidy of their leaders and the possibility of peace, "we may expect to see the southern army melting like snow in the summer heat." Not all rebels should therefore be subject to discriminatory legislation such as confiscation. Conservatives such as Senator Wright of Indiana wished the North to treat the individual rebel like a common criminal or a traitor.[12] They also feared, or at least argued, that confiscation would produce extreme results.

Opponents of the second act offered a pessimistic vision of what the South would become if confiscation were implemented. Their bleak assessment derived in part from the promise made by a few Republicans that confiscated land would go to freedmen and Union soldiers and in part from the Southern fear about confiscation. Doubtless some of the conservatives' rhetoric was also tactical; even so, the bleakness of their predictions was impressive. Senator Browning offered a grim picture of Southern life after confiscation. "It sweeps everything, even the most ordinary comforts and necessaries of domestic life, and reduces all to absolute poverty and nakedness," Browning predicted. Even if all Southerners resumed allegiance to the Union, Browning saw little hope for their future since they would "return bankrupts and beggars, with nothing on earth to make government desirable." Representative Benjamin Thomas, a Republican from Massachusetts, was no less alarmed. He predicted a "clean sweep of property" by confiscation, including even "the bed on which the wife sleeps, the cradel [*sic*] of the child, the pork or flour barrel." Thomas was concerned about how friendly nations would react to such devastation, while others worried about confiscation's effects on the mind of the South. Rather than prevent future rebellions, Senator Cowan said, the hatred bred among women and children by such a policy would encourage future revolts. Representative

Dunn, on the other hand, said that confiscation might lead the South to reject reunion after the war. Such predictions echoed the alarm offered in the *Memphis Argus* in January 1862, when it questioned how "a truly civilized and Christian nation could endorse" confiscation.[13] Even if there was much hyperbole in these dark forecasts, the intensity of the fear and anguish expressed suggested the profound misgivings held by many over confiscation's potential impact. Such anxiety clearly informed the emerging concern, later represented by the Copperhead movement, over changing goals for the war.

Many opponents also suggested that both the threat and implementation of confiscation would prolong the war, rather than hasten its end. A number reasoned that the South would grow bitter and fight to the last man once it knew that defeat would include the loss of all or much of its property. This certainly appeared to be the view of the *Atlanta Confederacy* in March 1862 when, in discussing the confiscation bill, it said: "Let any cruelties, any torments, any death that earth can inflict, come upon us in preference to the triumph of the Yankees!" Representative John Law (D.-Ind.) later provided an example of this fear. He asked the House to consider the results that "will follow such an act [as confiscation]—a war, the end of which no man can foresee—a contest, the end of which no one can calculate." Advocates of confiscation tried to reassure the worried that it would only affect unregenerate rebels and would leave loyal Southerners alone; anyone could escape confiscation by swearing allegiance to the Union. Law's prediction did not relieve those, like John Crittenden of Kentucky, caught between sympathy for the South and support of the North. He urged his colleagues to be more lenient and take a broader view of the whole issue. Adopt the one-sided policy of confiscation, he warned, and the war would continue to the point where rebels might begin to kill loyal Southerners.[14] Such alarmist arguments had little effect on the final vote, but they did reveal a view in the North that confiscation would exacerbate an already troubled war and make achieving peace problematic.

Although some conservatives did agree that confiscation could be implemented, they insisted that it remained an executive prerogative and was not within Congress's power. They assumed, correctly as it turned out, that Lincoln would not pursue confiscation if given the authority. Senator Cowan, for example, agreed that the Constitution permitted Congress to make the articles of war but felt that Congress could regulate only the internal affairs of the United States forces, with no authority over the treatment of the enemy. In fact, Cowan said, "the power of the Executive of this nation is absolutely despotic and unrestrained against the rebels." When pressed, Cowan conceded that the president could not retain the seized property beyond the life of the war, but argued that this provision applied to Congress, too. Even so, the fourth section of the proposed bill gave the president the authority to confiscate when propitious, which would probably mean when it suited the military. As Cowan noted, confiscation's advocates could pass their law, but it "is, then, law or no law, at his discretion, which is just the same as saying his discretion is the law." Moreover, the president could also subvert the will of Congress through the pardoning power.[15] Cowan and other conservatives realized, of course, that slavery was the key to all discussions of confiscation.

At the start of the debates over the second act, many in Congress appeared determined to preserve the institutions of the antebellum period. Many who supported confiscation did so only as a military necessity. As Senator James Dixon (R.-Conn.) observed, the fight to maintain the Union had induced some to forget that "the time may come when the just prerogatives of State authority may require defense." This would be necessary if the country agreed to govern the seceded states as territorial possessions, as some radicals advocated, but Dixon was confident that the "people" would reject such an idea. Others, from both parties and all regions other than the Northwest, repeated Dixon's point: the Civil War should not alter the status quo ante bellum. Representative John Killinger (R.-Pa.) succinctly summarized this position: "The moment that peace is restored law and order will take the place of military force, the States [will] resume their original place in the family of States, and be restored to their original rights and dignities." Many presumed that the "original rights" of the rebellious states would be restored after the war and this meant slavery could only be injured in the war out of military necessity. Representative Henry Grider, a Kentucky Unionist, urged delay on any discussion of slavery. The rebellion, he believed, would be defeated without the necessity of either confiscation or emancipation. If, after the war, emancipation was to be considered, Grider advised Congress to do it "when all the States shall be heard in our deliberations."[16] For some, of course, even suggesting this was too much of a concession. It also raised alarm.

Conservatives believed, in fact, that the war itself had arisen over just such a call for abolition. They despaired of more discussion about freeing the slaves while debating the second act. Wicked men in both the North and the South, said Representative Aaron Harding (D.-Ky.), had agitated the sectional issue in order to destroy the Union. Harding regretted that the "two or three hundred chosen leaders of this agitation" had not been hanged or exiled. Had they not interfered with the South's property rights, the secession crisis would have never developed in the first place. This rationalization, like that from Republican Senator Henry Wilson of Massachusetts, who said slavery had "perverted their [Southerners'] hearts, clouded their reason, blinded their consciences, and made them traitors," was too simple. If anything, however, as the confiscation debates illustrated, the war deepened the convictions behind these explanations. Senator Saulsbury, for example, argued that "abolitionism" continued to subvert constitutional liberty. Before abolition, he reminded his colleagues, "we did eat of the pleasant fruits of the tree of liberty and were content. It came, and with it death." Such recollections ignored the complex reasons the war began and revealed the desire on the part of many Northerners to leave the South as little changed as possible as the North defeated the Confederacy.[17]

Many conservatives, usually Democrats, insisted that Congress's frequently stated refusal to legislate on slavery must be honored. Unless and until the Constitution was amended, said Representative Law, it would continue to guarantee every slaveholder the right of property inherent in slaves. To do otherwise, he cautioned, would contradict the practice and opinions of all authorities since the Constitution's ratification. Supporters of this view usually cited the Crittenden-Johnson resolutions of July 1861 as a binding precedent against efforts at abolition, even if indirectly in the second act. John J. Crittenden of Kentucky in the House and Andrew Johnson of Tennessee in the Senate had sponsored the resolutions. The resolutions held that the war would not be waged for "any purpose of conquest or subjugation, nor purpose of overthrowing or interfering with the rights or established institutions of those States, but to defend and maintain the supremacy of the Constitution and to preserve the Union, with all the dignity, equality, and rights of the several States unimpaired." Those who used them as a bar against confiscation ignored the fact that the resolutions did not specifically mention slavery.[18]

Conservatives rightly saw that supporters of confiscation were attempting to abolish slavery by indirect means. Early 1862 was far too soon for most Republicans to support emancipation as an independent goal of the war. As Senator Powell of Kentucky said, the emancipation portion of the second act was nothing but "an insidious attempt to do indirectly what its advocates would not attempt to do directly." Representative Robert Mallory, also a Kentucky Unionist, actually believed that the bill's major goal was abolition, to be achieved through the confiscation of the rebels' estates. As his observation implies, slavery's defenders might have agreed to confiscation, at least for the leaders of the rebellion, had it not included the potential emancipation of so many slaves. Assuming that Congress would eventually pass a second act, defenders of slavery asked that it be consistent in the way it defined confiscation and property. In other words, said Senator Garrett Davis, a Kentucky Unionist, all the South asked was that "our slaves have the same fate with all property." If confiscated personal property and land counted toward the payment of war expenses, Davis demanded that the same apply for confiscated slaves. He expected that the proceeds from confiscation might then reach one billion dollars. Despite such suggestions, Representative Allen did not expect the policy to be approved because it would recognize "them [slaves] as property, which, I am quite sure, our Republican friends will never do." Allen and other Democrats asked that Republicans admit the obvious deceit in emancipating slaves under the second act.[19] The Democrats were deeply concerned about emancipation's impact upon the North, and they tried to use this fear to limit the reach of the second act.

To begin with, said Allen, the country would not permit itself to be "overrun by an ignorant and vicious population of worthless negroes," particularly since they would be competing against white labor. Representative Robert Nugent, another Ohio Democrat, echoed this view a month later. On the one hand, of course, this was simply racist rhetoric but to dismiss it on this basis ignores the widespread anxiety in the North over the possible influx of free blacks. Many assumed that abolition, by whatever means, was wrong because blacks were inferior. As Senator Saulsbury of Delaware observed, God, nature, and everything else indicated no legislation could elevate the "filthy" black to the level of the white people. His ancestors had treated their slaves humanely, which Saulsbury presumed testified to both his sympathy and understanding of their servitude. When he concluded that the United States would "not only be the white man's home, but the white man shall govern and the nigger shall never be his equal," he drew applause from the galleries. Although these comments may not have reflected those of a majority in Congress, they indicated the apprehension many felt over confiscation's granting of freedom to large numbers of slaves.[20]

Except for Representative Owen Lovejoy (R.-Ill.), legislators were pessimistic about the fate of slaves freed by confiscation.[21] If there were any who thought emancipation would not impose difficulties for either race, their optimism was not offered. For those less sanguine, colonization was the solution and the second act provided for willing former slaves to leave the United States for an undetermined location. The promise of colonization as a solution to America's racial problems had been discussed for some time, of course. Lincoln had long been a supporter of the idea, as had Thaddeus Stevens and Lyman Trumbull.[22] The refusal of most states in the North to admit freed blacks was a strong argument for colonization, according to Representative Mallory of Kentucky. But to colonize all the ex-slaves would be a very expensive project and, with an estimated cost of more than a billion dollars, Mallory implied it would be politic to keep blacks enslaved rather than bill the public for such a venture. Moreover, no one argued that freed slaves should be required to colonize. Senator Browning had no more faith in the public's altruism than did Mallory, but he believed colonization was far better than racial hatred, regardless of the cost. The alternatives were clear, said Browning: either "we admit the Negroes to full, free, and unqualified social equality, or we must separate them from us," to a country where they could decide their own future. However, Browning was not confident Congress would embrace either solution. Senator Samuel Pomeroy (R.-Kan.), on the other hand, favored colonization, but only if the masters were required to accompany the freed slaves. To send ex-slaves or masters from the country unattended would be foolish, he reasoned, since everyone knew neither could care for themselves. Earlier Pomeroy, in jest, had urged keeping ex-slaves in the country for common labor but forcing the masters to leave since they were incapable of work.[23] Even though none of these legislators had confidence in the ex-slaves' potential, they all worried about their future if it depended on the white man's sympathy. Lincoln, too, shared this concern.

Some congressmen believed that emancipation achieved through the second act would not lead blacks to either equality or colonization but back into slavery. The critical question, they said, would be the reaction of the North to emancipation. If northern states welcomed blacks, there would be an exodus of freedmen from the South and hope for the future. But some, such as Senator John Carlile of Virginia, who was no friend of abolition, believed that few if any states would admit any significant number of blacks. Unable to migrate to the North, Carlile declared, former slaves would constitute such a threat to Southern whites that their enslavement or extermination would be inevitable. Waitman Willey, the other Unionist senator from Virginia, added that all freedmen in the South before secession would have to suffer the same fate as those emancipated slaves or they too would threaten whites. In the end, Willey believed, all blacks would have to be killed or enslaved anew; none could go free. A border state representative, Republican Francis Blair of Missouri, believed that Northern states would pass discriminatory laws if they suspected that many ex-slaves would migrate to the North. These views, from Southern supporters of the Union, predicted with some accuracy the fate awaiting blacks after the Civil War, at least in the South.[24] Although clearly meant to scare those who supported abolition through confiscation, these prophecies also revealed a belief that the North's hypocrisy on race gave the South wide latitude in its conduct after the war.

In early 1862, doubts about the wisdom of abolition also appeared among Republicans outside of Congress. The *Indianapolis Gazette*, an Indiana Republican paper, noted that army volunteers were often heard to say that they would treat both secessionists and abolitionists in the same harsh way. Union meetings in Indiana were also emphasizing their support for the Crittenden-Johnson resolutions, which opposed antislavery legislation. In Pennsylvania opponents of the war became more aggressive as they sensed a shift in the war's goals that many in the public would not support. They began to embrace Senator Cowan, whom they had disparaged when he was first elected in 1861. Sidney George Fisher confided to his diary in mid-January that Republicans were now divided over abolishing slavery, with the "abolitionists" declaring "that slavery should be destroyed by right of war," whereas Lincoln had wisely "offered to the South protection in all their rights" if they will return to their allegiance. In Ohio, the Republican *Cleveland Herald* attacked Ben Wade's support for confiscation in an effort to deny him reelection to the Senate. Edward Everett did not yet see the wisdom or right of Congress to abolish slavery. "The Anti-slavery feeling of the North is strong enough for any measure which sound policy would warrant with reference to slavery," but he did not see how it could be achieved even under the war powers. Everett wondered "how can they be emancipated, by the general government, even as a war measure, considering that the war is waged to restore authority of the Constitution, which expressly recognizes slavery." Once a supporter of colonization, Everett now saw little hope of that scheme's succeeding. Few freed blacks embraced the idea, and the South saw it as "but another form of abolitionism." He had no hope for the intermingling of the two races, either: "There is some reason to think that there is a natural repulsion between the different types of our race," he concluded.[25] In sum, while a growing minority in Congress and in the North had come to support some form of emancipation, many remained deeply skeptical of that goal.

A few in Congress, like Senators Cowan and Browning, invoked the law of nations; they said that it prevented congressional confiscation but permitted Lincoln to pursue it. Even though never defined, the term suggested a body of laws that governed war and rebellion; these laws were unwritten but recognized, said supporters. Any law, said Cowan, in reference to the second act, was unconstitutional when it violated the law of nations. If the United States would live in the family of nations, enjoying national rights and privileges, Cowan believed that "nothing can be clearer than that we are bound by the law of nations." However, few supported this view. Senator Davis of Kentucky, for example, argued that in a domestic war such as the rebellion the nations involved were required only to avoid enacting laws that "outrage and shock the universal laws of humanity," which were not the same as the law of nations. For Davis this meant that all nations could prescribe any means necessary to quell an insurrection. Another conservative, Republican Senator Doolittle of Wisconsin, believed the Union was responsible to God alone for the type of confiscation employed because it affected only American citizens, including the rebels, and not those of other nations. It remained, however, for Representative Benjamin Thomas of Massachusetts, a Republican opposed to confiscation, to silence those who invoked the law of nations. After giving the House quotations and references for both sides of the argument, he dismissed the law of nations as anachronistic in a time of civil war.[26] To most legislators, for or against confiscation, the law of nations proved irrelevant because there was little agreement on how to define the fighting, though even fewer conceded to the South the status of a belligerent.

The confiscation debates often focused on the constitutionality of secession. This issue was integral to any definition of the war, and therefore to Reconstruction. Many argued that the Union was a compact in which each state was free to dissolve the bond at its pleasure. To recognize the legality of secession thus, however, would have created a belligerent status for the South. On the one hand, this would have allowed the North to confiscate without regard to the Constitution, other than how to define the war powers. Belligerent status for the South, however, would have legitimized foreign recognition for the South, which neither Democrats nor Republicans could accept. Belligerent status would have also allowed a victorious North to treat the South as a conquered territory, rather than as errant states defeated in battle, and accepted back in the Union. The potential for reconstructing the South through confiscation, therefore, depended to a large degree on the interpretation given secession. In the end, Congress restricted the definition of the war and this circumscribed the extent to which the South might have been changed after the fighting ended.[27]

Few faced the issue squarely, however. With refreshing realism, Representative Elijah Babbit (R.-Pa.) declared, "A body of men can do in fact that which they have no right to do. An admission that they have done the unlawful act is no acknowledgment of its being right." The rebel states were, Babbit conceded, clearly de facto belligerents, to be treated like any belligerent nation except that those in rebellion should be liable to prosecution as traitors, and those Southerners with no part in the rebellion should not be regarded as enemies. Perhaps there was too little sophistry in Babbit's argument for most congressmen. Only one other legislator, Representative Sam Blair (R.-Pa.), approached such a realistic appraisal of the country's condition. The federal government, said Blair, without any vestige of power in the seceded states, faced a hostile and organized government run by usurpers and traitors. In the face of such a foe, Blair believed, "we are compelled to act, in most respects, toward them as if they were a foreign government of a thousand years' existence, with whom and us hostilities have broken out." As Babbit realized, neither opponents nor supporters of confiscation could admit the reality of secession, because they would be conceding belligerent status to the rebel states during and after the fighting.[28] Belligerent status would allow Great Britain and France, among others, to recognize and aid the South, and perhaps help it win, while admitting that secession existed would allow reconstruction if the North won.

Confiscation's opponents believed the federal government could capture and try the traitors in their own states and that these rebels deserved the Constitution's protections. Supporters of confiscation, on the other hand, argued that the states ceased to function when they seceded and that those supporting the Confederacy no longer deserved the Constitution's benefits. State suicide or territorialization, as some called it, deeply upset conservatives. Senator James Dixon (R.-Conn.) asserted that only the South's victory could make secession legal. Representative Charles Wickliffe, Unionist from Kentucky, argued that the Constitution had to govern the conduct of the war; all citizens, including rebels, had to receive its privileges and blessings. Even though Wickliffe and others conceded that this could mean punishment for Southern traitors, this was a small penalty when compared to the results reconstruction might bring. Senator John Henderson (D.-Mo.) believed that since the Constitution did not authorize secession, not the states, their inhabitants, nor the federal government received new authority because of the unauthorized act. As Henderson put it, in perhaps the greatest understatement of the confiscation debates, "the act of secession itself is perfectly harmless." If an individual in a seceded state took up arms against the Union, he committed treason against the federal government, Henderson asserted. The government could punish only the individual traitors, not their heirs, and certainly not the states. The states, in other words, had done nothing wrong and therefore merited no punishment.[29] This view of secession, naturally, would have limited both confiscation and reconstruction, but it did not find many adherents.

About two-thirds of the way through the confiscation debates, outright opponents fell silent as it became obvious that Congress would eventually pass a second act in some form. Republicans controlled the second session of the thirty-seventh Congress, a reality that the Democrats understood.[30] Until then most speakers had begun their comments with a statement of the war's objectives, followed by evidence, either legal or historical, to support their views. The last third of the debates offered a very different form of discussion. Assuming that some form of confiscation law would be enacted, the legislators now argued over the legal issues involved in confiscation's application and what the law would achieve. The changed tenor of the comments only reinforced the impression that radicals wanted confiscation as both a means to win the war and start reconstruction, while the moderates and conservatives hoped to limit both its application and its duration to the life of those punished. These discussions also revealed difficulties, in particular the question of duration of forfeiture, that confiscation's supporters could not resolve in their effort to enact their bill.

3

The Second Act: Divided Republican Support and Flawed Result

Republican differences over the Second Confiscation Act reveal the limits of the radicals' influence in the Thirty-seventh Congress, at least on confiscation. The ineffective provisions of the second act also demonstrate the distaste for special legislation, as Michael Les Benedict has termed it, in mid-nineteenth century. If Senators Sumner, Wade, and Trumbull and Representatives Stevens, Ashley, and Julian had possessed a coherent plan and been able to orchestrate wartime measures, it would not have taken seven months to produce a measure as imperfect as the second act. The Senate Judiciary Committee, dominated by Republicans, circumscribed Trumbull's original proposal from its inception. And from the start of debate in both houses the moderates prevailed in both rhetoric and legislative compromises. In July, following more discussion than Congress had had on any other measure, a confused law that failed to achieve much confiscation and almost no change to the South emerged. The bill encouraged many, especially freed slaves, to expect land reform even as it scared others, particularly in the South, about the potential of confiscation and reconstruction and helped create a false reputation for radicals. It also increased partisanship between the parties and created alarm about a predicted migration of ex-slaves to the North. In addition, the debates and the law pushed Lincoln to a more direct assault upon slavery. Ironically, then, the Second Confiscation Act accomplished the most before becoming law and far less than expected or feared once enacted.[1]

For confiscation's true believers, among them Sumner and Trumbull, the power of Congress was wide indeed. Most who wrote to the two senators argued that Congress should now assert itself in the war since Lincoln appeared conciliatory to the South and unwilling to fight vigorously. The Massachusetts senator declared, "there can be nothing essential to its [the war's] success, which is not positively within the province of Congress. There is not one of the rights of war which Congress may not invoke." Congress, argued Trumbull, could employ whatever it thought "necessary and proper for the attainment of the end of the *war*, which is the suppression of *rebellion*." Trumbull maintained that there "is not a syllable in the Constitution conferring on the President war powers." Congress, therefore, could instruct the president to do as it wished. The president, as commander in chief of the armies and navies, Trumbull said, could "only govern and regulate them as Congress" instructed. The Constitution clearly stated that Congress "shall have the power to make rules for the government and regulation of the land and naval forces."[2] But both men realized that few in the party shared their expansive views about congressional power.

Trumbull designed his bill to meet those Republicans who opposed vigorous confiscation halfway on the question of emancipation. For senators such as Cowan, Browning, Doolittle, and Foster, who were doubtful about confiscation, emancipation if carried out by the executive for military necessity was tolerable.[3] To satisfy them, Trumbull said that his bill allowed masters who supported the rebellion to choose whether their slaves went free or not. Congress, he argued, by its war powers, could create a penalty for certain behavior in order to restore the Union. If the masters' support of the Confederacy continued after the act passed, their slaves would be freed through confiscation. The bill would therefore not be ex post facto and emancipation would only occur following a "voluntary act" of the "rebel master" to continue war upon the United States. Thus, Trumbull suggested, Congress would not violate its previous refusal to interfere with slavery. "I am not aware that the Republican party ever pledged itself not to allow the owners of slaves to make them free," he said. Trumbull's logic held that masters could retain their slaves by swearing an oath to support the Union before the act passed. Perhaps seeking to calm worried Republican colleagues, Trumbull predicted that his bill would confiscate the property of only one in ten rebels. By moving against slavery so indirectly in placing the onus on the unrepentant rebel owners, Trumbull revealed just how hesitant he was to advocate abolition in the midst of war. Even so, Browning and others opposed emancipation if it entailed transferring title and violating state laws on slavery. The issues were the same as for landed property. These senators also had concerns about lack of due process if slave owners were to lose their titles under the second act.[4]

There were, to be sure, Republicans who took Congress's power over confiscation and abolition for granted. Representative Charles Sedgwick of New York believed that "so far as the war power is concerned, Congress has an absolute despotism. They have the power to pass any law which they think best calculated to carry the war to a successful conclusion. They are absolute and sovereign." Senator Wade of Ohio maintained that Congress, as the repository of the people's will, was the final arbiter on any question, but particularly during a war. Those who believed that the president, "the moment that we are involved in a war, is a despotic magistrate, and is subject to no control from any quarter," were wrong. For Sumner, there could "be nothing essential to its [the war's] success, which is not positively within the province of Congress.

There is not one of the rights of war which Congress may not invoke," including confiscation. Sumner also believed the rebellious states had destroyed their status as states, so Congress could do as it wished. "Call it suicide, if you will, or suspended animation, or abeyance, they have nevertheless ceased to exist," he declared. State treason, Representative Thomas Eliot of Massachusetts observed, described what the secessionist states had done. As such, Congress has the duty "to make such fit enactments as will *declare a forfeiture of its power and functions as a State, and provide for its political reconstruction.*" By ignoring the Constitution's discussion of treason as an individual transgression and applying it to the states, Eliot attributed to Congress the power to punish treason as it wished. Another representative, Alfred Ely of New York, claimed that states became territories after they seceded, thereby destroying their claims to protection under the Constitution. These theories were part of the Reconstruction debates that began during the war, but they were certainly minority views in the deliberations over confiscation.[5]

Most Republicans took the middle ground: for confiscation but under executive control, for punishing rebels but worried about retribution's effect on reunion, for emancipation but also for colonization, and concerned about whether confiscation would last beyond the lives of the rebels. Senator John Sherman of Ohio, a moderate, believed in confiscation for "the prominent actors" in the rebellion and amnesty for "the great mass of citizens" in the Confederacy. Representative Roscoe Conkling of New York agreed. While "extravagant or passionate" legislation might be cathartic, a cautious application of confiscation would be more "practical." To punish "all who are legally guilty of treason," claimed Representative Eliakim Walton of Vermont, would not be just or helpful for reconciliation, since many Southerners had been led astray by a few. To help those less guilty realize their true loyalty, some legislators suggested a period of grace after the second act passed so that all the deluded Southerners could return to their former allegiance. "We should not close the door against" the rebels, said Representative Andrew Clements of Tennessee, "until they have had it in their power" to make the choice themselves. As the war and the confiscation debates continued into the spring and summer, however, this distinction found less support. Although most could not agree with Representative Dwight Loomis of Connecticut that in "the case of rebels in arms, every one is an actual enemy," many came to believe that more than the leaders should be punished. As the willingness to punish most rebels grew, so did the view that the president should have broad pardoning power to assist a swift reunion. Representative Albert Porter of Indiana wanted to extend it to those who failed to abandon their sympathy for the Confederacy. Some, like Senator Cowan, insisted that leniency be offered to all but the leaders, but most believed that the North should be harsh, if necessary. "Nobody supposes we would do it," Trumbull concluded, "but we are talking power."[6]

Even though advocates of a vigorous confiscation policy hoped that a reconstruction of the South would result from the second act, moderates were just as eager to prevent significant change, beyond perhaps emancipation, as a consequence of the war. Representative John Killinger of Pennsylvania well expressed the moderates' wish for a vigorous war with a mostly painless restoration. "I would reduce them to vassalage. Lay waste to their fields with fire and sword, and annihilate every living thing within their limits," he proclaimed in support of executive confiscation. But the "moment that peace is restored law and order will take the place of military force," he said, and the ex-Confederate states will "be restored to their original rights and dignities." Representatives like Henry Grider, a former Whig from Kentucky, hoped that confiscation would not harm slavery, but by early 1862 most moderates appeared to realize that this was inevitable. Senators William Pitt Fessenden of Maine and James W. Grimes of Iowa, both moderates on confiscation, were upset at Lincoln's refusal to attack slavery. Grimes even wanted to arm fugitive slaves. As Representative William Cutler of Ohio noted, the status of slavery before and during the war had dramatically changed. "You may as well ask me to regard with like complacency the quiet house cur sleeping at my feet, and the same animal raging the streets as a slabbering [*sic*] mad dog," he observed. For most, like Senator Henry Wilson of Massachusetts, slavery had caused secession, and it had to be destroyed. "It was slavery," he said, "nothing more, nothing less, that perverted their hearts, clouded their reason, blinded their consciences, and made them traitors." Wilson even went so far as to say that treason and slavery were synonymous. Representative Owen Lovejoy of Illinois likened slavery to a tiger with its fangs on the throat of the government. Unless killed, he predicted, it would suck, "vampire-like," the lifeblood of the republic. Radicals, on the other hand, hoped that confiscation would do considerably more than just put an end to slavery.[7]

Before the confiscation bill appeared in the Senate in December 1861, Sumner had written his friend Wendell Phillips, "The great end approaches. It cannot be postponed. . . . We have before us, as I assumed . . . the grand question of the reconstruction of southern society. Pray give me the benefit of your counsel," he urged. The radicals' plans for the South were grand indeed. Confiscation of the planters' property would eliminate that class and turn the South into a land of small farmers, said the radicals. To Senator Justin Morrill of Vermont, the "old struggle of a class for power and prestige" was "repeating itself in our history." The solution, said Senator David Wilmot of Pennsylvania, was to take the planters' property, land, and slaves. This would crush the rebellion and punish the class that fomented it. "Property is power," he concluded. If not ruined, Representative Ely predicted, the planter class would remember its loss; it would erupt again like "a political volcano, liable at any moment to belch forth smoke and fire and devastating lava." "It is only by the confiscation of the property of those who shall persist in rebellion," claimed Ely, "that society can be organized upon a loyal basis at the South." Confiscation would cause suffering for many, admitted Representative Aaron Sargent of California, but it was better to give land to the Southern poor, he argued, than to keep the South under constant military control. Confiscation's result, Sumner confidently predicted, would be to create small estates peopled by poor whites and Northern soldiers in the South, who "changing their swords into plowshares, will fill the land with northern industry and northern principles." Significantly, freed slaves were not yet part of the radicals' dream. That would come later. Even so, the radicals' presumption was impressive. As Justin Morrill concluded with considerable arrogance the South only needed "the privileges of free institutions, free schools, *homesteads*, even handed justice, and equality of rights" to realize its sovereignty.[8] A number of obstacles stood in the way of this utopia, not the least of which were the differences among radicals, moderates, and conservatives that surfaced in various Republican meetings. Moreover, although a number of newspapers supported confiscation, none discussed it as a means to reconstruct the South.[9]

For supporters of the second act, confiscation of property, including slaves, had to extend beyond the lives of the rebels to reconstruct the South. This proved the most contentious issue in the debates on the second act. The problems revolved around in rem proceedings, specifically provided for in the second act, and derived from revenue laws and admiralty procedure. In rem proceedings regarded the property, such as smuggled goods, as guilty and did not question the guilt of the owner. In *The Palmyra* (1827),[10] often cited as the leading case on the matter, Justice Joseph Story had upheld their use. "Many cases exist," Story observed, "where the forfeiture for acts done attaches solely *in rem*, and there is no accompanying penalty *in personam*." In other words, the owner need not be present or found guilty for forfeiture of the property. Moreover, Justice Storey said, "the practice has been, and so this Court understand the law to be, that the proceeding *in rem* stands independent of, and wholly unaffected by any criminal proceedings *in personam*."[11] Although few in Congress or the administration were well acquainted with in rem proceedings, the procedures raised a number of issues central to confiscation and reconstruction: how to describe slaves and the conflict, executive versus congressional power, the degree of punishment given rebels, and the means of restoration.[12]

Supporters of confiscation tried various arguments to assuage the critics' claims that in rem proceedings violated the Constitution, which requires that the trials of all crimes, other than impeachment cases, shall be by jury in the state where the crime occurred. Representative Eliot argued that in rem proceedings provided the chance to get at the rebels during the war and that "when this rebellion shall have ceased, the parties guilty as chief traitors will then be punished," as well. Punishing traitors in peace was one thing, said Representative Eliot, but we "all know that in time of war we cannot try a traitor." Even traitors who owned property in the North might be beyond reach, and it was most unlikely that Southern juries would convict traitors or rebels from their own states, assuming the Southern states still existed in law. To expect to reach traitors in the South would "be the very climax of absurdity," said Representative Elijah Babbit from Pennsylvania. Moderates said that the Constitution required that traitors should be tried after the war, whereas advocates of broad confiscation feared that too many would have been pardoned by then. So it was important to reach rebels during the war. As Representative John Noell, a radical Democrat from Missouri, said, in rem proceedings were "founded on public necessity and public convenience," similar to revenue cases where the perpetrators were often beyond the jurisdiction of the United States. This would allow, said Trumbull, "all the property belonging to rebels, as fast as we can get possession of it," to be "appropriated" for the government's use. Slaves would then be considered as property, echoing the majority opinion in *Dred Scott*. Moderates, however, rightly doubted that much property of any description could be seized, adjudicated, and sold fast enough to add to the North's treasury, undercutting one rationale advocates offered to support the second act.[13]

The very idea of in rem proceedings most troubled moderates. They believed such proceedings were simply a way to ignore the Constitution for the sake of confiscation. Although the Supreme Court would sustain their use after the war,[14] the arguments against them were telling on the shape of the final bill. Senator Cowan accepted the use of in rem proceedings when courts held property used or intended for unlawful or belligerent purposes, but "the property itself must have been the guilty instrument" and must exhibit evidence upon which the proceedings rest. The property to be confiscated under the second act, however, failed to meet these requirements. According to Senator Jacob Collamer of Vermont, there was, in fact, a "vast deal of *hocus pocus* in" the use of in rem proceedings for confiscation and it also violated due process. After all, he said, the Constitution clearly prohibited bills of attainder, taking property without due process, conviction without a jury, punishment twice for the same crime or corruption of blood for treason. Yet the confiscation bill, he claimed, would permit all this to occur for property owners in the South. The owner would be absent with in rem proceedings, there would be no jury, he could be tried for treason after the war, and the forfeiture would extend beyond his life. In addition, those pushing for broad confiscation were treating rebels inconsistently, both as citizens and as belligerents. If they were citizens, then the Constitution applied. If they were enemies, then confiscation was a military matter, best executed by Lincoln and the army and not to extend beyond the war.[15]

Many advocates of confiscation routinely described the rebels as enemies yet claimed they were to be treated as citizens who became traitors. Confiscation would occur during the war against enemies while trials for treason would occur only after the war by which time their property would have been confiscated, supporters hoped, beyond their lifetimes. Trumbull claimed the Constitution's prohibition against bills of attainder, however, had no relation to his bill. Confiscation was only meant to "reach the property of such rebels or traitors as are beyond the reach of judicial process, and can neither be arrested, tried, or convicted for treason or any other offense," while the war continued. As Trumbull noted, it was "because you have got no courts of justice in the South that this war is upon us." It would be absurd to apply this prohibition of bills of attainder to those who could only be tried for treason after the war, he claimed. In fact, Representative Noell declared, the bill "waives the crime of treason and undertakes to punish in another form and for another offense altogether different" than that in the attainder clause. The distinction to be emphasized, Representative Eliot argued, was that confiscation by in rem proceedings would not affect the person of the rebel, whereas a bill of attainder operated solely against the person. "It is the person alone that is attainted—it is the blood that is corrupted," he added. In addition, confiscation of an absent owner's property did not mean, according to Senator Wilmot, that the same man could not be tried for treason after the war. For the radicals, confiscation by in rem was but one of two ways the North could punish the South. As Noell concluded, confiscation penalized the rebel "in the thing seized and confiscated, not in person."[16]

Ironically, Noell, a Democrat from Missouri, became one of the most effective defenders of confiscation's constitutionality, which may help explain why a more effective measure was not enacted. Arguments against the second act were meaningless, he said, because the seizures only developed in response to the war and implied no preexisting condition, such as a contract or legal obligation. The government, he asserted, employed confiscation during a war because of crimes against its authority, for instance rebellion or attack, which violated no law but threatened the sovereign's authority. Therefore, the second act was not a criminal statute. As distinguished from forfeitures forbidden in the Constitution's article three, section three, which occurred upon the violation of a specific law or regulation involving commerce, Noel believed that confiscation was applicable against any conduct the sovereign—Congress or the president at its bidding—deemed contrary to its interests. To punish the individual for such crimes, continued Noell, the government penalized "him in the thing seized and confiscated, and not in person." The government appropriated this confiscated property, holding the fee simple absolutely, for its own use. Noell concluded that the absolute title owned by the individual transferred to the government absolutely through confiscation.[17]

Opponents of vigorous confiscation naturally scoffed at the argument that property could be considered guilty under the second act. Representative Eliot had argued that only "guilty property, made use of to destroy the Government" was to be confiscated, whereas Representative Benjamin Thomas, another Massachusetts Republican, saw no "guilty property" in the South compared with prize, booty, contraband of war, or property used for war. "It is private property outside the conflict of arms," Thomas declared, "forfeited not because it is the instrument of offense, but as a penalty for the crimes of the owner." Except for slaves used to aid the Confederacy, Thomas had a point. But proponents of broad confiscation could counter that plantations and farms, the other principal objects of confiscation, aided the rebellion insofar as they sustained the rebel armies in the field. Thomas was right, however, that supporters of in rem were not really interested in confiscating the guns, horses, and swords that rebels used to support the Confederacy. Senator Cowan, an opponent of any confiscation, declared that before in rem proceedings could be instituted, "the property itself must have been a guilty instrument" and manifested the evidence upon which the proceedings rested. But those who proposed a confiscation that would endure beyond the war ignored such critiques; they wanted to punish the rebels and initiate Reconstruction before the war ended and before requests for mercy and reconciliation began. Collamer, however, had been persuasive to many with his claim that arguments for in rem revealed a good deal of sophistry.[18]

Trumbull and other confiscation supporters faced the conundrum of reconciling their goals with the Constitution most of them revered. They believed Lincoln was unwilling or unable to act boldly against the South. Equally obvious, they thought, was the need to end slavery, which they saw as the curse of the nation and the cause of the war. Even Edward Everett, not yet a convert to confiscation, saw the demise of slavery as almost a certainty by mid-March 1862. The confiscators believed that allowing the planter class to survive, even without slaves, almost guaranteed that the sections would remain at odds after the war. As well, they believed that freed slaves would be at the mercy of their former masters, although this prospect bothered legislators very little. So, the South had to be changed and the process had to begin before the war ended, when a desire for peace and harmony would doubtless cloud the issues. Vigorous confiscation appeared to be one answer; the exigencies of the war would resolve whatever constitutional doubts might arise. But although there were many in favor of some confiscation, from Trumbull to Browning, they did not all sing from the same hymnal, particularly when legal issues were involved. When doubts arose about the second act's constitutionality, radicals like Representative Samuel Blair of Pennsylvania simply argued that confiscation was a congressional military measure, like the blockage of Southern ports or enforcement of the non-intercourse between the sections. It was nothing but "brazen impudence" for the rebels, or those who argued on their behalf, he said, to seek the benefits of the Constitution that they had repudiated by war. If that was an insufficient argument, Senator Jacob Howard of Michigan claimed that the due process clause of the Fifth Amendment did not apply to war legislation. Too much concern for due process in the midst of war was absurd anyway, he added. A Sumner correspondent echoed the sentiments of Blair and Howard. Referring to Senator Collamer's speech on confiscation, he argued, "the rebellion could not have received a more efficient support from any quarter."[19]

Most citizens who supported confiscation saw it primarily as a military measure, however. Some viewed it as a means to punish the South or its leaders but very few understood that its advocates hoped it would form the basis of Reconstruction. Although a few urged that the confiscated land should be given to Union soldiers, most suggested that the proceeds from the property seized be used to defray the war's cost. Many who wrote their congressmen associated confiscation with emancipation on the premise that slavery had caused the rebellion and now had to be abolished. Further, since the Union was at war, Congress could therefore ignore the ante bellum agreements not to interfere with slavery. Only a small number, though, appeared concerned about the fate of the freed slaves. As well, almost no one expressed doubt that broad and lasting confiscation was constitutional and none who wrote their congressmen on behalf of the second act suggested the Constitution be ignored. But unlike the experience of the Revolution, where support for confiscation arose from the people as much as the leaders, no groundswell arose in the North to urge passage of the second act.

Even so, the confiscation bill's introduction in December 1861 encouraged many to believe the North might finally strike at the South. "There is in that Bill the first streak of morning light that we have seen since the war commenced," John Russell wrote from Illinois. D. E. Clay thought the bill would "smother disloyalty" in the free states and "have a salutary effect in putting down the Rebellion in the slave states and eradicating the cause of it." At last, some said of the bill, something was being done. "Oh that our rulers, civil [and] military, would see & feel," said H. B. Stanton from New York, "how the people ache to have them begin the work of striking the rebellion in its vulnerable point" which was slavery. "Pray urge thro this Confiscation bill & give heart to the country," he wrote. From Ohio, Justin Hamilton, a recruiter, wrote that he was "anxiously watching the movements of the Administration and Congress" for some action. Even though he understood the need to be "prudent," he could not "see how, we, are to avoid Confiscating the Slaves of Rebels, and when confiscated," he advocated putting the freed slaves in Florida, perhaps. The people were "quite dissatisfied" with the administration's effort "to put down this accursed rebellion," reported Silas Potts, also from Ohio. The government should "capture at every opportunity any property, or means" used by those "who have taken up arms" or who are in any "manner either directly or indirectly assisting this *infernal* proslavery war," Potts added. If many Democrats had begun to believe that the administration was too eager to embrace abolition, many Republicans were just as upset at the sympathy it showed toward slavery.[20]

Only a minority who followed the confiscation debates realized that Trumbull's bill would take the rebels' landed property as well as their slaves. Like moderates in Congress who were not convinced that property could be considered guilty, most in the public did not appreciate the implications of taking the real property of rebels forever. For most, confiscation was a just punishment for those who instigated the rebellion or a way to end slavery, not a means to reform the South or assist freed slaves. E. L. Smith of Kentucky was typical of one group that supported a strong confiscation act. The "true Union men everywhere are the same in sentiment," Smith wrote to Ben Wade, and "that sentiment is as broad as the continent. If slavery stands in the way of the restoration of the Union destroy it. That is alone the true test of Unionism, all else is not." Another group wanted confiscation used to punish the rebels, as David Root from Vermont observed to Wade. He thought it "the supreme folly of some of your members who are afraid to touch the property of those villainous rebels who have remorsefully brought upon the country all the distress" of the war. "Nine tenths of the Northern people are expecting it, looking for it & will be awfully disappointed if it [the second act] should be defeated." A. Watson wrote Trumbull that he feared the war might end before slavery's death. "If the rebellion be put down, leaving slavery as at present, the slaveowners who have caused the rebellion will scarcely receive any detriment whatever," he concluded. Whether radicals in Congress should have discussed the importance of confiscation as a method of Reconstruction more fully to promote greater understanding within the public is difficult to determine. Certainly the lack of attention paid to confiscated land as a basis for Reconstruction during the war helps explain why there was so little support for the idea once the fighting ended.[21]

Some did understand that the freed slaves would need help after the war and that Union soldiers might well decide to settle in the South if given land there. Charles A. Dana, formerly of the *New York Herald*, endorsed the idea of giving "large bounties of captured lands to the soldiers to induce them" to settle in the South after the war. So, too, an anonymous correspondent recommended to Trumbull that South Carolina be set aside for freed slaves after the war to provide a place "where they can cultivate the soil and enjoy the benefit of schools," away from whites presumably. Several others also thought that freed slaves could use abandoned lands principally to provide crops to the government. But only W. G. Smith of Cincinnati specifically urged that parcels of confiscated land be leased to ex-slaves, for fifty years, to encourage "negroes to industry and enterprise." At the same time, however, he proposed protecting "union men in the Southern States in all their rights of Person & Property including slaves." A constituent urged Sherman to place ex-slaves "in possession of the confiscated Estates" and give them government protection, but the senator decidedly opposed harsh confiscation.[22]

Instead, almost all those who favored broad confiscation and discussed the aftermath of slavery urged colonization for ex-slaves. Colonization's appeal for the public, not to mention Lincoln and many in Congress, has been well documented. Trumbull's bill, of course, included a provision to encourage freed slaves to colonize. Even Thaddeus Stevens, with Sumner perhaps the strongest advocate for emancipation and equality in Congress, supported colonization.[23] Although William Lloyd Garrison found colonization "an absurd and preposterous scheme," as did other abolitionists and African Americans, many others, like Orestes Brownson, another notable reformer, supported the idea. He did so "as a concession to the prejudices of my countrymen." It may be that Brownson and others, like Lincoln, used this as a cover for their own racism. We should keep a number of factors in mind, however. Given the racism in the North at the time, colonization was not the totally impractical or insensitive idea that it might appear to be now. Only a very small minority, many of whom were seen as crackpots, believed social intercourse between white and black people was possible. As well, those who sincerely believed in emancipation and black equality then were perhaps not the hypocrites that some have thought since the 1960s. Although Democrats and Southerners were quick to condemn them in the 1860s, many honest and sincere people, like Lincoln, fervently believed slavery was wrong yet did not see how free blacks could succeed in white society after emancipation. Some urged colonization for freed slaves for fear they would move to the North; no one was naïve enough to suggest they would be welcomed there after the war. This was, of course, partly racist and self-serving, but it was also realistic. As an alternative to moving north, Uriah Boston wanted "them sent directly to Africa," for it was the "natural and God created home for all Africans." Most who endorsed colonization agreed with Thomas Lippincott that no one should be forced into it, especially when they were "dragged hither in chains. Justice would cry out against it."[24]

This is not to suggest that the proposal for colonization in the second act did not rest on a good deal of racism. Trumbull himself admitted that one of the main reasons to include it in the second act was to appease those worried about where freed slaves might migrate. "There is a very great aversion in the West—I know it to be so in my State—against having free negroes come among us. Our people want nothing to do with the negro," Trumbull conceded. Representative Samuel Blair, a Pennsylvania Republican, tried without much success to reassure nervous Northern colleagues who feared confiscation would loose millions of blacks upon the North. "These people are just as warmly attached to the land of their birth as their masters," he predicted. On the other hand, Representative William Cutler, an Ohio Republican, had no doubt that freed slaves would wish to flee the South and the cruelty of their former masters. "The blistered limb might as well trust a second time the burning heap of coals," he commented. As these comments suggest, there was much speculation about what emancipation might bring. No one, however, predicted it would lead to racial harmony, so some form of colonization seemed imperative if the just goal of abolition was to be accomplished through confiscation. As a compromise between neglect of freed slaves and foreign colonization, Senator John Ten Eyck of New Jersey suggested that they be separated from whites and given a special district somewhere in the country.[25] None of these ideas received much serious attention.

In a war far from won, Northerners gave little thought to the fate of freed slaves after the war, except to hope they stayed out of the North. However, the treatment accorded fugitives slaves and contrabands troubled some Northerners, who suggested ways, although not adopted, to ameliorate the transition to freedom. Even though their solutions may seem limited or naïve, these few did at least consider the matter. What is striking in that generation's attitudes about race is that so few considered the issue, as seen in the second act's failure to address race. John Jay, the grandson of the famous Federalist, for one, hoped the second act would provide a commissioner to help blacks as the Union armies moved southward. Some free black "citizens" in the North suggested to both Trumbull and Sumner that "agents" be appointed to inquire "into the feelings and wants of Contrabands" to secure "their future good." Secretary of War Edwin Stanton, Cameron's successor, felt that the issue of "Colored refugees from rebel service and how to provide for them is perhaps a ["the most" was crossed out] difficult question upon this Government." He thought a solution might be found at a "convention of Gentlemen whose exalted personal character, humanitarian behavior and freedom from party objections would give conclusive weight to whatever their judgment, after careful examination on the subject would recommend."[26] But advocates of emancipation by confiscation failed to heed these few entreaties. Little wonder, then, that no groundswell arose after the war to assist blacks in the South. Radical Republicans, not to mention abolitionists, had offered scant leadership on the issue during the war when they had the chance.

Although legislators spoke about how confiscation could transform the South, most outside Congress viewed it solely as a means to end slavery, with the added bonus of punishing the rebellion's leaders, the owners. And, with a few notable exceptions, they believed it was constitutional. Francis Lieber, a student of the rules of war, spoke for many when he said that those "who commenced this rebellion ought to have reflected upon this [abolition]. It is now too late to talk, *in the midst of war*, of rights made or guaranteed by municipal or constitutional law." Joseph Medill of the *Chicago Tribune* agreed that the rebels could claim no constitutional protection. "Those who *obey* the Constitution can discern its safeguards; those who trample upon it and make war upon it *cannot*." Others grew angry at the "sensitiveness," as G. S. Rynard expressed it, of some Republicans to confiscation and emancipation. The people, he claimed, wanted the government to "go to the very edge of the Constitution in confiscation" to make the rebels pay for "their monstrous rebellion." In fact, only one correspondent argued about the constitutionality of confiscation with its advocates in the Senate. Dr. Johnson H. Jordan, of Cincinnati and Pittsburgh, wrote Sherman, Sumner, and Trumbull a number of times that the Constitution would not permit emancipation through confiscation. As he explained to Sumner before the senator introduced his state suicide proposal, Congress could not liberate the slaves by confiscation if it treated the seceded states as part of the Union. Slavery remained a state matter until Congress admitted the reality of secession and treated the states as territories; only then could it emancipate through confiscation. But almost no one else, other than Democratic editors and Professor Joel Parker in the *North American Review*, challenged confiscation's advocates in such a manner.[27] In the end they had only to wrestle with their own Republican colleagues on what shape the bill would finally take.

Only four senators—Trumbull, Jacob Howard, Henry Wilson, and Wade—supported the original confiscation bill without qualification. In March, moderates had proposed referring the bill to a select committee that would write a measure a majority of Republicans could support, but radicals helped block the move. The *Detroit Daily Advertiser* wondered, "Why does the bill to confiscate the property of rebels so long hang fire in Congress?" The debate and the divisions continued. Without a new bill, moderates were able to defeat the radicals' efforts to pass their sweeping measure. In early May a new committee was chosen to resolve the stalemate. Trumbull, however, refused to serve on it; he did not "have much confidence in anything growing out of it." The Republican majority of the committee consisted of Daniel Clark of New Hampshire, Collamer of Vermont, John Harlan of Iowa, Ira Harris of New York, Sherman of Ohio, and Wilson of Massachusetts. Only Wilson and Harlan were considered radicals. Within a week the committee reported to the Senate a new version that satisfied only the moderates. The key provisions were that rebels convicted of treason would suffer death or five years in prison, a fine, and emancipation of their slaves. Those convicted of aiding the rebellion would forfeit their slaves and property but only for life. The president could "seize and sequester" the property of certain classes of rebels. He was also authorized to free the slaves of those who did not resume allegiance within sixty days of a proclamation, pardon rebels, and colonize freed slaves.[28]

The moderates had been successful; this bill bore slight resemblance to Trumbull's original measure. Trumbull said that the substitute "is not and does not profess to be a bill of confiscation." Advocates of confiscation particularly opposed the new bill's requirement that owners be present in courts following the seizure of their property and that a transfer of title could only occur if loyal judges and juries were found in the South to execute its provisions. Trumbull's bill, of course, had avoided such hurdles with in rem proceedings, which Collamer and other moderates had particularly opposed. Congress was, at the same time, considering impeachment for West H. Humphreys, a Tennessee district court judge, on a number of grounds including the enforcement of the Confederate Confiscation Act. The coincidence of the two events prompted Trumbull to inquire if the Senate wanted to authorize the judge "to say whether he shall fine and imprison Mr. Toombs, or whether he shall make him answer to the scaffold for the atrocious crimes he has committed against his country?" Beyond posing awkward questions about the moderates' objectives for their bill, the radicals in the Senate were able to postpone any vote on the measure.[29]

In the meantime, the House had created its own bill. Following three months of discussion, the Judiciary Committee rejected all confiscation measures under consideration. The House leadership, led by Thaddeus Stevens, then chose a fairly radical committee to consider the matter again. It included Republicans Eliot of Massachusetts and Sedgwick of New York, along with

Democrat Noell of Missouri, who had all expressed support for broad confiscation. Republicans Fernando Beaman of Michigan and John Hutchins of Ohio, both considered radical, were also on the committee. It returned two measures, both of which largely followed bills introduced earlier by Republican John Bingham of Ohio. The first confiscated all property owned by prominent rebels, who were in six classes, authorized the president to seize all property of rebels who did not resume allegiance within sixty days of a proclamation, and subjected all property confiscated to in rem proceedings. The second bill freed all slaves of persons who aided the rebellion but without any judicial process. If a person could prove he had not "in anyway aided, assisted, or countenanced" the rebellion, however, he could keep his slaves. Subsequently the House passed the confiscation bill 82–68. Only three non-Republicans voted for it, Noell, and two Unionists from Virginia. Nine Republicans, including five from Massachusetts, opposed the bill. The House then rejected the emancipation bill 78–74. All votes for were Republican, but seven other Republicans now joined the nine who opposed the confiscation bill, indicating that many still felt that Congress could not interfere with slavery. All seven Republicans were from states having a common boundary with at least one slave state.[30]

The Senate received the House bill but then ignored it. Instead, it returned to its own bill that had so disgusted Trumbull and passed it with most of the radicals, including Trumbull, reluctantly voting for it. Only Howard and Chandler of the radicals, both from Michigan, voted against it. Chandler said it "was utterly worthless as a bill to confiscate property." The House subsequently voted against concurring in the Senate bill. The Senate and House then chose colleagues for a conference committee. Senators Clark of Vermont, Harris of New York, and Joseph Wright of Indiana, none of whom were enthusiastic about confiscation, were chosen from the upper body, while Eliot of Massachusetts, James Wilson of Iowa, both radicals, and Democrat Erastus Corning of New York were chosen for the House. At first a deadlock developed in the conference committee but finally a compromise measure, similar to what passed in both the House and Senate, was reported. The new measure pleased most moderates, some radicals, and a few conservatives. It provided that a convicted traitor would suffer death or five years in prison, a $10,000 fine and emancipation of slaves. Fines would come from the sale of the traitor's property. Those convicted of aiding the rebellion would be imprisoned for ten years or fined $10,000. The president was instructed to seize all property of six classes of rebels and seize all the property of any rebel who did not cease aiding the rebellion within sixty days of a proclamation. In rem proceedings would be used for all confiscated property and all slaves entering the Union lines would be freed.

Finally, the president was authorized to colonize willing ex-slaves and given the power to pardon any rebel.[31] In the end, it was a bill full of compromises.

Although the new bill was a victory for moderate Republicans, since it was weaker than what Trumbull originally proposed, radicals were not displeased. The first four sections of the bill defined treason and its penalties but did not mention confiscation of property, although it did authorize freedom for the slaves of convicted traitors. Sections five through eight, on the other hand, enumerated who would be subject to confiscation of their property; these sections made no mention of treason. In effect, as supporters of confiscation would argue later, two separate measures were contained in one bill and the second had no relation to the attainder clause in the Constitution. Moderates obtained treason as a basis of punishment, confiscation for only six classes of rebels, broad authority, including the pardoning power, for the president and the opportunity for rebels to resume allegiance to the North and thus avoid the punishment of confiscation. The radicals obtained in rem proceedings and the liberation of slaves in Union-controlled areas, two central issues for them, but they failed to get an explicit provision for forfeiture beyond the lives of those whose property was confiscated and the bill authorized the president to implement the act. The House passed the conference bill 82–41. Bradley Granger of Michigan and Joseph Segar of Wisconsin were the only Republicans to oppose it. Four border-state Unionists voted with the Republican majority. The bill then passed the Senate 27–12, with only Republicans Browning and Cowan voting with the minority. The *New York Herald* reported that many radicals viewed the bill as impractical and thought its passage something of a defeat. Sumner, for example, incorrectly thought it "a practical act of emancipation. It was only in this respect that I valued it." On the other hand, Trumbull wrote his wife that he was pleased at what had just transpired in Congress. They had "passed a good confiscation bill. . . . It embraces the main features of my bill, & if only the President does his duty it will be very efficient."[32] The Second Confiscation Act, entitled a bill to "suppress insurrection, to punish treason and rebellion, to seize and confiscate property of rebels, and for other purposes," now only needed the president's signature to become law.

Congress knew that Lincoln favored less severe measures than the second act's provisions to subdue the South and emancipate the slaves. In early March 1862 he had asked Congress for money to implement gradual compensated emancipation so that "the more Northern shall, by such initiation, make it certain to the more Southern" that they would never "join the latter in their proposed confederacy." That realization would, he believed, persuade the rebels they could not achieve "independence" and the rebellion would "substantially" end. Lincoln thought this was "one of the most efficient means of self-preservation" the North could pursue and stressed that the "general government sets up no claim of a right . . . to interfere with slavery within" the states. Congress ignored the border-state representatives who opposed the president and subsequently agreed to his request for funds. In late March as Congress contemplated the abolition of slavery in the District of Columbia, Lincoln observed to Horace Greeley, the editor of the *New York Tribune*, that he did not oppose abolition in the Capitol in principle; he just worried "as to the time and manner of doing it." When Congress later passed the bill, Lincoln noted his concern was only "one of expediency, arising in view of all the circumstances." In other words, he wondered if it were necessary to move so quickly, even if toward a noble end.[33]

Lincoln's concern became clear on May 19, 1862, when he revoked Major General David Hunter's proclamation freeing the slaves in Georgia, Florida, and South Carolina, the area of his command. In early April Hunter had requested from the War Department permission to arm fifty thousand "loyal men," presumably blacks. In mid-April Hunter declared free all slaves owned by rebels in Fort Pulaski and Cockspur Island, Georgia. This drew little attention in the North and no official rebuke, perhaps because it involved few slaves. Less than a month later, Hunter far exceeded his April declaration and even Frémont's proclamation. Having already instituted martial law in the Department of the South, on May 9 Hunter proclaimed, "Slavery and martial law in a free country are altogether incompatible," adding that the slaves in these three states "are therefore declared forever free." He also conscripted all able-bodied black men between the ages of eighteen and forty-five. Reactions to Hunter's proclamation were not surprising; abolitionists and radicals thought it marvelous, while the more cautious believed it was too radical.[34]

Lincoln's view was all that counted, however. His proclamation of May 19 revoking Hunter's order was intended for the border states, not the North. Lincoln noted that Hunter had not consulted the administration before issuing the declaration. More important, Lincoln reserved to himself alone, as commander in chief, the question of whether to declare free the slaves as a "necessity indispensable to the maintenance" of the government. Having disposed of Hunter, he then returned to his message on gradual compensated abolition and Congress's support for this method in March. "I do not argue. I beseech you," he told the border states, "to make the arguments yourselves. You can not if you would be blind to the signs of the times." Gradual abolition "would come gently as the dews of heaven, not rending or wrecking anything" they truly held dear. If they did not accept gradual change then more dramatic alterations would be imposed, he predicted, in an apparent reference to what Congress had been discussing for some time. But Lincoln's offer in the revocation of Hunter's proclamation had no appeal to the influential citizens of the border states and they did not embrace it.[35]

This did not deter Lincoln from renewing his appeal on the day that Congress approved the Second Confiscation Act. On July 12 he wrote to the border states representatives, observing that had they accepted gradual compensated emancipation, "the war would now be substantially ended." Nothing less would be possible now, he said. The chance to return to the status quo ante bellum had certainly passed. "If the war continue long, as it must, if the object be not sooner attained, the institution in your states will be extinguished by mere friction and abrasion—by the mere incidents of war." But "substantial compensation" and colonization were still available if they would agree "at once to emancipate *gradually*. Room in South America for colonization, can be obtained cheaply, and in abundance," he assured them. Moreover, "when the numbers shall be large enough to be company and encouragement for one another, the freed people will not be so reluctant to go." His repudiation of Hunter's proclamation "gave dissatisfaction, if not offense, to many" whose support the Union needed; the "pressure in this direction, is still upon me, and is increasing." So, he concluded, "consider this proposition," since they "more than any others," had the opportunity "to bring" the country "speedy relief." Two days later, in a meeting with Lincoln, these same representatives rejected the offer once again.[36] Lincoln, by then, was running out of alternatives to emancipation by broader means.

At the same time, Lincoln conferred with Senator William Pitt Fessenden of Maine about the recently passed confiscation bill. Aware that the president objected to parts of the law, Fessenden conferred with colleagues who asked him to go the White House to discuss the matter. Although Fessenden had voted for the law, he was not an enthusiast. He told Senator Browning, who hoped Lincoln would veto the bill, he believed "it would have been better not to legislate upon the subject of confiscation at all." Yet he feared a veto would divide the Republican Party and damage its prospects in the fall elections. According to Fessenden, Lincoln's central concern was that forfeiture of real property should not extend beyond the lives of the offenders. The president also worried that widespread use of in rem proceedings would violate due process. In the meantime, Representative Horace Maynard of Tennessee, without any apparent prodding from Lincoln, as some later suspected, had proposed that Congress declare that the law be prospective throughout. According to Maynard, his resolution would mean "no judge or member of a State legislature shall be brought within its scope, unless he gave his adherence to the confederate State by oath to support the confederate constitution." The House agreed to Maynard's resolution by a voice vote without discussion. The issue then moved to the Senate without further clarification.[37]

In the Senate Clark of New Hampshire moved to amend Maynard's resolution by adding, "Nor shall any punishment or proceeding under said act be so construed as to work a forfeiture of the real estate of the offender beyond his life." Upon questioning, he admitted that the amendment was "to meet what I believe to be the objection of the President," namely Lincoln's concern that Congress could not confiscate real estate beyond a traitor's life. Radicals objected both to the president's methods and his request. Ben Wade, for example, demanded that the Senate not submit to such a procedure. Trumbull also protested Lincoln's methods but found the resolution itself even more disturbing. It would, he predicted correctly, seriously weaken the bill. He urged that Clark's amendment only apply to those convicted of treason, enumerated in the first four sections, not those guilty of rebellion, discussed in sections five through eight. This was a crucial distinction, as William Whiting, Solicitor of the War Department, observed.[38] But the Senate refused by a voice vote. It then agreed to Clark's amendment 25–15, with eight Republicans opposed. The Senate, however, did reject another amendment from Clark, also suggested by Lincoln, that would have authorized the president to combine amnesty for rebels with the restoration of "any property which may have been seized and condemned under any proceedings of this act, or the proceeds thereof." The amended joint resolution by Maynard and Clark then went back to the House, which accepted it 83–21. Only four Republicans, including Bingham and Stevens, opposed it.[39] These concessions, which many came to regret, substantially weakened the second act, already modified a good deal. The joint resolution allowed rebels to retain slaves even if they declared allegiance to the Union only a day before the bill became law. More significantly, the failure to accept Trumbull's distinction almost guaranteed that no forfeiture of real estate would occur beyond the life of any convicted under the act, even for those who had lost their property through in rem proceedings during the war. This removed any real chance that confiscation could produce a reconstructed South or that exslaves might obtain land with their freedom.

Lincoln signed the second act into law on July 17, 1862, but he remained troubled by the bill and sent his veto message, prepared before the joint resolution passed, to Congress. Sending his veto message made clear the division between him and the radicals on confiscation and emphasized how problematic he found the bill to be. In the message Lincoln expressed no objection to punishing persons for treason; they would receive due process and could be pardoned. Nor did he oppose the emancipation of slaves through confiscation although he strongly believed Congress had no power to free them until title of their ownership had been transferred to that body. He thought that the military already had the power to "seize and use whatever of real or personal property may be necessary or convenient" during the war, including slaves. But he believed that the confiscation contemplated was too sweeping. "The severest justice may not always be the best policy," he explained. "The principle of seizing, and appropriating the property of persons embraced within these sections is certainly not very objectionable; but a justly discriminating application of it, would be very difficult, and, to a great extent, impossible." His chief concerns, however, were forfeitures beyond the lives of the offenders and in rem procedures. Although he recognized that "no formal attainder" occurred by in rem proceedings, he wrote, "I still think the greater punishment can not be constitutionally inflicted, in a different form, for the same offense," expressing a concern for the rebels which the advocates of confiscation did not share. He preferred that "a reasonable time should be provided" for the owners of confiscable property "to appear and have personal hearings." In sum, he wanted confiscation carried out only for military purposes during the war and trials for treason afterward, with emancipation left to the executive, and more due process offered rebels.[40] Still, Lincoln approved the bill, whatever its flaws, because it reflected the growing sentiment within Congress and the public that more be done to end the rebellion, abolish slavery, and punish the rebel leaders.

4 Enforcement of the Second Act: Lincoln and Bates

Although Lincoln acknowledged the importance of the second act in a number of instances in the weeks after its passage, he and Attorney General Edward Bates chose not to implement the law vigorously. Lincoln used the second act in various ways, but not to punish those who aided the rebellion or to change the property relations in the South. In the end, the second act proved important before it became law as a threat of change and as a symbol to both slaves and Southerners of what the government could do if it wished to reconstruct the South. As a law, however, it accomplished little. It was a poorly designed measure without an enforcement mechanism, and the administration had little interest in using it to effect change in the South either during the war or as the basis of Reconstruction. Moreover, Congress paid almost no attention to whether or not the law was implemented.[1]

On July 13, the day after Congress passed the second act, Lincoln told Secretary of State William Seward and Secretary of the Navy Gideon Welles that he had decided to begin emancipation. Nine days later the cabinet heard the first draft of the preliminary proclamation. The first paragraph, issued three days later as a proclamation to the public, invoked the second act and its sixth section, warning "all persons . . . to cease participating in aiding, countenancing, or abetting the existing rebellion" against the United States. The emancipation proclamation would be announced on January 1, 1863. On July 22 Lincoln also wrote a memorandum authorizing the recruitment of "free negroes," slaves of disloyal owners, and slaves of loyal owners who had their owners' consent. An executive order to military commanders the same day authorized seizure and "use of any property, real or personal" for military purposes and the employment as wage laborers of "persons of African descent." It required an account "from whom both property, and such person shall have come" as the basis of future compensation. Three days later Lincoln issued a proclamation, which repeated the first paragraph of the preliminary emancipation.[2]

Lincoln also tried to pursue his colonization plans, which the second act had authorized. The bill to free blacks in the District of Columbia, passed in March 1862, provided $100,000, while the second act supplied $500,000 for the project. On August 4, Lincoln appointed Reverend James Mitchell as commissioner of emigration in the Interior Department. Mitchell then arranged a White House meeting for Lincoln on August 14 with a group of five black men, led by Edward M. Thomas, president of an institute to encourage black art and industry. This was the only time when Lincoln directly discussed colonization with blacks. The president urged them to embrace colonization because of the prejudice they would encounter "even when you cease to be slaves, [for] you are yet far removed from being placed on an equality with the white race. You are cut off from many of the advantages which the other race enjoys. The aspiration of men is to enjoy equality with the best when free, but on this broad continent, not a single man of your race is made the equal of a single of ours. . . . [But] for your race among us there could not be war, although many men engaged on either side do not care for you one way or the other."

And so, Lincoln concluded, it would be "better for both of us, therefore, to be separated." He then shifted much of the blame to whites, for there was "an unwillingness on the part of our people, harsh as it may be, for you free colored people to remain with us." Although some had once suggested Liberia as the place to colonize, Lincoln now urged them to consider Central America instead. He closed by asking if this appeared to them a practical plan. The reaction among both blacks and abolitionists was hostile, however. Although Lincoln continued to pursue this dream for several more months, nothing materialized from the plan or the money authorized in the second act.[3]

Nonetheless, the second act's passage in July clearly played a major part in that momentous summer when the focus of the war changed, as Mark Grimsley noted, from conciliation to hard war and the nation's politics became even more partisan. To be sure, a number of pressures encouraged Lincoln to consider emancipation, the use of ex-slaves as laborers and soldiers, and a more aggressive policy toward the South. By early July the clamor from the abolitionists, along with McClellan's failure to move against Richmond, increased demands in the North for more action. McClellan's tactics, on the other hand, might not have been interpreted as inaction had the confiscation debates not stretched over six months. It is clear that the prospect of confiscation was in the air. On July 7 McClellan himself offered Lincoln his unsolicited advice not to include confiscation of property or abolition as part of the war effort. Moreover, according to Joel Silbey, the bill to abolish slavery in the District of Columbia and the second act had increased the division between the parties; Democrats had come to believe by the summer the aims of the war had changed. As Senator John Sherman observed to his brother William in late August, "You can form no conception at the change of opinion here as to the Negro question." He, "for one," was now prepared "to meet the broad issue of universal emancipation" to hasten the war's end.[4] Yet there can be no doubt that the second act was a confused piece of legislation and that Lincoln, however much the act pushed him, showed no inclination to implement it as his intended veto message implied. The irony is that the law that attracted so much attention and produced so many hopes and fears about what it might accomplish was so poorly crafted and weakly implemented.

There are a number of reasons why the Second Confiscation Act was an imperfect instrument. Congress's expanded role during the war was new and unexpected. Perhaps because of this increased responsibility, the original intent of some legislation was not always fully realized. After all, the Thirty-seventh Congress had passed the largest number of laws up to that time, double the previous record. One contemporary also believed that too many lawyers, in the Senate at least, had a hand in drafting the confiscation bill. Legislation written by as many contributors as the second act was likely to contain some inconsistencies, as the act demonstrated. Moderates and radicals were forced to compromise to pass the law, which meant that practicality suffered. It was also evident that despite Congress's efforts to change the South, federalism, as Daniel J. Elazar has argued, came through the Civil War "substantially as it was before the war began." Most legislators remained wedded to the antebellum understanding of states' rights and the role of the central government. Herman Belz has shown how little interest there was in emancipation for the slaves' sake; freeing the slaves was primarily a military measure. In the end, whatever the rhetoric, most Republicans retained notions of property, like Lincoln's, that prevented them from embracing sweeping confiscation.[5] The result was an ineffective law.

If the prospect of confiscation encouraged hopes of emancipation, the law itself made it difficult to free slaves. Under the act, slaves of rebels were free only when they came within the military's control. The assumption was that emancipation would advance along with the army. However, slaves could be freed individually or in groups only when a federal court found their owners to be rebels; the military had no power to adjudicate the matter themselves. Doubts even arouse about whether the military had the power to transfer slaves to federal courts for such proceedings. The second act would have required hundreds of thousands of trials of individual masters. Furthermore, it did not affect slaves owned by nonrebels who could prove they had given no aid to the rebellion or by those who swore allegiance to the North, even minutes before the act became law. It also omitted a method for resolving the issue if slaves claimed freedom under the act while their masters insisted on their loyalty to the Union, a conflict that seemed likely to arise. During the debates some congressmen had expressed a desire to prevent reenslavement if slaves and owners differed in testimony, but the law did not include such a provision. Moreover, if slaves were confiscable as property through in rem proceedings in section seven, the second act reinforced the *Dred Scott* decision. As well, the law's declaration that slaves of convicted traitors were "made free" by section one violated the attainder clause of the Constitution. Either Congress could ignore this clause, because of the exigencies of war, or it could not. Both views could not be supported in the same act. In sum, if the second act moved Lincoln to recognize the North's desire for emancipation, it may also have persuaded him that a more effective and constitutional means to that end, for instance emancipation by executive proclamation, had to be found.[6]

The purpose of the second act was never made clear. It was a war measure intended to help defeat the South yet by requiring all offenders to be tried in federal courts, with due process provided, the law prevented extensive enforcement during the war. As against prize cases, where Congress passed legislation to assist the courts once the vessels had been captured, no provisions were made to simplify the confiscation process. As a result, prize cases realized over $10 million, whereas confiscation achieved less than $130,000. It was virtually impossible for federal courts to operate in the South while the fighting continued and had they been able to do so, it is doubtful that juries would have convicted their neighbors. As a consequence, even had Lincoln vigorously enforced the law, it might not have been used to help defeat the South other than by intimidating rebels who might have shifted their allegiance to the Union. The second act also meant to reconstruct the South, but in that it was equally inadequate. The moderates' insistence that forfeiture not extend beyond the lives of the offenders meant that no property would be available for distribution until long after the war ended. Senator Lyman Trumbull, among others, had argued that the Constitution's war powers gave Congress authority to punish, through in rem proceedings, those criminals who would not fall under the protection of the attainder clause for treason. In other words, confiscation in sections five through eight would not be for treason but for rebellion. But the majority refused to accept this reasoning, partly because they feared what it would achieve. As a result, the law extended the Constitution's protection to rebels while ignoring the possibilities for extraordinary powers the war had created. And, of course, the pardoning power given the president made such distribution of property unlikely, even during the lives of the offenders, except perhaps for the property of the rebellion's leaders.[7]

Attorney General Edward Bates's administration of the second act, like the first, also greatly determined the severity and breadth of confiscation during the Civil War. As noted in chapter 1, Bates was born in Virginia, rose to prominence in Missouri, was the brother-in-law of Unionist governor Hamilton R. Gamble, and, while opposed to slavery, had no wish to see the military emancipate slaves. Frémont's proclamation in August 1861 and Hunter's in May 1862 greatly troubled him. He nonetheless appreciated the growing desire for emancipation in the North and, with the president, believed that slave owners should be compensated for their freed slaves, who should be colonized immediately. Even after the preliminary emancipation proclamation Bates continued to advocate compulsory colonization. He believed that emancipation should be at the executive's discretion, but the idea of black equality was horrific to Bates. He was upset, for example, at the bill to abolish slavery in the Capitol. Nor was he pleased with the first act Trumbull introduced in December 1861, particularly the prospect that confiscation would enlarge and lengthen the war, rather than shorten it. He feared that the bill would increase the military's role in civil matters, a prospect that greatly troubled him. In addition, he believed the measure violated individual rights because a defendant need not be present to defend himself. Bates's opposition to the second act also stemmed from "his somewhat curious concern for the Southerners' individual property rights," as his biographer observed. In short, Bates saw almost no need for confiscation, except perhaps as punishment for the Confederacy's leaders, and thought Reconstruction should not be based on any widespread punishment such as the seizure and dispersal of property. For the most part these views were similar to Lincoln's, of course, which made Bates's conservative implementation of the second act amenable to the president.[8]

In August Lincoln took up an invitation to express his views on confiscation publicly and thus suggested how he might implement the second act. Horace Greeley, editor of the *New York Tribune,* had urged, as secession began, that the "erring sisters" be allowed to leave in peace. By the summer of 1862, however, Greeley had changed his views. On August 19 he wrote the president a public letter, "the Prayer of Twenty Million," to urge, among other things, emancipation of the slaves by the second act. Greeley wrote, "Those provisions were designed to fight Slavery with Liberty. They prescribe that men loyal to the Union, and willing to shed their blood in her behalf, shall no longer be held, with the nation's consent, in bondage to persistent, malignant traitors, who for twenty years have been plotting and for sixteen months have been fighting to divide and destroy our country." He also complained "that the Confiscation Act which you had approved is habitually disregarded by your Generals, and that no word of rebuke for them from you has yet reached the public ear." In closing, Greeley reminded Lincoln that all "an immense majority of the loyal millions of your countrymen require of you is a frank, declared, unqualified, ungrudging execution of the laws of the land, more especially of the Second Confiscation Act."[9] Significantly, Greeley, like so many others, associated the second act primarily with emancipation, not the seizure of landed property, the destruction of the planter class and the use of its land for freed slaves.

Lincoln's equally famous reply was conciliatory in tone. He could find no "erroneous" facts or statements, nor did he see any "inferences" that were "falsely drawn." And even if "there be perceptable [*sic*] in it an impatient and dictatorial tone," he would "waive it in deference to an old friend," whose heart he "always supposed to be right." Even so, he would save the Union in "the shortest way under the Constitution." And if that meant not disturbing slavery, then so it would be. "What I do about slavery, and the colored race, I do because I believe it helps to save the Union; and what I forbear, I forbear because I do not believe it would help save the Union. I shall do *less* whenever I shall believe what I am doing hurts the cause, and I shall no *more* whenever I shall believe doing more will help the cause." At the same time, however, he intended "no modification of my oft-expressed *personal* wish that all men every where could be free." Unbeknownst to Greeley and the public, of course, Lincoln had already announced to his Cabinet that he would offer preliminary emancipation when a propitious moment arrived. But his public reply to Greeley made it clear that he would not implement the second act for punishment or reconstruction; it would be used only if it could be seen to help win the war. The president had even quoted the Democratic phrase "the Union as it was" to emphasize that he would do nothing more than was needed to secure victory.[10] Yet Lincoln also realized that time was running out for those who wished to restore the Union as it had been in 1860, even if he did not wish to pursue the ends sought in the second act.

In the middle of September, Lincoln met with a religious delegation eager for emancipation and again suggested the limitations he felt in prosecuting the war, even while armed with the second act. If God's design was clear to these men, Lincoln wondered why the same had not been imparted to him; nor was it evident to him that a proclamation would have the effect they proposed. "Would *my word* free the slaves, if I cannot even enforce the Constitution in the rebel States. Is there a single court, or magistrate, or individual that would be influenced by it there? And what reason is there to think that it would have any greater effect upon the slaves than the law of Congress, which I approved, and which offers protection and freedom to the slaves of rebel masters who come within our lines? Yet I cannot learn that law has caused a single slave to come over to us." He was no less worried about what would happen if the slaves, freed by proclamation, threw themselves upon the Union. "How can we feed and care for the multitude?" Moreover, the rebels had already reenslaved free blacks they had captured. Still, he could see the merit of a proclamation and ended the meeting by indicating that he might offer one.[11] The meeting prompted an interesting discussion that Lincoln appeared to have with himself about the limitations on what he would soon do.

Lincoln publicly announced his preliminary proclamation of emancipation on September 22, after the Union victory at Antietam. It repeated his wish to offer "pecuniary aid" to loyal states that freed slaves as well as his hope that freed slaves would voluntarily "colonize" on "this continent" or some other place willing to have them. Next Lincoln promised to free "all persons held as slaves" in states still in rebellion, thereby excluding all slaves in border states, slaves in any state that abandoned the Confederacy and rejoined the Union, and all slaves beyond the reach of Union armies. Then Lincoln noted the March 1862 law that prohibited the military from returning fugitive slaves and referred to the ninth and tenth sections of the second act that freed slaves of those in rebellion. Last, the proclamation promised to compensate loyal Southerners "for those losses by acts of the United States, including the loss of slaves."[12] The proclamation was, in sum, both a revolutionary and a conservative promise by Lincoln.

It was revolutionary that Lincoln, even though acting as commander in chief, had finally turned the federal government against the institution of slavery in states that had had their peculiar institution constitutionally protected. Moreover, he did so despite some doubts about this use of the war powers. By this proclamation, the nation began the task of abolishing slavery, which, when the war began, was unthinkable for most everyone in the North except abolitionists. The transformation in Northern thinking had been swift and startling. As the delegation that visited Lincoln on September 13 noted, the North's view had changed dramatically from that of December 1861. Many now agreed, because of the war, pressure from constituents, and the debates over the second act, that if slavery continued the Union could not be restored and the war could not be won. The reaction to the proclamation, while predictable, also suggested the radical step Lincoln had taken. Many in the border states were appalled. Most Republicans welcomed the promise, while abolitionists were, for the most part, pleased if not ecstatic. They had long asked for such a declaration.[13]

Some supporters of the administration, however, had doubts about the proclamation. In August, Secretary of the Treasury Salmon Chase had asked Edward Everett to comment on the prospects of such a declaration. Everett replied he had no constitutional concerns about Lincoln's authority under the war powers to make such a declaration, but he thought many would take offense even though the army was already accomplishing what the declaration would announce. He wondered then what point there was "to issue orders to terminate what we have no force to carry into effect?" After the announcement Everett observed that it "seriously divided opinions" and was a "triumph for the radical wing of the Republican party." Moreover he noted that where the Union armies "are *not* in force, proclamations will not give them [slaves] freedom." Senator Browning recorded in his diary that both he and Senator Fessenden doubted the wisdom of the proclamation, although they agreed with its goal. Richard Henry Dana Jr., the U.S. attorney for the district of Massachusetts, hoped the proclamation would succeed but doubted its "statesmanship," although he would not say so publicly. Nor was Governor John Andrew of Massachusetts enthusiastic. A peace Democrat, H. B. Whiting of Connecticut, however, welcomed the proclamation, for it "removes the scales from the eyes of those stupid" people "who persisted in thinking that the President was a conservative man and the war was for the restoration of the Union under the Constitution." All of these observations were essentially correct, of course. Lincoln did nothing not already being accomplished by the military in the field and actually postponed implementing the second act, promising not to free the slaves until January. At the same time, his declaration acknowledged the changed goals of the North as expressed in the second act.[14]

Of course, the proclamation and the second act drew criticism from administration opponents. Perhaps the most notable was Professor Joel Parker of the Harvard Law School, who had already argued against Sumner's state suicide thesis and was a staunch opponent of the administration. In October Parker published in the *North American Review* a detailed attack on both Lincoln's proclamation and the second act. Parker was hardly sympathetic to the South or slavery; he wanted a war waged more vigorously and the peculiar institution ended, if constitutionally permissible. He even agreed to arm freed slaves. Yet he did not view slavery as the cause of the war, could not agree that victory depended upon its abolition, and dismissed Lincoln's proclamation as an unwarranted exercise against a constitutionally protected state institution. Moreover, Congress appeared to agree that a proclamation was insufficient since it had passed the second act. This measure, Parker argued, was also unconstitutional since there could "be no confiscation for treason" under the Constitution "without a trial for treason," although this misread the act, which said confiscation would not occur because of treason. Nor could slaves be made free, Parker said, for that would constitute a bill of attainder, which the Constitution forbade. In addition, he believed Union soldiers had no wish to fight a war for emancipation and pursuing such a goal would, he predicted, divide the North and lengthen the war. He pointed to the second act's confusion over the method of securing freedom for slaves.[15] Parker's analysis repeated much of what opponents had said during the debates over the second act and identified its limited power to free slaves.

In the end, although for different reasons, the second act's provisions for freeing slaves proved as ineffective as the first act and Lincoln's proclamation. In 1864 Trumbull had admitted in Congress that he believed no slave had been freed by the first act, which had only implied it would free slaves employed in Confederate military service. The second act also failed to provide a procedure by which slaves entering Union lines would secure their freedom. Although the act stated that slaves entering Union-controlled areas had to prove their masters' support of the rebellion in order to be freed, it did not specify how they could do so. As James G. Randall noted, the courts would have had to decide the truth of the slaves' testimony concerning their masters' aid to the rebellion since all questions involving forfeiture of property under federal law had to be decided in a court. The army was not given the authority to assess the testimony of slaves. Furthermore, the second act did not refer to slaves as property and omitted them from the provisions for confiscating it. If Congress had considered slaves to be property, it should have provided for their confiscation along with the rest of the rebels' property. Since military authorities never enforced the sections of the act relating to emancipation, despite Lincoln's order in the proclamation of September 22, the final authority for verifying the slaves' claims to freedom was never determined and the second act freed few, if any, slaves.[16]

The irony in all this is considerable. The second act attracted significant attention in and out of Congress because of its assumed attack upon slavery. The public in the North came to support emancipation as a new goal in the war in part because of the debates, while it ignored the other parts of the bill. The second act was also designed to confiscate real property other than slaves, and this probably scared the South more than any other part of the measure. The confiscation of lots of real property did not take place, however, which greatly disappointed the former slaves and some radicals, not to mention some historians. The second act had two symbolic lives at the time then. The first was in Congress and the North; both grew to appreciate the need to destroy slavery in order to save the Union. The second act, though, played little part in securing that end except as part of a larger discussion over ends and means. The second life occurred in the minds of Southerners and opponents of confiscation in the North. Many predicted that confiscation would destroy property relations in the South and produce a bitter peace. But it failed to accomplish the former and had almost no part in the latter, except as a ploy used by white Southerners to attack the North's intentions. Confiscation also failed to destroy the planter class and thereby help freed slaves achieve economic independence after the war by acquiring land. Lincoln's conservative implementation of the second act gave the South no reason to think confiscation would be used to punish them and the failure to pursue the act's goals deprived freed slaves of the chance to begin new lives with more security and hope.[17]

Lincoln's preliminary proclamation of emancipation revealed his determination to ignore all questions not related to restoring the Union. As many have noted, his reference to the second act in the proclamation rested on military necessity and the need to address antislavery feeling in the North. In the months after the proclamation, Lincoln worked simply to win the war and restore those states containing a loyal minority to the Union. In late October, Solicitor of the Treasury Edward Jordan noted to Salmon Chase that Lincoln had yet to issue any order to enforce the second act. Only after he began reunification proceedings in Louisiana, North Carolina, Tennessee, and the recently formed state of West Virginia did the president turn to the confiscatory provisions of the second act. The success of the Democrats in the fall elections may also have encouraged Lincoln to delay authorizing the second act. In mid-November, almost four months after Lincoln signed the second act into law, Bates drew up a rough draft of orders for the president to approve. Bates's directive, written at Lincoln's behest to guide the attorney general's office, was tentative at best. In his draft, Bates wrote he was "authorized and required to give" the district attorney or marshal "all needful instructions and directions as he may find useful" for seizures. However, he crossed out "all needful," so its force was further diminished. It now read that Bates was authorized to give "such instructions and directions as he [a marshal or district attorney] may find useful and convenient touching all such seizures, prosecutions and condemnations." Although Bates had not welcomed the law, regarding it as "a repressive measure" according to his biographer, he was delighted that Lincoln allowed him to implement it as he saw fit. It was clear to the attorney general that Lincoln had no wish for widespread confiscation to occur and did not see it as the basis of reconstruction.[18]

Bates also took pleasure from the complete control that Lincoln allowed his office over the second act, particularly by making the military subordinate to Bates and his colleagues. Although it is doubtful the military would have wished to pursue confiscation as Trumbull and other advocates had hoped, Bates nonetheless made sure the directive Lincoln authorized put the attorney general in charge. No suggestion that the military should initiate confiscation as it moved forward appeared. Attorneys and marshals could "call upon any military officers" to aid them in a seizure and "to give them such aid, protection and support as may be necessary to enable them safely and efficiently to discharge their respective duties." Moreover, all commanding officers were "required, promptly, to obey such a call, and render the necessary service," if it did not violate other duties. The fact that Congress was divided at the time about whether or not the military should have a role in confiscation made Bates's assertion of control even easier.[19]

Bates and his assistant Titian J. Coffey prepared instructions for a limited number of district attorneys on December 1, 1862, shortly after Lincoln signed the directive the attorney general had drafted. The instructions, which were cautious, went only to district attorneys in Boston, New York, Philadelphia, and Baltimore. Marshals could seize property only if directed by a district attorney, and no seizure could occur unless the latter was sure a condemnation of the property would result. Bates felt that unless "some responsible legal mind" controlled the seizures "great abuses" that might damage the administration's standing would result. He added that further instructions would be drawn up to secure "efficient and uniform methods" for enforcing the law. No discussion of the law's constitutionality or purpose was included in this first set of instructions. Nor was an actual policy offered; only the mechanics of how the law should be observed, emphasizing Bates's control, were outlined.[20]

Bates, with Coffey's assistance, sent out a more comprehensive set of instructions to all district attorneys and marshals on January 8, 1863. They went out shortly after the Emancipation Proclamation, almost six months after the second act became law. They were perhaps also a response to complaints from Speaker of the House Galusha A. Grow about lax enforcement of the second act in the Capitol district. The instructions governed the procedures to be used in the seizure of property liable to confiscation. If unforeseen procedural problems developed, officials were to request direction from the attorney general's office. Local discretion, on this issue at least, was thereby discouraged. No marshals could seize property without a written order from district attorneys. Naturally, Bates wrote, he expected them to execute the law vigilantly but with care to "avoid hasty and improvident seizures." No orders for confiscation were to be issued unless the evidence guaranteed the property's condemnation. Otherwise, said Bates, local officials would jeopardize cases, do injustice to potentially innocent owners, and create expense and embarrassment for the government. Although the attorney general believed that local officials were the best judges of whether to confiscate, he felt it necessary to discourage them from implementing the law vigorously lest they waste money and annoy the public. (This concern obviously referred to the North at the time, since the military had yet to occupy much of the South.) In addition, district attorneys were to ask the military to turn over any property they had seized and then begin condemnation proceedings against it once in their custody. These instructions were also to cover proceedings under the first act.[21]

Unlike the first act, however, which provided for a percentage of the confiscated property's proceeds to an informer, neither the second act nor Bates's directives contained any provision for paying informers even though they remained important to a successful confiscation policy. By the terms of the second act the courts had the responsibility to pay such fees and charges "as shall be reasonable and proper," but this was an uncertain and unsatisfactory method for both officials and informers. The first act had wisely provided a set fee for both. Congress clearly hoped that district attorneys and marshals enforcing the second act would confiscate as much property as possible because they depended upon their prosecutions for payment. Instead, the reverse occurred; part of the blame rests on Bates's warnings against attempting doubtful cases, as well as on Congress' failure to create set fees.[22]

For the most part, district attorneys worried far more about securing their fees than enforcing the second act. Although this attitude might have developed without more encouragement from Washington, Bates's reluctance to enforce the second act did not help. When officials lacked sufficient evidence to prove that the potential defendant supported the rebellion, they were naturally reluctant to press the case. When district attorneys requested assistance, such as documentation of an individual's participation in the rebellion, or advice on presenting a difficult case, they discovered that the attorney general's office granted funds for preparing a case only when notified in advance and condemnation seemed probable. In the end, Bates authorized financial help in only two cases. The first was a complicated one under the first act in which the property had been sold and the case had to be retried because of errors in the admission of evidence. The other involved the need for travel money to obtain evidence of a prominent rebel's position in the Confederacy. These, however, were the exceptions. Most pleas for money received little sympathy from the attorney general. On one occasion Bates lost his temper with a request for money from a district attorney. "Really, sir, I do not know how to state the matter plainer than it is stated in the letter of instructions," Bates replied. Bates expected local officials to make their financial arrangements with the courts and not depend upon his office for funds to help implement the law.[23]

Given the lack of set fees, the failure of Congress to appropriate money to enforce the acts, and the reluctance of the attorney general to risk money on doubtful cases, it was hardly surprising that some district attorneys decided not to waste time and money on confiscation. E. L. Larned of the northern district of Illinois knew of rebel-owned property in Chicago, yet he would not prosecute unless the attorney general's office authorized his expenses. To prove rebel ownership Larned had to buy abstracts of the property's title. This was expensive and, with the complicated procedures required in every case, there was no guarantee the court would condemn the property. District attorneys had too little money to finance such a risk, reasoned Larned, and since the act provided no money for an informer, "no one is interested in hunting up the necessary evidence in the class of cases." At least three district attorneys—one from Connecticut and two from eastern Pennsylvania—may have shared Larned's view on expenses. No successful prosecutions occurred in their districts, and there is no evidence that they wrote the attorney general for assistance. The greatest responsibility for the lack of funds to enforce the act belonged to Congress, which failed to provide money for its enforcement. Although Speaker Grow complained about the lack of enforcement in early 1863, Congress made no effort either to monitor the law's enforcement or to rectify the problems of fees. Bates, of course, could have asked for funds, but he had not passed the second act and had no interest in a successful confiscation policy.[24]

Bates had numerous opportunities to explain his policy on enforcement to officials who found his directives an inadequate guide. The directives had been written for district attorneys to determine which property to seize without losing cases on technicalities. As Bates realized, the second act did not stipulate the procedures to be followed. It was the attorney general's view that his instructions answered all the questions his office could properly consider, and he told inquiring officials they would have to suffice. To almost all those who wrote about problems with individual cases not covered by the instructions, Bates advised presenting the questions to local officials. When he received requests that specific property be confiscated, Bates advised consulting the district attorney in whose district the property lay. Even when Chase, who expressed interest in a "thorough execution of the Confiscation law," told him about large amounts of confiscable property, Bates's instructions to the district attorney through Coffey avoided an explicit direction for confiscation. Instead, Coffey simply reported that Bates wanted, for example, John Trimble in Nashville to give his "earnest consideration and attention to the subject." Even though there is no doubt that Bates expected Trimble and all officials to enforce the second act, he declined to encourage them to do so. Effective enforcement of the law, which Ira Berlin and his colleagues have aptly described as "unwieldy," demanded that the attorney general encourage a wider and more vigorous application, but Bates had no inclination or instructions to do so.[25]

The attorney general's office primarily aided implementation of the two acts by transmitting information about property thought to be confiscable. Residents from all sections of the country, including the upper South, wrote Bates or other government agencies about property they believed should be confiscated. (This indicates that there were many who realized that both acts were meant to do more than abolish slavery.) Often the correspondents knew the rebels personally and some were quite angry at their support of the Confederacy and wished them punished. The attorney general or his assistant directed the correspondent to the local district attorney or sent that official the information with directions to investigate the allegation. Levi Hooker, a native of West

Virginia who moved to Connecticut, informed Bates about four men in his former state and one in Alexandria, Virginia, who, he claimed, supported the rebellion. Bates's assistant relayed this information to the district attorneys in both districts and told Hooker he should be prepared to substantiate the charges. Colleagues like Chase, Seward, and Stanton also sent Bates information about property they believed confiscable. In each case he or his staff forwarded it to local officials. As in other instances, Bates or his assistants directed the officials to investigate the cases and take the steps they considered necessary. No sense of urgency or concern, however, appeared in these directives.[26]

Bates presented a clear policy only when local officials ignored his instructions on the proper method for seizing property. To protect those subject to confiscation, mostly rebels wealthy enough to own property in the North, the attorney general directed marshals to seize the right, title, and interest of real estate and to give a written notice of such seizure to any tenants on the property. Officials Bates suspected of violating this rule received quick and explicit commands from the attorney general's office. In the fall of 1863 Bates received reports that James Close, a marshal in eastern Virginia, had taken actual possession of some property in Alexandria, ejected the tenants, and committed trespass, "amounting to oppression if not outrage upon aged and infirm women," according to the attorney general. Bates's language suggested that he placed more credence in the charges against Close than he did in his subordinate's integrity. Bates required Close to submit a report in which the latter denied seizure of one piece of property but admitted taking possession of another in order to protect personal property, as the attorney general had directed. This explanation, however, failed to satisfy Bates; he replaced Close as marshal with John Underwood. The dismissal of Close was later justified when Bates learned the marshal had not only evicted tenants but became the landlord of the property seized. But when he dismissed Close, Bates only had the word of one elderly woman against the testimony of a government official. In this instance, at least, the attorney general's solicitude for individuals subject to confiscation was apparent.[27]

Following Close's dismissal, Bates had to reiterate his order several times against physically seizing real estate. In a case involving Close's successor, Bates forbade John Underwood to eject a tenant when seizing property or guarding it against injury between its condemnation and sale. To avoid abridging the supposed rights of the tenant, he instructed Underwood not to interfere with the property after its sale. Although Bates conceded that court orders to sell property would undoubtedly injure tenants, he insisted officials abide by the court's decision once the property had been seized. As Bates's instructions implied and as he emphasized throughout his correspondence, district attorneys had only the power to direct marshals in the seizure of property, which would be in name only if real estate. One district attorney, Benjamin Smith of Virginia, did argue that Bates was wrong to construe the first and second acts so narrowly. According to Smith, whose position the Supreme Court later affirmed, neither act forbade taking possession of real estate; both simply required seizure of property and said nothing about seizing only a property's right, title, and interest.[28] Several local officials also disagreed with the attorney general's effort to limit the role to a theoretical seizure of real estate, thereby likely protecting the rental fees to owners, but they conformed to his interpretation of the laws.[29]

Bates also demonstrated considerable caution involving the confiscation of intangible property like stocks and mortgages. In his instructions of January 1863 the attorney general told district attorneys that where there was "no specific method prescribed by the state law" to have the marshal "describe the property as plainly as he can in his return" and let the court "determine the sufficiency of the seizure." Bates was even conservative in actual practice. John Maffit, a commander in the Confederate navy, owned more than $75,000 worth of mortgages in Minnesota, and District Attorney H. S. Moss was eager to confiscate them. Bates appeared to share his enthusiasm, perhaps because of Moss's prominent position in the Confederacy, "but the way to reach his right and credits is not plain to me," he confessed to Moss. Bates saw no way to get at the property except by garnishment or attachment, neither of which Congress had provided for in the second act. Although Congress could have been more explicit about the ways intangible property might be described as seized, Bates could also have been more willing, in practice, to risk failure in court.[30] In the end, Moss decided there was no way to seize Maffit's property, and so it escaped confiscation. Bates also doubted that Samuel Browne, the district attorney in Denver, could seize confiscable money from a bailee. Since the second act had no provision for the garnishment of such money, Bates saw no solution. "It presents a case of omission or defect in the law," he observed. If Browne could not seize the money by local law, Bates was unable to offer him "a remedy for the apparent evil." But, as demonstrated in *Miller v. United States* (1870), to be discussed in chapter 10, a majority of the Supreme Court was willing to grant local officials considerable leeway in their seizure of intangible property.[31]

In New York City, where confiscation has been more closely examined than in any other region of the North, the problems of the second act and the impact of Bates's caution were clear.[32] Most of the property liable to confiscation in the city consisted of stock, owned by Southerners still in the South, in companies with charters from states other than New York but whose head offices were in the city. E. Delafield Smith, the city's district attorney, was reluctant to institute proceedings against such property because of the supposed difficulty of seizure; nor did Bates encourage him to pursue such a potentially rewarding form of confiscable property. Finally, after both an informer and a private citizen made persistent requests that he act, Smith instituted proceedings against the property of Hugh W. Mercer, who owned considerable stock in a Minnesota mining company. District Judge Betts, who was also involved in a more famous case at the same time,[33] agreed to the condemnation and the sale of the property in the summer of 1863, netting the United States over $29,000, by far the largest amount realized from a confiscation case in the city. Thereafter, however, as Henry D. Shapiro noted, suits "were instituted irregularly throughout the remainder" of Smith's term. In the end, only about $30,000 more was realized in the city.

The lack of authority granted district attorneys over the property after its seizure and condemnation was another reason the second act was not more successful. Often district attorneys wanted to prevent auctions of confiscated property if the bids would not realize their value. In the case of property owned by Albert Jenkins, a former congressman who became a Confederate army officer, Flamen Ball, a district attorney in Ohio, advised Bates that the sale of Jenkins's property would fall below its real value. Ball asked if he could stop the sale or buy the property in the government's name. Although Bates acknowledged Ball's right to halt the sale if it failed to conform to the court's order, he did not believe the second act permitted anyone to interfere with the sale after the property had been condemned even if it would not reach its value. A year later, in a similar case, Bates reiterated this view. William Grover, a Missouri district attorney, asked Solicitor of the Treasury Edward Jordan if there were some means by which he could achieve a higher price for the sale of confiscated property. Annoyed that Grover had directed the question to the Treasury, Bates told Grover that his office would issue no instructions contrary to the decree of the court. "We are prosecuting attorneys for the public property," he reminded Grover, "and not outside agents and managers of the public property." Bates was, of course, correct; his office had no authority to authorize local officials to maximize the proceeds from confiscation. Yet Bates made no effort to persuade Congress to empower officials like Ball and Grover who wished to raise the revenue the second act had been designed to achieve. In the end, Bates had the good bureaucratic fortune to supervise an inadequate statute whose principles and goals he did not support.[34]

There were few instances during Bates's administration when he directed local officials to confiscate the property of rebels. When he did, the owners were always prominent supporters of the rebellion like Trusten Polk, a former Senator who became a rebel, or W. W. Hunter, a Confederate navy commander, or

Samuel L. French, a Confederate army major, or John Maffit, also a Confederate navy commander. The attorney general made little effort to pursue the property of those rebels who served the Confederacy in less conspicuous positions.[35] In January 1863 Bates had suggested to R. J. Lackey, a district attorney in Missouri, his general view of who should be prosecuted for treason and why:

> It is not desirable to try many cases of treason. It is a crime hard to prove, being guarded by a variety of legal technics. . . . In a clear case against a person of eminence, of notoriety, I would be glad to see a conviction for the public effect rather than the punishment of the individual. But it would be unfortunate to be defeated in such cases. It is far better policy I think when you have the option to prosecute offenders for vulgar felonies and misdemeanors than for romantic and genteel treason.[36]

The attorney general's office often received information about less than prominent rebels, but there was apparently little desire to instruct local officials to confiscate their property. William Alexander of Brownsville, Texas, for example, wrote to Bates five detailed letters about confiscable property in his region but failed to receive even an acknowledgment. Bland Ballard, who later became a marshal, estimated that there were "hundreds of thousand[s,] possibly millions of dollars" of confiscable property in Kentucky but Joshua Tevis, the district attorney there, received no direction to investigate the claim. W. F. M. Arny, the acting territorial governor of New Mexico, wrote Secretary of State Seward that Theodore Wheaton, the district attorney for the territory, appeared unwilling to pursue the large amounts of confiscable property in the territory. No evidence has been found that Bates made any effort to investigate this claim, such as writing to Wheaton.[37] The failure to investigate possibilities for confiscation does not mean Bates did not implement the first and second acts, of course, but it does suggest a lack of interest in the success of the laws.

Bates also advised local officials to dismiss doubtful cases, but only after first assuring officials that they were in the best position to make such decisions. After Flamen Ball had confiscated Albert Jenkins's property, he seized that of his brother William but could not obtain the evidence to prove, what he knew, that William had supported the rebellion. Ball wanted to prosecute the case and asked Bates for advice. At first the attorney general said he could issue no instructions on the case, because the "responsibilities of its conduct devolve upon you." Reversing himself, he then told Ball to press the case if he had the necessary proof, which, of course, he did not or drop the case if "after every proper and reasonable effort" Ball could not find the requisite evidence. When Joshua Tevis suggested that the proceedings be dismissed against a prominent rebel because he had transferred his title before the second act became law, Bates responded as he had to Ball. He readily acknowledged Tevis's complete discretion over the matter. Nonetheless, Bates added, if Tevis thought he could not obtain a decree of condemnation, he was free to dismiss the proceedings. In New York, William A. Dart, the district attorney, had been unaware that the rebel owner of property confiscated had sold it to a loyal resident of Texas before the second act became law. J. Hubley Ashton gave the usual disclaimer that only Dart could dismiss the case, but also felt it necessary to urge Dart not to allow the proceedings to continue. In these and other similar cases, the attorney general's office began by denying that it would give direction but then suggested dismissal of the proceedings. Doubtless the advice was sound but not once did the attorney general's office suggest proceedings should be continued. The evidence suggests that Bates was more worried about losing cases than pressing for confiscation.[38]

Edward Bates served as attorney general until December 1, 1864, when he resigned because of exhaustion and disappointment he had not been named to the Supreme Court. Although conscientious, he exerted no more than a minimal effort to make the first and second confiscation acts work, just as Lincoln expected.[39] Confiscation, the attorney general thought, should apply only to the leading rebels and serve as a symbol of punishment. It was not used to raise revenue, emancipate the slaves, or destroy the planter class and begin the reconstruction of the South, where he had been born. Bates acted slowly, reluctant to give advice, and suggested only a narrow interpretation of the law. When he finally prepared instructions for enforcement of the second act, they exuded caution and circumspection on the mechanics of confiscation and said nothing about policy. His administration of the second act was as restrained and careful as that of the first; he never encouraged subordinates to disregard the laws but urged their application only upon the most conspicuous rebels who owned property easily confiscated. Whenever he faced a choice involving energetic or restrained use of the laws, Bates chose the latter course. Although Bates's administration of the laws was honest, sincere and careful, it lacked any conviction they were just or useful laws. The problems of implementing confiscation also involved the roles of the military and Treasury Department. And Bates worried they would in some way with his conservative application of the two acts.

5 Early Military Confiscation

The military commanders and troops who conquered and occupied the South were potentially the best enforcers of the confiscation acts. They encountered confiscable property before any other government officials and, through martial law, could have prevented transfers of property titles. However, they could not confiscate property without going through the courts. Although Secretary of War Edwin Stanton and a few of his commanders, such as General Ben Butler, demonstrated some sympathy for confiscation, most officers were reluctant to disturb Southerners' property, except slaves, or enforce a measure the president did not believe directly related to their military mission. Attorney General Bates, with Lincoln's support, also opposed military confiscation except as related to slavery. Even though Stanton often aroused Bates's concern over military interference involving confiscation, the amount of property the military confiscated under either act was not large. The discord between Bates and Stanton, added to the president's support of a conservative confiscation policy, meant that the military played a minor part in the enforcement of either act, except in New Orleans. As a result, there was no substantial confiscation of Southern property. However, the second act did encourage the military to act with growing assertiveness toward the property of rebels and in this way played a significant part in the development of more aggressive tactics toward the Confederacy.[1]

Without any guidance from either the White House or the attorney general's office, the military began making decisions and promises about property in the South, especially slaves, soon after the war began. As we have seen, General Butler in late May 1861 decided not to return fugitive slaves and thereby helped to create a "contraband" policy that led to the first act.[2] Others in the military, however, presumed the North would not interfere with the peculiar institution. In late May, for example, Major General George McClellan in Ohio ordered a subordinate to ensure the property rights of those he encountered "are respected, and [to] repress all attempts at negro insurrection." He also promised the slaveholders of western Virginia that he would not interfere with slavery. In mid July McClellan could boast that he had "protected all private property, by whomsoever owned" in all of Virginia. At the same time, the

House of Representatives joined the discussion and passed a resolution that forbade the military from capturing or returning fugitive slaves.[3]

Without orders from either Lincoln or Bates to enforce the first act, little changed for the military after the first act was signed into law on August 6. (The First Confiscation Act authorized seizure of property used to aid the insurrection.) Some officers ignored it, while only a few tried to use it. Two days after the act became law, for example, Major General John A. Dix in Maryland, in a letter to Secretary of War Simon Cameron, wrote that he assumed that the military "would not meddle with slaves even of secessionists." Dix, who did not hear back from Cameron, continued to believe that having anything to do with the slaves of secessionists would "expose ourselves to the imputation of intermeddling" in an issue "foreign to the great questions of political right and duty" inherent in the war. As we have seen in chapter 1, General John C. Frémont in Missouri arrived at a much different view of his power over slavery under the first act. On September 12 Frémont, in fact, declared Frank Lewis, a slave, free because his master had participated in the insurrection. The deed of manumission did not claim that Lewis had been used to aid the Confederacy so Frémont had gone beyond the scope of the first act. When Frémont refused to accede, at Lincoln's request, to the limits of the first act the president removed him. Frémont's dismissal doubtless deepened the views of men like McClellan, Dix, and Brigadier General William T. Sherman. As the latter observed, he had "no instructions from Government on the subject of negroes" and so presumed Kentucky's laws on fugitives had to be observed. As others have noted, the First Confiscation Act was a limited way to achieve liberation. Even so, the military could have been more aggressive in its implementation had they been encouraged to do so. Although determining if property, including slaves, had been employed to aid the insurrection would have been complicated, it was not an impossible task. Room did exist between Frémont's broad view and the caution of most others generals in the fall of 1861.[4]

But, as Mark Grimsley has argued, at this stage in the conflict the military hoped that a war of conciliation would be successful. In mid-September, for example, a proclamation to the people of North Carolina by Colonel Rush Hawkins promised that the "rights of property and persons" would be protected by Union forces. Acting Secretary of War Thomas A. Scott suggested this delicate policy in mid-October to General Thomas W. Sherman, who soon would occupy the islands around Port Royal, South Carolina. Sherman's own "discretion" should govern how he employed slaves in the region and all loyal masters would be justly compensated. At the same time, Scott said, the military's conduct should also "avoid all interference with the social systems or local institutions," if possible, so as to secure a peaceful restoration of the Union. Sherman found this a difficult policy to execute, however, for the abundance of property abandoned led to much destruction, particularly by "blacks." At the same time, in orders to Brigadier General Don Carlos Buell, in charge of Tennessee and Kentucky, McClellan said he firmly believed that "we are fighting only to preserve" the Union. He urged Buell, so long as military needs permitted, to "respect the constitutional rights of all." Later in November, in Missouri, Major General Henry W. Halleck, the author of a book on the rules of war, ordered all slaves barred from entering Union lines. He did so to prevent fugitive slaves from conveying information to the enemy, which meant that his order ignored the first act, since slaves used as spies would obviously aid the insurrection. In Maryland, on the other hand, Major General Dix informed Lincoln that he had given a copy of the first act to his subordinate and had "instructed him to enforce its provisions as far as practicable." Yet there is no evidence that Dix and his colleagues pursued confiscable property at all. They appeared far more anxious about the excessive demands Union supporters were making upon them.[5]

This conciliatory policy toward Southern property was followed into the spring and early summer of 1862 by most military officers, although a few began to chafe at these limits, reflecting the growing desire in the North and Congress for a more vigorous war. Continued protection of property was evident in the border state of Tennessee. Commander A. H. Foote informed the inhabitants of Clarkesville in February 1862 that the property of "all peaceably-disposed persons" would not be harmed and that they could resume their businesses without fear. That February, Buell, too, reminded his troops that the war's purpose was to "maintain" the Union's integrity, not to invade the rights of "fellow-countrymen" in Tennessee or elsewhere. "Peaceable citizens," Buell noted, were "not to be molested in their persons or property." Although Buell's primary concern was to prevent "depredations" against property by soldiers, his order also denied the military any role in discovering confiscable property. Buell acknowledged this three weeks later when he claimed the power to confiscate private property lay with authorities created by Congress; the military could only seize property owned by the "rebel Government." He was misreading the language of the first act, of course, which did not deny the military the right to seize property suspected of use in the insurrection. In Nashville, in accordance with Buell's approach, a number of people had time to take the oath and insure their property was not confiscated. By late June 1862, Brigadier General George W. Morgan was pleased to report to the secretary of war that the "conciliatory policy" in East Tennessee and Lee County, Virginia, had inspired confidence among the people, but he confessed that many of his troops were not as pleased.[6]

Conciliation also remained the policy in Virginia up until the passage of the second act. Under General Nathaniel Banks's authority, troops were cautioned in March 1862 to avoid "any injury to private or public property or any interference with the rights of citizens." The military meant to "re-establish the privileges" enjoyed by all classes of Virginians. No property, the order said, could be seized without a direct order from headquarters or the provost marshal. Omitted was any mention that the military should seek out confiscable property for seizure. Almost a month later Brigadier General William S. Rosecrans proposed that the government try to impress upon Virginians, through the military's policy on property, that it acknowledged "the true interests and feelings of the people," presumably those who might side with the Union. By early May General McClellan was insisting to his subordinate that no property was "to be taken except in extreme cases" and then only if seized for an immediate purpose. Orders immediately followed this directive that required officers, even if they knew of property owned by disloyal persons, not to seize it for the military "or upon any other pretense." Only provost marshals could give the necessary orders for such seizures. Provost marshals were, in fact, to "give protection to the private property" of Virginians and treat them "with courtesy and kindness." Such directives transformed the military's role to one completely outside the intent of the first act, the result of a narrow and constricted understanding of the measure. In early June Major General Irwin McDowell reinforced this understanding of the first act to the troops in the Department of the Rappahannock with an order that no one had "the right to take private property for public purposes," except with his authority. On the eve of the second act's passage, McClellan summarized, in a letter to a Virginian, the conciliatory position taken toward property by most military commanders: "I have not come here to wage war upon the defenseless, upon non-combatants, upon private property, nor upon the domestic institutions of the land." McClellan's letter ended with an expression of thanks "for the noble spirit of humanity" the probable Confederate supporter, to whom the letter was addressed, had shown to McClellan's sick and wounded soldiers.[7]

There were three exceptions to this conciliatory attitude toward southern property between the enactment of the first act and the passage of the second act, not including General Frémont's act in Missouri. As we saw in chapter 3, in May 1862 Major General David Hunter proclaimed the slaves in Georgia, Florida, and South Carolina free as a result of his declaration of martial law. Lincoln quickly revoked Hunter's decree.[8] The second was in Arkansas, where General Samuel R. Curtis, a former Iowa antislavery congressman, freed slaves under the first act. Curtis's pursuit of the Confederates began in southwestern Missouri and ended in the battle of Pea Ridge, in northwestern Arkansas, in March 1862. As he moved east across Arkansas, Curtis received orders from Halleck to free slaves working at a Confederate saltpeter works in Marion County. Once he reached Helena, Arkansas, Curtis informed Halleck that he had given "free papers to negroes" who had been employed by rebels to build obstacles to the Union's supplies. His action, Curtis reported, had created a "general stampede in this region" of blacks in reaction against the rebellion. Many of the freed slaves followed Curtis's soldiers. A slave from Jefferson County later claimed, "Iffen you could get to the Yankee's camp you was free right now."[9]

The third and most important military confiscation under the first act occurred in and around New Orleans. In May 1862, Major General Ben Butler had assumed command of the region and, contrary to his reputation in Virginia, pursued a lenient policy toward the inhabitants of New Orleans. Butler's primary official goal was to restore Louisiana to the Union, as Lincoln directed; he also presumed this would help his career. On May 1 he promised protection of "persons and property," except as military necessity might require, for all inhabitants who renewed their allegiance to the Union or ceased aiding the Confederacy. Butler did not anticipate the problems associated with the many slaves who labored for those who had "been passive rather than active in the rebellion," as he put it. While he was "hunting out" the confiscable property of the minority still "actively" helping the insurrection, Butler was not sure how to treat the slaves of those masters who professed loyalty to the Union and asked for the return of their property. "Now," he asked Stanton, "what am I to do?" Unless he confiscated "all the personal property of all rebels," something he thought no military officer was authorized to do, he believed it "unjust to make a virtual confiscation" of slaves within the reach of the military. In other words, he could not agree to grant freedom only for those who might have been used to aid the rebellion. Nor did military necessity suggest arming blacks, as Butler assumed had been true under General Hunter. It took Stanton more than a month to reply to Butler's question. In the meantime the general had to confront the decisions of his subordinate Brigadier John W. Phelps.[10]

Phelps, a Vermont abolitionist who commanded Camp Parapet, seven miles west of New Orleans, differed markedly with Butler on what to do with slaves in Louisiana. In early May, Phelps began to accept slaves who entered his lines. Butler then directed Phelps to turn away any unemployed person, black or white, and announced that no officer was authorized to "take the property of any citizen" without a special order. Many planters, whose allegiance the general wished to retain, informed Butler that without slaves their crops could not be harvested and that acceptance of slaves into Union lines was creating unrest. A report soon reached Butler that Phelps's subordinates had been urging slaves, particularly those claiming punishment at the hands of owners, to leave plantations. Acting upon the report, Butler admonished Phelps not to interfere with the property, meaning slaves, of loyal owners; Phelps appeared to comply. But in mid-June Phelps heard that more than 150 slaves had arrived at his picket lines. One report said Phelps's men informed the slaves owned by Babbillard Lablanche, a plantation owner who claimed neutrality in the war but whose son was in the Confederate army, that they would be free if they went to Union lines. Another version said that Lablanche urged them to abandon his plantation or face fifty lashes each. Phelps, in a letter to Butler, claimed Lablanche had sent the slaves away with clothes, furniture, and threats of punishment if they returned, indicating his ownership had ended. Because of Congress's March order prohibiting the return of fugitives and his inability to feed and clothe them, Phelps implied he had no choice but to set them free. In closing, Phelps asked that his interpretation of the situation be made known to Lincoln. Although Phelps nowhere mentioned the first act, his decision reflected a liberal interpretation of the measure: slaves who worked even for loyal masters were aiding the Confederacy and should be freed. In forwarding Phelps's letter to Stanton, however, Butler argued Phelps had offered "the negro side of the story," which he did not accept. He believed Lablanche was "a humane man" and had not urged his slaves to leave and, further, that Phelps wanted to "make this a test case" for the government. If so, Butler trusted that the government would side with him, in which case Phelps's services "are worse than useless here."[11]

Finally, in late June Stanton responded to Butler. The delay reflected, in part, the changing perspective of the administration as the pressures mounted in the North for a more vigorous military policy. The Secretary of War urged Butler, perhaps ironically, to use his "accustomed skill and discretion" to handle his disagreement with Phelps but without causing the government any embarrassment. Then, in early July, Stanton reported that the president agreed that Congress's March law prohibited the return of the slaves to their masters and that "common humanity" required that unemployable slaves should not suffer for the lack of "food, shelter, or other" necessities. No directive about Phelps's decision to free the slaves ever came. In fact, just two weeks before the second act was passed and signed into law, Stanton wrote Butler that the president did not mean "to settle any general rule in respect to slaves or slavery" in regard to Phelps, nor did Stanton or anyone else communicate with Phelps. It seems clear that Lincoln did not wish to rescind Phelps's decision. Shortly after signing the second act, the president observed to Senator Reverdy Johnson of Maryland that the people of Louisiana had only themselves to blame for the presence of the Union armies and Phelps in particular. They "know the way to avert all this is simply to take their place in the Union upon the old terms," Lincoln observed. Two days later he reiterated his view that "military necessity" explained Phelps's action and reflected on "the pressure in this direction" that he, Lincoln, and Congress felt. If those in Louisiana wished "protection to person and property," Lincoln said they had only to rejoin the Union.[12]

Butler could do nothing about Phelps's policy of accepting slaves. By late July the Confederates learned that Phelps was "arming negroes." In the absence of direction, Phelps had organized five companies of black troops. Butler requested that the troops only chop down trees and not be issued guns, but Phelps refused to change his views and finally resigned. He resigned over a principle that Butler and the leaders in Washington would soon themselves embrace. Shortly after Phelps's departure, for example, Butler began recruiting free blacks, but not slaves, for the military. From both Secretary of the Treasury Chase and his wife, Butler learned that attitudes in Washington about the use of blacks had changed, in part because of the second act and officers like Phelps. Phelps, Frémont, Curtis, and Hunter constituted a small minority, exceptional in their view of how the first act allowed the military to handle property, particularly slaves, in the South. Yet they anticipated the course the war would soon take and to some degree influenced that direction. Phelps was the most significant of the four insofar as his freeing and arming of slaves occurred just as the second act became law, in itself a reflection of how the war had changed.[13]

On the surface, at least, Lincoln appeared to encourage military enforcement of the Second Confiscation Act, which he signed into law on July 17. The second act provided for the president to confiscate the property from six classes of rebels as well as anyone who failed to cease aiding the rebellion sixty days after a proclamation. Slaves of traitors were to be freed as were slaves who entered Union lines; this was already taking place in New Orleans under Phelps's initiative.[14] On July 23 Lincoln authorized the military recruitment of "free negroes," slaves of disloyal owners, and slaves of loyal owners who had their owners' consent, nearly the policy Phelps had been pursuing. That same day Lincoln ordered the military to seize and use "any property, real or personal" for military purposes and authorized the hiring of freed slaves as military laborers. In these directives, as Burrus M. Carnahan has noted, lay the core of Lincoln's view of how the military should implement any law relating to property. In New Orleans Butler saw this clearly, aided by advice from his wife back in the East. Military necessity was the governing principle about rebel property for Lincoln. If confiscating property helped the military, then Lincoln was willing to do so, and ever more so as the war continued. He refused, however, to allow the military to confiscate for political objectives, as he believed Frémont had done. He did not agree with many of confiscation's supporters who hoped the second act would achieve these political ends. This distinction helps explain why the officers under Lincoln's command rarely engaged in confiscation except in case of military necessity. Although Lincoln allowed the second act to push him toward a limited emancipation, as proclaimed on September 22, he refused to accept the premises of the second act, which saw it as a way to punish the South, provide land for slaves or reconstruct the region.[15]

Many presumed, then and later, that Butler pursued his own policy on confiscation. But in all but one instance, his conduct coincided with the president's wish to subdue the residents of the Gulf and encourage them to rejoin the Union. If Butler's confiscation orders at times appeared sensational and harsh, they did not interfere with the administration's goals and Washington offered little complaint. At first, upon arrival in May, Butler had expressed a desire to protect property, but within three weeks he had threatened to confiscate property sold in consideration of Confederate currency and to confiscate banks if they refused to redeem certain forms of money.[16] This was followed in early June with an order that any persons who possessed Confederate property would have it confiscated unless they reported it within three days. Four days later he required everyone, including foreigners, to take an oath to the United States if they wished their property protected. Solomon Benjamin, brother of the Confederacy's secretary of state, for example, had to take this oath in order to stay in business. Then in late June Butler "sequestered" all the property of General David E. Twiggs, including his house, which Butler used as office and residence. Butler's rationale was that Twiggs had become an officer in the Confederate forces. He also seized the house of John Slidell, the Confederate ambassador to France.[17] The first act did not authorize any of these threats or seizures by Butler, of course, but that did not deter him. Confiscation, for Butler, was both a means to persuade the population to accept federal authority and a way to make money.[18]

Only Butler's treatment of foreigners disturbed the administration. The disagreement over how to treat foreigners was significant for two reasons. First, it led to Lincoln's decision to replace Butler with General Nathaniel Banks in early November 1862, and second, it involved foreign nationals rather than those born in New Orleans. On June 10 Butler issued General Orders No. 41, which required, in effect, that foreigners take an oath not to aid the Confederacy. It was part of a larger requirement that residents willing to work for the Union or wishing its protection had to take an oath of allegiance. Foreign consuls protested to Butler and then Secretary of State William Seward that this order required them to become American subjects in order to protect their property. Lincoln appointed Reverdy Johnson of Maryland, who had just been elected to the Senate, as a special agent of the State Department to investigate. Johnson arrived in July and decided that most of the property seized from the foreigners should be returned. In his defense, Butler argued that many foreign nationals had already forfeited their nationality by aiding the Confederacy. Lincoln subsequently replaced Butler, but he did so only after many foreigners had taken an oath to support the Union. Lincoln's concern over Butler's actions arose because they drew protests from other nations, not because he was concerned about confiscation per se.[19]

Butler's interest in confiscating property, particularly that of prominent rebels, increased after the second act became law. Butler's seizures arose from his own greed and that of his brother, Andrew, not from a desire for punishment or reform.[20] In the end, the Butler brothers secured millions of dollars during their time in New Orleans and much of it came from the proceeds of confiscated property, which should have been delivered to the government. Under the second act Andrew, with his brother's permission, set about confiscating with alacrity the property of any Confederate civil or military officer. However, Butler did allow these owners to transfer their property after July 25, the day that Lincoln had authorized the seizure of property for those who did not resume allegiance to the Union within sixty days. This delay was in keeping with Lincoln's wish not to challenge the property relations that had operated for so long in that region and thus hurt the chances for Louisiana's restoration to the Union.[21] In other words, Butler and his brother confiscated what they could but only if it did not damage Lincoln's plans for reunion.

Butler was less eager, for example, to punish those who had not yet demonstrated an overt enthusiasm for the Confederacy. He delayed until September 13 an order that all "neutral" foreigners in the Department of the Gulf had to register with the provost marshal, indicating their place of residence and a description thereof. And he waited until September 18 to prohibit any transfers of property by those who had not yet returned to their allegiance to the Union. The lateness of this important order gave many in New Orleans time to protect their property, and Butler was doubtless aware that he had given the great mass of citizens a grace period. On September 24, sixty days after the second act became law, Butler ordered former citizens of the United States to take an oath of allegiance on or before October 1 as well as to submit a list of their property. Those who failed to do so subjected their property to confiscation "as a punishment for such neglect." About four thousand refused the oath and registered as enemies; Butler allowed them to leave the city with only a little personal property. Those who fled the city or were soldiers in the Confederate military and had not transferred their property before the September 18 deadline also suffered the confiscation of their property, much of it personal. Most of this property was soon sold below value at public auction. More important, it is estimated that as many as 68,000 in New Orleans swore allegiance to the Union by the end of the year. Many residents realized that some took the oath to protect their property; such deceit was accepted under the circumstances. Butler certainly realized that many were insincere in taking the oath; he simply wished to force a choice on the assumption it would aid restoration. Dr. William Mercer, for example, refused to take the oath and asked that his neutrality be respected since he had never sworn allegiance to the Confederacy. Butler denied the request. "There can be no such thing as neutrality by a citizen of the United States," he claimed, "in this contest for the life of the government." In mid-October Butler prohibited attorneys from transferring property owned by any persons who had not sworn allegiance to the United States. However, the seizures contemplated under these orders could apparently be avoided if Andrew Butler was paid to persuade his brother not to confiscate. Although many in New Orleans hated Butler for his confiscation policies, they were, except for those directed at prominent rebels, not very harsh.[22]

Butler, on the other hand, considerably broadened the range of his confiscation when he "sequestered" all the property of the District of Lafourche west of New Orleans. Several reasons have been offered for Butler's effort to seize the district in October 1862. The three parishes of this district, Assumption, Lafourche, and Terrebonne, had wealthy plantation owners, many of whom were disloyal or had fled. These owners were inviting targets for Butler. Lafourche also posed a threat to New Orleans if fully controlled by the Confederates. Butler had done little fighting of late and the district was not well guarded at the time. As well, Butler no longer faced a threat from Baton Rouge. Union forces encountered little resistance in Lafourche and captured abandoned plantations whose slaves were eager to be received within Union lines. Miles Taylor, manager of Stephen Douglas's 1860 campaign and himself a plantation owner, recalled that Union officers told his servants that they "were now free," presumably under the second act. Taylor also estimated that at least nine thousand freed slaves had entered Union lines by late October. After subduing Lafourche, Butler ordered that all property in the district be "sequestered" under the second act and that no transfers of property be allowed. All personal property not used by the military was to be sold at auction in New Orleans. This included thousands of hogsheads of sugar. Slaves in Lafourche, however, were not necessarily set free. The order allowed for their continued employment on plantations, owned by both loyal and disloyal owners, with wages and hours set by the government in order to ensure the success of the crops. In effect, then, the sequestration of Lafourche revolved around personal, not real, property owned by disloyal or absent owners and the use of plantations' former slaves for crop production. It was hardly the confiscation contemplated by the second act, but it received no criticism in Washington. Butler had cleverly reacted to the shifting attitudes of the administration by arming free blacks and creating a quasi-free labor force. At the same time he did not disturb property relations in the Gulf, except when it came to personal property and crops that could be quickly auctioned for profit.[23]

Despite Butler's reputation at the time, his administration of the Department of the Gulf was hardly radical. His seizure of Lafourche, like many of his orders, used harsh language that obscured modest measures and limited results. Little more than imposition of martial law occurred in Lafourche and individuals could avoid confiscation by taking the oath of allegiance and complying with the new labor system, which many found to their liking. His confiscation efforts ignored the procedures of the second act and illustrated his twin objectives of pacifying the region and enriching himself and his brother. Moreover, the volume of property confiscated in Lafourche and the amount money realized from its sale, money that should have gone to the government, has never been clearly determined. To Stanton, Butler estimated that the hogsheads of sugar alone would be worth a million dollars; to Treasury Secretary Chase he calculated that his seizures would realize "a million of dollars worth of property" for the government. In 1864 Stanton asked Butler how much the seizure had realized; Butler expressed surprise that Stanton had not seen the figures that surely had been transmitted to the government. Butler then suggested that "something like three-quarters of a million dollars" in personal property had been taken, but much of this, he said, had been restored to the owners. Later Butler informed Stanton that no more than $100,000 appeared to have been realized from the property confiscated in Lafourche. Furthermore, much of this sum, the general claimed, had not reached the Treasury because Banks, his successor, had mixed this sum in with other funds to pay for the army in the Gulf.[24] Yet the Butler brothers appeared to have become quite wealthy as a result of their time in Louisiana. In the end, although perhaps no region of the South provided a better place in which to implement the second act, it failed to occur, for Lincoln had no wish to annoy potential Union supporters and Butler only confiscated that which he could sell quickly, thereby excluding land.[25]

Beyond New Orleans, there were two military views on confiscation after Congress had passed the second act. One followed the general outlines of the administration's policy. Lincoln wanted the second act used solely for military reasons and authorized only Attorney General Bates to implement it, allowing only a minimal role for the military. This made for some odd bedfellows on the question of confiscation. In the absence of instructions, General George

McClellan could disparage "the civil policy inaugurated by recent acts of Congress" and maintain the view that "private property and persons" should be protected as much as possible. Later, upon receipt of Lincoln's July 22 executive order, which authorized that property be seized only for military purposes, McClellan smugly informed his subordinates that the order "accords so substantially" with his previous instructions that no change in direction was needed. Nonetheless, he emphasized that officers and soldiers were to "abstain from all seizures of private property" except to meet military needs. In Memphis, Major General William T. Sherman also rejected the chance to involve the military in confiscation at that time. Sherman understood that General U. S. Grant had not taken the opportunity to confiscate property; instead, he rented it, and Sherman proposed to do the same. If the residents of Memphis "remain quiet and conform" to the laws, Sherman would protect their property and lives. "We have nothing to do with confiscation," he concluded. In time, he believed, courts would be established to execute the laws, like confiscation. Until then, however, every chance should be offered the "wavering and disloyal" to resume their allegiance. Although Sherman had made it clear that all masters "who are in open hostility to the Constitution" would lose their slaves, he did not declare them free. Henry Halleck, General-in-Chief of the Army, also offered strict rules on the seizure of property in mid-August but omitted any mention of the second act. At the same time, however, Halleck reported hearing that after the second act became law some in the military were willing to have blacks die for the Union in place of whites.[26]

In early September on his own initiative, however, Secretary of War Stanton instructed Brigadier General John M. Schofield of the District of Missouri to begin proceedings under the second act. Stanton had learned of many disloyal persons in Schofield's district and thought it "expedient to enforce" the second act against them. Schofield's orders anticipated the careful instructions Bates himself issued three months later except that army personnel rather than marshals were to seize the property and secure evidence against the owners. There is no evidence, however, that any property was confiscated under these orders. Brigadier General George Wright in the Department of the Pacific also followed orders to enforce the act, but with little apparent success. His department included California and Oregon plus the territories of Washington, Utah, Nevada, and present-day Arizona. It is doubtful that much property in this district met the requirements of the second act. Both these directives regarded confiscation as anticipated by the second act's authors—seizure as a consequence of aiding the rebellion, not as a means of aiding the military or coercing the rebels.[27]

The military also used confiscation to justify the destruction or seizure of other forms of rebel property as they moved deeper into the South. In early August Henry Halleck instructed Major General U. S. Grant to "clean out" portions of Tennessee and Mississippi and treat "active sympathizers" "without gloves and take their property for public use." This led to an order four days later that General James D. Morgan in Mississippi was to inform the residents that any hostile acts would render them enemies "whose property belongs to the United States." In addition, all women and children were to move beyond his lines, and their property was to be seized and "their houses burned." In Virginia, Major General John Pope in late July signaled an end to a lenient property policy. Soldiers in his command were no longer to be "wasted in protecting private property" of rebels. By mid-August, however, Pope was forced to offer several admonitions against those soldiers who had taken more private property than was needed for their own subsistence.[28]

The decision by some to allow an assault upon property did not please all military commanders. McClellan, in the orders noted above, reacted against the increasing damage visited upon all kinds of property in Virginia and ordered no seizures without specific authorization and enjoined those under his command to abstain from plunder. Major General John A. Dix also believed "the inhabitants" of Virginia should "be protected against all disturbance" and warned those who ignored this rule would "be visited with the most extreme rigor of the law." But such solicitude for Southerners was not widespread after the summer and fall of 1862. Instead, as the documents in the *Official Records* demonstrate, commanders found it increasingly difficult to prevent "depredations" against property. They spent much time instructing subordinates how to behave. In early October, for example, McClellan noted "the frequent orders" issued about "stragglers and pillagers" and regretted that he had to remind his commanders of the matter again. It became a consistent theme for officers.[29]

As Wayne K. Durrill has suggested, the authority given under the first and second acts, which the preliminary emancipation proclamation of September 22 expanded, attacked secessionists' "absolute claims to property." Not only did slaves become objects of the military, so too did cotton, livestock, houses, and just about anything else owned by rebels. Beginning in the summer of 1862, the Civil War became a "property war." Confiscation or destruction of property became a way to defeat the South, although not to reconstruct it, as the authors of the second act had hoped. In August, for example, the Union forces under General Curtis in Arkansas began seizing livestock, food, and slaves around Helena. Some soldiers and officers even complained if asked to protect the property of rebels. When Curtis left to command the Department of Missouri, his replacement, Frederick Steele, continued to allow confiscation of cotton and food but did not follow his predecessor's liberal policy toward confiscating slaves. Many in his command criticized Steele for defending slavery and violating the second act. Soldiers from Illinois wrote back to their hometown newspapers in the summer and fall of 1862 that a harsher military policy should be implemented against the South, including particularly confiscation of property and emancipation. Having witnessed slavery firsthand, these soldiers felt both were morally justified. In October and November 1862 unionists in North Carolina, citing the authority of the second act, threatened to confiscate the property of secessionist planters if they did not take an oath to the Union.[30]

The second act's most significant impact on Southern property involved the military's changed view of slavery and contrabands from July 1862 on. Yet just how critical the second act was to slavery's demise is difficult to assess. Tennessee offered the earliest example of how the mixture of the law, the public, the army, and slaves led to the disruption of the peculiar institution. When the Union forces first entered Tennessee in February 1862, Halleck had ordered Grant to exclude runaway slaves from federal lines. By the spring some officers were bending the rule where military necessity dictated while others, like Buell, adhered strictly to the policy. Others with strong antislavery convictions ignored the rule. During the summer a number of factors changed the military's view. Some Tennessee unionists began to criticize Buell and others for protecting secessionists' property, Congress passed the second act, legitimizing those eager to attack rebel property, and Halleck was elevated to general in chief. With Halleck now in Washington, officers felt less constrained to obey the exclusion policy. Grant, for example, became more responsive to the needs of blacks entering his lines. Finally, in November 1862 Grant received permission to use contrabands as he wished. By early 1863 most commanders in Tennessee were using freed slaves as laborers, and this created a surge of slaves into the Union lines. However, few commanders tried to free the slaves under the second act; a resident of Lawrence County, Alabama, just south of Tennessee, wrote in February 1863 that he and others suffered "under the military enforcements of the Confiscation Act, and the orders to subsist on the country by the Federals."[31]

It is clear, then, that by late 1862 and early 1863 the war had changed dramatically. Most in the army now saw the value of using free blacks and freed slaves as laborers and soldiers, both of which the second act and Lincoln authorized. However, that is not to say the second act was central to the demise of slavery. Slaves could not be freed under the second act unless a court adjudicated the issue. What the second act did was support the changing views on how to conduct the war. General William T. Sherman was a good example of this transformation. In June 1862, for example, he observed that the military use of private property was "a delicate right" that should be "exercised by as few as possible." In August 1862, as we have seen, he said the military has "nothing to do with confiscation" and that it was "neither his duty nor pleasure to disturb" slavery. But soon his attitude changed, and by October 1863 he ordered the destruction of private property of those citizens who did not oppose guerilla warfare in West Tennessee. He did all this to change residents' attitudes in order to facilitate a Union victory, not to prepare the South for reconstruction after the war. The difference is central to how the second act should be viewed in relation to the military.[32]

6 Rules of War and Later Military Confiscation

The military's participation in confiscation occurred during a period of critical discussion about the rules of war. This discussion was clearly important for the conduct of the Civil War and later conflicts, but it did not have much effect on how the military involved itself with confiscation. The debate over the rules of war was, nonetheless, for it explains how both civilians and military viewed the right to seize private property during the Civil War. This debate is central to understanding why the confiscation acts failed to realize the goals of their supporters.

When the Civil War began, the Union forces possessed no adequate military code to guide their conduct in the conflict. The only available American guides were *General Regulations for the Army*, written by Winfield Scott and published in 1821, and *Regulations for the Army of the United States 1861*, which were inadequate to the problems that arose in the war. Both concentrated on the internal workings of the American army and did not address the issues that other, more notable, commentators such as Emerich de Vattel, Cornelius van Bynkershoek, and Hugo Grotius had discussed—for instance, the rules as they related to international law. Early in the war, most Americans who considered that subject assumed that municipal, not international, law should govern the conflict. West Point graduates did not have any greater understanding of the issues involved. In 1859 it had been suggested that Francis Lieber, a scholar on the rules of war, offer a course at the military academy, but the commandant had rejected the idea. As a consequence, many officers were ignorant of the laws of war, as were civilian officials. There were exceptions, though, such as Henry Halleck, who succeeded General John C. Frémont in Missouri in 1861.[1]

Halleck graduated from West Point in 1839 and became both an engineer and lawyer before the Civil War. In 1846 he wrote a treatise on fortifications and in 1861 published a study on international law, which discussed the laws of war but did not anticipate the questions that soon emerged in the fight between the North and South. As Frémont's replacement, Halleck instituted regulations that brought some order out of the chaos in Missouri and protected private property, angering some radicals in Congress. In the fall of 1861 Halleck asked Lieber, who was teaching law at Columbia University, to send him the lectures he was then giving on the rules of war. Born in Germany, Lieber had been a soldier in the Prussian army before he immigrated to the United States. He arrived in Boston in 1827 but later moved to the South, where he lived for twenty years, teaching at South Carolina College. During that time he owned a few slaves, although he professed to dislike the peculiar institution. While in South Carolina Lieber had published important works as a political philosopher. He moved in 1857 to New York City. His three sons served in the war; one died for the Confederacy while the other two fought for the Union side. A longtime correspondent of Charles Sumner, with whom he often agreed on the objectives of the war, Lieber was devoted to the Union.[2]

In September 1861, Lieber, like many Northerners, applauded Frémont's proclamation, but, like Lincoln, he doubted that the general had the power to free slaves. Lieber had already expressed concern that the military did not understand the problems surrounding slavery as it moved into the South. For example, he had opposed the word "contraband" used in connection with General Ben Butler at Fort Monroe because it suggested that slaves were property. Although he had long disliked slavery, he believed only Congress could authorize confiscation of slaves; this was effectively Lincoln's position in 1861. Lieber wanted to write a treatise to assist the military on such questions and in March 1862 received encouragement for the project when he met Halleck on a trip west in March 1862 to see one of his sons, who had lost an arm. In May, again agreeing with Lincoln, Lieber found fault with Hunter's proclamation freeing slaves along the seacoast. According to Lieber, Hunter had not consulted with his superiors and had based his proclamation on martial law, when the army did not control the area in question. At the request of Attorney General Bates, Lieber agreed to have his views on Hunter made public in early July. He also corresponded with Secretary of War Edwin Stanton and Judge Advocate General Joseph Holt on other military matters. In November Halleck, now general in chief, accepted Lieber's suggestion that Lincoln should "issue a set of rules and definitions" to guide the military. A committee chaired by Halleck was created and, with Lieber as the principal author, wrote General Orders 100, issued in April 1863. It is noteworthy that Lieber's work, justly hailed then and since, appeared after the military had adopted a more aggressive policy toward property. Presumably Lieber knew of the new military behavior and supported it. Moreover, Lincoln and Lieber fundamentally agreed on the need to protect property during the war and on confiscation's implementation during the conflict. It may be that Lincoln agreed that Lieber should write the Orders insofar as they appeared to be of the same mind on the protection of all property except slavery. Burrus M. Carnahan, in fact, argues that Lieber rested his thesis of military necessity on Lincoln's earlier proclamations.[3] The impact of General Orders 100, therefore, was to complement what Lincoln had already set in motion, the liberation of slaves by the military and the protection of most other property unless needed by the military.

Lieber's Orders came to seventeen pages, but only one of the ten sections concerned private and public property. As Lieber noted in another instance, the central principle that had emerged in land war over the years was that the "unarmed citizen is to be spared in person, property and honor, as much as the exigencies of war will admit." In other words, military necessity allowed for the confiscation of property except where specifically authorized or prohibited. In fact, the Orders said that the North should protect "strictly private property; the persons of inhabitants, especially those of women; and the sacredness of domestic relations." Moreover, the property of peaceful citizens should not be destroyed, pillaged, or in any way molested. Significantly, Lieber authorized confiscation only by a narrow authority: "Private property, unless forfeited by crimes or by offenses of the owner, can be seized only by way of military necessity" for the Union army. And Lieber emphasized that those who violated personal property should "be rigorously punished." As Phillip Paludan has observed, Lieber's belief that "nationalism and private property" were closely connected protected almost all property not public and slavery. Thus, confiscation that would last beyond the fighting, whether taken for treason or support of the rebellion, had no place in Lieber's understanding of the rules of war.[4]

Although Lieber's Orders were conservative on property, they were much less so on slavery. This reflected Lieber's willingness to sidestep the Constitution on this issue and, for the most part, coincided with the changes Lincoln's views had undergone by the summer of 1862. As Michael Les Benedict and Allen C. Guelzo have argued, Lincoln took a broad view of his power as commander in chief. Lieber had objected to a description of fugitive slaves as contraband because that defined them as property, a concession, he believed, the federal government did not have to make to masters whose slaves escaped the municipal laws that governed them. At the same time, Lieber deplored the proclamations of Frémont and Hunter, since they extended federal authority where it could not be sustained by the military. Yet he also worried about the government's hesitancy over those who escaped into Union lines. In December 1861 Sumner expressed concern about the status of fugitives in a civil war, but Lieber brushed his worry aside. The conflict was an international war, Lieber said, governed by "the Law of Nature" which did "not acknowledge the difference of skin" color. The slaves were therefore free as soon as they left the municipal law that bound them to slavery. "Those who commenced this rebellion" should have considered this fact. "It is now too late to talk, *in the midst of war*, of rights made or guaranteed by municipal or constitutional law," he concluded. This reflected Lieber's fear that the Union would be imperiled if it strictly adhered to the Constitution's protection of slavery. The Orders stated that "a person held in bondage" who came under "protection of the military forces" of the Union would be "immediately entitled to the rights and privileges of a freeman." (This exceeded what the second act promised slaves who came into Union control.) To return a fugitive slave, the Orders said, would "amount to enslaving a free person" and the Union could not countenance that. Such promises of freedom, of course, went beyond what Lincoln contemplated under the Emancipation Proclamation, which emancipated slaves only in states beyond the Union's reach but did not confer any privileges upon freed slaves or abolish slavery. It appears, however, that the Orders were often more observed and understood after the Civil War, not during it.[5] Nonetheless, Lieber and his orders reflected the importance the North placed on the protection of private property, other than slaves, in the South. Furthermore, slaves were not confiscated under the Orders so much as self-emancipated by entering Union lines.[6] And once emancipated, freed slaves enjoyed far less than the freedom promised in Lieber's Orders. This was certainly true in New Orleans.

The replacement of Ben Butler by Nathaniel Banks in New Orleans in December 1862 emphasized the president's moderate position on confiscating private property that was also seen in Lieber's Orders. Even though Butler had accomplished a good deal, the Lincoln administration decided to replace him in November with the less flamboyant Banks, largely because of the dispute over foreigners that Butler had initiated. Whereas Butler had the support of many radicals, Banks, a former speaker of the House from Massachusetts, had a reputation for moderation. Significantly, among Banks's first acts in mid-December was an order to suspend all sales of property. This suggested a more conciliatory policy than his predecessor's. Banks hoped it would facilitate restoration of the Union and enhance his political prospects. In addition, he ordered a report on the sequestration of Lafourche, which later led him to withdraw the military from further confiscation of property. No more seizures were to occur without his permission. If Banks presumed his lenient approach would encourage cooperation in and around New Orleans, where Butler's bellicose behavior had created discord, historians are agreed that it failed. Planters, blacks engaged in his labor system, and many Unionists found fault with Banks's administration for a variety or reasons.[7]

Banks's administration of confiscation also came into conflict with the court system that had been created in New Orleans just before his arrival. This squabble illustrated the administration's inattention to any confiscation that did not involve slavery. In October 1862 Lincoln had appointed Charles A. Peabody as a judge of a provisional court to "hear, try, and determine all causes, civil and criminal" and his judgment was "to be final and conclusive."[8] This removed even the Supreme Court from the power of review; only Lincoln had the authority to overturn the provisional court's decisions, although he apparently forgot about the appointment. Peabody and his associates, a prosecuting attorney, marshal, and clerk, were to serve at the president's pleasure in the area occupied by the military only and they were to be paid by the War Department, not the attorney general's office. Nor did Peabody, who owed his appointment to Secretary of State William Seward, face Senate confirmation for his position. The decision to create this extraordinary court with sweeping powers derived from Lincoln's concern, prompted by Seward, that someone address the complaints of foreign residents in New Orleans, who felt abused under Butler's regime. Problems soon developed when Peabody exercised some of his extraordinary powers, particularly over confiscation.[9]

Peabody's court initially heard only federal cases, but soon it became involved in civil cases under Louisiana law, to the annoyance of the New Orleans legal community. Banks, like many others, grew concerned at the breadth of Peabody's reach and, in particular, the judge's enforcement of the confiscation acts. Peabody authorized widespread seizures of moveable property to be sold at auction in New Orleans. The court officers often received military assistance in the search for confiscable property. Although Banks conceded Peabody's authority to confiscate, he complained that the seizures were interfering with the work of the military. Specifically, they were taking property, largely foodstuffs, away from the military that it needed to sustain itself in the field. "This is inconsistent with the laws of war," Banks complained, and has reduced the "army to the standard of a marshal's *posse comitatus*," a group of men authorized to aid the court. "In a department under martial law the army cannot be held subordinate to a civil tribunal," Banks argued. The provisional court had stripped him, claimed Banks, of the powers enjoyed by Butler and so he asked that it be made subordinate to the military. Halleck subsequently agreed. "Neither this court nor its officers should be permitted to interfere with or embarrass" Banks's movements, Halleck ordered. If the court interfered with Banks's operations, Halleck gave him the power to "send them [the court's officials] back to the city, or, if necessary, out of the department." In May, on the advice of two Republicans in New Orleans, Lincoln appointed Edward H. Durell as a federal judge for the Eastern District of New Orleans, and thereafter Peabody confined himself largely to cases involving Louisiana law. By late June the *New Orleans Delta* concluded "the establishment of really civil courts denoted the retirement of the military" rule in the city,[10] but this did not mean conflict would disappear with the courts over confiscation.

If anything, Banks had more problems with Durell's court. In November 1863 Durell and District Attorney Rufus Waples demonstrated a reluctance to accede to Banks's control over an issue involving confiscation.[11] Even though the issue, like others before Peabody's court, was not that important, it illustrated the confused and tangled arguments between the military and civil officials in New Orleans as well as the way Lincoln's administration largely ignored the second act. The dispute involved the *Alabama*, a steamer the navy had offered the army to transport troops to Banks in Texas. Durell, however, ordered a marshal and his deputies to seize the ship on November 12; they then forced civilian workers to abandon their work on the vessel. Brigadier General Charles Stone, Banks's chief of staff, then had the marshal and his men arrested, and the ship shortly thereafter left with reinforcements for Banks. Stone subsequently reported to Banks that Waples and Marshal James Graham "seem to have gone demented in your absence," with the apparent approval of Durell. After the *Alabama* episode, Waples and Graham, according to Stone, threw New Orleans "into confusion by a general seizure of cotton," which created "more excitement" than he had yet seen. In fact, if "more confusion and trouble should ensue, I think these gentlemen will have to be arrested." Apparently, however, this did not occur. After Stone had written a "respectful letter" to Durell, the judge summoned him to appear in court, where Waples tried to prove that the brigadier general had shown contempt for the court. Finally, after Durell gave what Stone characterized as "a long reprimand" about his supposed wish "to override civil authority," he dismissed the case.[12] The *Alabama* affair exemplified the obstacles Banks and the military faced dealing with New Orleans civil authorities such as Peabody, Durell, and Waples, all of whom were involved in both confiscation and local politics.[13]

As historians have noted, Banks faced a bewildering set of pressures as he struggled to devise a strategy that would achieve restoration and simultaneously help his political career. It is hardly surprising that for Banks confiscation became a means to achieve ends that had not been envisioned by either act. In May 1863 he planned for the military to confiscate "mules, horses, cattle, and the staple products of the country—cotton, sugar, and tobacco" in order to deprive the Confederacy of their use. If he reached Alexandria, Louisiana, however, he would allow the residents there to retain half of all proceeds from their staple products sold in New Orleans. The goal was to add 50,000–100,000 bales of cotton to the market and perhaps realize between $10 million and $12 million. "I am aware that at first thought this may seem in conflict with the act of confiscation," he observed to Halleck, but since cotton was particularly perishable, easily destroyed by hostile parties, or hidden, he assumed that it was not the property the second act meant to confiscate. Moreover, it would take the military "valuable time" to transport these goods to the market if confiscated. So, rather than destroy the cotton or let it rot, Banks believed it "necessary to give the people possessing it some interest in its preservation" and ultimate sale. Banks conceded that the policy might not be successful, but he saw no other choice. Banks's attempts to resolve this problem highlighted the limitations of the second act and the administration's inconsistent and limited implementation of it. In the end, Secretary of Chase, for his own reasons, vetoed Banks's plans for seizing the cotton.[14]

Undeterred, Banks proposed to take the cotton and compensate those who could prove they were not secessionists. To implement his scheme, he explained to Lincoln that he planned to bribe those in the Confederate military who held the property and might prevent the seizure. He claimed that "the impoverished condition" of Confederate "officers west of the Mississippi" was such that they would agree to this kind of confiscation if they received eighteen cents per pound, once it was clear they would not use the money against the Union. Banks also proposed allowing the importation of cotton held by private individuals, from the Confederacy into Union lines, with the owners allowed to profit from the sales. He claimed that perhaps 300,000 bales would be sold by these two plans. Banks's schemes were innovative uses of the second act, yet both failed when the Confederate officer in charge decided to burn the cotton rather than have Banks take possession of it. As will be discussed in the next chapter on the Treasury, Banks's handling of confiscation, like other issues he confronted in Louisiana, was less about the immediate issue. Instead, confiscation had to fit into the larger goal of achieving restoration while fending off Banks's political enemies and thus not damaging his career. In the end, Banks succeeded in accomplishing little while in Louisiana, in contrast to his more flamboyant and corrupt yet more effective predecessor.[15]

While Banks struggled with confiscation in Louisiana, without either interference or assistance from Bates, the attorney general had his first important dispute with the military over confiscation. In late October 1862 General James S. Wadsworth, military governor of the District of Columbia, had ordered Provost-Marshal W. E. Doster to take possession of the furniture in the house of John A. Campbell. A former justice of the Supreme Court from Alabama, Campbell had resigned from the Court and became the Confederate assistant secretary of war.[16] The military guarded the furniture for over two weeks until December 18 when the district's circuit court issued a writ of replevin under the second act to Marshal Ward Lamon of the district. This writ required that the furniture be restored to Campbell if he provided security and pledged to surrender it if he lost the case in court. When Lamon went to inventory and seize the property, General John H. Martindale, Wadsworth's successor, directed Doster to stop Lamon from issuing the writ, by force if necessary, and report to Bates. Lamon also informed Bates of the incident and said that similar interference by the military had occurred on numerous occasions before. Bates then told Martindale that he had asked the president "to suppress such dangerous irregularity." Before answering Bates, Martindale made an effort to resolve the problem himself.[17]

Martindale first told Lamon that he could issue the writ of replevin because the property had originally been seized by the military in order to turn it over to the civil authorities. Then, in reply to Bates, Martindale blamed the confusion on his predecessor who "supposed he was acting in conformity to principles of public law . . . and in furtherance of the confiscation act." Martindale, of course, failed to point out that he had ordered the marshal to stop Lamon from issuing the writ. In his reply, Bates also ignored this fact. Instead, he wanted to make certain that the property Martindale promised to relinquish was indeed confiscable and not seized for military use. If anything, Bates was most concerned about the military's apparent interest in confiscation. He later warned District Attorney Edward Carrington against conducting any business with the military except in writing so "whatever is done in *our* Department upon this delicate subject, may be capable of perfect explanation hereafter."[18]

Although Campbell's furniture eventually reached Carrington and realized the government almost two thousand dollars, both Carrington and Secretary of War Stanton believed the episode had exposed weaknesses in the second act that had to be remedied for it to be successful. Carrington, in fact, believed the act's deficiencies so grave "that no satisfactory results" could be attained in either current or future confiscation cases. Early in 1863, Carrington wrote to Bates to suggest an amendment to the act's fifth and sixth sections. Carrington proposed that owners of confiscable property in the North who failed to appear at their trials would have their property rights adjudicated on the assumption that their absence proved support for the rebellion. He also proposed the government consider as rebels those who had moved to secessionist states after the war began and had failed to renew their original allegiance before the passage of the second act. Both Bates and Congress wisely failed to pursue either of these suggestions. These proposals certainly would have enlarged the amount of property liable to confiscation in the North, but under both the absence of a person would be taken as proof of Confederate loyalty. Although this might have been fair in Campbell's case, since he was a prominent Confederate, it probably would have been unfair to less prominent citizens absent for unknown reasons. Moreover, the second act's primary intent was not to punish those in the North suspected of supporting the Confederacy.[19] Even so, it is significant that Bates ignored these suggestions to modify the act. The attorney general consistently refused to approach Congress about amending an act his subordinates found difficult to implement.

In response to a House request, Stanton also made two suggestions following the Campbell furniture case. First, he wanted the military authorized to confiscate property without direction from civil officials. The military would report the seizure to civil officials in areas where the courts functioned and turn the matter over to the civil authorities. Second, where courts did not exist, a massive area by early 1863, the military would regulate condemnation and sale of confiscated property through court martial proceedings. This proposal resembled Carrington's first suggestion insofar as it placed the burden of proof upon the property's owner, not the government. According to Stanton, anyone who abandoned property, remained a rebel, or had a "general reputation" for disloyalty should be presumed guilty and, unless proved otherwise, have his property confiscated. While Carrington's suggestion was directed at owners in the North, Stanton's targeted those in the South known to support the Confederacy and was therefore easier to defend. However, Congress took no action on either of Stanton's ideas. Nothing as radical had been proposed during the debates over either confiscation acts. As well, Congress had proved unwilling to supervise the confiscation acts, and was not inclined to increase their scope drastically. It is significant that Stanton made these suggestions only to the House, at their request, and left no record of lobbying Lincoln, Bates or others Cabinet members for more widespread confiscation.[20]

Even though Stanton made no concerted effort to expand the military's role in confiscation, Bates still expressed concern about the military's encroachment upon his responsibility. When Bates received word that military authorities had seized confiscable property on several occasions, he sent Stanton a copy of his instructions and observed that, by the terms of the second act and Lincoln's authorization, confiscation belonged in the hands of civil officers. In January 1863 Bates specifically asked Stanton to "order all military officers who hold such property to deliver it over to the civil authorities, to be proceeded against according to law." The attorney general, however, did concede the military's right to retain possession of seized property where the courts did not yet function. Stanton apparently ignored this request. A month later Bates received word from the marshal in Nashville that General William S. Rosecrans had taken property already confiscated by civil authorities. Bates quickly relayed this complaint to Lincoln, who directed the secretary of war to correct this jurisdictional conflict. In his directive to Rosecrans, Stanton presumed the military had acted "in conflict" with the Marshal "through misapprehension," not intentionally. In any case, the president had directed Stanton to request that Rosecrans's officers "avoid any interference with the civil officers in the performance of their duties" as requested by Bates.[21]

Rosecrans, however, refused to acknowledge any conflict with civil authorities over the second act, illustrating again the problems surrounding the military's interpretation of the confiscation act. No one, claimed Rosecrans, "has been more careful and anxious to give strength and vigor" to the civil authorities than he had been. Nor had there been any "collision" between civil and military authorities on "any important principle involved." The complaints had arisen only where the military had taken property "for public service" and the U.S. Marshal had objected "on account of his personal liability" for it. Insofar as Nashville was "a camp, a garrison, and a great depot," Rosecrans had deemed it necessary to impose a "species of martial law" to limit the "smuggling, spying, and knavery." Some goods had been confiscated for violating his orders, but he did not believe there had been any effort "to enforce by military means" the confiscation acts. At the same time, Rosecrans required the residents of Nashville to take an oath to support the Union or face searches, arrests, or seizure of their property. By requiring such oaths, of course, Rosecrans was enforcing a form of military confiscation and precluding the work of civil officials. After all, both the circuit court and the U.S. District Court for the Eighth Circuit were in operation by April 1863. Had Bates wanted a vigorous enforcement of the second act, he doubtless would have objected to this kind of military confiscation.[22]

Bates also could have lobbied Lincoln to expand the reach of civil officials in areas where the military had gained control and martial law may not have been appropriate. There is no evidence that the attorney general wished to challenge the military's sovereignty in these areas in order to gain power for those civilians authorized to enforce the second act. With a dearth of direction for civil officials, military commanders duplicated the example of Rosecrans and dealt with confiscable property as they saw fit, without consulting the attorney general. In March 1863, for example, Major General Dix authorized his quartermaster at Fort Monroe, Virginia, to possess and rent the farm of Jefferson Sinclair, "an absentee disloyalist," to one William H. Lynch if the latter would take an oath of allegiance. Fifteen other farms in the region, also apparently owned by absent rebels were to be handled in the same manner, presumably under the power of martial law.[23] Noel C. Fisher has also found that the military used confiscation, among other means, to induce loyalty among civilians in East Tennessee in late 1863 and early 1864, again without any effort by the attorney general's office to contest such rule. As Fisher indicates, much rebelliousness remained in this region. Civil authority would have had a hard time asserting its right to enforce the confiscation acts, but under Bates civil authorities failed even to make the effort.[24]

Another instance of military confiscation replacing that by civil authority occurred in Virginia in the summer of 1863. Lincoln had given Governor Francis H. Pierpont civil authority over all of occupied Virginia, but he made an exception in a dispute involving property in Portsmouth. In late July the city officials of Portsmouth had decided to raise funds for its destitute families from the rents of property abandoned by those who refused to take an oath of allegiance. Brigadier General Henry M. Naglee conferred with the mayor of Portsmouth, who, said Naglee, admitted that the city had no power to confiscate the property and collect rents from them. Naglee agreed to collect the rents for the mayor, but the city council then passed a resolution claiming that the military had interfered with their civil authority. The council asked Pierpont to uphold their claim. According to Naglee, Pierpont conceded that the council had no authority "to condemn property and collect the rents," so he asked Naglee to confiscate the property if the owners failed to take the oath. Naglee's response was to issue special orders directing the provost marshals of both cities to "take possession" of houses and real property of "disloyal citizens," but only if they took an "active part" against the Union or violated military orders. Moreover, no property would be condemned without written evidence and approval from the commanding general.[25] There was no question that the military's right to exercise authority superseded civil officials when military necessity arose. Both Lincoln and Lieber certainly adhered to this view. Military necessity was not the issue in Fort Monroe or Portsmouth, however. In this case, as in others, neither Congress nor the administration expressed an interest in confiscation other than for military purposes.

Bates's concerns about the military remained focused on protecting his administration of confiscation, not on the extent of seizures. As he noted in his diary in March 1864, "it is my duty, above all other" Cabinet members, "to uphold the Law, and to resist all encroachments, from whatever quarter . . . upon the province of the law." Moreover, the attorney general appeared most concerned about conflicts in the vicinity of Washington, as in his argument with General Ben Butler that began in March 1864. In November 1863 Butler took command of the eastern district of Virginia and North Carolina. In contrast to his actions in New Orleans, he proceeded with moderation on questions of property. Butler directed the seizure of private property only for the use of troops or from known enemies, in which case the Treasury Department would receive it with the understanding the military could reclaim it. Then in March Bates received a report from Charles M. Butts, a Norfolk lawyer, that Brigadier General Edward Wild had confiscated the property of John A. Williams in Portsmouth. Without waiting for more information on the case, Bates once again reminded Stanton that the confiscation laws were a civil matter and asked him to investigate the incident and report. As he noted in his diary: "It is only yesterday that I sent the Secretary of War, a strong remonstrance against a sweeping order of confiscation" by Wild.[26]

This incident, like others, provoked Bates to "to denounce, if I cannot prevent, the frequent instances of needless, groundless and wanton" military interference in areas where it had no concern. It seemed to Bates "as if the object were to contemn and degrade civil power." Doubtless Stanton felt equally irritated at his colleague, for he simply forwarded the attorney general's letter to Butler without directions or comment. Butler's reply went to Stanton rather than Bates. In it he questioned Butts's integrity and blamed the incident on Wild's ignorance of the law and the latter's use of the word "confiscate" when he should have used "sequestrate." His subordinate's order, therefore, appeared incorrectly to be a military confiscation under a civil law. According to Wild's report, there had been ample justification for a military confiscation of the property in that Williams openly displayed his allegiance to the South and took the prescribed oath only to protect his property. Butler concluded on the basis of Lieber's General Orders 100 and his professional legal experience that Wild's action was perfectly legal, and he presumed the "learned" attorney general would concur. Apparently satisfied with this report, Stanton ignored Bates's letter. After waiting more than two weeks for a reply, the attorney general sent Stanton a long letter, again explaining the civil responsibility for the confiscation laws. When Bates finally received Butler's letter of explanation and Wild's report from the War Department, he privately expressed astonishment. He realized that "upstarts" like Wild had done similar things before, "but I never knew before, such monstrosities [to be] deliberately reduced to writing and embodied in formal[,] official reports." Bates decided not to press the issue, however, because Wild and Butler made it clear that they did not intend to confiscate any property under the two laws. That was what Bates ultimately hoped to accomplish.[27]

The military's most blatant effort to take over the enforcement of the confiscation acts took place in the spring of 1864 in Maryland. Major General Lew Wallace, commander of the Middle Department, believed that many citizens had left the state and their property either to join the rebel army or to aid the rebellion in some way. Moreover, many residents of the South who supported the rebellion apparently owned property in Maryland. In late April Wallace ordered that all the proceeds from their property, including real estate, slaves, stocks, debts, and bonds in railroads, banks, manufacturing companies, and public corporations, be withheld and turned over to the military. On May 1, Wallace then ordered all banks, insurance companies, railroads, turnpikes, ferries, and manufacturers to submit lists of stockholders or proprietors. Upon receiving a complaint about the first order and then reading about it in a clipping from a Baltimore newspaper, Bates responded. (It was not until later that he learned about the second order.) In addition to noting "a very large power over persons, contracts, and property purely civil" that the military had "no lawful authority" over, Bates had four complaints, which illustrated his conservative views on confiscation, his anxiety about the military's role, and the problems with the law itself.[28]

Bates's first concern, significantly, was that the order produced "a painful conflict of jurisdictions." Secondly, he feared it would produce "a crop of future litigation" once peace returned, since he believed there was no law that authorized such military seizures. And even though Bates claimed that all "readily acquiesce" in the use of extraordinary powers for military necessity, few would agree to transfer the application of statute law to the military without congressional authorization. And, last, the attorney general believed that Wallace's order would supply grounds for those who claimed that the president and his administration had "set themselves up as above the law" and ceded all power to the military. Moreover, the first and second acts provided "another and different method" to confiscate property. Most important, the laws required "the proceedings to be judicial" and in courts. Bates further informed Wallace that Lincoln had twice ordered that the attorney general alone implement the two laws. In closing, he informed Wallace that Lincoln knew and approved of this letter of admonition.[29] Like all of Bates's statements on the attorney general's role as the sole administrator of the confiscation laws, this letter all but ruled out any assistance the military might offer in pursuing confiscable property.

Wallace replied at length to Bates five days later. He believed that his answer would allow the attorney general to see "why I cannot agree to the view you have taken" over his orders. In fact, Wallace noted that he had issued two orders on the subject, but only after having read the first and second act. The orders rested "upon certain laws of war" that gave him as much right to stop "money going to rebel soldiers" as he had to prevent clothing and medical supplies being sent to the South. In addition, he believed his orders did not conflict with the two confiscation measures since neither of his orders sought to confiscate property or money. Instead, the money obtained from rents, interest on debts, and dividends from stocks would go to his quartermaster. As well, the orders were meant to discover those properties for confiscation by civilian officials. Indeed, in a rebuke to the attorney general, he admitted "an energetic execution" of the confiscation acts would make his "orders superfluous." To his knowledge there had been only one judgment by the United States attorney in Maryland in three years, whereas the work of his subordinate had already discovered much confiscable property in Maryland. For example, said Wallace, General George H. Steuart had an estate valued at $250,000. His son, "by a flimsy deed of trust" signed in Richmond, falsely owned the property and sent its profits to his father. If he were to accede to Bates's request and revoke his orders, this "wretched traitor" would have means to "devote himself at elegant leisure to his accursed work." Wallace closed by offering his officers' assistance to Bates for his work in confiscation and asked that the president be shown his letter.[30]

On June 11 Bates reported the correspondence to Lincoln and presented his position in the controversy. In Bates's view, Wallace's orders "were not only without law, but flatly against law" and contrary to the president's authorization that the attorney general administer the laws. The justification for his orders was even more egregious, since it defended an illegal act "upon grounds most absurd," presumably that he could assist Bates in detecting property to be confiscated. Perhaps more significant to Bates, the general had put "weapons in the hands" of the administration's enemies by "assuming arbitrary and illegal powers" in the absence of military necessity. The matter so exercised Bates that he threatened to resign if Lincoln did not revoke the orders and end this "military usurpation." Two days later Lincoln directed Bates to have Stanton issue such an order. But, complained Bates to his diary, the president did so without discussing "the legal merits" of the issue. In conveying the president's order to Stanton, Bates observed that "it was an easy thing" to denounce "men as rebels and disloyalists" and that some did so to hide oppressive conduct. Moreover, and most significantly, he dismissed Wallace's argument that many Maryland residents fell under the confiscation act.[31]

On June 14, at the president's request, Stanton directed Wallace to revoke his orders and Wallace immediately did so. Stanton's language to Wallace illustrated both the laws' weakness and the administration's reluctance to employ confiscation except to attack slavery. In Lincoln's view, Wallace "transcended the power" he possessed as a commander of a department when he issued the orders. Only the president had the authority to make such orders. If Wallace believed the orders were necessary, then he should "make representations thereof" to the president through the proper military channels and wait for instructions. Until then, however, he was to have the orders annulled and do nothing more to execute them. In his message Stanton did not discuss the merits or defects of confiscation, nor did he suggest that it might be employed at some future date. He simply said confiscation occurred at the discretion of the president, echoing the observation of Senator John Sherman, no fan of confiscation, to his brother a year earlier, on the weakness of the law. But Wallace's adherence to the president's order was not sufficient for Bates. He complained to his diary that Stanton "hates to give the order" and that Wallace had "ostentatiously" published his orders, "assuming very broad jurisdiction." thereby calling into question Bates's performance but then "silently abstains from executing" the orders. "And thus," the attorney general lamented, "the Government lies under the odium of assuming the power, without the spirit to enforce it!"[32]

Bates's arguments over the definition of military confiscation with Wallace and Butler typified the conflict between the civil and military branches under the confiscation acts. Even though Bates appeared to ignore military interference in confiscation when it occurred at a distance, with Butler and Banks in New Orleans, the attorney general was generally overzealous in guarding his office's power and jurisdiction in disputes with the military. Part of his defensiveness undoubtedly resulted from his office's lack of departmental status. As Bates's diary reveals, he was extremely worried about what he termed "encroachments" upon his area of responsibility. As the administration's legal advisor, his vigilance was understandable. However, it also stemmed from a limited vision of the war's ends and a desire for a narrow enforcement of the confiscation acts. The attorney general grew so concerned with restricting the military's role that he never sought their aid in enforcing the acts. And, with the exception of General Lew Wallace, most in the military agreed with Lieber's view that confiscation of property, other than slaves, should only be pursued out of military necessity. The letters and orders from officers, in fact, are replete with admonitions against what they called the "depredations" against property that had become all too common. Although the war did become grim and hard, the military's concern for the protection of private property, other than slaves, remains impressive. Under the second act, once the military had subdued an area and martial law was no longer required, as was true in ever larger parts of the South as the war progressed, confiscation could have been carried out with the assistance of these officers. As Wallace realized and demonstrated, it was not difficult to determine who owned confiscable property. The military could have easily assisted district attorneys and marshals in implementing the second act. In late 1864, for instance, the commanding officer in New Mexico complained to a local judge that he had written Bates two years earlier about "large amounts of property" in Texas that could have been confiscated but had received no reply.[33] Cooperation to this end would have required Stanton and Bates to work well together and that proved unrealistic. In the end, the confiscation acts proved inefficient for implementation in the wake of the military, the military had little interest in them, and the attorney general was too conservative to allow their implementation except by his officials. Largely because of Bates, the military proved of limited help in transforming the South or punishing its leaders through confiscation.

7 The Treasury's Part in Confiscation

If anyone in the administration might have had sympathy for confiscation and its aims, it should have been Secretary of the Treasury Salmon P. Chase. He certainly had the greatest antislavery and radical reputation of the men Lincoln chose for the Cabinet.[1] As well, the Treasury Department was authorized to handle a diverse assortment of property in the South as it followed in the wake of the military. Treasury agents had excellent opportunities to evaluate what might be confiscable in the considerable amount of captured and abandoned property they encountered, thereby helping the implementation of the confiscation acts. But, for a number of reasons, Chase and his agents did not exert themselves on behalf of confiscation. Most significantly, Chase decided that for political reasons he could not be seen as ahead of Lincoln on the abolition question. Like many others, Chase also came to believe that freedmen needed to participate first in the economy as workers rather than as landowners. Furthermore, the system Chase and his agents set up to handle land in the South worked against any concerted interest in confiscable property. In addition, Attorney General Bates was as worried about Chase's and his officers' interfering in his administration of the confiscation acts as he was about Secretary of War Stanton and his officers. Finally, there were conflicts between Treasury agents and other officials, particularly in New Orleans, that limited the success of confiscation.

The first indication of Chase's cautious attitude toward using confiscation for abolition came in the fall of 1861. Following John C. Frémont's proclamation Chase wrote to Green Adams, a Kentucky friend, that Lincoln had "had some difficulty in consenting" to the First Confiscation Act for fear it might be "construed" as an attack upon slavery. No one in the administration, Chase asserted, wished "to convert this War" into an attack upon any state institution. Nonetheless, should the war be prolonged, as it would if "Secessionism shall gain the upper hand" in Kentucky, then slavery's death was almost inevitable. "But certainly," Chase proclaimed, "the Govt. is seeking no such result." In the meantime, the administration would observe the policy inaugurated by Cameron's response to Butler in May with the result that eventually freed slaves would be "sent out of the country, or in some other way reconciling" their freedom with the general good. Freed slaves, in other words, would not necessarily be treated as equal to whites. Beyond employing those slaves who volunteered to assist the government, "no interference with Slavery is thought of." More than three weeks later, Chase explained to a former colleague in the antislavery cause that it was almost impossible to discriminate between slaves of loyal and disloyal masters. The military, he said, should not be involved in "catching & returning slaves at all." "You may rely upon it that Acts, not Proclamns., will advance the cause,"[2] but events soon outstripped this confident prediction. By early January 1862, Chase and the Treasury Department were handling the land and freed slaves of rebels.

In early November 1861, a number of islands off the coast of South Carolina fell to Union forces. Plantation owners there had fled to the mainland, leaving about eight thousand slaves and their property. Because the land had been abandoned and the cotton crop needed to be harvested, the Treasury Department assumed responsibility for the islands under an act Congress had passed in July to supervise commerce in formerly rebellious portions of the South. Several correspondents urged Chase to use the Sea Islands as a means to attack slavery, just as many simultaneously wrote Trumbull and his colleagues to attack slavery as the cause of the war. The administration, however, ignored these proposals. In his message to Congress on December 3, 1861, Lincoln suggested these slaves be colonized; it was not clear that he believed they were free. At the same time Chase appointed Edward L. Pierce, an abolitionist friend from Boston, to administer the islands. Chase hoped Pierce could prevent the "deterioration of the estates" and realize "the greatest possible benefit" to those who labored on them, a vague way of alluding to the slaves' the future on the islands. In February, the reformer George William Curtis noted to Chase the "novel" duties the government had assumed under the first act in South Carolina. He urged that Chase appoint Frederick Law Olmsted to care for the "many thousands of persons held as slaves" under the authority of a "Sub-Department or Bureau," perhaps like the later Freedmen's Bureau, but Chase had already appointed Pierce to administer the islands. He also ignored Curtis's suggestion that the first act be used to free the slaves.[3]

Instead, Pierce and a large group of volunteers supported by wealthy abolitionists began work in the spring of 1862 to create schools and churches for the blacks and supervise the production of cotton on the plantations. These Northerners were the first to confront, under the authority of Chase and then Secretary of War Stanton, the issue of former slaves and the land they worked. As Willie Lee Rose and Akiko Ochiai have discussed, the ideas that emerged on the islands revealed much about Northerners' and abolitionists' beliefs concerning what the relationship between freed slaves and Southern land should be after the fighting ceased. Both the Northern whites and the islands' blacks agreed that the plantation system should be abolished but differed on what should replace it. Whites presumed the blacks should work upon the plantations as paid laborers, at least initially. Pierce told Chase in January 1862, for example, that the "Negroes seem very well disposed, & quite well pleased with the new order of things here," with most willing to remain on their plantations if they were paid for their work. The secretary concurred. "It is, indeed, in the highest degree essential to the commercial intercourse" of that area, Chase responded, "that the abandoned estates be cultivated, and the laborers upon them employed." The possibility blacks might want land rather than be paid for their labor did not apparently occur to Chase. Profits from the large 1861 cotton crop, harvested with free black labor, impressed many in the North and helped defeat what little chance blacks had had to acquire land. In April 1862 the War Department took over administration of the Sea Islands, and Stanton's instructions to General Rufus Saxton were similar to the ones Pierce had received. Saxton was to "make such rules and regulations for the cultivation of the land, and for the protection, employment, and government" of the islands' inhabitants "as circumstances may seem to require."[4] In other words, Saxton was to harvest cotton, using blacks as laborers.

Chase's response to General David Hunter's proclamation of May 9 freeing slaves in Georgia, Florida, and South Carolina illustrated his belief at the time that former slaves only should assist the war, nothing more. Perhaps he would not have made the proclamation, Chase admitted to Horace Greeley, but Lincoln should not have rescinded it until Hunter had a chance to explain his reasons. To Murat Halstead of the *Cincinnati Commercial* he went farther. Similar orders "should be promulgated in all the Gulf States at least," for he did not "believe in fighting rebellion & upholding" slavery. But Chase confessed he was "unable to do much outside my own department." In late June, the Secretary admitted to Ben Butler in New Orleans that for some time after the war began he had "clung to my old ideas of non interference" with slavery and hoped that it would "gradually" be eradicated by local governments. In time it became clear to him that restoration of the Union with slavery was impossible. Now he believed that not using the military to free slaves "was simply to contribute the whole moral & physical power" of the government to their subjugation by the rebels. This did not lead Chase, however, to embrace confiscation of rebel landed property.[5]

At the special Cabinet meeting on July 21, 1862, Chase raised objections to the confiscation of property based on his fears that proper accounts would not be kept, which hardly suggests a large view of the subject. The next day, however, Chase expressed support for the president's plan to announce emancipation based on the second act, although Stanton characterized Chase as silent during the meeting. It is significant that Chase continued to focus on slavery, however, to the exclusion of other aspects of the second act. In a letter to Butler at the end of July he examined the second act's impact on slavery only, concluding that slavery would probably not survive if both acts were executed. He also informed Butler, who was worried about Phelps's arming of freed slaves at the time, that there had been "a great change in the public mind within a few weeks" on the question of slavery. If "negro slavery" stood in the way of victory, the people now were resolved that "it must be abolished." He urged Butler to prevent the return of slaves even to masters loyal to the Union. As for the confiscation acts, Chase believed that they did threaten slavery. However, he did not address the confiscation of real property owned by rebels.[6] It is therefore not surprising that Bates and Lincoln faced no pressure from Chase to enforce the second act vigorously.

Labor and commerce, not land, were central to Chase and others who supported the emancipation but not colonization in the summer of 1862. This view helps explain their reluctance to embrace confiscation of real property under the second act, for it would have enraged Southern whites and made it more difficult to establish trade, for instance, in the Mississippi Valley. In his letter to Butler, Chase assumed that after military emancipation in the Gulf States freed slaves would remain there. If, on the other hand, "they behave themselves and work industriously & honestly," Chase had no objection to their presence in the North. But because "many honest men" in the North believed they should not reside there, Chase hoped the South would be "opened to negro emigration," thus solving the problem for the North. This solution would not be viable, however, if Southern whites had their property confiscated by the North. At the time, many congressmen, including George W. Julian, Owen Lovejoy, Lyman Trumbull, and James M. Ashley, supported emancipation, colonization, and confiscation.[7] By colonizing freed slaves, the Midwest would be spared further race problems while the South's landholding class would be destroyed. But Chase and others, who supported emancipation but not colonization or confiscation, imagined free blacks as landless laborers in the South after the war. As Heather Cox Richardson has argued, during consideration of the second act many Republicans, both inside and outside Congress, began to see former slaves as free laborers and as part of their party's ideology. Many had come to believe slavery had to be abolished yet understood Republican voters in the North would not countenance an influx of freed slaves. Their solution was to enlarge the free labor ideology to envision a role for freed slaves as laborers in the South, but not as owners of property confiscated from plantation owners. Many Republicans even persuaded themselves that white Southerners would welcome free blacks as laborers so long as they were allowed to retain their property.[8]

The Treasury Department's responsibilities under the Direct Tax Act of June 7, 1862, and the Captured and Abandoned Property Act of March 12, 1863, also shaped its attitude toward confiscable property. Under the tax act, special commissioners were to follow the military into the South and assess taxes in rebellious states, based on 1861 property valuations. In addition to the tax, property owners were to pay a hefty penalty. Failure to pay both led to the sale of the property at public auction to the highest bidder or to the government. The act provided that those purchasing the land received it in fee simple, unlike provisions for the sale of confiscated land. In the end, perhaps as much as $5,100,000 was collected in taxes and sales of forfeited lands under this law, far more than was achieved under confiscation.[9] The Captured and Abandoned Property Act required even more work from the Treasury Department than the direct tax act. Special agents were to collect property, other than war munitions, that had been abandoned or captured in the rebellious states. The property collected could be appropriated for public use or, if portable, sent to the North for sale at auction. The money realized from captured and abandoned property, mostly from the sale of cotton, was over $25 million, five times that realized under the tax act and considerably more than under the confiscation acts.[10] Although these acts required Treasury agents to follow behind the military into formerly rebellious areas of the South, thereby providing them the opportunity to find confiscable property before marshals and district attorneys arrived, it was not one of their primary obligations, nor was it as lucrative.

Chase was under pressure almost from the start of the war to establish a system that regulated and facilitated trade, particularly cotton, in the South. Pursuit of confiscable property would have interfered with such commerce and with the military, with which Treasury agents had an uneasy relationship. In March 1862 Chase offered general guidelines to govern commerce in the South. In September 1863, following passage of the Captured and Abandoned Property Act, Chase introduced a more detailed set of rules to regulate trade in those parts of the South now occupied by Union forces. Agents were authorized only to dispose of confiscable property after it had been turned over to them or if they discovered it deserted or abandoned. Chase, as did his successors William Pitt Fessenden and Hugh McCulloch, also instructed agents to cooperate with the attorney general's plans for administering the act, particularly his wish that marshals and district attorneys have primary responsibility for initiating confiscation. Treasury officials, therefore, had no authority to direct agents to seek out confiscable property. In contrast with the War Department, which had no overall methods for handling property, the Treasury Department also set up a well defined, if often ignored, system to handle confiscable property. Because it frequently stifled individual initiative, this attempt to establish uniform procedures for confiscation helped reduce the amount of confiscable property agents encountered. As well, Treasury agents worked mostly in the cities and made few trips to the country looking for property of any kind. By remaining in the commercial areas, they became dependent for information about rural areas on the military, which had no more interest or authority in confiscation than they did. Finally, the Treasury agents saw little reason to enforce the confiscation acts since the proceeds were small and they could not profit from it personally. All of these conditions worked to eliminate the agents, with the exception of Benjamin F. Flanders of New Orleans, from the process of confiscation. Like the military, the Treasury Department could have been instrumental in the enforcement of the acts. Abandoned and captured property might have been confiscable, too, but Treasury agents had no incentives to inquire if this might have been true. Instead, the Treasury Department, beginning with Chase, deliberately excluded itself from assisting in the enforcement of the confiscation acts, thereby restricting their scope.[11]

The Treasury Department issued numerous detailed instructions to agents on what should be done with property received during the Civil War. These instructions were meant to both produce an orderly system and reduce the opportunities for corruption, which were numerous according to observers at the time. Agents were responsible for four types of property found within the formerly rebellious states: abandoned, captured, commercial, and confiscable. In a circular of July 3, 1863, Chase reminded agents that "great care must be exercised in properly classifying all the property" into these categories. They should also remember "that with property included in the fourth class, unless found deserted and abandoned, the Agents of the Treasury have no authority to interfere." Abandoned property included that which owners had left voluntarily to participate in the rebellion; captured property mostly meant cotton. It is estimated, in fact, that over 95 percent of the captured and abandoned property was cotton. The government could obtain possession of captured and abandoned property, as distinguished from confiscable property, without proving the owner's support of the rebellion. Plantations came into the Treasury's possession this way, and it was often easier to take the property as abandoned without the bother of proving the owner's participation in the rebellion. After the military had used personal property, they often turned it over to Treasury agents to sell it, the proceeds going to the United States Treasury. The third class of property was commercial and was the basis of the trading system whereby agents issued permits for commerce to individuals who pledged their loyalty to the Union.[12]

The Treasury Department did not allow special agents to deal with confiscable property as defined in the first act, nor to seize confiscable property under the second act unless it had been deserted or abandoned. These restrictions limited the amount of property that could be confiscated in the Special Agencies the Treasury Department set up in the South. The department established these agencies, which were simply geographical divisions in the South, primarily to collect and manage or dispose of captured and abandoned property. Without Treasury agents participating in the enforcement of the confiscation acts, rebels had time and opportunity to transfer property titles before district attorneys and courts arrived in Union-controlled areas. When lawful owners of landed property left to fight for the Confederacy, relatives remained to pose as the property's owners, preventing agents from seizing it as confiscable, as happened to General Lew Wallace in Maryland. The only way to prevent this deceit was to examine property titles, something Treasury agents were in a position to do if they had been authorized to do so. Unless they received specific information about confiscable property, agents were strongly inclined to view all property they encountered as abandoned. They could profit from the sale of abandoned property, such as cotton, while confiscable property had to be turned over to district attorneys.[13]

Leasing abandoned farms and plantations was a major part of Chase's efforts to restore commerce. As part of the process, he also hoped to remove freed slaves from contraband camps, sell or lease them small parcels of land and remove plantations from liability of confiscation.[14] In late 1863 Chase promoted William Mellen, his close friend and political ally in Ohio, to Supervising Special Agent for the Mississippi Valley with instructions to lease to "colored people" when possible. "They should all be got out of the [Contraband] Camps and restored to their accustomed employments under the free labor system" as soon as possible. Ten days later he urged Mellen to encourage "proprietors of plantations" to sell "small parcels of forty, eighty or a hundred and twenty acres" to those freedmen who could raise the funds. Of equal importance, he was "very confident" that the president wanted the Treasury Department "to relieve the plantations of any proprietor" whose conduct might have made his property liable to confiscation. In other words, Chase thought it best to limit confiscation because it interfered with the leasing of farms and plantations to revive the region's economy.[15]

This policy encouraged agents to lease plantations that might have been confiscable rather then report them as such. They could profit from their rents if they were in good condition, employ former slaves upon them, and help revive the local economy. The agents' desire to rent or lease property led them to make deals for confiscable property that disloyal owners still occupied before district attorneys could seize them. Agents also enriched themselves with fees earned illegally by returning abandoned or confiscable property to owners, loyal or disloyal, who came back to the region. This practice was widespread and clearly limited the number of properties that could be confiscated. Although Treasury officials worried about this corruption, they appeared more concerned when captured and abandoned, and not confiscated, property was involved.[16]

The methods developed to collect property within the Special Agencies naturally led to a greater acquisition of captured and abandoned property as compared to confiscable property. Although assistant special agents earned six dollars a day and ten cents a mile working for the government—a reasonable salary at the time for such labor—many agents made little effort to discover property that could not realize a profit. Special Agencies were large; the ninth, for instance, covered all of Florida and the southern half of Alabama. Given their size and the lack of adequate transportation, the largest proportion of property collected came from the region's biggest cities to the exclusion of the rest of the territory. Moreover, both business and the Treasury Department were interested in shipping out captured and abandoned property, mostly cotton, from Union controlled areas as soon as it was possible, not in finding confiscable property. In January 1862, for example, William H. Reynolds, an agent in Port Royal, South Carolina, reported to Chase that he had discovered over a million pounds of cotton. Soon thereafter Chase appointed Reynolds to be the agent for Florida on the assumption that vast quantities of cotton had been abandoned in the port cities. Almost as soon as he arrived, Reynolds began sending cotton, turpentine, and resin back to New York. Agents were also encouraged to promote commerce, even if that meant they failed to inquire about a property's ownership. In October 1862, Chase informed William Mellen that although he did not "countenance any evasion of the confiscation act," he did not wish any "unnecessary interruption of commerce" in cotton that might arise by too much investigation into the "morals of any transaction." As Chase made clear in a report to Congress in early 1863, Treasury agents had two major tasks in captured areas. They were to send abandoned property to New York for auction by Hiram Barney, Collector of the Port, and return the abandoned plantations to production.[17]

Treasury agents generally relied upon the military to supply them with information about abandoned and confiscable property, but the military's knowledge of this property was incomplete since they occupied only some areas within a Special Agency. Nor did the military have a good reputation for observing the rights of property owners. Even though the military was supposed to turn captured and abandoned property over to the Special Agencies, a task they performed fitfully, they had no obligation to inform the agencies of abandoned or confiscable property. As Carl Moneyhon has argued, few military or Treasury officials in the field were interested in assisting a social revolution. As a result, little confiscable property found outside the cities came into the agents' possession except in the rare instances when commanders ordered troops to collect and deliver such property to the proper officials. The military was more cordial to the Treasury agents than they were to district attorneys but the military often felt, in fact, that Treasury officials were in the way. In March 1862, for example, Henry Halleck wrote Chase that William Mellen was thwarting the military "in order to exhibit his own authority" and threatened to seek his removal. Mellen, however, remained in office and worked closely with General U. S. Grant on disposal of the property, including cotton and abandoned plantations in Tennessee, and to regulate the commerce that developed. The military's criticisms of Mellen and the Treasury did not abate. In October 1863, Rear Admiral David D. Porter expressed dismay at both Mellen and the "pack of knaves" who worked for the Treasury Department along the Mississippi. By late 1863 General Lorenzo Thomas had succeeded in pushing freed slaves back onto plantations along the Mississippi between Memphis and Vicksburg. Complaints reached Chase and he interceded to help freed slaves lease abandoned plantations, under Mellen's supervision. Word of this reached Lincoln in early 1864 and he authorized General Thomas to handle the problem. If left alone Mellen's contraband and leasing system "would fall dead within its own entangling details," the president said. Almost two months later, Thomas remained persuaded that Mellen's regulations were "beautiful in theory, but utterly impracticable."[18]

For the most part the military did as it wished with regard to the Treasury's regulations. Major General John M. Schoefield, for example, reminded a subordinate that property "still held by the army may be returned [to the Treasury officials] at the discretion of the commanding officer" but the army "cannot settle any questions of confiscation." General Grant expressed a more dismissive view of the Treasury's authority on the eve of Mobile's fall. "Let the Treasury agents have nothing to do with your captures," he wrote General E. R. Canby in February 1865. "They have no business with the army, if you desire to be clear of them." Grant gave Canby permission to do whatever he wished with property he encountered. In one instance Grant and Sherman halted the Treasury's cotton trade, since it was incompatible with their plans. Major General James B. McPherson in Alabama, on the other hand, pursued a different policy. He ordered his troops to take no property other than horses, mules, and food so that they would not be burdened with anything, confiscable or abandoned, to turn over to Treasury agents. Other generals ordered that all private property be returned to owners, that refugees occupy abandoned property, and that confiscable property be reported to district attorneys rather than to Treasury agents. The majority of generals, however, appeared to comply with the regulations regarding property taken by the military and conveyed whatever the military did not require to Treasury agents. A number of commanders even reminded their officers that the military had no authority to determine the validity of property titles. Whether officers heeded these admonitions made little difference, since most of the confiscable property transferred from the military to the Treasury agents was personal property of little value.[19]

Commodore, a famous stallion worth at least sixteen thousand dollars, was the most valuable piece of property the military turned over to Treasury agents. The army captured the horse in Nashville after he had been wrongly confiscated from his owner and sold to a colonel in the rebel army. With his owner unable to escape from the South, finding someone to own and care for the horse posed a problem. Although Chase received a report on the matter, the decision to turn the horse over to the Treasury came from Stanton, who believed Commodore was too valuable to be used by the military. Commodore went to the Treasury for sale on the assumption that his owner could sue for compensation or the horse. The absence of any court decision on the property's liability for confiscation only compounded the odd nature of the case. The only normal part of Commodore's confiscation was the manner in which Stanton decided to dispose of him without consulting Bates.[20]

Most confiscation cases involving the military and the Treasury followed the pattern of the Commodore case, with the Treasury in the subordinate position, beseeching the army for facts or receiving reports of actions the army had taken without any consultation. In one case the army ordered a rebel south of its lines and then confiscated his cotton. When the officer in charge learned that the man's cotton had already been sold but not paid for, he demanded that the buyer pay the money to the Treasury or have the cotton seized from the field. Treasury Agent Charles Fuller heard of these orders just before the army moved out. He reported the facts to his superior in embarrassment and frustration. In another instance, a provost marshal took it upon himself to decide the loyalty of all people within his district whose property was subject to confiscation; his explanation for assuming this authority was the convenient military necessity. Even powerful Treasury agents found the military a difficult partner. For instance, William G. Brownlow, appointed to his position in late 1862, also found time to be a newspaper editor and, according to his biographer, the dictator of commercial affairs in East Tennessee. Yet, he too found the military's arbitrary rule so frustrating that he could only malign them. "There are, as a matter of course," Brownlow observed, "others [in the army] who are thieves, and make themselves the intimate associates of Negro women." Racial attacks like this demonstrated Brownlow's contempt for blacks but they had, of course, no effect on the military's conduct. The latter remained cooperative during the war only when it suited them and turned only a small amount of confiscable property over to the Treasury.[21]

Without assistance from the army or orders to seize property liable to confiscation, Treasury agents generally handled only small amounts of confiscable personal property that had been abandoned. One agent in Texas resigned because there was no abandoned or confiscable property in his district. Another agent in Mississippi knew of "a great deal of abandoned and confiscable property" in and around Jackson but feared the Treasury would never get it because the titles had been transferred and no agents were in the area. Except for one farm outside Nashville, the confiscable property reported to Treasury agents consisted of animal stock, furniture, liquor, and other items of little value. One agent reported some confiscated property only because he wished to be paid for informing about it. In a case that illustrated the haphazard way Treasury agents came upon confiscable property, J. F. Simonds, who was both an agent and a port inspector in Memphis, searched a boat in the latter capacity and found cotton, mattresses, and sugar. By the time he had determined these goods were confiscable, however, they had been sold by order of the military. He reported the matter only because he believed himself entitled to some portion of the money paid for the goods. Unless they happened upon it, as Simonds did, or received detailed information about confiscable property within their immediate area, agents made little effort to seek it out.[22] Treasury agents, in fact, handled so little confiscable property that they had almost no contact with the attorney general's office or local district attorneys. If they communicated with marshals or district attorneys, it was only to relate or receive routine information concerning the property they held.[23]

For a number of reasons New Orleans was the only significant exception to this pattern. The city fell to the Union early in the war—in May 1862—so there was ample time to attempt confiscation. Many in New Orleans, as noted, also remained loyal to the Confederacy even after Butler offered them the chance to keep their property by taking the oath of allegiance to the Union. In addition, New Orleans was the largest and wealthiest city in the South. Finally, the political and ethical differences among Union men in New Orleans, in this case Treasury Agent Benjamin F. Flanders and District Attorney Rufus Waples produced a number of problems. As scholars have observed, the politics in New Orleans during and after the war were complicated, intense, and often nasty. Treasury officials in particular were central to this political atmosphere, in part because of Secretary Chase's influence through his use of patronage, his interest in restoring Louisiana to the Union, and his plans to run for the presidency in 1864. Moreover, New Orleans was one of the first seceded areas to begin the process of restoration as the war continued. All of this contributed to the city's volatile politics, which spilled over into the local officials' handling of confiscable property that came into their possession.[24]

A native of New Hampshire and a Dartmouth graduate, Benjamin F. Flanders had lived in New Orleans for some years before the war. In 1862 George S. Dennison, a Vermont-born special agent for the Treasury, as well as a relative and confidant of Secretary Chase, appointed Flanders as a Treasury agent. By the end of 1862, Flanders had also won the election to House of Representatives as a Unionist, along with Michael Hahn; they served out the remaining days of the Thirty-seventh Congress. (In February 1864, Hahn defeated Flanders for governor of Louisiana.) Upon recommendations from Flanders and Hahn, in early 1863 Chase secured the appointment of Rufus Waples as the U.S. district attorney for the eastern district of Louisiana, a decision he soon regretted. Born in Delaware, Waples came to Louisiana in 1849 where he obtained his law degree. While district attorney, Waples went so far as to purchase some of the confiscated property himself, which raised concerns about his honesty for Attorney General Bates. (He was also involved in a number of cases that reached the Supreme Court, discussed in chapters 10 and 11.)[25] By late April 1863 Flanders wrote Chase, in reference to an open judgeship, that Waples was now "considered eccentrick [*sic*], sometimes flighty, and hence an unsafe man for that appointment." In May 1863 Chase appointed Flanders the supervising special agent for the Treasury over the lower Mississippi Valley.[26]

By late 1863 two factions had emerged in New Orleans to contest how best to restore Louisiana to the Union. Onc group, under the leadership of General Nathaniel Banks and Representative Hahn, opposed slavery but was not enthusiastic about a fundamental change in the power structure in Louisiana. Lincoln eventually threw his support to them. The other faction, perhaps a bit more radical, followed the leadership of Thomas J. Durant, originally from Philadelphia and a former slaveholder who now supported abolition. This faction was allied with Chase's presidential ambitions.[27] Most of those in the Durant faction believed in black suffrage, although Flanders, its nominee for governor, did not. Many like Flanders and Hahn became closely allied with the factions' leaders, but others, such as George Denison, Rufus Waples, Edward Durell, and John S. Whitaker, apparently did not have fixed allegiances, in part because the two groups differed less over goals than over leadership. In December 1863, for example, Flanders wrote Chase that "Hahn has behaved well" and he "is thoroughly with us in our free state movement, and in other matters he will be right." Shortly thereafter, the faction's political differences became sharper, but their permeable nature revealed itself in the conflicting assessments Denison made to Chase about both General Banks and Flanders. These different political evaluations illuminate how the confiscation of property, among other issues, was important in New Orleans only insofar as it enhanced a person's power and wealth.[28]

The first major dispute between Treasury agent Flanders and District Attorney Waples arose over the control of confiscable property between its seizure and the court's decision. In May 1863 Chase informed Secretary of War Stanton that four classes of property were to be found in New Orleans—confiscated, abandoned, captured, and purchased. As for confiscable property, he argued it "includes much that may be also regarded, until confiscation is enforced through judicial proceedings, as belonging to one or more of the other classes." This, of course, was a questionable opinion. In August, however, Flanders, acted on this premise after Waples ordered the property of John Parham Jr. seized and notified the tenant, Mr. Otis, of this fact. Flanders then seized the property and installed a new tenant, Mr. Bush. Although Waples ordered the marshal to notify the owner, Parham, that the right, title, and interest of the property had been seized, Bush took actual possession of the property. This angered and worried Waples because condemnation of the property through in rem proceedings depended on proving clear possession; transfers of control invalidated the original seizure. To remedy this problem, Waples issued another order for seizure in September and had the marshal again notify Parnham of the theoretical seizure. This action, in turn, upset Flanders who had assumed, as did Chase, that such property could remain in the Treasury's possession until the court ruled on it. Flanders had wanted control of the property before its sale so he could rent it and perhaps keep the money. At the time Bates was informed that Flanders and others "occupy the best houses" in New Orleans, and did not pay rent. Perhaps not coincidentally, Denison urged Chase in September to define "the extent of Mr. Flanders's jurisdiction" more precisely.[29]

Before he reissued the order of seizure, Waples made repeated efforts to confer with both Flanders and General Banks over the jurisdiction in cases like this. Flanders, however, avoided a meeting and followed his own counsel in handling all the confiscated property that he encountered. Waples insisted, nonetheless, that Flanders report the property that he had seized for confiscation and inform Waples how much money he had made from any unauthorized sales of property in New Orleans. In an effort to guard his authority, Waples emphasized that no matter who seized it, all property taken for confiscation had to be reported to him, the district attorney, for proper seizure and condemnation before sale. Waples wanted Flanders to obey Bates's instructions and what he understood the Treasury regulations to be, not to act as if he were engaged in a competition for the city's confiscable property. Although one historian has claimed that Flanders and Waples shared a wish for sweeping confiscation, Waples's anxiety over Flanders's methods suggests the district attorney was more interested in control over the confiscation process than its success.[30]

Waples's supposed interference greatly upset Flanders, who complained to Chase about the district attorney's conduct. Most damning was the false accusation that Waples had tried to seize captured and abandoned plantations, which Flanders had rightfully received from the military. When Bates received Flanders's accusations, sent to him from the Treasury Department, he at first assumed the agent had confused the confiscation acts with the 1863 Captured and Abandoned Property Act. Soon, however, with only Flanders's charges as evidence, Bates became convinced that Waples had taken physical possession of plantations in contravention of the law and his own instructions. Having misunderstood Flanders's complaint, which only alleged Waples's "intention" to seize the plantations, Bates ironically presumed his understanding of the subject had resolved the dispute and decided not to write Waples himself. There the matter rested until Waples, the only district attorney who regularly reported on his confiscation work, wrote Bates himself to enlighten and reassure his superior.[31]

In the month between Flanders's complaint and Waples's report, two more incidents served to discredit the behavior of the Treasury officials in New Orleans and lend support to Waples's position. It also revealed the tangled relations among the Union men in New Orleans. The first involved a petition from Charles Lillenburger that officials under Flanders's instructions, without cause, used force to enter and occupy his house for a night. The same men returned the next day, again occupied the house by force, and did "wanton damage" to it. Lillenburger knew of no grounds for this action and the men gave none. He demanded that Flanders's men be enjoined to vacate the dwelling and pay damages of ten thousand dollars. District Court Judge John S. Whitaker, later rumored to be a candidate for governor from the Banks faction, granted the injunction two days after the first trespass occurred. The second incident is mentioned in a petition by Waples that alleged George Denison, whom many at the time and since believed was corrupt, had failed to report the seizure of more than $4,000 worth of goods. The petition noted Denison's failure to inform Waples of the facts despite a written request for the information. District Court Judge Edward H. Durell, recommended for his position by Hahn and Flanders, accepted Waples's petition and issued a writ of mandamus ordering Denison to supply the facts so the district attorney could determine the property's liability for confiscation.[32]

In late December 1863, when the contest for governor and control of New Orleans was taking shape, Flanders finally sent Waples a list of the confiscable property under his control. This was two days before Waples wrote his report on confiscation to Bates. In the report Waples muted his criticism of Flanders, but not his annoyance. He recounted that Flanders had seized thirteen properties without informing him. Not knowing about Flanders's seizures, Waples had instructed the marshal to seize some of the same properties. These double seizures resulted in a loss of revenue for the government and, by disturbing his system of rents, a loss to Flanders. Even though Waples regretted the money lost to the Treasury, he asserted that it "it was not the fault of this office if the government has lost any revenue by these proceedings." The district attorney put the blame on Flanders for his failure to report his seizures. Although Flanders had not directly halted the process of confiscation in New Orleans, his eagerness to expand his authority and obtain rental properties had certainly made Waples's job more difficult.[33]

Waples's report to Bates mentioned the thirteen cases but ignored specific conflicts between his office and the Treasury officials in New Orleans and minimized their disagreements. "I have found less difficulty and embarrassment here in carrying out the Confiscation Acts than I had suspected," he wrote to Bates. However, the district attorney was unaware of Flanders's accusations that he had seized captured and abandoned plantations, as he tried to reassure Bates that he had consistently observed the instructions prohibiting physical possession of landed property. Yet he speculated that some of the plantations held by Flanders as abandoned or captured would prove to be confiscable if he could see the relevant facts. Even with his estimate that "nine tenths of the property under seizure in this city" remained in military or treasury hands, Waples remained optimistic. The only note of discouragement came in his veiled request for direction on his jurisdictional problems with other government officials. In the absence of a specific question, however, Bates followed his custom and did not reply to Waples, and thus did not inform him of Flanders's charges.[34]

Waples formally learned of Flanders's accusations from the Treasury agent himself. The district attorney vigorously denied that he ever attempted a physical seizure of property held by the Treasury or removed a tenant from property at the time of seizure. Even though, Waples admitted, the Treasury Department was entitled to such rents in instances where the district attorney knew of the confiscable property, Waples rejected Flanders's charge of interference with the renting system. To support his claim, Waples cited instructions to the marshals against such seizures and offered all records of confiscation for Flanders's examination. The Treasury agent apparently declined the invitation, and the dispute ended with Waples's conceding Flanders's right to collect rents and Flanders's agreeing to report to his colleague on matters of confiscation. Occasionally thereafter Waples felt the need to remind Flanders to report relevant information, but their contact diminished after 1863 and they apparently continued to work at arm's length. It is impossible to determine how much the differences between Waples and Flanders hindered the confiscation of property in New Orleans, but their disagreement illustrated the problems that even a vigorous district attorney faced when confronting a Treasury agent determined to be involved with confiscation.[35]

One further example demonstrates the Treasury Department's involvement in the complexity of confiscation in New Orleans. In February 1864 Lincoln, after a visit from Mrs. J. Q. A. Fellows, asked General Banks to investigate her claim that she and her husband had been evicted from their house in the city. The president's request came in the midst of the gubernatorial election, in which J. Q. A. Fellows was the candidate of the Conservative Unionist party, many of whose supporters hoped that slavery would be retained. Banks reported that Flanders, also a candidate for governor, apparently evicted the couple from the property for political reasons. Fellows, said Banks, "was politically unacceptable to Mr. Flanders and his friends." Flanders then rented the house to the family of Colonel Dudley, who "is now commanding" forces against the rebels; Banks could not interfere with the matter any further since the property was under the Treasury's jurisdiction. Instead, Secretary Chase "should be required to give such orders" to Flanders to sort out the problem. Within three weeks of Banks's letter, Chase admonished Flanders. Treasury officials should only seize and rent property, he reminded the agent, "actually *deserted* and *abandoned*." Nor was property abandoned if the owner possessed it, "even if he be disloyal and his property clearly liable to confiscation." Flanders had no cause to evict Fellows, regardless of his politics or supposed loyalty to the rebel cause.[36] The episode was remarkable for Flanders's audacious eviction of Fellows and the failure, on the part of all involved, to correspond with either Bates or Waples about the affair.

Following Chase's admonition, Flanders abstained from interfering with enforcement of the confiscation acts for the rest of the war. The amount of property confiscated showed no increase because Flanders abstained from interfering with Waples's work, but the administration of the laws became less difficult.[37] Even with the conflict between these two officials, however, the property confiscated from New Orleans and surrounding areas realized the government over sixty thousand dollars, easily the largest sum obtained from the confiscation acts, and one-fifth of the total revenue they achieved. Except for Virginia where significant confiscation occurred after the war's end, New

Orleans proved the best area for enforcing the laws, for no other region of the South had such wealth or endured such a long occupation. No other place in the South had as energetic a district attorney as Waples, who wrote six reports to Attorney General Bates about confiscation in the city, only one of which was answered.[38] Had Flanders been instructed early on to assist Waples in confiscation, the totals from New Orleans would doubtless have been greater. That would have required rare cooperation between Bates and Chase over confiscation. Treasury agents had the opportunity to be a major asset in the enforcement of confiscation, as they often arrived in the Union areas long before district attorney or marshals. Like the military, the Treasury Department had little incentive to pursue confiscable property except, as in the case of Flanders in New Orleans, when it could be used for rents. In the end, except in New Orleans the Treasury Department played a very small role in confiscation, just as Lincoln and Bates wished.

8 The Politics of Confiscation

The failure of the confiscation acts, particularly the second, owed much to the inattention and declining interest of the Republicans in Congress. Except for one inquiry about implementation in the District of Columbia in early 1863, Republicans ignored the acts until early 1864. Although Congress had created the Committee on the Conduct of the War to monitor military progress, it had yet to adopt the practice of using congressional hearings to oversee legislation. Those responsible for implementing the acts, notably Attorney General Bates, were therefore not asked to report to Congress on the success or failure of the acts. The public also expressed serious doubts about altering the goals of the war, as reaction to Lincoln's proclamation of September 22 on freeing slaves and the fall elections in 1862 made clear. Congress doubtless understood this attitude. Although Republicans supported Lincoln's call for emancipation, many noted the public's concerns over a harsh peace. Perhaps for this reason the plans of distributing Southern land faded. In 1864 and 1865 Republicans in Congress did try to remove the limitations on forfeiture contained in the 1862 joint resolution but failed to coordinate their efforts, and no revision occurred. By the spring and summer of 1864, most had abandoned the land issue as a central assumption about the Reconstruction. And, finally, by the spring of 1865 Lincoln's efforts to create a swift and relatively painless restoration of the Union had found more favor than did those of others advocating reconstruction through confiscation. As a result, with the war's end and Lincoln's death, confiscation as a war measure had largely failed.[1]

The reaction to Lincoln's September 22 preliminary emancipation proclamation revealed the North's divisions over this limited assault upon slavery. Using his powers as commander in chief and citing the confiscation acts, Lincoln declared free those slaves in states that remained in rebellion after January 1 but protected the property of loyal slave owners and offered colonization for freedmen. Abolitionists were generally enthusiastic and most Republicans supported the proclamation, if somewhat reluctantly. The proposal troubled many others, however. In New Hampshire, Democrats argued that Lincoln had fallen into the hands of radical supporters of confiscation. Republicans in Massachusetts and New Jersey were divided over the proclamation, while Democrats discussed their fears about forced equality with blacks. New York Republicans supported the president, although they often employed racist arguments to persuade their conservative colleagues to embrace emancipation. Responses in the Midwest were similar. Some Republicans, such as Governor Oliver P. Morton of Indiana, expressed doubts or justified the proclamation on military grounds, while Democrats were vociferous in their condemnation.[2]

Like the Indiana governor, many soldiers supported the call for emancipation as a military necessity. Others, though, had doubts about what slavery's end might entail. Even though some soldiers were abolitionists before the war, most had never presumed that the war would lead to slavery's abolition. If many found the logic of Lincoln's proclamation of September 22 powerful, others worried about its consequences. The number who supported the call for emancipation is impossible to determine, but it is doubtless greater than Bell Irvin Wiley's estimate that not more than one in ten had "any real interest" in emancipation. Nonetheless, many Union soldiers would not support a war that abolished slavery, no matter what the rationale because they feared that freed slaves would move to the North. The flood of contrabands into Union camps gave many soldiers their first contact with African Americans and persuaded them that former slaves could not benefit from freedom. A minority, however, believed that slaves and other property of Southerners should be confiscated both to end slavery and to punish the South. Some who had now witnessed slavery believed both emancipation and confiscation were morally justified, even if they did not believe in racial equality. However, after September 22 morale in the Union forces declined and the rate of desertion increased, reflecting the anxieties felt in the North that fall.[3]

The most critical and widespread assessment of both emancipation and confiscation before the fall elections came from Professor Joel Parker of Harvard in the *North American Review*.[4] A conservative constitutional scholar and an opponent of confiscation during the debates of 1862, Parker believed that slavery was a local institution beyond the reach of either the president by proclamation or the Congress by law, even in time of war. Since the rebellious states retained all their rights, no infringement upon them was constitutional, nor could their authority be denied once the rebellion had ended. Although Parker vigorously opposed slavery, he also presumed "seven eighths" of emancipated slaves "would not know how to use" their freedom if granted. Moreover, the Constitution did not allow forfeiture of property beyond the life of a person convicted of treason, be the property slaves or real estate. And so the second act was a bill of attainder prohibited by the Constitution. (This ignored the distinction Trumbull and others made that only the first four sections of the act related to treason.) Parker concluded that he, too, wanted the war prosecuted "with the greatest possible vigor" and supported the use of "negro regiments and brigades" but he could not countenance subversion of the Constitution for these ends.[5]

A defense of emancipation and confiscation also appeared that same month in the *Atlantic Monthly*, but it was a weak counter to Parker's views. Elias H. Derby's analysis ignored the constitutional questions involved in the war. Instead, he said, slaveholders had no defense against emancipation if they relied upon slaves to oppose the Union. For Derby and much of the North, the chief anxiety was where African Americans might live following the war. He believed that emancipation during the war would encourage blacks to remain in the South, whereas slaves would flee north and west if slavery survived the North's ultimate victory. Further, freed slaves should not be exiled by colonization, but should be given Southern land through "eminent domain" by the "nation either directly after conquest, or through the States and Territories it may establish." Planters would be compensated at ten dollars an acre, paid by the tenant over a period of years, during which time "he will soon have every incentive to exertion." Derby's essay was attractive to Northerners worried about emancipation and confiscation. It conveniently ignored the legal issues, embraced emancipation, predicted freed slaves would remain in the South, where they would contribute to the national economy, and promised compensation to those whose land was taken.[6]

A number of issues, including the fears surrounding emancipation, the president's suspension of the writ of habeas corpus two days after September 22, and military setbacks, hurt the Republicans in the fall elections of 1862. Throughout the North, Democrats used Lincoln's proclamation to argue that emancipation, often linked with confiscation, demonstrated Republican plans to elevate the blacks, permit miscegenation, and promote the exodus of freed slaves to the North. Republicans countered that freed slaves would want to remain where they were born and would even lure blacks from the North to the South. Although the Democrats' racist appeals had an effect, they did not overwhelm their opponents. Republican losses were nonetheless significant. Democrats did very well in almost all states, electing governors in New York, New Jersey, Delaware, Indiana, and Illinois and reelecting the governor of Rhode Island. Democrats in the Midwest received large votes in Illinois, Ohio, Indiana, Wisconsin, and Minnesota. In all, Democrats gained thirty-one congressional seats and raised their vote total significantly, while Republicans gained five Senate seats.[7]

Two contests illustrated the problems faced by Republicans who vigorously supported confiscation. In addition to the reason cited earlier, many of the Republican losses have been attributed to conservative candidates, a failure of Republicans to vote, and the absence of the soldier vote. But Galusha Grow,

Speaker of the House, and John Bingham appear to have lost in large part because of their radicalism, including their support for confiscation. Grow's district in northeast Pennsylvania had been reapportioned in early 1862; it also experienced the proximity of the war in Virginia. As a result, he came under increased attack for his positions on confiscation, emancipation, and civil liberties issues. Even some of those opposed to Grow's positions were moderate Republicans. Grow refused to move to the center as others in the Pennsylvania party had done when voters grew worried about the radical bills in Congress. One local newspaper dubbed Grow the "prince of fanatics" and attacked him for allegedly saying that the South should be made a desert, as Thaddeus Stevens, also a Pennsylvania representative, had advocated. There were also other, more local issues that contributed to Grow's surprising loss to a relative newcomer, but the concern over emancipation and confiscation played a major part in his defeat. In Ohio Bingham was renominated in August with a pledge to employ the "sweeping confiscation and emancipation" measures to force the rebels to pay for their own demise. His district had also been reapportioned and was now more Democratic than before. Some Republicans in eastern Ohio, near West Virginia, also found his positions too radical. Many had grown tired of the war, were worried about the outcome, including a migration of blacks into Ohio, and no longer wished to volunteer for the military. Reports circulated that Bingham had vowed that the war would not end until the slave owners had been destroyed, a far cry from Lincoln's terms of reunion. Democrat newspapers in the district ignored their own candidate, who was proslavery and inexperienced, and instead printed articles about Bingham's support for the war and emancipation. The result was a dramatic loss in which Bingham's vote totals declined from 1860 throughout the district.[8]

Little was heard of confiscation after the fall elections until 1863. In early February, journalist Jane Grey Swisshelm expressed dismay over Republican weakness in a letter from Washington to the *St. Cloud Democrat* in Minnesota. Democrats, she said, were planning to invalidate both the Second Confiscation Act and the Emancipation Proclamation and were "met by the most disgraceful, unmanly, halting timidity on the part of the Republicans." Abolitionists and a few others tried to raise the issue of land for freedmen. Senator Charles Sumner of Massachusetts introduced a bill to allot ten acres each to black soldiers, while Wendell Phillips urged that the plantations in states bordering the Gulf of Mexico be divided up for the freed slaves. Representative George Julian of Indiana, later the author of the Homestead Act, proposed a homestead policy based on creating small parcels from plantations. This policy would benefit the "freed-men" rather than speculators who would try to snatch up large tracts and create another "land monopoly" similar to slavery. Seizure of the traitors' property, Julian said, would also defray the war's expenses.[9] Few Republicans, however, supported these proposals.

An experiment with abandoned lands on the Sea Islands off South Carolina exposed the presumptions Northerners had about how freed slaves would live after the war. The Sea Islands came under Union control in November 1861. In June 1862, Congress passed the Direct Tax Act that authorized the president to have taxes assessed in Union-held areas in the South and to sell at public auction the land of those who had not paid their taxes. Having assessed the value of the plantations on the Sea Islands, the auction was scheduled for February 1863 until worry about speculators postponed the sale until March. At that time private purchasers bought 21,000 acres of the 80,000 that had gone on sale. Although freedmen were able to purchase more than two thousand acres, the majority, over seven thousand acres, went to Edward Philbrick, a Boston businessman who represented other entrepreneurs from that city, for $7,000, or less than a dollar an acre. They also leased two plantations from the government. These men, however, were unwilling to consider the sale of their newly bought acres to freedmen. Instead, they believed it was in the best interests of the African Americans to work on the land and learn the virtues of free labor. A number of observers, however, doubted their altruistic motives. The profits made from the work of former slaves were not much different from the money made by plantation owners before the war.[10] This disposition of the abandoned lands on the Sea Islands clearly illustrated the emerging interest in allowing former slaves a role as laborers, not landowners.

The elections of 1863, which began in the winter and spring, demonstrated the growing acceptance of Lincoln's position on slavery, the importance of military success for Republican political prospects, and the decreased support for radical measures like confiscation. Although Republicans supported emancipation in the 1863 contests, there were no calls for enforcement of the confiscation acts. Republicans in the New Hampshire governor's election, held in February 1863, weakly defended the emancipation proclamation and prevailed only because a third party candidate allowed them to control the legislature. In the Connecticut governor's race in April the Republican speakers ignored emancipation, stressed that a Confederate victory would hurt the working class and only narrowly won. In the fall, Republicans won major victories in Pennsylvania, Ohio, and Wisconsin, but confiscation played no part, although it was implied in the Democratic charge of administration despotism. Only in Ohio, where the notorious Clement L. Vallandigham was the Democratic nominee for governor, and in Pennsylvania did Republicans have wide margins over their opponents. In the fall elections, Republicans depended upon good military news from Gettysburg and Vicksburg, the soldier vote, and charges that Democrats were willing to sue for peace on any terms. Even though attacks on both abolitionism and racism had declined, the idea of a harsh peace visited upon the South, through a policy such as confiscation, had little if any support in the 1863 elections.[11]

By late 1863, Lincoln had begun to dominate the Republicans' discussion on Reconstruction. The president had orchestrated the administration's support for Republicans during the 1863 elections and had given considerable attention to what Reconstruction would entail. Although he had hoped emancipation would be part of Reconstruction, by September he doubted that freeing the slaves was legal except as military necessity. Emancipation, he noted to Secretary of the Treasury Chase, could not be applied to those areas already occupied by Union forces. Confiscation was therefore still far removed from his Reconstruction plans. With the war going well and radicals posing no significant challenge, he felt confident in giving his views on Reconstruction in December.[12]

Lincoln's Proclamation of Amnesty and Reconstruction, issued on December 8, 1863, offered policies for pardons and the restoration of rebellious states to the Union. Its liberal provisions, however, also helped revive interest in confiscation and provoked a wider discussion of Reconstruction. Lincoln proposed that all participants in the rebellion, except for those in a few categories, receive pardons and have all rights restored except the ownership of slaves. Former rebels had only to take an oath of allegiance to the Union and "abide by and faithfully support all acts of Congress passed during the existing rebellion with reference to slaves" as well as Lincoln's proclamations. Much of the Southern elite, however, whose property was liable to confiscation, was unable to take advantage of the pardons offered. Lincoln's order excluded civil and diplomatic members of the Confederate government, army and navy officers, those who had resigned a United States service commission to aid the rebellion, those who left the judiciary for the Confederacy, and all who had treated prisoners of war unlawfully. These exclusions left state government officials, low-ranking military men, judges, and all private individuals owning property in the loyal areas who had aided the rebellion free to seek pardons. Although the proclamation did not explain how a rebel might obtain a pardon, it soon became clear that appeal to the president was a successful method. In the following year, in fact, Lincoln pardoned even those from the excluded categories who applied. In the end, Lincoln's attitude on pardons was generous and clearly limited confiscation's potential.[13]

Lincoln's pardon offer affected the process of confiscation in direct proportion to the speed at which the Union forces took control in the South. In areas already under Northern control, such as New Orleans, east Tennessee, and parts of Virginia and North Carolina, the president's proclamation exempted those who took the oath from confiscation. Those within Confederate lines eligible to take the oath could have escaped to areas under Union control but there was nothing to be gained by doing so. Their property remained safe from confiscation until the North took control of the area where they lived. When this did occur, they could then take the oath and avoid confiscation. Persons whose property had already been sold through confiscation proceedings could not recover their possessions if pardoned but their survivors could reclaim the real estate upon the offenders' deaths. Even though Lincoln's proclamation allowed pardons to a significant number of rebels, it excluded the prominent rebels who had been the primary targets under Bates's administration. Its immediate effect on confiscation was not significant, but with the Union's advance, more prominent rebels could obtain pardons and confiscation was further restricted.[14]

Lincoln's December 8 message also explained how those involved in the rebellion could "reinaugurate loyal State governments" with measures as lenient as his pardon policy. When one-tenth of a rebellious state's voters, based on the 1860 presidential election, took the oath of allegiance and abided by it, they could "re-establish a State government." Lincoln only required that the new governments be "republican" in nature consistent with the Constitution's republican guaranty clause, and that they honor the loyalty oaths taken by the voters. As noted, these oaths required adherence to the laws, like the confiscation acts, and proclamations on slavery and thereby obligated states to accept the abolition of slavery. However, Lincoln also said he would accept "any provision" a state adopted that "shall recognize and declare" former slaves' freedom and "provide for their education, and which may yet be consistent, as a temporary arrangement, with their present condition as a laboring, landless, and homeless class." He was doubtless alluding to the arrangements already made by General Nathaniel Banks in Louisiana, where, in effect, freed slaves were contracted to remain on the land as laborers. In other words, Lincoln's Reconstruction plans explicitly assumed that blacks would not be assisted in acquiring land, either confiscated or abandoned, but would become laborers in the newly reorganized states, with the approval of the federal government.[15]

Republicans generally applauded Lincoln's proclamation, but many realized that his policies would limit confiscation. Since the second act expressly provided the president with pardoning power, Republicans could hardly complain about Lincoln's use of that authority. Instead, House members like Thaddeus Stevens of Pennsylvania and Thomas Eliot of Massachusetts tried to insure that the real estate already confiscated would be forfeited in fee, and not just for the life of the owner. The day after Lincoln's proclamation they introduced measures to repeal the joint explanatory resolution of July 17, 1862, in which Republicans, under the threat of a veto from the president, had agreed that forfeiture of real estate under the second act would not continue beyond the owner's life. In the following weeks other representatives offered similar measures, all of which went to the House Judiciary Committee. Repeal of the joint resolution became a last and unsuccessful effort to guarantee that confiscation would have an effect beyond the reconciliation of the combatants. Repeal of the joint resolution would not have stopped the granting of pardons, but it would have allowed for permanent confiscation of all property seized and sold before its owners had obtained pardons.[16]

In early January, Representative James Wilson, a Republican from Iowa and chair of the Judiciary Committee, offered a motion to amend, not repeal, the joint resolution in an effort to bridge the differences on the question. Wilson's proposal limited the operation and effect of the second act. Forfeiture would conform to the Constitution's provision that "the Congress shall have the power to declare the punishment of treason, but no attainder of treason shall work corruption of blood, or forfeiture during the life of the person attainted" (article three, section three). But Wilson explained his proposal did not specify whether Congress could provide for forfeiture in fee or for life only. "In other words," Wilson admitted, "we simply submit the section of the Constitution relating to the forfeiture of real estate to the courts of the country to determine whether forfeiture may be in fee or only for life." Although he supported forfeiture in fee, Wilson did not offer an answer to the question he proposed Congress evade and pass onto the courts.[17] His proposal also revealed how little support existed in early 1864 for a repeal of the joint resolution and a challenge to Lincoln.

Before considering Wilson's measure, the House passed a resolution that both revealed the concern many felt over Lincoln's handling of confiscation and their own unwillingness to attack the president openly. The Republican majority prohibited further proclamations under the authority of the second act and recognized Lincoln's order of July 25, 1862, as "sufficient in all cases now pending or which may hereafter arise under said act." In other words, the House voted against further executive interference in confiscation or Lincoln's use of the second act, as in the proclamations of September 1862 and January 1863, to curtail slavery. No mention was made of the administration's enforcement of the confiscation acts, although it was obvious that Lincoln had only embraced the acts when it suited his purposes regarding slavery. Republicans were also worried about the future of confiscation now that Lincoln had begun to pardon all but the most prominent rebels. Since Lincoln and most Republicans agreed upon the broad outlines of Reconstruction, no member of the party attacked his offer of pardons, but the vote did reflect concern over the future.[18]

The House debate over Wilson's bill followed the pattern of discussions on the second act. The Democrats predicted a calamity if Wilson's motion passed and reminded supporters that it was their president who had insisted upon the joint resolution. Francis Kernan of New York believed the measure would force the mass of Southerners into the ranks of the leading rebels. On the other hand, Republican James Garfield of Ohio, the future president, believed confiscating the landed aristocracy's property was the only way to prevent future rebellions. Thaddeus Stevens, however, opposed Wilson's measure because it did not repeal the joint resolution. Forfeiture in fee, Stevens argued, was permissible under the second act since it sought to punish alien enemies, the rebels, not citizens protected by the attainder clause. Only Henry Winter Davis, a Unionist from Maryland, supported Stevens's view. Many Republicans agreed with their colleague Nathaniel Smithers of Delaware, who felt that rebels were not aliens but criminals who were protected by the Constitution. In the end, much of the debate revolved around what the attainder clause meant. Most who supported Wilson's bill contended it allowed forfeiture of fee before the owner's death but not afterward. These arguments, of course, had been heard before and probably altered few positions. When the House finally voted, Wilson's measure passed with only six Republicans opposed.[19]

Remarkably, a number of radicals assumed that Lincoln generally shared their views on how to reconstruct the South even though they were concerned about his attitude toward confiscation. After the president's December proclamation, Senator Charles Sumner of Massachusetts had focused on Lincoln's attack on slavery and his deference to Congress in seating representatives from reconstituted states. Thaddeus Stevens went even further, in January, observing that the president now wanted to treat "the rebel territory as a conqueror alone would treat it." Stevens concluded that Lincoln's "legal mind has carefully studied the law of nations and reached a just conclusion." Such reasoning was unrealistic, however, and may have rested on the impression that the positions of William Whiting, the War Department's solicitor, had persuaded Lincoln. Despite the radicals' hopes, there was no indication that Lincoln had changed his mind about Reconstruction or forfeiture in fee. Nor was the Senate willing to accept Wilson's proposed revision to the joint resolution. The Senate Judiciary Committee, controlled by Republican conservatives who very much favored Lincoln's ideas on Reconstruction, adversely reported the resolution to the full Senate, which accepted the recommendation without discussion.[20]

Attorney General Bates certainly agreed with the president's policy on pardons and restoration of the states. Harsh measures like confiscation against the South, he believed, would produce an embittered peace and jeopardize a swift reconciliation. He hoped for a full pardon and the return of property rights.

Bates had long been dubious about the use of treason to punish rebels believing it would create martyrs. In February 1864, Bates directed that instructions to district attorneys be published in the *New York Times* and elsewhere. The instructions stressed his understanding of the president's amnesty provisions. "The President's pardon of a person guilty of acts of rebellion will, of course, relieve that person from the penalties incurred by his crime," Bates advised his subordinates. If a person were pardoned, Bates directed that "a *bona fide* acceptance of the terms of the President's Proclamation by persons guilty of acts of rebellion . . . will secure to such a person a restoration of all rights of property" except as to slaves and the intervention of third parties' rights. To reassure those who questioned the wisdom of pardoning those punishable by the second act, Bates cited the thirteenth section of the second act. The "purpose of this section" was "to vest the President with full power to relieve such persons on such conditions he should prescribe from the penalty of loss of their property by confiscation." In other words, Lincoln had the power to redress what the act prescribed. Bates, of course, had not enforced the second act with any vigor, as Lincoln wished. He was therefore not defensive over his announcement that proper pardons would protect confiscable property.[21]

Bates further informed district attorneys that the presentation of valid pardons should halt all judicial proceedings instituted under the confiscation acts on the incorrect analysis that "under both acts the ground of condemnation is the personal guilt of the owner in aiding the rebellion." As the attorney general himself had often reminded his subordinates, confiscation under the first act could only occur if the property itself had been used to aid the rebellion. "By the pardon and amnesty," Bates continued, "not only is the punishment of that personal guilt remitted, but the offense itself is effaced, that being the effect of amnesty of the government." Bates thereby declared that pardons restored rebels to their status before the war. According to Bates, Lincoln had authorized him to instruct district attorneys to "discontinue and put to an end" any judicial proceedings for confiscation initiated, pending, or undetermined in their districts "whenever the person so charged" offered proof that he had taken the oath and abided by it. Bates had consistently advocated great care in undertaking prosecutions under the confiscation acts lest district attorneys lose their cases. In 1863, for example, Bates had reminded R. J. Lackey in Missouri that it would be a "far better policy . . . to prosecute offenders for felonies and misdemeanors, than for *romantic* and *genteel* treason."[22] After Lincoln's proclamation on amnesty, however, Bates shunned a cautious use of the power to pardon rebels and restore property.

The policy adopted by the attorney general's office, without complaint from the president, gave district attorneys considerable authority in determining valid pardons. At the same time, however, Lincoln hoped that the threat of confiscation would induce leading rebels to take the oath. After December 1863, Lincoln saw confiscation as punishment with the potential to induce prominent rebels to abandon the rebellion and rejoin the Union. Since it was "quite impossible," said Bates, that Lincoln could sign all the pardons issued, district attorneys were authorized to terminate confiscation cases if the owner proved that they had taken the oath in good faith. It was therefore not necessary for a former rebel to have a pardon signed by the president in order to recover property being confiscated. Bates thereby turned the pardoning process over to the local officials to determine what constituted proof of pardon. Earlier in his tenure Bates had tried to control the implementation of the confiscation acts from his office; now he moved to decentralize the process of pardons. At the end of his instructions Bates warned against halting proceedings or restoring property where evidence existed that the oath had been taken only to protect property. This admonition, however, may have been lost among the many details Bates gave to halt confiscation proceedings when possible.[23]

Not everyone was pleased with the effect that Lincoln's pardon policy and Bates's instructions might have on confiscation. Some supporters of the Union feared that Southerners would simply lie, take the oath, and avoid confiscation. They were doubtful that these policies were effective strategies to end allegiance to the Confederacy or to halt the rebellion. William A. Sorrells of Tennessee wrote Governor Andrew Johnson in June 1864 about this. Rebels who fought against the government for three years only to take "a hypocritical oath to save property," predicted Sorrels, might create "an awful doom" for the rest who had remained loyal. Reports surfaced that some women were taking the oath to avoid confiscation, although they were discreet about it. In Arkansas, William Woodruff admitted his willingness "to take the oath to Old Abe's" government to protect his property and he would be "quite as strong a Rebel after taking it as I ever have been." Woodruff's letter became known to a Union general who had him expelled and had his property seized again, this time for military use.[24]

In any event, the intent of Lincoln's amnesty proclamation and Bates's instructions was to provide for full restoration of property rights except those involving slaves and where a third party's rights intervened. Lincoln's proclamation protected the rights of those who had purchased confiscated property, whose titles would last until the rebel owner died in the case of real estate. Bates's instructions, on the other hand, only dealt with property rights before the cases had been adjudicated. If Bates's instructions had been followed by district attorneys or embraced by those rebels liable to confiscation, the property rights of third parties would not have been an issue; confiscable property would not have reached the condemnation stage if the owner could prove he deserved a pardon. Bates intended to prevent sales of confiscable property to third parties yet unknown and to protect the property rights of those prominent rebels entitled to pardons by Lincoln. In sum, Bates directed district attorneys to end all court proceedings against confiscable property whenever they thought a pardon might be obtained. In the case of rebels who were exempt from pardons under Lincoln's proclamation, district attorneys could end the proceedings before condemnation and sale occurred or a pardon had been issued. If Bates's administration of the confiscation acts had lacked ingenuity, he more than made up for this in his instructions on how to implement pardons for confiscation.[25]

Whatever Lincoln's intent or Bates's efforts, few rebels came forward to take the oath and secure their property. Although Lincoln added more officials to administer the oath of allegiance, few rebels used the proclamation to avoid confiscation. The attorney general's office received several reports of oaths taken, but they came from areas with few prominent rebels.[26] Moreover, not many rebels were in a position to take oaths. Very few Confederates within Union lines wanted to do so, even in early 1864. Nor were there district attorneys or courts in the seceded states to verify pardons granted. Lincoln's amnesty proclamation, therefore, spoke about the future possibilities in relation to confiscation rather than the present.[27]

The small number of rebels who sought pardons did not persuade the minority in Congress, who opposed the joint resolution of 1862, to abandon their hope for permanent confiscation of real estate. They knew that more would ask for pardons as the North occupied larger parts of the South, thus reducing the land liable to permanent forfeiture. Only a repeal of the 1862 joint resolution could alter this process, and the chances of persuading Congress to do so would diminish as victory over the South appeared more likely and prospects of a painless reconciliation between the North and South increased.[28] Since Lincoln's threatened veto had precipitated the joint resolution in the first place, it was presumed his position had to change for repeal to pass. In February 1864, during a discussion of the Freedmen's Bureau Act, Thomas Eliot of Massachusetts said that Lincoln would now support a measure to remove the joint resolution, but he offered no evidence for this claim. In March the House heard again—this time from Representative George Julian, almost certainly incorrectly—that Lincoln had changed his mind about the constitutional problems surrounding permanent confiscation and was now willing see the joint resolution repealed.[29]

In January 1864 Julian had introduced a homestead bill. The measure proposed to secure homesteads of forty and eighty acres in the South for military personnel, black or white, from the confiscated and forfeited estates. The bill declared that the fee of all lands lying outside the limits of Southern towns, cities, or villages, confiscated under the second act, would be transferred to the authority of the secretary of the interior as public lands. In late March, Julian asserted that Lincoln's insistence upon the joint resolution "was the saddest and greatest mistake of his life." Moreover, said Julian, the president, "as I am well advised, now stands ready to join" in the repeal of the joint resolution. Julian, however, did not reveal the basis for Lincoln's supposed conversion; nor did he do so in his memoirs after the war. In 1884 he claimed that he saw Lincoln in July and not March of 1864, when the president had supposedly said that Solicitor Whiting's arguments had changed his position. The fact is that in February 1864 Whiting had written an eight-page letter to Julian that argued confiscation in fee was constitutional. Perhaps that is what persuaded Julian to say that Lincoln had changed his mind. There is no evidence to suggest that Lincoln agreed with either Julian or Whiting, however. The Republican convention in June 1864, over which Lincoln had considerable control, opposed permanent confiscation. Furthermore, there is no doubt that Lincoln disagreed with Whiting's views about the effects of secession on the status of states. Whatever the origins of Julian's comments about Lincoln, the House passed his bill by eleven votes, but the Senate refused to consider the measure in late June 1864.[30]

Nonetheless, Whiting's arguments were important, whether they persuaded Lincoln to change his position on forfeiture or not. A patent lawyer in Boston, Whiting came to Washington in December 1862 as Solicitor of the War Department and by mid-1863 had acquired a reputation as influential within the government as a whole. Secretary of the Navy Gideon Welles observed in August 1863 that the State Department, Stanton, and Lincoln all thought well of Whiting. A month earlier Charles Sumner wrote a friend in England that Whiting was "in the full confidence of the President." In addition, Democrat Samuel S. Cox of Ohio noted Whiting's influence with disapproval. In 1862 Whiting had written a pamphlet on the war powers of the executive and Congress that argued that both had the authority to emancipate the slaves in response to the rebellion. This pamphlet was later published as a book, with more than forty editions by 1871.[31]

Whiting also wrote in 1862 that the second act was "one of the most important penal acts ever passed," and that the joint resolution had been wrongly accepted on the faulty premise that Congress could not confiscate property from rebels permanently, in fee. Whiting offered two arguments to support his conclusion. First, the Constitution did not bar Congress from punishing treason by confiscating real estate beyond the life of the offender. Had the authors of the Constitution wished to do so, Whiting claimed, Congress would have been barred from taking the property of traitors following their executions. According to Whiting "Congress has the power . . . to declare as the penalty for treason the forfeiture of all real and personal estate of the offender, and is not limited, as has been supposed by some, to a forfeiture of real estate for life only." To limit the punishment of treason to death but not forfeiture was illogical. "If the framers of the Constitution were willing that a traitor should forfeit his life," he asked, "how could they have intended to shelter his property?" Second, Whiting claimed the second act was not even a bill of attainder, as its opponents, including Lincoln, had claimed. Although the first four sections of the act discussed treason and listed two punishments, death with freedom for one's slaves or imprisonment, or a fine and the loss of one's slaves, the following sections did not mention treason at all. The sixth section of the bill, said Whiting, directed those engaged in rebellion to cease such activity or face the loss of property; it did not even relate to treason. The attainder clause therefore had no bearing on the loss of property by those who chose, sixty days after the president's proclamation, not to return to their former allegiance to the Union. Whiting therefore believed the forfeitures under the sixth section could be permanent.[32]

Trumbull had voted against the joint resolution in 1862 and did not need Whiting's argument to persuade him that confiscation under the second act could be permanent. In June 1864 he sought to repeal the joint resolution. Following the Senate's rejection of Julian's homestead bill, Trumbull inserted an amendment into the Freedmen's Bureau Bill then under consideration to repeal the joint resolution. Following an odd scenario where first one body and then the other agreed to repeal the joint resolution but never in the same bill, the Senate accepted Trumbull's amendment and the Freedmen's Bureau bill. The House, however, could not agree to the Senate's version of the Freedmen's Bureau Act, and no compromise over the differences could be reached before the end of the first session of the Thirty-eighth Congress in July. Republicans differed about how much protection and assistance should be afforded the freedmen after slavery, while Democrats and Republicans from the Midwest raised objections about whether there should be protection for freed slaves in the bill at all. The Wade-Davis bill on Reconstruction, for instance, had no provision for property distribution after the war, and Senator James Grimes of Iowa expressed the laissez-faire approach when he asked, "Are they free men or not?" These worries also found expression in the work of the American Freedmen's Inquiry Commission, made up of Robert Dale Owen, Samuel Gridley Howe, and James McKaye, whose report appeared in May. In addition, differences arose about whether the Freedmen's Bureau should be located in the War or Treasury departments. These problems carried over into the second session that began in December 1864. It is also noteworthy that in December Representative John M. Ashley of Ohio, a pronounced radical, introduced a Reconstruction bill that made no mention of land for blacks after the war and reflected much of Lincoln's approach.[33]

In February 1865 a conference committee led by Thomas Eliot and Charles Sumner reported a compromise Freedmen's Bureau Act that contained ambiguous provisions about freedmen and their right to permanent title. Under the law, freedmen were given first chance to lease or rent abandoned and confiscated lands for a year and might own them thereafter, but nothing was said about obtaining permanent title to confiscated lands. As Herman Belz notes, there is little evidence to suggest that the conference bill meant to allow permanent forfeiture. There was no discussion in either chamber specifically about forfeiture and no suggestion, despite Julian's later claim, that the president now supported permanent confiscation. Instead, debate focused on the degree to which the federal government should be the guardian of the freed slaves. Sumner and Eliot both stressed the need to assist freedmen and protect their basic rights. Other Republicans, such as William D. Kelley of Pennsylvania, emphasized that such assistance would not be needed for a long period. At the same time, some Republicans and most Democrats questioned the assumption that freed slaves would need guardianship at all. As well, both in and out of Congress, many questioned why the legislation gave preference to blacks over whites.[34]

After a long debate the House accepted the conference committee's Freedmen's Bureau bill in early February, by two votes, with only four Republicans, including Robert C. Schenck of Ohio, opposed. He had already proposed an alternative measure to treat both freed slaves and loyal whites alike, providing limited assistance until the war's end, with no mention of permanent forfeiture. His version found considerable support as an alternative to the recently passed conference bill. Nine days after approving the compromise bill, the House passed the Schenck measure without debate and by a large majority in a voice vote. It then sent both measures to the Senate. The Senate rejected the compromise bill and took no vote on the Schenck measure. All this reflected the growing conviction that the government should not do much to help freed slaves and indicated the lack of support that permanent confiscation now had in Congress.[35]

Both chambers then chose a new conference committee that was more conservative than its predecessor. Schenck was among its members and, not surprisingly, it reported a measure similar to his original House bill, with no promise of permanent forfeiture. The new measure proposed a bureau for refugees, freedmen, and abandoned lands to last for the remainder of the war and a year thereafter. Confiscated and abandoned lands were also to be set aside, forty acres of which would be assigned to each male freed slave or refugee. At the end of three years occupants could purchase the land and receive "such title as the United States can convey." It remained unclear what title the government could "convey" from confiscated lands insofar as the Republicans had failed to amend or remove the 1862 joint resolution. In early March 1865 both the House and Senate agreed to the compromise measure.[36]

Some historians believe the Republicans had come close to repealing the joint resolution and guaranteeing permanent confiscation with the possibility of redistribution of land in the South after the war.[37] The evidence suggests instead that they failed repeatedly because at any one time they could not persuade a majority that permanent confiscation and redistribution were important enough even to discuss or act upon in concert. If there were regrets over bowing to Lincoln's threat in July 1862 or a willingness to accept Whiting's argument about the constitutionality of permanent forfeiture, they did not lead to a united action. Congress had never expressed concern over Bates's implementation of the laws. The failure of Congress to revise the joint resolution also owed less to missed opportunities than it did to the country's different views on the treatment of freed slaves and restoration of the Union. Emancipation, with an emphasis upon former slaves as free laborers became the foundation for Reconstruction; there were no guarantees of land. The prospect of pardoning a growing number of rebels began to appear likely as first Lincoln and then Bates moved to lessen the impact of confiscation.

On four occasions the House and Senate separately expressed interest in permitting permanent forfeiture for confiscated land. In early 1864 the House asked the courts to decide the issue, but the Senate ignored the suggestion. In March 1864 the House passed Julian's homestead measure, which included permanent forfeiture, but the Senate did not even vote on the bill. In June the Senate accepted Trumbull's amendment to repeal the joint resolution, but the House refused to agree to the full act. Finally, a Freedmen's Bureau Act did pass, but it was narrower than the original proposal and it contained only an ambiguous provision on permanent forfeiture. Because the legislators did not discuss forfeiture, it is impossible to say why the Republicans did not unite and accept this idea, about which they circled a number of times. Their repeated failure to amend or repeal the joint resolution makes clear that even before the end of the war Republicans did not believe that the Reconstruction should rest upon a redistribution of Southern land. Republicans had moved away from the idea that so animated them up to July 1862: that a vigorous confiscation should punish the rebels and provide significant assistance to the freedmen. Instead, by late 1864 and early 1865 they had largely accepted what William C. Harris has characterized as Lincoln's "conservative" Reconstruction policy. This accommodation was perhaps logical, particularly given Lincoln's skill in presenting his ideas on the Reconstruction and the aftermath of his assassination. However, the Republicans' inability or unwillingness to move together on the land issue needs to be seen clearly: by April 1865, Republican support for the original premises of confiscation had eroded.[38]

9 Andrew Johnson and the End of Confiscation

The succession of Andrew Johnson to the presidency in April 1865 produced a shift in the enforcement of the confiscation acts. Lincoln had implemented the acts conservatively with the willing assistance of Attorney General Bates. When it suited his plans for emancipation, Lincoln had invoked the second act. Otherwise, until his December 1863 proclamation on restoration, he had not encouraged implementation of the acts as a means of war, a punishment for rebels, or a basis for reconstruction. He hoped that his proclamation would encourage leading rebels to take the oath of allegiance. By January 1865, as the war neared its end, Lincoln favored using confiscation only against those who still encouraged the rebellion. As for the rest, as Attorney General James Speed said that month, it was "greatly to be desired that the community should not be harassed by proceedings in confiscation, as that was an active war measure."[1]

There were two final indications about how Lincoln might have used confiscation had he not been assassinated. At the Hampton Roads Conference on February 3, 1865, according to Confederate Vice President Alexander H. Stephens, Lincoln assured the Southern representatives he would use the confiscation acts "with utmost liberality." Stephens concluded that meant no confiscation would occur if the war ended. Two months later, after the fall of Richmond, Lincoln met there with John A. Campbell, former Justice of the Supreme Court and a conferee at Hampton Roads. With the end in sight, Lincoln made two promises. If the war continued, Lincoln reportedly said, confiscation would be used to support the Union army. Confiscated property, except for slaves, "will be remitted," however, "to the people of any State" which promptly "withdrew" its troops and ended "further resistance to the government."[2] From 1861 on Lincoln had distrusted confiscation's effects on all but the most prominent rebels and had insisted on a limited enforcement except where it might induce a faster, less painful restoration. Lincoln remained consistently opposed to using the confiscation acts to distribute lands to either poor whites or freed slaves.

At least superficially, Andrew Johnson seemed to be an advocate of vigorous confiscation before and after he became president. As a congressman Johnson had voted for the First Confiscation Act. In the spring of 1862, appointed by

Lincoln as the military governor of Tennessee, Johnson promised an audience in Nashville that treason "must be crushed out and traitors must be punished," presumably by confiscation and hanging. For "the leading traitors" Johnson would "extend no terms of compromise." Yet he did not believe "Reconstruction" was "the proper term" for the process of restoration, because the rebellious states had not left the Union. Just before the second act passed in 1862, Johnson said in a Fourth of July oration that "treason must be made odious, traitors impoverished." Moreover, "their property should be taken from them to defray the expenses of war." His views were widely quoted in the North thereafter. In February 1864, Johnson, despite his evident antipathy to blacks, promised a group of African Americans in Nashville that he would be their "Moses leading them from slavery to freedom." On other occasions he declared that the large properties in the South should be broken up and distributed to small farmers, and in August 1863 he defended the second act. In April 1864, in a comment that persuaded many Republicans that he was a radical, Johnson told Senator Benjamin Wade that "treason is crime, and the crime must be punished." In his June 1864 acceptance speech as the vice presidential nominee, Johnson was most explicit about confiscating the property of traitors. "Their great plantations must be seized and divided into small farms," he said, "and sold to honest, industrious men." But Johnson supported confiscation only against leading Confederates—and not if it meant freed slaves would be allowed to obtain the property. Although he accepted the necessity of abolition as a military measure, he believed that former slaves should be landless laborers and below whites in the social order. Johnson also supported confiscation as a means to raise revenue to pay for the war. Shortly after becoming president, Johnson told Governor Oliver P. Morton and the Indiana delegation that "after making treason odious, every Union man and the Government should be remunerated out of the pockets of those who have inflicted this great suffering upon the country."[3] This appears to have been the last public comment Johnson made on confiscation, and it suggested a more narrow application than his previous pronouncements.

Any man who followed Lincoln to the presidency after the Civil War would have suffered in comparison, but Johnson was particularly ill suited to the task. Not the least of Johnson's problems was his ignorance about Lincoln's plans for reconstruction. In addition to winning a war, a feat that had not looked promising in early 1864, Lincoln had also pointed the way to restoring the Union. Notwithstanding the complaints of radicals, by his death Lincoln had unified much of the North and the Republican Party behind his reconstruction plans. Editors Henry Raymond of the *New York Times*, Horace Greeley of the *New York Tribune*, and James G. Bennett of the *New York Herald* supported

Lincoln's conciliatory policy, as did the *Chicago Tribune*. And despite their bluster, as seen in the Wade-Davis bill, the radicals' efforts to control reconstruction had not succeeded by the time of Lincoln's death.

Lincoln's administration was difficult for the former Democrat from Tennessee to follow. Johnson had to decipher Lincoln's plans without having been in the Cabinet or privy to them. Lincoln and Johnson, in fact, had only one brief meeting after the election, on the very day of the assassination. While Lincoln had been the most criticized president until that time, his death and Johnson's performance soon suggested how wonderfully talented he had been. The willingness to let events influence policy was among greatest Lincoln's strengths and was perhaps one of Johnson's major shortcomings. Johnson often misread the ambiguous situations that Lincoln had handled so well. Many Republicans had concluded by the end of the war, for example, that the government should guarantee blacks at least minimal rights in the South, but Johnson could not see past his own assumptions on race and was unable to shift his position on this crucial issue.[4]

Unlike Lincoln, Johnson instituted a vigorous, if selective, confiscation policy soon after he became president, although acquiring property for poor whites and former slaves was not his objective. Instead, he wanted to use confiscation to intimidate leading rebels, forcing them to ask for pardons. On the surface his pardon policy appeared harsh, particularly to the planter elite, but it was actually quite soft and enabled most rebels to protect their property. When asked, he was consistently willing to grant pardons. Moreover, even as he directed the attorney general to enforce the confiscation acts, Johnson tried to deny land to freedmen, restrict the role of the Freedmen's Bureau as a land agency, and force it to give back land to pardoned rebels. A vigorous confiscation policy was not intended to acquire land. In fact, he demanded that the bureau restore land as soon as rebels were pardoned. In sum, confiscation was a tool Johnson used to humiliate some rebels and, later, to assist his plans for restoration of the Union.[5]

Johnson, however, did not initially link confiscation with restoration. Instead, he saw enforcement as a way to help some rebels and threaten others. On April 22, less than a month after the war ended, Johnson, through Speed, curtailed enforcement of the second act in Missouri, Kentucky, and Tennessee, three border states. It may be significant that Kentucky and Tennessee were the native states of the attorney general and president. Johnson's goal was to help those involved in confiscation proceedings retain their property until he announced his amnesty plans a month later. The attorney general's office directed the three district attorneys to "omit proceeding further in all cases" under the confiscation acts "pending in your District, until further instruction from this office." When Missouri District Attorney William Grover asked if the order prohibited the development of future cases, Speed sought to clarify the directive. Disclaiming any intent to stop preparation of present or future cases, Speed said, "I only mean that you shall not press trials and sales till further orders."[6] Speed offered no further explanation, but the effect of his order was to protect rebels in these states who were already involved in confiscation proceedings. Even if they failed to receive a blanket pardon later on, they would still be able to apply for special pardons and need not worry about losing their property. However, rebels in the other states, who Johnson seemed to believe had demonstrated more sympathy for the Confederacy, did not receive such an opportunity.

Less than three weeks later Speed sent another instruction, but only to Lucius H. Chandler, the district attorney of Virginia, which had a large class of property holders that supported the Confederacy. Referring to the president's proclamation of May 9 ordering the reestablishment of federal authority in Virginia, Speed instructed Chandler "to libel and bring to judgment, confiscation and sale all property within the geographical limits of the State of Virginia that may be subject to confiscation." Although Johnson expected other district attorneys to administer the confiscation acts, Speed's letter to Chandler was the only specific order following one of Johnson's general instructions. It was, in fact, the only time that the attorney general's office gave a direct order for confiscation. When numerous men of wealth and position in Virginia complained to Johnson in September about Chandler's enforcement, the president relented and instructed Chandler, through Speed, not to confiscate any more property in the state. Johnson, it seemed, had achieved his purpose with this selective and brief enforcement. The proposed confiscation frightened that portion of the Virginia elite that had supported the Confederacy and encouraged them to ask Johnson for consideration.[7]

Johnson began enforcing confiscation, albeit selectively, soon after taking office, but many were troubled because he took so long to announce his reconstruction plans. Lincoln might have been able to get away with this; his successor was under much closer scrutiny, in part because he had led various groups to believe he supported their reconstruction views. On May 29, more than a month and a half after Congress adjourned, Johnson announced his proclamation on amnesty and restoration, prepared in consultation with Speed. The president offered a pardon, with fourteen classes of exemptions, "to all persons who have, directly or indirectly, participated in the existing rebellion" with full restoration of all property rights except those involving slaves and where proceedings under the confiscation acts had been instituted. In addition to the groups prohibited by Lincoln from taking the oath of allegiance, Johnson excluded the following: those who left Congress and became Confederates; those who went abroad to assist the South; supporters of the rebellion who attended West Point or Annapolis; those who had interfered with the Union's maritime commerce; those who took Lincoln's December 8 oath of amnesty and then violated it; and all in the rebellion whose property's taxable value exceeded $20,000. The last exemption, representing the South's wealthiest elite, might have proven the most significant in terms of confiscation had they not been able to obtain pardons. At the same time, Johnson allowed anyone in the exempted classes to make a "special application" for pardon.[8] This was an important concession from the president. All, but particularly wealthy Southerners, could personally ask him for a pardon, thereby escaping confiscation and returning to their former allegiance.

Less than two weeks after Johnson's proclamation on amnesty, the attorney general's office revoked the order to the district attorneys in Missouri, Kentucky, and Tennessee that they cease trials and sales of confiscated property. Instead, they were told, "you are directed to press those cases forward to an early determination." The two-week interval had presumably been enough time for those pardoned to rescue their property. At the same time, however, Speed's assistant J. Hubley Ashton rebuked Edward Bradford, Delaware's district attorney, who had assumed he should follow the instructions sent to the three border states. "The Government desires you," Ashton lectured, "to pursue the requirements of the Statutes of the United States until you are officially directed to take a different course."[9] And from this time forward—from mid-June until late September 1865—the attorney general's office directed a strict and vigorous application of the confiscation acts with no more preferences shown for one part of the South or the nation. This was the most consistent and explicit enforcement the confiscation laws received, but it was not, of course, designed to achieve the goals Trumbull and other supporters envisioned for the second act.

The irony of a consistent enforcement of the confiscation acts, which had been passed as war measures, taking place only after hostilities ceased is significant and highlights Johnson's interest in their use as a means of punishment, not as part of land reform or reconstruction. With one exception, the attorney general's office under Johnson responded to questions on confiscation with instructions to proceed against all confiscable property.[10] District Attorney Wingate Hays of Rhode Island, for example, wondered whether he should confiscate property under the second act now that the rebellion had ended. Ashton promptly replied that Hays "undoubtedly" had the authority to seize property of anyone who had aided the South following the act's passage. "The suppression of the rebellion does not stop the execution of the [First] Confiscation act," Ashton declared. The attorney general's office was as forceful with District Attorney Bennett Pike of St. Joseph, Missouri, who was confused over the order revoking the suspension of sales for confiscated property. Pike, William Stewart instructed, should "institute legal proceedings against all property in your district liable to confiscation and prosecute the same with due diligence."[11] Confiscation's advocates therefore suffered under Bates's weak enforcement of the acts during the war, perhaps the best time to confiscate, and Speed's forceful implementation, at a time of diminished opportunities for confiscation, as former rebels behaved pragmatically and pardons proliferated.[12]

Even though Johnson designated more classes ineligible for amnesty than did Lincoln, three circumstances provided incentives for the overwhelming majority of the rebellion's participants to ask the president for a pardon. The first involved the widely publicized Special Orders No. 15 issued by General William T. Sherman on January 15, 1865, which set aside land on the Sea Islands off Georgia and South Carolina to freedmen. This unexpected decision both encouraged many freed slaves to believe they might obtain land after the war and made obvious to Southern whites that land redistribution, from either abandoned or confiscated property, was still a real threat. An oath of allegiance to the Union to protect one's property therefore was pragmatic, no matter how unpleasant taking it might be so soon after hostilities ended. The war's conclusion was the second compelling reason to seek a pardon. The Confederacy's defeat removed the last practical impediment that most rebels might have had for not swearing allegiance to the Union. It soon became clear that Johnson would respond generously to requests for pardon, except from those involved in confiscation cases, those with land liable to confiscation, and thereby excluded from receiving pardons, and the very wealthy. The third reason was Johnson's demonstrated willingness to grant pardons, despite his promises to punish the Southern elite, those most vulnerable to confiscation. A year after Johnson's proclamation, Representative John Longyear, a Michigan Republican hostile to permanent confiscation, estimated that the few rebels who remained unpardoned would receive the benefit shortly.[13]

General Sherman's Special Orders were significant for the history of confiscation, even though they involved only abandoned lands. In March 1863, Congress authorized the Treasury Department to collect and to administer captured and abandoned property in the South. As noted in chapter 7, perhaps as much as 95 percent of the property collected under this act was cotton, but some abandoned lands were involved. They were often leased to local whites and worked by freedmen. Only a few whites, such as General Rufus Saxton, who became involved in the Sea Islands in 1861, however, had assumed that the titles of these lands could be transferred after the Civil War to former slaves themselves.[14]

This assumption about black ownership changed in January 1865. Just as contrabands entering the Union lines provoked interest in abolition through confiscation in 1861, so too did slaves and the military provoke a wider discussion of land near the war's end. In November 1864 General Sherman's famous march through Georgia began, and as many as 17,000 slaves may have left their masters to follow in his wake, in order to gain their freedom but with some hope of acquiring land. Secretary of War Edwin Stanton, who had been eager to use the second act in 1862 to employ freedmen as laborers, went to confer with Sherman in Savannah about the plight of these freedmen. On January 12, 1865, Stanton and Sherman held a conference with twenty African American ministers, nine of them just freed from slavery, to inquire as to their wishes for the freedmen. Garrison Frazier, a Baptist minister chosen to speak for the freedmen, said the best way to "take care of ourselves is to have land, and turn in and till it by our labor. . . . We want to be placed on land until we are able to buy it and make it our own." Stanton and Saxton then assisted Sherman in preparation of Field Orders No. 15, issued four days later. It set aside the Sea Islands and the low country area thirty miles inland from Jacksonville, Florida, up to Charleston, South Carolina, and granted freedmen forty acres each, even though it left the ownership question murky. Freedmen were to be given "possessory titles" until Congress "shall regulate the title." Sherman later mentioned that the army would provide mules and horses to the freedmen. It was from these promises that many freedmen came to believe that the government had guaranteed that they would receive "forty acres and a mule."[15]

Although Sherman has been credited with these orders, Stanton and Saxton were doubtless chiefly responsible for their content. Sherman had never evinced much interest in slavery itself and had not been bothered about the reports, some of which had reached the North, that the freedmen following him had been poorly treated. It was thought that many would starve if they were not fed soon. Sherman appeared more interested in being rid of the freedmen whereas Stanton was worried about them. Sherman later explained to President Johnson that he had bowed to Stanton's wishes to set aside the land. "I merely aimed to make provisions for the negroes who were absolutely dependent on us, leaving the validity of their possession to be determined by after events or legislation." Even later, in his memoirs, Sherman said he only meant to give the freedmen temporary possession of the land. The evidence indicates that Stanton and Saxton, however, meant to have the titles made permanent by Congress later on. The order put Saxton in charge of the new colony of freedmen and, he hoped, as he noted to Stanton, that they would be able to gain permanent possession of their lands, unlike the freedmen on the Sea Islands. The Special Orders were also important because they offered evidence, however false it later proved to be, to former slaves that the government would actually provide them with permanent possession of land in the South upon which they could reconstruct their lives after the Civil War. This dream, begun on the Sea Islands in 1861, was revived by Sherman's orders, and reappeared in legislation creating the Freedmen's Bureau.[16]

The Freedmen's Bureau appeared to offer the opportunity for former slaves to acquire land, either confiscated or abandoned, but this hope, like that inherent in Sherman's Special Orders, also proved illusory. As noted in the preceding chapter, Congress passed the Freedmen's Bureau Act in early March 1865, creating the Bureau of Refugees, Freedmen and Abandoned Lands. It was to be a temporary agency, in the War Department, to "continue during the present war of rebellion, and one year thereafter." To administer the Freedmen's Bureau, Johnson chose General Oliver Otis Howard, a professional soldier from Maine, who had come to believe the government had the obligation to help the freed slaves. Howard began his work in early May 1865, more than two weeks before Johnson's proclamation on amnesty. By the terms of the act Howard had the authority, "under the direction of the President," to allocate forty acres of the property, to which the government had acquired title, to each freedmen or loyal refugee. The law also guaranteed the tenant occupancy for three years at which time he could buy the land and receive "such title as the United States can convey."[17] This was, however, a vague promise at best. Moreover, there was nowhere near enough land available to the bureau to fulfill this lofty mission, nor the power to gain more. Only about 850,000 acres were in the bureau's possession, less than one percent of the land in the Confederacy. Still, it was enough land to start thousands of freedmen toward independent lives after the war if Johnson had not proved most reluctant to let them take possession of what little land the bureau controlled. In addition, Howard and most of his colleagues, as well as many Northerners, believed in what has been called the "free labor ideology," which held that freedmen needed to learn the lessons of free labor before they became property owners. All these factors prevented the Freedmen's Bureau from distributing much confiscated or abandoned land to the freedmen.[18]

Even though Howard instructed Saxton on May 20, 1865, the day of Johnson's amnesty proclamation, not to give up land held by "disloyal persons," he did not immediately see the implications of the president's offer of pardons. It was not until early June, when General Quincy A. Gilmore, commander of the Department of the South, threatened to take away the property under General Saxton's supervision, as a result of Sherman's orders, that Howard realized the import of the president's message. Apprised by Stanton of Gilmore's order, Howard rescinded the command, although he agreed to let whites take up lands under Sherman's orders also, itself a major concession. Howard then asked Attorney General Speed for clarification of his authority and responsibility as commissioner of confiscated and abandoned lands. Like Bates, Speed resented requests for his opinion from anyone other than the president or another Cabinet member, so he responded to Howard's query by writing Stanton, Howard's superior. His analysis in late June was both cautionary and ambiguous.[19]

The attorney general gave Stanton a general view of what he thought the Freedmen's Act required the commissioner to do and a specific definition of Howard's control over lands. According to Speed, Congress meant for the Freedmen's Bureau "primarily" to look after "the personal and social interests of the loyal refugees and freedmen." The Freedmen's Bureau, therefore, was only secondarily concerned with land. Howard's "authority with regard to the lands is . . . an incident of his power in regard to the persons" the act was designed to assist. The Freedmen's Bureau Act, said Speed, gave Howard "control of all subjects relating to refugees and freedmen," but he then noted that his control of abandoned lands was limited. Howard had "the *authority*, under the direction of the President, to set apart *for the use* of loyal refugees and freedmen the lands in question" and was also "*required* to assign to every male of that class of persons not more than forty acres of land." But, observed Speed, Howard had no control over those lands he did not use or set aside for freedmen or refugees. Although this interpretation limited Howard's authority over lands not used for the freedmen or refugees, it implied he had the power to take possession of abandoned and confiscated land and deny restoration of these occupied lands to the original owners who obtained pardons. However, Speed did not address the question of whether or not an absolute title could be given to the occupants of the land, particularly abandoned land. Whereas the title to confiscated land had passed to the government, owners of abandoned property retained title to it. Only confiscation proceedings against abandoned property, therefore, could wrest the title from the landowner and perhaps prevent its restoration under Johnson's amnesty proclamation or by special pardon.[20]

Soon after receiving Speed's analysis, Howard moved to discover what lands the bureau had assigned to freedmen and to enlarge the holdings wherever possible for their immediate needs. On June 26, instructions went out to assistant commissioners to enumerate lands, including hospitals, being used for the freedmen, and to do so quickly. On July 1 Howard informed Speed that he would "refuse to give up any property held by or for the use of loyal refugees or freedmen" unless Speed, the courts, Stanton, or Johnson requested otherwise. When his subordinates returned the requested lists of property in their control, Howard sent them to Speed on July 11 so the attorney general could institute proceedings against property that had not yet been confiscated. By mid-July, then, the commissioner realized that a more comprehensive policy was needed to ensure freedmen with more than temporary facilities and deter the rate at which land was being restored. But, as he noted to Freedmen's Bureau official Orlando Brown in Virginia, "it is extremely difficult for me to arrive at any well determined course when there are so many opinions." He therefore asked Stanton to raise the issue in the Cabinet.[21]

On August 1 Circular No. 13, the most aggressive action by the Freedmen's Bureau over confiscated and abandoned lands, was issued. It had not received Johnson's approval, however; he had been ill when Howard hoped he might review it. Worried that land would be lost to the Freedmen's Bureau by the time Johnson had a chance to review the circular, Howard authorized it anyway. Howard's assistant added the disclaimer that officials were "to be guided by it as an expression of General Howard's views, pending submission to the President." The circular instructed subordinates to "select and set apart such confiscated and abandoned lands and property as may be deemed necessary for the immediate use of refugees and freedmen" and to rent or sell them according to the Freedmen's Bureau Act. The directive implied that land that had been "set apart" could be purchased within three years and could not be restored to former owners even if the president had pardoned them. Circular 13 removed the ambiguity of the original act with Howard's assertion that freedmen and refugees could not have their property taken back by pardoned rebels during the three years of tenancy. Nor could a pardon, Howard suggested, prevent the sale of the land following the years of tenancy. "The pardon of the President," outlined in the Amnesty Proclamation, "will not be understood to extend to the surrender of abandoned or confiscated property, which by law has been 'set apart for refugees and freedmen,'" Howard concluded. Having issued a bold policy that might have permitted the transfer of much land to poor whites and former slaves, Howard left Washington for a vacation in Maine. Within days his policy began to unravel, however.[22]

Secretary of the Treasury Hugh McCulloch had written Howard, before Circular 13 was issued, that the courts might not sustain the title transfer contemplated if pardoned rebels challenged it. With Howard absent, McCulloch's concern prompted his assistant William Fowler to write Orlando Brown in Virginia that the commissioner wanted the orders followed "until its actual approval or disapproval" by Johnson. The president made his views very clear soon thereafter. B. B. Leake of Tennessee had received "a special pardon" from Johnson four days before Circular 13 took effect. In accordance with the circular, the Freedmen's Bureau in Nashville refused to return Leake's property, whereupon the former rebel asked his aunt to appeal his case. Knowing of this personal appeal to Johnson in mid-August, Fowler wired the Nashville agent, General Clinton Fisk, to return Leake's property before the president intervened. Fisk, however, said he could not return the property, prompting Johnson to write Fisk himself that Leake had been pardoned "and thereby restored to all his rights of property, except as to slaves." Johnson added that the "same action will be had in similar cases," negating Howard's directive that bureau officials ignore the pardoned rebels' pleas when they asked for the return of confiscated or abandoned property. Johnson also ordered bureau officials in Mississippi to restore the property of another person he had pardoned, and noted that he had received many such complaints. Within two weeks Johnson had abrogated Howard's policy on land for the freedmen.[23]

During Howard's absence that August, the Freedmen's Bureau in Washington acceded to the president's views on restoration. Howard's assistant, James Fullerton, observed to one official that Johnson wanted "the country to know that his proclamation of Amnesty is more than wind" and that restoration of abandoned property should follow a pardon. The president also made it clear to bureau officials that he considered its agents in some states, particularly Tennessee, too responsive to needs of former slaves. Some officials, like Thomas W. Conway in Louisiana, tried to ignore Johnson's aversion to former slaves occupying land that might soon be pardoned. But most, like General E. A. Wild in South Carolina and Fisk in Tennessee, thought they had little choice. Wild wrote Saxton in late August, "The *reports of* lands amount to nothing at all. We have no plantations whatsoever," while Fisk, under orders, ended the Freedmen's Bureau work in east Tennessee and returned the lands in its possession. Bureau officials in Washington presumed that Howard would accept Johnson's orders and bow to the president's wish to restore the land to those he was pardoning.[24]

Howard, however, believed he could develop a policy to replace Circular 13 that would both satisfy the president, who wished full restoration, and subordinates like Saxton and Conway, who wanted to help the freedmen secure land. Upon his return to Washington in early September, Howard proposed that rebels with property worth more than $20,000 be granted a pardon if they allowed freedmen already tilling parcels between five and ten acres the right to secure a title to the property for their lifetimes. Whereas Circular 13 authorized the government to grant the title, Howard's new formula gave the pardoned rebels power to grant the fee simple. The shift reflected Howard's appreciation of how eager Johnson was to pardon the elite and his own willingness to allow freedmen to resume subordinate positions under their former masters. In

Howard's subsequent meeting with Johnson on September 8, it became clear that the president would not accept his compromise plan, which had already been published in newspapers. Following the meeting Howard wrote his wife, "President Johnson is giving up the law pretty fast and I begin to tremble with anxiety for the freedman." According to Howard's later recollection, at his suggestion that pardoned landowners "provide a small homestead or something equivalent" to freedmen, "President Johnson was amused and gave no heed to this recommendation." Instead, Johnson directed that he write Circular 15, which Howard signed and sent out on September 12.[25]

The new policy significantly narrowed the definition of both abandoned and confiscable property, thereby reducing the land the Freedmen's Bureau could retain and increasing the amount it had to restore to pardoned rebels. Under the new circular, abandoned property existed when the lawful owner was absent and engaged in aiding or encouraging the rebellion, which the war's end had eliminated. Little land, if any, could therefore now be classified as abandoned. The circular also defined confiscable property as only that sold under court decree, so that even lands seized and or condemned but not sold were to be returned to their pardoned owners. Beyond contravening his own provision in the May amnesty proclamation, which forbade interference with property already in confiscation proceedings, Johnson's circular, under Howard's name, effectively authorized restoration of all property in the Freedmen's Bureau's possession that might have been confiscated. By limiting confiscable property to that condemned and sold before the circular appeared, it excluded property still in the bureau's hands that had been confiscable under the two acts. Johnson also limited Howard's opportunity to distribute land by directing that no more property be transferred from the Treasury Department or the military to the Freedmen's Bureau. As Speed explained to a district attorney at the time, the president no longer wanted "to keep open the sores made in & by the late struggle." Unless individuals were of "sufficient national consequence" to impair restoration without the threat of confiscation, Speed reported that Johnson wanted no further enforcement of the second act. Howard confided to his wife that he was "quite apprehensive that the freedmen's rights will not be care[d] for as much as I would wish." In other words, by early September 1865 Johnson saw no further purpose in enforcing the second act.[26]

Johnson also expected Howard to take his plans for restoring property to the South and the freedmen. In early October the president sent Howard to South Carolina, Florida, and Georgia "to effect an arrangement mutually satisfactory to freedmen and landowners," meaning that whites would have their land and Howard would deliver this blow to the freedmen himself. Even though Howard delivered the message, he also encouraged subordinates like

Saxton and Alexander Ketchum to delay the process of restoration where possible and to assist the freedmen in various ways. In addition, the commissioner promised before more than two thousand freedmen at a famous meeting on Edisto Island, off South Carolina, that he would urge Congress when it next met to secure land for them. But Howard's suggestions to Congress and the efforts of Saxton, Ketchum, and others in the South to prevent the removal of blacks from lands restored to pardoned rebels in late 1865 and early 1866 could not stop the momentum of Johnson's policy. As Howard observed to Senator Henry Wilson in late November, he was "sorry for the policy adopted of restoring lands to pardoned owners without affixing conditions" but could do nothing about it.[27] In December 1865 the Freedmen's Bureau possessed 786,000 acres; by late 1868 pardons had reduced that number to 139,000 acres, much of which was land not worth cultivating. As Speed observed in regard to confiscation and restoration in November 1865, the government "desires to act with magnaninity [*sic*] and generosity" consistent with a quick return to peace and order, with the result that Johnson and Speed favored pardoned whites over freedmen. It became clear that the best freedmen could expect was a favorable labor contract from the owner of the land they formerly occupied. In December 1865 Speed reiterated Johnson's policy; it was not "the wish of the Government to harass or impoverish any of the citizens who desire in good faith to return to their allegiance & duty." The freedmen's hope of receiving confiscated or abandoned land continued to dwindle.[28]

The conduct of Freedmen's Bureaus in the former Confederate states naturally differed, but the results involving land for freedmen were similar in the end, as Johnson directed. In Texas and Alabama, at one extreme, the bureau had almost no abandoned or confiscated land to distribute after the war. Despite the expectations of many former slaves that they would receive land, from the start the bureau could only function, at best, as a mediator between white landlords and black labor. By August 1865 the Tennessee Bureau had acquired about 42,000 acres, a relatively small amount, of which a fourth was worth farming without significant clearing to make it productive. In Mississippi the bureau, with the smallest staff of any state, faced a particularly hostile white planter class.[29] Although the bureau held some land in Arkansas, the results were largely the same as in Texas and Alabama. Some freedmen in Arkansas were able to buy land after the war, but not through the bureau's administration. By late 1866 Johnson's pardon policy had returned over 95,000 acres to former owners, leaving only 29,000 acres still in the bureau's possession. In North Carolina the bureau had about 100,000 acres in the fall of 1865 but controlled only around 11,000 by the end of the year.[30]

Although the Freedmen's Bureau controlled significantly more land in Florida, Virginia, and Louisiana, the results were the same as in other states. The bureau did not begin effective operation in Florida until September 1865, by which time William Marvin, the provisional governor appointed by Johnson, had already received permission to suspend the sale of confiscated property. Thereafter the bureau did not deter the return of land to former owners and won praise from Florida conservatives in 1866.[31] In Virginia some bureau agents, like Charles B. Wilder and Orlando Brown, tried without success to resist Johnson's restoration policy. And although freedmen openly resented the bureau's policy, the return of confiscated and abandoned lands to former owners proceeded nonetheless.[32] In Louisiana, Thomas D. Conway of the bureau at first enjoyed some success in securing lands for freedmen, although many blacks felt Conway was too paternalistic. Benjamin F. Flanders of the Treasury Department surrendered more than 250 properties, valued at $5 million, to Conway in July 1865. In the same month Conway asked Howard to help him obtain money the Treasury Department had earned from renting abandoned land to be used to secure testimony so he could "confiscate a vast amount of property." Conway also created strict procedures to impede restoration to those with pardons. All this greatly angered Johnson, who insisted in October 1865 that Conway be removed, with James Fullerton taking his place. Although it took some time to reverse Conway's work, restoration of property to pardoned rebels in Louisiana did proceed by early 1866.[33]

The restoration of property in South Carolina, including land put aside by Sherman's orders, ended as it had in other states but was a more complicated and longer process. Rufus Saxton was in charge of both the mainland and the Sea Islands and had worked hard to secure land for freedmen. In June 1865 the Freedmen's Bureau there had over 300,000 acres, much of it under Sherman's Special Orders, and perhaps one thousand pieces of town property. Saxton and his assistants thereupon sold or leased forty-acre plots to the freedmen. About forty thousand freedmen occupied land on the Sea Islands off South Carolina, Georgia, and northern Florida by the end of the summer in 1865. In response to requests for restoration in September, Saxton said that he could not accede. "It is of vital importance," he informed Howard, "that our promises made to the freedmen [of land on the islands] should be faithfully kept." Saxton, on the other hand, agreed to restore by December confiscated and abandoned property on the mainland. It was Saxton's position on the Sea Islands that prompted Johnson to send Howard to South Carolina in October to inform the freedmen they would have to give back their land on the islands. Saxton and his colleague, Alexander Ketchum, however, only complied by restoring plantations to which freedmen did not hold possessory titles. In December, Saxton was offered a transfer from South Carolina to another post, but he refused. Finally, on orders from Johnson, in early January 1866 Saxton was relieved of his position. Although Ketchum then began restoring more property, he still protected land held by some freedmen. Howard then relieved Ketchum, and the process of restoration increased under his successors.[34]

Land controlled by the Freedmen's Bureau in Georgia, much of it included in Sherman's Orders, met a fate similar to land in South Carolina. Saxton remained in charge of the Georgia Bureau until September when Howard appointed Davis Tillson to supervise all but the lands in the Sherman grant. The Georgia Sea Islands remained under Saxton's supervision until he was removed in early 1866. As in South Carolina, through the spring and summer of 1865 thousands of former slaves had been granted lands on the Georgia islands and encouraged by bureau officials to stay. Also, as in South Carolina, restoration of the Sherman grant lands in Georgia only began after Saxton was removed. Although Tillson, too, wished to find land for freedmen, as he demonstrated in Dougherty County, in the southwest near Albany, he wanted to do so only on land that was not abandoned or confiscated. Nor did Tillson share the willingness of Saxton, Ketchum, and Howard to resist the instructions to restore land to pardoned owners. And like so many in the Freedmen's Bureau, Tillson believed that freedmen, if unable to obtain land, would have to adapt to rigors of free labor when they did not have a clear title to the land they coveted. To this end he tried in early 1866 to help most of the freedmen on the Sea Islands adjust to the necessity of becoming laborers. He appreciated, however, as did most by the spring of 1866, that the freedmen's dream of title to confiscated or abandoned land had been lost.[35]

A few Republicans and public figures continued to insist that confiscated land be put aside for the former slaves, but their efforts met with almost no support in Congress after the war. In September 1865 Thaddeus Stevens had argued to his constituents that 400 million acres in the South should be seized from the wealthy, with forty acres given to each adult freedman. He repeated this call in subsequent years. Even though a few others, like Charles Sumner and Wendell Phillips, still gave at least rhetorical support to such pleas, most Republicans no longer supported confiscation. Instead, they advocated the virtues of the free labor ideology and homestead legislation. The decline of confiscation's appeal became clear, yet again, in the effort to pass a new Freedmen's Bureau Bill in late 1866. In January Lyman Trumbull, who had consulted Howard about the bureau and was, at the time, persuaded that Johnson and Congress could work "harmoniously," reported from the Judiciary Committee a new Freedmen's Bureau bill. Its goals were to prolong the bureau's existence and protect freedmen from the emerging Black Codes. As for land, freedmen would have a three-year occupancy of the Sherman lands, and three million acres in the South would be obtained for homesteading. In the Senate Trumbull claimed that "a homestead is worth more to these people than almost anything else," but it would not be taken from confiscated land. When Stevens moved in the House to acquire "forfeited estates of the enemy" for the freedmen, the Republican majority voted it down. Instead, two days later Republicans supported George Julian's bill to create homesteads for those able to purchase them. Republicans, including Trumbull, had again abandoned the premise of confiscation—that freedmen needed special help and that the property of those who supported the rebellion should be expropriated for that purpose. Instead, freedmen would now be expected to compete with whites for land in the South.[36]

There can be no doubt that freedmen wanted land after the Civil War. Many slaves and former slaves believed it only just that they receive land after suffering in slavery. Moreover, many realized they would need land to succeed after the war. The belief in "forty acres and a mule," to be provided by Lincoln, then Johnson, was widespread at the war's end and for some time thereafter. Freedmen frequently resisted when asked to leave the land they occupied or when forced off plots allotted after the war. In addition, their reluctance to become contract laborers was often intense and reflected their desire to be free; for many that meant the opportunity to cultivate their own plot of land. This desire for land did not die quietly among freedmen during Reconstruction. There were numerous indications that freedmen held onto their dream of receiving confiscated and abandoned land long after Johnson succeeded in restoring this property to pardoned rebels.[37]

By 1867, however, most black leaders evinced little or no interest in confiscation even if a few appreciated the importance of land reform in the South for the freedmen's future. This reluctance to push for confiscation reflected an understanding of its lack of support among whites and the fact that few leaders were themselves former slaves. Many black leaders from the middle and upper classes shared the assumptions of the free labor ideology as well as the Victorian assumptions about self-help. These leaders also frequently accepted what most white friends, other than staunch advocates like Thaddeus Stevens, now believed was their proper place in the South and the Republican Party. Various black leaders across the South took the position, sometime in defiance of the freedmen who chose them, that confiscation should no longer be encouraged or demanded. In various state conventions, where black leaders had a significant voice, confiscation was either not mentioned or was at best a secondary issue.[38]

By 1867 most white leaders of the Republican Party had decided that confiscation could no longer be part of their platform. Although Benjamin Butler had now joined Thaddeus Stevens to insist on confiscation as part of Reconstruction, almost no other prominent Republican echoed their views. Senator Henry Wilson of Massachusetts expressed the party's majority view during a tour of the South in the spring of 1867 when he announced that confiscation would only occur if former rebels attempted to undermine Reconstruction. It was Wilson's hope that such a promise would attract planter support to the party. Wilson and other Republicans worried that confiscation would harm their party in the South and urged that it not be part of any campaign. After the party suffered significant losses in the North in the 1867 election, including Senator Ben Wade's seat in Ohio, a number of Republicans singled out confiscation as one of the reasons. After the elections, legislation on confiscation found little support. Although many freedmen continued to believe and hope that the federal government would honor its commitment to confiscation, by the end of 1867 Republicans had abandoned the issue forever.[39]

Whether or not the distribution of confiscated lands to former slaves would have made a significant difference in their lives after the Civil War cannot be determined. Too little confiscation of rebel property occurred during and after the Civil War even to allow for widespread distribution. Moreover, had Lincoln lived to implement his reconstruction plans, there is no evidence to suggest he would have abandoned his aversion to confiscation either as a punishment or a method of assisting freedmen. In April 1865, for example, Lydia Maria Child observed that she was "much afraid that Lincoln's good-nature" would prevent him from understanding the importance of reconstructing the South on the basis of confiscation. Certainly Andrew Johnson believed distributing the property already confiscated would have permanently injured those rebels he wished to pardon, and hurt his plans for restoring the Union. As Attorney General Speed said to a district attorney in the spring of 1866, the administration no longer wished to implement war measures. They regarded it as "bad policy to keep up an indiscriminate persecution of those engaged in the late rebellion," and so Speed officially instructed the official "to make no further seizures of property."[40] Although the Freedmen's Bureau did not have the authority to pass on permanent titles to the small amount of land they did possess, several in the bureau nonetheless tried, for a short time, to offer the freedmen some hope of occupying land they could farm. This slim chance for freedmen to possess confiscated land also failed to materialize as Johnson intervened to assist those pardoned rebels who wished their land returned. The fervor for confiscation as both a punishment for rebels and a means to alter the South waned, in fact, as we have seen, among Republicans themselves as the war progressed.

Enthusiasm for permanent forfeiture revived for a short time in 1864, but no agreement on amending the joint resolution could be achieved. The failure to pursue this goal of permanent forfeiture as the party attacked Johnson over Reconstruction illustrated that confiscation had attracted a majority of the party, in fact, only during the year the second act passed. Johnson, therefore, was not responsible for the failure to provide land to freed slaves, although he did everything he could to prevent it. Within a few years after the war ended most Republicans came to believe that their goals for reconstruction no longer required confiscation. Many Republicans and philanthropists now argued that free labor and education would be the best means for blacks to achieve independence in the South.[41]

10 Confiscation and the Courts: Jurisdiction and Procedures

Despite the expectations of both confiscation's supporters and opponents, the Supreme Court liberally interpreted the First and Second Confiscation Acts. It granted Congress the benefit of the doubt on jurisdictional and procedural questions and accepted the constitutional argument for confiscation, thereby permitting the acts as broad a scope as their advocates could have desired. In fact, the Court often suggested that confiscation, particularly under the second act, could have been more extensive and that property taken from pardoned rebels need not have been returned. These interpretations failed to increase the effectiveness of the two acts, however, since all but a few were decided after President Andrew Johnson and Attorney General James Speed had ceased enforcing the acts. Nonetheless, the Court's interpretation of the acts was significant. It undercut President Abraham Lincoln's anxiety about duration of forfeiture and Attorney General Edward Bates's worries about procedures. Perhaps more important, the Court's discussion of the acts, particularly the second, illustrated the sloppy craftsmanship of the measures themselves, the problems that local officials faced when implementing them, and the radicals' inattention to their enforcement and failure to rescind the joint resolution governing duration. Judicial acceptance of confiscation suggested that a broader and longer confiscation of Southern property would have been acceptable had congressional Republicans been less timid and had pushed the Lincoln administration on these issues.[1]

The first major question before the courts involving confiscation was whether Congress meant to limit proceedings to admiralty, the term mentioned in both acts, or if the legislation was meant to be under common law, thus extending to a broader range of property and involving jury trials.[2] In 1863, a Tennessee resident claimed that the First Confiscation Act did not reach his real estate, because Congress had stipulated the property liable to confiscation "to be lawful subject of prize and capture wherever found," meaning only personal property found at sea. The Circuit Court of Tennessee disagreed in *United States v. Republican Banner Officers* (1863).[3] It ruled that the "mere technical sense" of the words "prize and capture" should not limit the act because Congress obviously sought to confiscate more than property at sea. Instead, Congress's intention "must have been to deter persons from using and employing" all manner of property to aid the rebellion, including real estate. The court concluded that Congress intended "prize and capture" to have the same meaning as "seizure" in the Second Confiscation Act, demonstrating its willingness to accept the broad aims of both acts.[4]

A year later, in *Mrs. Alexander's Cotton* (1864),[5] the Supreme Court expanded the definition of property liable to military capture and confiscation. According to Chief Justice Salmon P. Chase, who as secretary of the treasury was familiar with issues surrounding both confiscated and abandoned property, Mrs. Alexander's seventy-two bales of cotton constituted enemy property, even if she was not a supporter of the rebellion. (Chase, however, had made it clear he had no doubt Mrs. Alexander had been "a rebel enemy" when the second act passed.) He wrote that all people of a region in insurrection against the United States—her plantation was near Alexandria, Louisiana—had to be considered enemies until that region returned to its former allegiance. Chase cited Justice Robert Grier's opinion in the *Prize Cases* (1862)[6] to uphold the right of confiscation during a state of war and concluded that the cotton, as enemies' property, "was liable to capture and confiscation by the adverse party." Of equal importance, the chief justice dismissed Mrs. Alexander's claim that the seizure of her property by naval forces on land denied the court jurisdiction. Instead, Chase cited both the first and second acts to justify the seizure. The "capture was justified by legislation," Chase said, "as well as by public policy" as expressed in the two laws.[7] Thus, even before the war ended the Court embraced a generous view of jurisdiction under the confiscation acts.

The Supreme Court reaffirmed this broad interpretation of jurisdiction after the war in several decisions concerned with jurisdiction under the first and second act. In *Union Insurance Company v. United States* (1867)[8] the appellant argued that the Circuit Court of Louisiana had no jurisdiction over the first act because the proceedings were in admiralty, thus held without a jury, when the property seized was landed real estate. In dismissing both contentions, Chase argued the first act "must be construed with reference" to its "general purpose" which was to seize "all descriptions of property, real or personal, on land or on water" used to aid the rebellion. Even though Chase conceded the language in the first act on jurisdiction was "certainly not clear," he argued that "when we look beyond the mere words to the obvious intent," it was evident what "the sense of the law" permitted. The first act granted jurisdiction "to any District or Circuit Court having jurisdiction of the amount, or in admiralty, in any district where the property is found." Chase said the act should have used the conjunctive "and," not the disjunctive "or." Thus, said Chase, the law meant "both the Circuit and District Courts [to] have jurisdiction 'according to the amount' *and* 'in admiralty.'" Not only did this construction not injure any parties, he asserted, it also met the requirements of the second act, which said proceedings should conform as nearly as possible to "proceedings in admiralty or revenue cases."[9] In three subsequent confiscation cases Chase used the same reasoning as in *Union Insurance Company*. In effect, Chase amended the language of the first act and related it to the second, thereby giving both more latitude.[10]

In order to consider *Union Insurance Company*, the Court had ignored the normal process of appeal. District courts had original jurisdiction of cases in admiralty that could be heard by the Supreme Court on appeal. The Supreme Court normally heard cases from circuit courts only upon a writ of error.[11] But *Union Insurance Company*, a case in admiralty, came from the circuit court on appeal. Chase said the majority wanted to hear the appeal "only for the purpose of reversing the decree of the Circuit Court as irregular," thereby directing a new trial, with a jury to determine the issues of fact according to common law procedure involving property seized on land.[12] Chase and the Court, therefore, believed that proceedings under the confiscation acts could follow admiralty proceedings while the substance was of common law, although the acts did not say this.

This view received forceful expression the next year in *United States v. Athens* (1868)[13] from a district court in Georgia. In supporting the seizure of the Athens Armory, Judge Erskine ruled that Congress did not intend "to confine" prize and capture under the first act to ships and their cargoes. Congress had passed the first act, he said, to confiscate property used "in aid of the Rebellion; whether the contaminated property be found afloat, or even on shore, or even if it be land itself." To limit the proceedings to admiralty would change the intent of the law. "Statutes must not be so construed," Erskine concluded, "as to produce a result different from what was intended by the lawgiver." The proceedings under the first act, therefore, should "conform to proceedings in admiralty" only "to initiate the cause and shape it for trial." It was not within the district court's power, Erskine concluded, to say that Congress, through the first act, "contemplated the expansion of the jurisdiction of the admiralty" so that "the right of trial by jury" was removed and "the determination of the cause" by a single judge occurred. As James G. Randall noted, Erskine's position not only preserved the common law remedy "on the grounds of general justice" but also because the Judiciary Act of 1789 required that district courts should, in forfeiture cases, provide "a common law remedy" wherever possible.[14]

Chase made this issue clear in *Semple v. United States* (1868),[15] a case before the Circuit Court of Virginia under the second act. In contrast to *Union Insurance Company*, the plaintiff in *Semple* was within Confederate lines when the trial occurred in the district court, and he failed to contest any issue of fact. The case was brought to the circuit court on a writ of error, which claimed that since the proceedings on real estate were in admiralty, they were incorrect. Chase ruled in *Semple* that the trial, although in admiralty, had followed common law procedures. In other words, had the plaintiff appeared and made an issue of fact, the circuit court would have required a new trial, as in *Union Insurance Company*.[16] By these two rulings, Chase allowed district courts to decide cases of confiscated property on land where neither party raised issues of fact and guaranteed the protection of trial by jury in those cases where the parties made claims of fact on the seizure of their property. These decisions both protected individual rights when asserted and simultaneously permitted a wide application of both confiscation acts.

A year later, the Court narrowed the *Semple* view of jurisdiction in *Morris's Cotton* (1869).[17] In *Union Insurance Company* the Court had agreed to hear the appeal of an admiralty case from the circuit court so that it could remand the case for the lower court to provide a jury trial. In *Semple* no complaint about a jury could be entertained because the property owner was behind Confederate lines and did not appear. In *Morris's Cotton* the Supreme Court heard the appeal from a district court in Alabama in an admiralty case. The defendant, Morris, had asked for a jury trial regarding the facts of the seizure; the district court denied his request, although it took testimony about the cotton and its seizure. Justice Nathan Clifford, for the Supreme Court, ruled that the district court had exceeded its jurisdiction when it conducted a trial in admiralty and took testimony about the alleged facts but did not permit their evaluation by a jury. When the seizure is made on land, said Clifford, it must be prosecuted as other common law suits: with a jury. Thus, the district court lacked jurisdiction "of the cause in admiralty to render any decree upon the merits." Even though the district court lacked jurisdiction originally, the Supreme Court had the right to remand the case to that court with instructions to grant a new trial, with a jury, if the money dispersed from the sale of the cotton could be returned. Clifford's opinion affected only the procedural rights of confiscation defendants and did not limit the confiscation acts themselves.[18]

In *Ex parte Graham* (1870)[19] the Court again took a generous view of jurisdiction under the second act. Proceedings against Duncan Kenner's property in New Orleans had been held in the district court; part of the property was later sold to Marshal James Graham and L. Madison Day.[20] In February 1869 Kenner asked that the decision be reversed since, he claimed, the proceedings had been in admiralty. In November 1869 Kenner further asked that all rents and profits since the sale of the property be paid to him. The Louisiana district judge agreed that he had the jurisdiction to grant Kenner's request for "a libel of review" since the original case had been in admiralty. Justice Noah Swayne, for a unanimous Court, cited the thirteenth section of the Judiciary Act of 1789 that authorized the Court "to issue writes of prohibition to District Courts when proceeding as courts of admiralty." He also noted the second act stated that proceedings shall be in rem and "shall conform as nearly as may be to proceedings in admiralty or in revenue cases." But Swayne concluded the proceedings in district court were not in admiralty. "It is too clear to admit of doubt," Swayne concluded, that the original case against Kenner's property had not been in admiralty, so the district court could not entertain a libel of review in Kenner's behalf. The court that presided over the confiscation had therefore exercised proper jurisdiction when it proceeded against Kenner's property, even if it did not proceed as in admiralty.[21]

When property owners were denied the right to contest the seizure of their property, however, the courts did express concern. In August 1863 the government filed a libel of information under the first and second acts against 1,756 shares of the Great Western Railroad Company of Illinois owned by Leroy M. Wiley, an Alabama resident. Although Wiley submitted replies to the allegations in the information, Judge Betts of the District Court of New York ignored them, because the defendant was an "alien enemy" and was "incapable of maintaining a suit while he retains that character." Representatives of the railroad attempted to speak on Wiley's behalf, but Betts would not hear them either.[22] The case was appealed to the circuit court, where Justice Samuel Nelson reversed the decision and ordered the libel of information dismissed. Nelson observed that Betts incorrectly condemned the property under proof that was only relevant to the second act while the libel of information was issued under the first act. Moreover, the district court never acquired jurisdiction of the res, the property in Illinois, through a lawful seizure, an issue the Supreme Court would return to in later cases. The most compelling reason for Nelson's reversal, however, was the striking of Wiley's response. According to Nelson the district court should have heard the defendant's response because "the principle that an alien enemy has no standing in court . . . does not appear to have ever been applied to a claimant in admiralty." Even if Wiley was an alien enemy, "he is entitled to appear as a claimant, and contest the allegations of the libel."[23]

The issue of a rebel's standing came before the Supreme Court six years after the war in *McVeigh v. United States* (1871).[24] William McVeigh's home in Alexandria, Virginia, had been seized in 1863 on the grounds that he had been an elected official of a Confederate state, a Confederate military officer, and had not ceased his support of the Confederacy following Lincoln's proclamation of July 25, 1862. Counsel for McVeigh appeared to contest the seizure, but the government's attorney moved "that the appearance, answer, and claim" should be removed because McVeigh was a Richmond resident, now lived in the Confederacy, and was a rebel. District Judge John C. Underwood, who became known for his vigorous and improper enforcement of the second act, agreed with the government that as an enemy McVeigh had no standing unless he disavowed his allegiance to the Confederacy and ordered the property sold. A writ of error took the case to the circuit court, where Chief Justice Chase affirmed the decision in November 1864, thus allowing the case to come before the Supreme Court.[25]

Attorney General Amos Akerman argued two points for the government before the Court in 1870. An enemy had no standing in court, he said, and McVeigh's voluntary residence within the Confederate lines, which his counsel had admitted, made him an enemy. On the other hand, Akerman said, the proceedings in the district court were against the property, not McVeigh. McVeigh's counsel maintained that although his client might be a rebel and even an enemy, for the purposes of confiscating his property he also remained a citizen of the United States. As well, the second act did not authorize "a sweeping condemnation" of all rebels or enemies but "singled out persons guilty of certain offenses" and therefore McVeigh had a right to a hearing to assert his innocence. His counsel also argued that McVeigh's supposed guilt, not the property's, was in question.[26]

The Court unanimously reversed the lower court's decision. It also questioned Underwood's logic, highlighted a weakness of the second act, and remanded the case to the circuit court. Justice Swayne said that McVeigh had a right to contest the charges brought against him in district court. The case against McVeigh was "wholly unlike a proceeding purely in rem" since the court identified him as the claimant and he, through counsel, had appeared before the judgment. Swayne was also critical of Underwood's ruling. The lower court, Swayne said, "committed a serious error" in preventing McVeigh's claim from being heard. Once the government assailed him in the district court, according to Swayne, he had a right to defend himself. "The liability and the right are inseparable. A different result would be a blot upon our jurisprudence and civilization," Swayne concluded. Whether McVeigh was an alien enemy, as the government claimed, was irrelevant; being sued brought with it the right "to use all means and appliance of defense."[27] Although this decision protected those in McVeigh's position, it did not help those who had left during the war, perhaps to aid the rebellion, and were ignorant of a libel against their property. Confiscation's supporters obviously wanted to confiscate the property of men like McVeigh, but they had not written the law so as to deny them standing, except as interpreted by judges like Underwood. The second act wrongly assumed those liable to confiscation would be unaware of a libel against their property. This might have been true for those within Confederate lines, who owned property in the North, but not for someone like McVeigh, who supported the Confederacy but was aware of proceedings against his property in Virginia. Nor did the second act anticipate the Court's willingness to allow rebels to use the Constitution for protection even as they were attempting to overthrow it by force.

In October 1871 the circuit court heard the McVeigh case on remand and decided in his favor. A Mr. Gregory now occupied McVeigh's house and refused to vacate the premises. Various appeals in Virginia courts ensued and led to the case returning to the Supreme Court as *Gregory v. McVeigh* (1875).[28] The confiscation issue in *Gregory* turned on how to interpret the decision by Underwood against McVeigh. McVeigh's counsel now argued that the criticism of Underwood in *McVeigh v. United States*, which had been scathing, made the decision in the district court "a nullity." Therefore Gregory could not acquire possession and any federal question involving the second act ceased. Gregory's lawyer replied that a federal question, involving ownership gained under the second act, did exist and could be pursued. Chief Justice Morrison Waite, for a unanimous Court, supported Gregory, which meant the issue returned to Virginia yet again.[29]

The case then came back to the Supreme Court in 1876 as *Windsor v. McVeigh*,[30] with a Mr. Windsor, who occupied property originally owned by McVeigh, as the plaintiff. Where *McVeigh v. United States* involved a rebel's standing in court, *Windsor* involved the powers conferred by jurisdiction. Justice Stephen J. Field noted that Windsor's counsel believed that when the district court "has once acquired jurisdiction," it has "a right to decide every question" that arises. Even if the court's judgment was wrong it could not "be collaterally assailed," the counsel claimed. If Underwood's decision to strike McVeigh's appearance had been wrong, the court's jurisdiction still gave it the right to confiscate, to sell, and to transfer the property to Windsor and the latter's title could not be challenged. Field admitted that while such a "doctrine" was "undoubtedly right as a general proposition," it was also open to qualification. Although the court may have possessed jurisdiction of the case, and "of the parties," it was still limited in the procedures it took and judgments it reached. In other words, it had to "act judicially in all things" and not transcend the power conferred upon it. When a court ignored the "established modes" of procedure "governing" a certain type of case, then it exceeded its jurisdiction. This was true of Underwood's ruling. "It was not within the power" of the district court's jurisdiction "to proceed with the case, so as to effect" McVeigh's rights. Field concluded that by Underwood's ruling, McVeigh "was excluded from its jurisdiction."[31] *Windsor* therefore affirmed the ruling of *McVeigh v. United States* that proceedings under the second act had to admit the testimony of rebels when it was offered, in McVeigh's case by counsel, and underscored the rebels' legal protections that confiscation under the second act could not ignore.

Five years later, and sixteen years after the war ended, the New York Court of Appeals, ruling in *Chapman v. Phoenix National Bank* (1881), went even further to protect testimony from rebels.[32] Although the ruling had no impact on confiscation, it demonstrated the complications inherent in confiscating property in the United States and the persistent and perhaps misplaced concern over protecting the common law rights of supposed rebels. In 1854 Verina S. Moore, a native of Ireland teaching in North Carolina, had purchased stock in the Phoenix Bank of New York. In 1861 Moore married a Reverend Chapman. Mrs. Chapman took no part in the rebellion except, as she later said, "in common with all the better class of my sex" she "sympathized" with the South and tried "to alleviate suffering among our soldiers, and others of the needy" whenever possible. In 1864 a district attorney ordered the seizure of bank stock owned by "Ver. S. Moore," who was alleged to be an officer in the rebel army, a member of the Confederate Congress, and a state judge. When no one answered the charges in the monition, the local New York court condemned the property under the first act and its owner's liability under the second act. In reversing the lower court Judge Earl ruled the "fatal defect" of the proceedings was that "the owner of the property was in no way brought into court" and thus could not address the mistakes in the libel of information. In addition, it was the district attorney's responsibility to know the facts of the case "and until he did have such knowledge he had no right whatever, in law or morals, to take the proceeding." Earl, however, did not explain how Mrs. Chapman might have learned of the information, though he conceded that she would have found it impossible to cross enemy lines to appear. Nor did Earl correctly apply the precedents he cited on behalf of his own decision, none of which involved the pertinent issues in *Chapman*. Earl rightly observed that insufficient evidence and incorrect monition invalidated the forfeiture, but his view that no confiscation proceedings could be held without the owner's presence ignored *Semple v. United States*.[33]

Sufficiency of seizure was one of the most difficult procedural problems arising from confiscation, and it directly related to jurisdiction. The Court's sufficiency of seizure rulings also documented the difficulties officials faced in implementing the confiscation acts. One issue concerned what constituted seizure of intangible property. The initial discussion of this occurred in *Miller v. United States* (1971),[34] the most important case on confiscation. (*Miller v. United*

States also upheld the constitutionality of the confiscation acts in a split decision, which will be discussed in the next chapter.) In 1863 Michigan District Attorney Alfred Russell instructed Marshal Charles Dickey to seize, under the first and second acts, the shares in two railroad companies owned by Samuel Miller, who lived in Virginia, and leave a copy of the "said seizure" with an officer of each company. Dickey reported that he "seized said stock by serving a notice of said seizure personally upon" a vice president of one company and the president of the other. The court later instructed Dickey "to hold the said stock" and publish a notice of the seizure in a Detroit newspaper. In April 1864 Dickey reported, "I have seized and now hold all the property described" in the writ. The court subsequently condemned the property on evidence that Miller had used it to aid the rebellion and that he had served in the Confederacy in violation of the second act. Miller was not aware of the suit until August 1865, when he appealed largely on the grounds that the proceedings were invalid since Dickey never actually seized the property.[35]

The majority of the Court, in Justice William Strong's opinion, rejected Miller's contention and held that Dickey's seizure was sufficient to give the district court jurisdiction. Strong conceded that Dickey's "return did not describe the mode of seizure," but the second act required no "more than the fact [of seizure] should be stated." Proceedings under the second act were to conform to admiralty or revenue cases, where the res was usually moveable property, "as near as may be" possible. The second act sought stocks and credits but "it gave no directions respecting the mode of seizure." Although stocks prevented actual "manucaption," that did not mean they were "incapable of being seized" by the act. "Seizure may be either actual or constructive," Strong observed. "It does not always involve taking into manual possession." Strong concluded that Dickey's seizure was legitimate because the notification to the companies bound them as trustees of Miller's property to hold the stock until the court's determination, even if Miller remained ignorant of the notification until after the war. In other words, when Dickey notified the companies' officials, he seized Miller's stock and brought it under the court's control, thus establishing jurisdiction.[36] This was a generous interpretation of Congress's intentions regarding seizure under the second act and it mostly applied to intangible property in the North.

Justices Field and David Davis dissented and offered a more conservative view of how seizure should have been implemented under the second act.[37] Field argued that a valid seizure for a proceeding in rem had to dispossess the owner so that he was unable to "exercise dominion over the property." This did not occur in *Miller*, Field said, since those informed by Dickey did not possess the stocks and were not agents for Miller. Moreover, notice to the owner, which was essential, did not occur either. The notice given to the officers of the companies, said Field, could, "with equal propriety, have been given to any other strangers to the owner." Attorney General Bates, according to Field, had instructed district attorneys to seize stocks according to the laws of the states. Since Michigan had no such law, no seizure of stocks was possible. Field concluded that with such a "highly penal" law custom required that "it should be strictly construed" by the court "and a rigid compliance with its provision exacted." He did not believe this had been done. Davis, an old friend of President Lincoln, also dissented because a seizure had not occurred. Intangible property, unlike land, is not left in the care of others, Davis said; stocks travel with the owner. How then, he asked, can information to a company official give notice to the owner or bring the res, the property, within the court's control? Like Field, Davis concluded that only state law, absent in Michigan, could have satisfied the legal requirements in such a case, particularly the seizure of stocks and notice to Miller behind Confederate lines.[38]

Two later Supreme Court decisions narrowly modified the majority opinion on seizure in *Miller* but failed to reverse it. In *Alexandria v. Fairfax* (1877)[39] the Court ruled unanimously through Justice Samuel F. Miller that in proceedings against intangible property, where the owner was absent, the notice of seizure had to be served upon a specific company official in conformity with state law. Orlando Fairfax owned stock in the city of Alexandria but resided within enemy lines during the war. In 1864 the district attorney ordered the marshal to seize the stock. The marshal then gave notice of the seizure to the auditor of Alexandria. After the war Fairfax claimed the notice of seizure was invalid and had denied jurisdiction to the district court. The Supreme Court agreed; the Virginia law specified that many other officers of the corporation, but not the auditor, could have been served with such a notice. Where "actual manucaption is impossible," the Court reasoned, the seizure should be carefully examined. In *Phoenix Bank v. Risley* (1884)[40] the Court continued this line of reasoning and held that the notice of seizure had to indicate correctly whose property was subject to confiscation. The marshal's notice described the property seized as $15,000 on deposit in New York's Phoenix Bank but owned by a South Carolina bank and used to aid the rebellion. The libel of information, the Court said, suggested "the idea of tangible property, actual cash" to be taken "by manual seizure, in the hands of the Phoenix Bank," was owned by the bank in South Carolina. The reality was that Phoenix Bank had borrowed the money from the South Carolina bank, making it the owner. There was a debt, then, in the bank but no cash from the South Carolina bank; so the libel of information was incorrect. No seizure of the debt occurred; therefore, the district court did not acquire jurisdiction. Even though both decisions demonstrated the Court's annoyance at sloppy research by local officials, neither addressed the concern raised by Field and Davis over in rem proceedings of intangible property.

The Court was also asked to decide if seizing the evidence of a debt was the same as seizure of the debt itself. In *Pelham v. Rose* (1870)[41] a libel of information under the second act was issued in Indiana against some "credits and effects" of Henry Pelham, specifically a promissory note for $7,000. Pelham and his note remained in Kentucky during the war, however. The marshal, Rose, was ordered to attach the promissory note and retain it in his custody. In his return, Rose reported that he had "arrested the property" as required. The promissory note was later sold to the debtor for $3,000. After the war Pelham claimed Rose had not seized his note so the court had no jurisdiction. The Court disagreed. According to Justice Field, Rose had taken custody of the promissory note, the res "against which the proceeding" was begun, and not " 'a credit' or debt, which the note is supposed" to represent. Rose had "actual custody and control" of the note, Field said, as was evident in the return in which he said he had "arrested the property," using terms from admiralty law. In other words, Rose had seized the evidence of the debt, not the debt itself. Two years later the case returned to the court as *Pelham v. Way* (1873)[42] when Pelham asked the court for the interest that accrued after his debt had been confiscated. Justice Strong, for the Court, affirmed the first case and ruled that Pelham could not receive the debt or the interest upon it. Rose had not seized the debt, only the promissory note, "and consequently the debt was not confiscated." The debt, then, was "distinguishable from any instrument of evidence of the debt," in this case the promissory note. After the war Pelham could not, then, obtain interest on a debt that had not been confiscated. In both cases brought by Pelham the Court interpreted seizure and jurisdiction under the second act broadly.

The Court's majority reaffirmed its generous interpretation of seizure in *Tyler v. Defrees* (1871),[43] announced a week after *Miller*. Henry Tyler had left the District of Columbia and served in the Confederate navy. In 1863 Marshal Ward Lamon, an old friend of Lincoln, by authority of the district attorney, gave notice to the occupant of Tyler's house that it had been seized. However, he failed to serve the court's order of attachment on the property, which Tyler claimed in 1867 denied the court jurisdiction. Even though Justice Miller said Lamon had erred,[44] Tyler's claim had to be rejected given the second act's purpose during an "internal civil war." Alluding to the Court's support for the confiscation acts in *Miller*, Justice Miller claimed that the Court could not be governed "by a system of procedure so captious, so narrow, so difficult to understand or to execute, as to amount to a nullification of the statute." Congress could have given, Miller said, a "full code of procedure" for confiscation cases, but it chose instead to invest "the courts with discretion in that regard." Since Lamon had already seized the property, had it in his possession, and held it subject to the court's order, Miller viewed the objection by Tyler "to be as narrow and unsubstantial as the second seizure [serving the notice of attachment] would be useless." The omitted act was not necessary, Miller concluded, in this expansive interpretation of both jurisdiction and procedure under the second act.[45]

Justice Field, with Clifford concurring, strongly dissented again.[46] Field argued that Lamon had only acted as an agent of the executive under the second act when he notified the tenants and filed the libel of information with the court. His failure to follow the court's instruction to "attach the property and detain the same in his custody" meant that the court never took the res into its custody and Lamon did not become an agent of the court. For Field, "no objection is narrow and unsubstantial" when it involved jurisdiction of a court over property where the owner was incapable of appearance or defense. Lamon's second seizure was required by law, said Field, and its absence denied the court jurisdiction. The second act, he said echoing his view in *Miller*, was "highly penal" and its "every requirement should be rigidly exacted." Field's anger at the majority's relaxed attitudes on procedure may have owed more to his disagreement over the larger issue of the Court's acceptance of confiscation's constitutionality. Lamon, after all, had published a notice of the property's seizure for Tyler's benefit. Tyler's failure to appear and defend himself did not result from Lamon's neglect in serving notice of attachment to the tenants. Whatever prevented Tyler from appearing and defending himself, it was not the court's lack of jurisdiction.

A year later, *Brown v. Kennedy* (1872)[47] presented the Court with a case similar to *Pelham* and the question of whether jurisdiction had been achieved with the seizure of an absentee owner's property. In 1859–60, Virginian Edward S. Brown had made loans to a number of people in Leavenworth, Kansas, including Lawrence and Eliza Kennedy. In 1863 a Kansas marshal was instructed to seize "the estate, property, claim, credits and rights thereto and therein belonging" to Brown, who remained in Virginia during the war. Brown received a pardon in 1868 and, citing the *Pelham* decisions, claimed that the court had not acquired jurisdiction since no seizure had occurred of his bond and mortgage, which had been in Virginia. The Court, in the opinion by Justice Strong, disagreed. Whereas the debt in *Pelham v. Rose* had not been part of the marshal's warrant, that was not true in *Brown*, Strong said. The marshal had been explicitly directed to seize both the debt and "the written evidence of the debt." The marshal's return said he had "attached the bond, mortgage, and credit," and the court then condemned all three. Strong cited the *Miller* ruling that, as he wrote, "seizure could be made without manual caption of the visible evidences of the credit." "What is the credit in a bond and mortgage," Strong asked, "if it is not the debt secured or evidence by them?" Moreover, Brown in effect had accepted the validity of the property's condemnation when he had asked the court for the proceeds from it. The majority in *Brown* went well beyond the *Pelham* cases in its willingness to grant jurisdiction by interpreting seizure in a way that facilitated confiscation in ambiguous circumstances the second act had failed to anticipate.[48]

The court's tolerance for procedural errors in *Tyler* was even more pronounced in *The Confiscation Cases* (1873),[49] in which the Court affirmed the confiscation of John Slidell's property, and others, in New Orleans. (Slidell had been a principal in the *Trent* affair and the Confederate ambassador to France.) The case came to the Court on appeal from the circuit court decision of Justice Joseph Bradley in favor of Slidell, who claimed, among other things, that District Attorney Rufus Waples's libel of information against him had been defective.[50] Bradley certainly agreed. Waples's libel of information, said Bradley, "is one of the most remarkable specimens of loose pleading and uncertain statement that I remember ever to have seen." The justice wondered if "from this allegation any mortal can tell what John Slidell did" to have his property seized under the second act. "The extreme ambiguity of these charges is something more than a matter of form," Bradley observed, "it amounts to a substantial defect." "There is no charge that Slidell acted as a foreign minister of the Confederacy. The allegation is that he either did that or something else," Bradley concluded, "but we are not informed what." When the case came to the Supreme Court, however, Bradley took no part in the decision.[51]

Justice Strong, in a 5–3 decision, swept aside Bradley's concerns over the libel of information, the basis for his decision.[52] Since the second act specified classes of people whose property was liable to confiscation, the government only had "to aver or prove" that the property in question belonged to someone identified in the act. "It may be," Strong conceded, "the information might have been more" carefully drawn by Waples, but the failure of Slidell and the others to appear and question the information's errors rendered them "mere formal faults" that were "of no importance." These faults "cannot have injured any one." In arguing his case before the Supreme Court Slidell had also claimed that other procedural errors denied the original court jurisdiction and invalidated the seizure of his property. Although on each point Strong admitted the substance of Slidell's complaint, he dismissed them all as insignificant, harmless, or already decided in *Miller*. Slidell, for instance, argued that the district court had conducted the suit in admiralty and not in common law. Strong agreed that seizures on land should be conducted on "the common law side of the court, and such, *in substance*, was, we think, the case here." To Slidell's objection that the clerk of the court had failed to sign the requisite documents, Strong said the signature of the deputy clerk "was sufficient." For the Court's majority the numerous technical problems with the procedures followed in seizing Slidell's property were not that important in the wake of *Miller* and the obvious role that Slidell had in the Confederacy. Justices Clifford and Field could not agree and dissented over these very failures to observe strict procedural requirements.[53]

Except for concerns about the right of rebels to testify against the confiscation of their property, the solicitude of the lower courts and the Supreme Court over jurisdiction and procedure under the first and second acts was pronounced. Although all but one of the decisions came after the war and could not have enlarged the scope of enforcement, they demonstrated strong support for the goals of confiscation so long as basic common law guarantees prevailed. The courts permitted a wide jurisdiction for in rem proceedings against all types of property seized and, for the most part, generously interpreted Congress's intent even when its language had not been clear or appropriate to the task. The decisions also expressed sympathy for those authorized to administer confiscation, accepted a variety of procedures to do so, and demonstrated that both the legislative and executive branches need not have been so timid in drafting and enforcing the First and Second Confiscation Acts. This support of confiscation was just as pronounced on the issue of constitutionality.

11 Confiscation and the Courts: Constitutionality and Duration

The Supreme Court's decisions on substantive confiscation issues were important for several reasons. The support for confiscation's constitutionality in *Miller v. United States* (1870)[1] vindicated those who had proposed and supported the First and Second Confiscation Acts in Congress. Although two justices did dissent in *Miller* over its constitutionality, the majority's view demonstrated a support for wider measures on behalf of the North's cause. Support for its constitutionality did not increase the amount confiscated during the war, but it did curtail the number of rebels who contested the loss of their property. Of equal significance, other substantive decisions on forfeiture of fee and pardons indicated the Court believed Congress had not reached the constitutional limits of what could have been achieved through confiscation. Although the Court nowhere endorsed permanent confiscation or limited the benefits due pardoned rebels, its decisions demonstrated an acceptance of congressional intent as a justification for constitutionality. The Court's decisions implied, in other words, that had Congress explicitly enacted confiscation beyond the life of the offender, it would have received a sympathetic hearing. In the end, the Court's decisions on substantive confiscation, like those on jurisdiction and procedure, demonstrated the timidity of the laws' authors.

The central constitutional issue in *Miller v. United States* was whether the confiscation acts were criminal statutes enacted under the municipal power of Congress to punish crimes against the United States or legislated under the war powers of the government. In the *Prize Cases* (1863),[2] the Court had ruled, albeit by a bare majority, that the United States was a belligerent power in the Civil War and competent to use its war powers to defeat the rebellion. Moreover, said Justice Robert Grier, the government had the right "to cripple" the enemy's resources "by the seizure or destruction of his property" as "a necessary result of a state of war." Justice William Strong observed at the start of his majority opinion in *Miller*[3] that if the acts were simply municipal regulations there "would be force" to Samuel Miller's claim that his rights under the Fifth and Sixth amendments had been violated. (The Fifth Amendment guarantees that no person shall "be deprived of life, liberty, or property, without due process of law," while the Sixth Amendment guarantees "the accused shall enjoy the right to a speedy and public trial, by an impartial jury" in the state where the crime supposedly occurred.) Strong found no justice in Miller's claim, however. "The whole doctrine of confiscation," he argued, rested "upon the foundation" that it was an "instrument of coercion" used to deprive the enemy of property. That certainly defined the intent of the first act; it "was aimed exclusively at the seizure and confiscation of property" meant "to aid, abet, or promote the rebellion, then a war, or to maintain the war against the government." Only the property was guilty under the first act. "It cannot be maintained," Strong concluded on the first act, "that there is no power to seize property actually employed" in a war against the government.

It was the constitutionality of the second act, Strong observed, that was most "assailed."[4] He conceded that the first four sections of the act were "aimed at individual offenders" and "undoubtedly" derived from "the sovereign, not the belligerent rights of the government." These four sections of the act involved criminal law, authorizing prosecution of offenders for their behavior. Unlike the first four sections, which were meant to "punish treason and rebellion," sections five through ten were to seize and confiscate the property of rebels. The "avowed purpose" of these sections was not "to reach any criminal personally," but to end the rebellion "then present, which was a war," as both Congress and the Court had recognized. These six sections involved civil law.[5] Nor did the omission of the word *enemy* make the second act a municipal measure, as Justice Field would claim in his dissent. The rebellion was a war, Strong said, and "those engaged in it were public enemies." And "they are not less such because they are also rebels." Rebels and enemies were synonymous in this rebellion, Strong concluded. He also dismissed the argument that confiscating the property of those living outside the Confederacy rendered the measure invalid because the laws of war did not view these persons as enemies. Those who united "themselves to the cause of a foreign enemy," said Strong, could not be "permitted to claim exemptions" which those inside the Confederacy did not possess. To take their property was to "strike a blow against the hostile power" equal to that of "confiscating the property of a non-combatant resident." Strong was impressed that the Constitution had been written after confiscating the property of various classes during the Revolution. Those confiscation laws demonstrated then "the general understanding that aiders and abettors of the public enemy were themselves enemies" and their property therefore liable to seizure, but not for treason. Following the Revolution, the Constitution prohibited ex post facto laws and bills of attainder but "it imposed no restriction upon the power to prosecute war or confiscate enemy's property." Finally, Strong rejected the claim that the description of certain persons whose property was liable to confiscation, in section five, proved Congress meant to punish criminal acts rather than to seize enemy property. "Plainly it was competent for Congress to determine how far it would exert belligerent rights" and it was "too large a deduction" to conclude Congress meant not "to confiscate the property of enemies at all" simply because it limited those liable under the act.

James G. Randall, the most important scholar on the history of confiscation, was very critical of Strong's argument and praised Field's dissent.[6] For Randall, Strong's decision suffered because it "plainly rested the authorization for the acts upon the law of nations" and thus relied upon a controversial "presumption." Randall's reading of the authorities on confiscation—Hugo Grotius, Emerich de Vattell, and Baron von Pufendorf—persuaded him that there was no "noticeable preponderance of legal opinion on the side of confiscation as a belligerent right." Instead, it required a "sympathetic editing" of these scholars for Strong and others to conclude that the Union had the belligerent right, based on international law, to confiscate the private property of those who supported the Confederacy. Randall was equally doubtful of the American precedents that supporters of confiscation invoked. Although he conceded that *Ware v. Hylton* (1796)[7] supported confiscation, at least of moveable property, Randall was critical of the central precedent, *Brown v. United States*,[8] which many supporters of confiscation invoked. In Randall's view John Marshall's majority opinion and Joseph Story's dissent in *Brown*, both of which upheld the right to confiscate, relied upon authorities that authorized capture during war, not confiscation. Finally, Randall argued that while Chancellor Kent in the 1820s generally supported confiscation, Henry Wheaton, writing in the 1850s, believed the executive had only a qualified right to implement confiscation. Randall's conclusion was, therefore, that Congress's right to pass the confiscation acts, despite Strong's opinion, was ambiguous at best.

Notwithstanding Randall's excellent scholarship on confiscation's history before the Civil War, his analysis of Strong's opinion was flawed. Randall rightly noted that Strong said that confiscation had always been "an undoubted belligerent right," but the justice based his claim on the Constitution, not on the law of nations. As Strong observed, "any uncertainty" about the belligerent right was "set at rest by the express grant" in the Constitution "to make rules respecting captures on land and water." The argument that the law of nations governed the prosecution of that power was simply not relevant. "Whether this is so or not we do not care to inquire," Strong concluded, "for it is not necessary to the present case."[9] Nor did Strong discuss *Brown v. United States*. Instead, Strong argued that the right to capture and confiscate "in a foreign war" was applicable to "a civil war of equal dimensions" and required "the employment of all means to weaken the belligerent" armed against the government. "Every reason" to confiscate in a foreign war "exists in full force when the war is domestic or civil," the justice concluded.[10] Randall's antipathy to the premise of confiscation led him to cite precedents against the right to confiscation that even the acts' opponents in Congress and Justices Field and Clifford, who dissented in *Miller*, did not use in their own arguments.

Strong's decision also indicated that the Court's majority might have supported a more comprehensive law. Congressional moderates, of course, had forced confiscation's advocates to limit those whose property could be liable to seizure depending on whether or not they resumed allegiance to the Union sixty days after a presidential proclamation. Moderates argued that not all Southerners should be punished for the crimes of a few and that the North would win just as quickly if only prominent rebels suffered confiscation. Believing they lacked sufficient support in the House or Senate for a more inclusive measure, confiscation's advocates compromised and reduced the number of individuals unconditionally liable under the second act. The majority in *Miller*, however, suggested that the Court might have accepted a stronger measure if moderates had accepted unconditional confiscation of Southern property. As Strong observed near the end of his opinion, it was wrong to infer from the limited reach of the second act that Congress could not have defined enemies more broadly and confiscated a wider swath of property. "Plainly," he said, "it was competent for Congress to determine how far it would exert belligerent rights," and that meant it could have enlarged the number of enemies enumerated in the fifth, sixth and seventh sections of the law.[11] The possibilities for confiscation, and therefore for Reconstruction, under such a measure would obviously have been greater than occurred under the second act, assuming Lincoln would have implemented such a law.

In his lengthy dissent, Justice Field ignored the first act and attacked the majority's opinion that the second act related to enemies and not individuals criminally liable under the law.[12] Field readily conceded that the inhabitants of the Confederacy were public enemies and that the Constitution granted Congress the authority to "apply to them all the harsh measures justified by the rules of war," including confiscation, so long as the measures conformed to the law of nations. However, the second act confiscated property only because certain individuals committed overt acts of treason, Field said, not because they were enemies. Even the act's title, Field noted, failed to mention enemies. The stated purpose was "to suppress insurrection, to punish treason and rebellion, to seize and confiscate the property of rebels, and for other purposes." The second act therefore confiscated property only because certain individuals committed treason. It contained no directions to seize the property of enemies, the justice explained, "but only of persons who may thereafter violate provisions of the act." Field argued that "there is not a single clause" in the act to signify that "it was against public enemies [that] its provisions were directed." Clearly, then, Congress enacted the act under its municipal power to punish offenses against the United States, not by authority of its war powers. Field found further support for this view in the joint resolution Congress passed, under the threat of Lincoln's veto, to prevent forfeiture beyond the life of the offender. Under the law of nations, Field observed, words such as *forfeiture* and *offender* are not found in the confiscation of enemies' property; they are "exclusively applicable to punishment of crimes." If Congress had not agreed with Lincoln that the second act was penal, Field concluded, it would not have agreed to the joint resolution. In sum, for Field the second act violated Miller's criminal rights under the Fifth and Sixth Amendments, guaranteeing due process and a speedy and public trial by an impartial jury in the locale where the offense was committed, and was therefore unconstitutional.[13]

Field's dissent revolved around the definition of "enemy," whether the act of rebellion constituted a criminal offense and an apparent misreading of the act itself. As he noted, the word "enemy" only appeared in the seventh section, which authorized the courts to condemn those things seized "as enemies' property."[14] He believed, incorrectly it appears, that this was conclusive evidence that Congress passed the act to punish "offences against the United States," not to confiscate the property of public enemies. Justice Strong had conceded that the first four sections enumerated specific crimes but emphasized that the fifth through the tenth sections proposed confiscation of property for those who participated in the rebellion or gave aid and comfort to it, with the implication that those who did so were enemies. Field failed to observe that sections one through four defined treason but did not mention confiscation, while sections five through seven made no mention of treason but enumerated those liable to confiscation by their support of the rebellion. These sections defined no other offenses that warranted confiscation. Although section five listed six categories of individuals subject to confiscation, Congress enumerated these persons so they would not have the opportunity to escape confiscation by returning to their former allegiance within sixty days of the president's proclamation as would the rest of the Confederate supporters described in section six. It seems clear, then, that Congress viewed all those enumerated in sections five through ten as rebels and/or enemies and their property as subject to confiscation for the same offense: aid and comfort for the rebellion. In Congress's view, they were waging war, by armed rebellion, against the United States. Congress made only one exception in this group: the most prominent rebels could not escape confiscation even if they did not return to their former allegiance within sixty days after the president's proclamation. In conformity with the second act's purpose—"to insure the speedy termination of the present rebellion"—Congress afforded the majority of Confederate sympathizers the opportunity to renew their former allegiance, thereby hastening the war's end.

It followed from Field's dissent over constitutionality that he would also enumerate the supposed due process violations of the in rem proceedings in the second act.[15] According to Field, property subject to in rem proceedings was that which was guilty. "The thing is the instrument of wrong, and is forfeited by reason of the unlawful use," he said. Smuggled goods, for example, were subject to in rem proceedings. Proceedings could also occur against the smuggler, if caught, but "the proceedings in rem are wholly independent of, and unaffected by, the criminal proceedings against the person." Field's interpretation of the second act required that the guilt of the person had to be established in order to confiscate the property and that guilt could be established only with the conviction of the offender "according to the forms of the Constitution." In other words, Field denied that property could be condemned upon evidence taken by default because the owner was absent and had not been described as an enemy in the act. To accept Field's position would have eliminated in rem proceedings and rendered the second act virtually inoperative. His interpretation would have enlarged the *McVeigh* ruling to insure that no condemnation occurred unless the court heard the owner's defense. It also suggested that Field failed to appreciate the circumstances of the Civil War that prompted the confiscation acts or accept the Court's opinion in the *Prize Cases*, where the court said one could be both a rebel and a belligerent.[16] Although he conceded that rebels in the Confederacy were public enemies and that Congress had the authority to confiscate their property for the act of rebellion, he demanded that they be treated as if no war existed or they could appear for proceedings if notified. Except for Clifford's concurrence, the majority of the court rejected Field's interpretation of in rem proceedings under the second act.[17]

The question of duration of forfeiture was almost as important an issue as that of the second act's constitutionality and was certainly more complicated. Congress, of course, had passed the joint resolution to satisfy Lincoln's concern over this issue, although at the time a number of senators claimed the resolution had no bearing on duration and dealt only with treason. Later William Whiting, L. Madison Day, and Rufus Waples also argued that the joint resolution only related to treason and was not applicable to sections five through ten of the second act, which involved confiscation for support of the rebellion. Although their interest in confiscation during the war raises doubts about their objectivity, their arguments about duration are still impressive.[18] In November 1863 Judge John C. Underwood of the United States District Court for the eastern district of Virginia had also decided in *United States v. Latham* that absolute forfeiture was permissible. According to Underwood, the Constitution, the second act, and the joint resolution all allowed forfeiture beyond the life of the offender. For Underwood, the Constitution's phrase "no attainder of treason shall work corruption of blood or forfeiture, except during the life of the person attainted," simply meant that the actual forfeiture should occur during the life of the person, not after his death. To Underwood, "except during" indicated the legal act of forfeiture and did not relate to its length. The joint resolution, by Underwood's logic, simply made the second act consistent with this clause. As a result, Underwood ruled that the fee simple had been confiscated and went to the highest bidder when the property was sold. No other judges, however, followed Underwood's reasoning.[19]

Bigelow v. Forrest (1869)[20] was the first case involving duration the Supreme Court heard, and the Court unanimously ruled that the joint resolution limited confiscation to the offender's life. The case involved property seized from French Forrest, who had served in the Confederate navy. Following Forrest's death, his son Douglass asked the court to eject Mr. Bigelow from the property he had purchased following its confiscation. Bigelow, however, claimed that he had lawfully purchased "all the right, title, and interest" of Forrest's property and used Underwood's reasoning on bills of attainder to support his plea. According to Bigelow, the "true construction" of the attainder clause should be that "no attainder of treason should work a forfeiture *except during* the life of the person attainted; that is, that it should be done during his life." He also contended that because the joint resolution had been "passed out of superfluous caution" by Congress, "to keep the act within the limits of the Constitution," it should be ignored. Any "construction" of Congress's intent that limited the purchase of all Forrest's property "would defeat the object of the bill, which was to raise money for the support of the army." The act declared that "*all* the property shall be seized, and the *same* shall be condemned," said Bigelow. He closed with a prediction that any decision that deprived him of the fee would lead "into difficulties which cannot be solved by any known rules of law."[21] Subsequent decisions by the Court on possession of the fee proved Forrest's prediction accurate.

Justice Strong rejected Bigelow's claims and concluded that Congress clearly meant to limit the duration of forfeiture. Although the district court had said that the case involved the "United States against all the right, title, interest and estate" of Forrest, this language was merely descriptive according to Strong. The lower court, argued Strong, had no power to sell the fee simple. The court's proceeding was only against the property, not the estate of Forrest and the confiscation was only of Forrest's land, not his fee. The history surrounding the joint resolution, Strong said, left no doubt that "the act and the resolution are to be construed together" and that only "a right to the property seized" could be conveyed to the purchaser. This right, therefore, ended upon the death of the person from whom the property had been confiscated, as the joint resolution stipulated. "The punishment inflicted upon" Forrest, Strong said, "is not to descend upon his children. His heritable blood is not corrupted." The justice ended his opinion with a swipe at those, like Underwood, who suggested the fee had been seized during the owner's life. "Such speculations may be curious," Strong concluded, "but they are not practical, and they can give no aid in ascertaining the meaning of the statute."[22] In addition to dismissing Underwood's logic and separating the property from the fee, Strong's opinion established the inseparability of the second act and the joint resolution, thereby limiting the duration of forfeiture to the offender's life. Strong ignored the argument, made at the time and subsequently by Whiting, Day, and Waples, that the first four sections of the second act were directed at treason and the next five sections at enemies' property. Strong's implication that the resolution necessitated the court's interpretation on duration highlighted confiscation supporters' failure to repeal the joint resolution.[23]

The Court refused to speculate in *Bigelow* on where the fee resided during the life of the offender, although it was crucial to the question of duration. Those who bought confiscated property claimed that the fee remained with the property's owner and could be sold. The Court subsequently struggled with this issue and resolved it with a novel interpretation of the joint resolution. In *Day v. Micou* (1873),[24] property owned by Judah P. Benjamin, a high official in the Confederacy, had been mortgaged to Mrs. William Micou before the war. The property was then confiscated, condemned by in rem proceedings, and sold to L. Madison Day in 1865.[25] When Micou filed a foreclosure against the property in 1868, Day claimed that his deed from the sale had given him the fee. According to Day, the joint resolution only applied to the first four sections of the second act that were designed to punish "treason and rebellion." These sections were "an exercise of sovereign authority" and constituted "the criminal portion of the act." The other sections provided "for the seizure and condemnation" of enemies' property as a "belligerent right" in time of war. Day therefore claimed that the fee had been confiscated and he had subsequently purchased it. Justice Strong, for a unanimous Court, disagreed; Micou's mortgage had not been part of the property and estate that Day had purchased. The second act "manifestly contemplated no seizure of anything more than that which belonged to the offending person," Strong concluded. Unlike admiralty and revenue cases where the fee could be sold, only Benjamin's property and estate could be passed to Day.[26] The implication in *Bigelow* and more so in *Day*, however, was that the fee remained in the offender's possession after the property's sale, a finding that would have surprised those who supported confiscation.

The Court appeared to solve the question of the fee's location in *Wallach et al. v. Van Riswick* (1875),[27] but the ruling proved too problematic to endure. Justice Strong, for a unanimous court, now held that the fee remained suspended between the property's condemnation and the offender's death, whereupon it went to the offenders' heirs. Before the seizure of his property, Charles Wallach, a Confederate army officer, had mortgaged it to Van Riswick in partial payment of a promissory note the former had borrowed. Van Riswick then bought the remaining interest of the property in the confiscation sale. After the war Van Riswick purchased a deed from Wallach that he claimed conveyed the fee simple of the property to him. But upon Wallach's death in 1872 his heirs demanded the property, claiming that the estate, the fee, had been vested in the United States after confiscation and that it reverted to them when he died. Van Riswick countered that the confiscation proceedings "carved a life estate out of the fee," leaving the fee with Wallach, who had the power to convey it to him, the defendant. Van Riswick also argued that the joint resolution only prohibited confiscation proceedings from forfeiting real estate beyond Wallach's life but had no effect on Wallach's ownership of the fee.[28]

Strong's opinion supported Wallach's heirs by declaring that the act and the joint resolution should be considered as one and ruled that Wallach retained no connection to the fee after the property had been confiscated.[29] The joint resolution had to be understood "in accord with the general and leading purpose" of the act, which "was to strengthen the government and enfeeble the public enemy," by taking away his property. The Court, therefore, could not agree that the joint resolution allowed Wallach to possess the fee after the condemnation and sale of his life estate. The joint resolution "made no attempt to divide the estate confiscated into one for life, and another in fee." The act of confiscation, Strong said, left Wallach "no estate or interest of any description which he could convey by deed." Congress meant the joint resolution "exclusively" for the benefit of the heirs, to acquire the property upon the offender's death. *Bigelow* and *Day* had unfortunately created the impression, Strong said, that "what was sold under the confiscation acts was a life-estate carved out of a fee," which repeated the phrase used by Van Riswick. Strong now regretted his "language" in these two opinions that "was, perhaps, incautiously used." The Court did not mean to say that there was "anything left in the person [Wallach] whose estate had been confiscated." However, Strong did not say where the fee resided. It was noteworthy that in *Wallach* the Court used the second act to interpret the joint resolution, not the other way around, as Lincoln and Congress had intended.[30]

In divesting the fee from Wallach and ruling for the heirs, Strong devised the notion—contrary to the common law, as he himself observed in *Wallach*—

that a fee could be in abeyance.[31] That is, the fee existed in Wallach, but no one, least of all Wallach, could exercise it until his death. This did not resolve the issue of what rights, if any, heirs had to the property before their ancestor's death and from whom the heirs received the fee. This issue was decided in *Pike v. Wassell* (1876).[32] Albert Pike's property in Arkansas had been confiscated and sold to Wassell, who refused to pay taxes on it, whereupon Luther Pike, Albert's son, sued to have the taxes paid. To block the suit Wassell claimed Pike's children had no interest in the property while Albert Pike still lived. Chief Justice Morrison Waite, for a unanimous Court, disagreed; Pike's prospective heirs had a legal right to demand payment of the taxes until they acquired the property following their father's death. Failure to pay taxes, the court ruled, would subject the property to encumbrance and jeopardize the heirs' rights to inheritance. If Pike's children "do not hold the fee," Waite said, "they are certainly the only persons now living who represent those for whose benefit" Congress passed the joint resolution.[33] With *Pike* the mystery in *Wallach* of the fee's location was narrowed; *Pike* suggested that it resided with the heirs.

Three further cases clarified the status of the fee after the confiscated property was sold. In *French v. Wade* (1880),[34] the Court held that an offender under the second act who bought his own property after its condemnation could not thereby possess the fee and therefore could not sell it. "Another [person] could not, after purchase, have sold and conveyed the interest of the heirs in the property; neither can" Wade do so, the Court concluded. Apparently the fee did not reside with the offender during his life. *Avengo v. Schmidt* (1884)[35] and *Shields v. Schiff* (1887)[36] held that the fee devolved upon the heirs at the death of the offender as a right of descent and was not held in special trust by the government. This meant that the heirs had to honor the mortgages their ancestors made before the property was confiscated. As the lower court in Louisiana noted in *Shields*, "it matters not where the fee resided. Wherever it was . . . it remained subject to prior mortgages and privileges in favor of third persons" who held the mortgages.[37] The question of what happened to the fee after condemnation proceedings remained unanswered, however.

The court tried to resolve the confusion in *Illinois Central Railroad Company v. Bosworth* (1889).[38] A. W. Bosworth, whose property had been confiscated and sold, received a special pardon from President Johnson in 1865 and was included in the proclamation of amnesty and pardon in 1868. In 1871 Bosworth sold his property, which Illinois Central Railroad eventually came to own. After Bosworth died in 1885, his sons filed for possession of the land, claiming that confiscation left their father no power over the fee and the pardon did not allow him abrogate the joint resolution, which guaranteed their possession of confiscated property upon their father's death. For Justice Joseph Bradley, the central question was whether the pardon and amnesty restored control over the fee to Bosworth. After reviewing the Court's previous interpretations of the disposition of the fee, Bradley said that "the naked fee," after the confiscation of the property, "remained in the offender himself; otherwise how could his heirs take it from him by inheritance?" However, the offender was unable to touch the fee during his life and so it remained "a mere dead estate, or in a condition of suspended animation." The pardon, however, restored to him "the control of his property" as if it had "never been forfeited or vested in" someone else by sale. Thus Bosworth's heirs had no claim to the property, whose fee had been rightfully sold by Bosworth himself in 1871.[39] The irony of *Illinois Central* was that it located the fee in abeyance as *Wallach* had done, but at the expense of the heirs after a pardon, thus reversing the outcome of *Wallach* and ignoring the joint resolution.

Two more cases completed the reversal of *Wallach* and the destruction of the joint resolution. In *Jenkins v. Collard* (1891)[40] Justice Field, the only remaining member of the Court who had heard the first confiscation cases, ruled that the pardon Thomas Jenkins received, granted after he deeded his confiscated property, entitled him to transfer the fee. Jenkins's property had been confiscated and then sold during the war to Edward Bepler. In August 1865 Jenkins deeded his fee simple to William Collard. Upon Jenkins's death in 1872, his heirs claimed the property. The Court, however, held that the pardon of December 1865 and the general amnesty of 1868 had removed the inability of Jenkins to deed his fee and allowed him, in effect, to disinherit his heirs. Although Jenkins had no power to dispose of the fee during his life, the fee remained with him after confiscation and he could deed it as he wished. In other words, Bepler retained the life estate until Jenkins's death, whereupon the deed to Collard took effect.

In *United States v. Dunnington* (1892)[41] the reversal of *Wallach* was completed. Charles Dunnington, a supporter of the Confederacy, had property in the District of Columbia, near the Capitol, confiscated during the war; A. R. Shepherd purchased it. In 1872 Congress authorized the purchase of the property, including the fee, to enlarge the grounds of the Capitol. Neither Dunnington nor his heirs appeared in 1873 to contest the sale or question its appraised value. When Dunnington died in 1887 his heirs claimed that their father and they had had no right to intervene in 1873, since they had no interest in the forfeited estate. They now required the government to pay them what the property cost. Justice Henry Brown disagreed in a unanimous decision against the Dunnington heirs. He proclaimed that "we think the doctrine was too broadly stated" in *Wallach* that the owner lost "every vestige of propriety right over the property" because of confiscation. In other words, Charles Dunnington and his heirs had a right to appear at the sale in 1873. Their failure to do so waived any future claims. Even though the theory "that the fee can never be in abeyance" was "somewhat fanciful," Brown said, it derived from the sound idea that there should "always be someone in existence to represent it" and protect it for the heirs. Moreover, President Johnson's amnesty and pardon proclamation of 1868 had restored to Dunnington the power to dispose of the fee. The failure of Dunnington to do so, therefore, vested the fee in the United States at that time, depriving his heirs of it when he died in 1883.[42] Like *Illinois Central* and *Bigelow*, *Dunnington* ignored the joint resolution, which had been seen in *Forrest* as a means to insure that heirs inherited the offender's property upon his death. The irony of all this was considerable. The second act had been enacted to deprive rebels of the ability to use property during their lives yet these decisions allowed them to dispose of their property before death. The decisions also denied what the joint resolution had intended, that heirs receive the property that had been confiscated. At the same time, of course, the ruling came thirty years after the second act had been enacted.

The Supreme Court only ruled on duration of fee under the first act in *Kirk v. Lynd* (1882).[43] For a unanimous Court, Chief Justice Waite said that the fee passed absolutely to the purchaser of the property seized, condemned, and sold under the act of August 6, 1861. The Constitution, said Waite, gave Congress "express authority" to make the rules about captures on both land and water, and the first act was "manifestly an exercise of this power." Waite quoted part of Justice Strong's opinion in *Miller* to explain the first act and its treatment of the property, not the person, as the guilty subject. Once the "hostile use with the owner's consent was established" in court, Waite said, then the title to the property, the fee, could be sold. Under the first act, Waite observed, property was not taken, no "more than the life of a soldier slain in battle," to punish the owner. Both were taken only to decrease the enemy's strength. Near the end of his opinion Waite implied, in fact, that the majority in *Miller* had been wrong to accept the second act's constitutionality, since its intent "was to punish the owner for countenancing the rebellion." That was why the joint resolution had been passed, Waite argued. Such a resolution was unnecessary with the first act, however, "because that had reference only to the capture and condemnation of property for its unlawful use."[44]

The irony of the *Kirk* ruling was that it sustained forfeitures of fee under the first act, even though the second act was passed to replace the first act because it appeared ineffective to confiscation's supporters. *Kirk* thereby underscored the sloppy thinking of confiscation's supporters. They believed the first act unsuccessful, but the Court held that it, not the second act, accomplished the absolute forfeiture they believed essential to punish and reconstruct the South.

Confiscation's advocates tried, without notable success, to design the second act to confiscate property and the fee beyond the life of the offender but then succumbed to pressure and adopted a joint resolution that, the Court said, nullified these ends. Even the joint resolution proved less effective than anticipated when Van Riswick argued that it allowed a convicted rebel to retain the fee after his property had been condemned. Over time, in fact, the Court came to agree with Van Riswick's argument that the second act, when understood in the light of the joint resolution, did not divest the rebel of the fee until his death. In *Collard* and *Dunnington* the fee remained with the offender, which directly contradicted one of the goals of the second act. Although confiscation's advocates were obviously not responsible for the Supreme Court's interpretation of fee under the second act and joint resolution, their lack of precision in drafting the law and joint resolution certainly allowed the Court to find its own conclusion on where the fee resided after condemnation.

The last major confiscation question before the Supreme Court concerned how pardons affected the property rights of those who suffered confiscation.[45] Before the Court had an opportunity to consider this issue, however, Congress moved to limit President Johnson's pardoning power.[46] In May 1865 Johnson had offered plans for Reconstruction and amnesty that many Republicans thought were too generous. In the spring of 1866, in discussions of the Fourteenth Amendment, a number of House members had expressed concern over the number of pardons Johnson had issued. On December 3, 1866, the first day of the Thirty-ninth Congress's second session, Representative Thomas Eliot (R.-Mass.), a supporter of confiscation, proposed repeal of the second act's thirteenth section, which authorized the president to pardon rebels at his discretion. The House passed the measure the same day without discussion. It had been evident from earlier debates that many were willing to restrict Johnson's authority to pardon.[47] The Senate, by contrast, discussed the measure, but only a few members believed that the president's power could be curtailed. Republican Jacob Howard of Michigan was alone in the view that the thirteenth section of the second act gave the president powers not conferred upon him by the Constitution. Democrat Reverdy Johnson of Maryland, on the other hand, thought the Constitution gave the president absolute pardon authority and that any effort to diminish it was meaningless. Although Lyman Trumbull, the author of the second act, agreed with Senator Johnson's position, he believed that Congress should pass the repeal to register opposition to the president's restoration of property to pardoned rebels. At the same time Trumbull expressed his disappointment over how confiscation had unfolded: "The confiscation bill which did pass was emasculated and not effective; such as it was, it has never been sufficiently executed." On January 4, 1867, the Senate also agreed to the repeal the thirteenth section of the act.[48] Congress's failure to rescind the joint resolution prohibiting permanent confiscation made their desire to limit Johnson's pardoning power academic, however.[49]

The first significant confiscation case involving pardon was perhaps the most remarkable. Although there had been widespread agreement in Congress and the Supreme Court that forfeiture under the first act was absolute due to the property's guilt, the ruling in *Armstrong's Foundry* (1867)[50] held that a pardon allowed for the restoration of confiscated property. Attorney General Stanbery argued for the government that no pardon could restore Armstrong's property since he had committed no wrong. It was the "unlawful predicament in which the property" was found which prompted the forfeiture, said Stanbery. Salmon P. Chase, onetime secretary of the treasury and now chief justice of the Supreme Court, disagreed. Clearly, he said, the first act "regarded the consent of the owner to the employment of his property as an offence" and its forfeiture was the penalty.[51] Subsequent decisions by the Court in *Miller v. United States* (1870) and *Kirk v. Lynd* (1882), however, ignored Chase's novel interpretation of the first act.

The Supreme Court's decisions on pardon under the second act were more logical than Chase's in *Armstrong*, and they generally weakened the goal of those who supported confiscation. In *Semmes v. United States* (1875)[52] Justice Nathan Clifford for a unanimous Court that the conditional pardon Raphael Semmes accepted in October 1865 denied him the right to retrieve his confiscated property. Semmes's pardon had specified that he could not claim any property that had been condemned and sold under the second act. Nor, the Court said, had it been superseded by the subsequent grants of amnesty by Johnson in 1867 and 1868. Moreover, Clifford added, the second act confiscated property as a belligerent right, not as a punishment for treason, a position that Whiting, Day, and later Waples argued. Pardons for treason, therefore, did not restore property condemned under the second act.[53]

In *Osborn v. United States* (1875),[54] however, the Court upheld a pardoned rebel's right to have his property restored when no one acquired possession of it after its condemnation. In 1863 bonds owned by Edward S. Brown of Virginia, secured by mortgages to property in Kansas, had been confiscated. The debtors were then ordered to pay the money due to the court, which some did. Property that defaulted was sold and over $20,000 came into the court, which maintained control of it. In September 1865 Brown obtained a conditional pardon that prohibited him from claiming any proceeds from the sale of his property. However, Brown claimed his bond had never been sold. Justice Field, for a unanimous Court, agreed and affirmed the decision of Justice Samuel Miller in the lower court, *Brown v. United States*.[55] The mortgages had been collected by various means, but that, said Field, did "not pass the title of the property mortgaged" in Kansas. "The property mortgaged was not confiscated or sold under the confiscation laws," he said, nor did the money pass into the U.S. Treasury. The conditions on Brown's pardon as in others granted had been intended to protect anyone who might have purchased his confiscated bonds. Since none had been sold, there was no purchaser whose right Brown would injure by claiming his property under the pardon. As Field observed, the president's power to pardon carried with it the authority to "release penalties and forfeitures which might accrue from the offenses."[56]

In *Knote v. United States* (1877),[57] the Court broadly affirmed the implication in *Osborn* that no restoration could occur if proceeds from confiscated property had become vested in another party. More important, *Knote* denied most rebels the opportunity to reclaim property once pardoned. John Knote of West Virginia claimed the amnesty proclamation by President Johnson of December 25, 1868, required the government to restore to him the proceeds realized from his confiscated property, deposited into the federal treasury. Johnson's proclamation granted "unconditionally, and without reservation" to all rebels "a full pardon and amnesty," with "the restoration of all rights, privileges, and immunities under the Constitution and the laws which have been made pursuance thereof." Justice Field, however, ruled for a unanimous Court that this proclamation did not permit Knote's claim. Although Field agreed that a pardon "releases the offender from all disabilities imposed by the offense, and restores to him all his civil rights," he claimed it "does not make amends for the past." Knote's pardon, therefore, returned to him all the rights not affected by his property's condemnation and sale that he had enjoyed before becoming a rebel. The pardon also signified that the punishment for his offense was justly suffered and had no effect on the rights acquired by others through the sale of his property, in this case the U.S. Treasury. "However large, therefore, may be the power of pardon" held by the president, it could not reach the money realized from the sale of Knote's property and placed in the U.S. Treasury, except by an act of Congress.[58] *Knote* thereby confirmed the intent of those who supported vigorous confiscation; it denied pardoned rebels the return of property so long as it had been correctly seized, condemned, and sold to another party. It could not prevent the heirs of these same rebels from receiving the property upon their ancestors' deaths.

Nor did *Knote* remove the right of a pardoned rebel to sell or transfer the fee of his confiscated property before his death. As noted earlier, the Court later decided in *Illinois Central Railroad v. Bosworth* (1889)[59] that pardons restored all rights and privileges not acquired by third parties from the purchase of the confiscated property, including the right to dispose of the fee. After the war

Bosworth had been pardoned, and before his death in 1885, to the dismay of his heirs, he had sold his fee to the confiscated property. The Court unanimously held that between the property's condemnation and sale and Bosworth's pardon, the fee remained in "a state of suspended animation." Even though Bosworth had not touched the fee, it belonged to him as a result of the confiscation proceedings. The pardon, Justice Bradley said, restored Bosworth's power to dispose of the fee. Had Bosworth died without a pardon, the fee would have reverted to his heirs, since the joint resolution stipulated that there could be no forfeiture beyond the offender's life. The pardon, however, removed "the guilty party's disabilities," Bradley said, and restored "all his rights, powers and privileges, not absolutely lost or vested" in some other party. A pardoned Bosworth was thus able to prevent his heirs from inheriting his fee and thereby negate the joint resolution.[60]

The *Illinois Central* ruling amply illustrated some of the inadequacies of the confiscation acts. Although the first act did call for property to be forfeited beyond the life of the rebel, little property was confiscated under it. The second act and the joint resolution, however, failed to divest the owner's fee. As Justice Field observed in *Jenkins v. Collard* (1881),[61] which reaffirmed Bosworth, the pardon removed the disability of disposing of the remaining estate—the fee that had not been confiscated—and the former rebel "stood, with reference to the estate, precisely as though no confiscation proceedings had ever been had."[62] Moreover, the confiscation acts realized only a small sum of money for the government's use in suppressing the rebellion and were completely unsuccessful in reconstructing the South through a distribution of confiscated property. Those who wrote the first and second acts deserve the blame for the failure of confiscation. Although the Lincoln administration could have enforced the laws more vigorously, Congress knew before their enactment that neither the president nor the attorney general supported confiscation. Furthermore, the judicial interpretation the laws received demonstrated they were not well crafted. With some minor exceptions, such as *Armstrong's Foundry*, which returned a pardoned rebel property confiscated under the first act, the Supreme Court viewed the laws in a balanced manner. The Court, however, could not interpret what Congress had not provided for in the laws. Nor could it ignore Lincoln's reason for demanding the joint resolution, which was to prevent forfeiture of confiscated lands beyond the offender's life.

12 Conclusion

Although the confiscation acts did not accomplish their goals, they were still important measures that represented many Northerners' concerns about how the war should be prosecuted and applied pressure on President Lincoln to expand the Union's objectives. They promised a radical alteration of property relations in the South and the prospect of distributing land to the freed slaves. The failure of these two fundamental initiatives (for the texts of which see the appendix) did not diminish fears among Southerners about confiscation nor the slaves' hopes that they might become independent farmers. The threat of confiscation became part of the North's mythical plan to destroy the Southern way of life, while the expectation of confiscation became the failed promise to give land to freed slaves. The prospect of confiscation was illusory from the start: the acts were not well written, the administration had no interest in their enforcement, and Republicans soon abandoned the idea of land for freedmen. By the time Andrew Johnson became president, the Republican majority's Reconstruction plans consistently omitted turning over confiscated land to freedmen. In the end, ironically, it was the Supreme Court that viewed the acts favorably and suggested that Congress had been timid in their formulation.

Congress passed the first act quickly in the summer of 1861 in reaction to the contraband question and early military reverses in the war. Intended to confiscate rebel property, primarily slaves, used to assist the rebellion, the act accomplished little in part because Lincoln did not authorize military enforcement. However, the measure did encourage many in the North to insist that the Union attack slavery, the cornerstone of the Confederacy, more directly, even at the risk of alienating the border states. The anger many Northerners felt at Lincoln's revocation of Frémont's order in Missouri suggested that the Republican Party and the administration did not share their willingness to punish the South even as it restored the Union. By late 1861 Senator Trumbull and many other Republicans came to believe that it was necessary to enact a second, broader confiscation act. Their original measure was intended to punish rebels by confiscating their property, including slaves, for perpetuity, thereby destroying the planter class and reconstructing the South. The real estate would be sold to help defray the costs of the rebellion.

It took Congress over six months to discuss and pass the second act. During that time the differences among Republicans about how to punish the rebels, end slavery, and restore the Union became apparent. The result was a bill full of compromises that promised more than it could ever produce. The first four sections defined treason and its punishment, including the loss of slaves, but did not mention confiscation. The next four sections authorized the president to confiscate all the property, including slaves, of most rebels who continued to support the rebellion after an executive proclamation ordering them to cease such activity. Confiscation in these sections was punishment for support of the rebellion, not for treason. Proceedings against the "enemies' property" were to be in rem—that is, without the owners present—with the property sold so that purchasers obtained "good and valid titles thereto." The remaining sections of the measure specified how rebels' slaves would be made free, enrolled in the Union's military, and, if they wished, colonized in another country.

Lincoln feared the repercussions of the second act and, by threatening a veto, forced Congress to adopt a joint resolution (see the appendix) that further limited the potential for confiscation. Despite the different punishments authorized for treason and for support of the rebellion, Lincoln conflated the two and persuaded Congress to guarantee that no "punishment or proceedings under" the act would violate Article III, Section 3, of the Constitution, which says that "no attainder of Treason shall work Corruption of Blood, or Forfeiture except during the Life of the Person attained." According to the joint resolution, the second act would not "be so construed as to work a forfeiture of the real estate of the offender beyond his natural life." This meant confiscation would not be permanent even for those punished for supporting the rebellion. So, in effect, by the summer of 1862 Republicans had rejected the idea of giving land to ex-slaves.

The Lincoln administration also implemented the confiscation acts late, minimally, and with tight controls. Although the president used the second act to lay the foundations for his own emancipation proclamation, he did not intend to enforce the confiscation provisions vigorously. Attorney General Bates of Missouri shared Lincoln's aversion to harsh punishments except for the most prominent rebels and opposed using confiscation for social reform. Instructions from the attorney general's office to district attorneys in the North, where many rebels owned various types of property, were very cautious, and they urged a conservative application of the law so that the prosecution of doubtful cases would not embarrass the government. Nor did Bates did encourage a vigorous application of the laws as portions of the South fell into Union hands. Moreover, Congress did not complain about the weak implementation of the laws.

Both military and Treasury officials could have been valuable allies in the pursuit of confiscable property as the Union occupied the South. That did not occur, and for several reasons. From the start of the war only a few generals, such as John C. Frémont or Ben Butler, were willing even to disturb slavery. Most declared that they would not interfere with the property of rebels. Although the military's conciliatory policy changed in the summer of 1862, Lincoln continued to authorize seizure of property only for military purposes. Even in New Orleans, which the Union controlled for a long time and where Butler achieved a fearsome reputation, relatively little confiscation occurred. Francis Lieber, whose General Orders 100 appeared in April 1863 and was widely hailed as a guide to military behavior in the war, agreed with Lincoln's restrained approach to confiscating Southern property. The military's reluctance, with a few exceptions, to enforce the confiscation acts greatly pleased Bates, both because he did not want to share their implementation and wished for limited results.

Despite his support for abolition before the war, Secretary of Treasury Chase was also reluctant to involve his department in confiscation. This aversion became evident when Treasury officials took control of the Sea Islands off South Carolina in early 1862. Very soon concerns for restoring the plantation economy there took precedence over parceling land out to the former slaves. As more of the South fell to Union forces, Treasury officials under Chase's directions set up a system to collect various forms of property, abandoned, captured, and confiscable, to promote the revitalization of a region's commerce, particularly that involving cotton. Treasury officials often had to rely upon the military for assistance in obtaining property, and this, too, limited the opportunities for detection of confiscable property. In New Orleans, several Treasury officials were involved with confiscable property, but Bates, as he often did, failed to support the local district attorney there. Nor did he attempt to work with Chase to seize as much of the city's property as possible.

The declining support among Republicans for confiscation after the summer of 1862 may in part explain Bates's weak enforcement of the acts. Republicans did not do well in the fall elections, and many attributed their losses to Lincoln's preliminary proclamation on emancipation and other supposedly radical programs such as confiscation. Although the party rebounded in the 1863 elections, many attributed these victories to success on battlefield and reduced attention to emancipation. Republicans hardly mentioned confiscation during the elections. In December, Lincoln offered a proclamation on amnesty and Reconstruction, in which some Republicans found his terms for reconciliation and pardon too generous; they proposed a repeal of the 1862 joint resolution on permanent confiscation to prevent the restoration of property to rebels. Various proposals came before both the Senate and House through 1864 and early 1865, but, in the end, the Republican majority failed to repeal or amend the joint resolution. Just as the party omitted provisions to redistribute land from their various Reconstruction plans, so it rejected confiscation that would last beyond the lives of those who had supported the rebellion. This decision revealed the growing Republican enchantment with the free labor ideology rather than a commitment to land for the freedmen.

With Lincoln's death came the possibility of a change in confiscation policy. Andrew Johnson had given some the impression that he wanted to punish the planter elite, and, at least for a while, he embraced vigorous confiscation even though the war had ended. However, it soon became clear that Johnson only wanted to use confiscation as a threat to some rebels while he allowed others a chance to protect their property. He was even more willing to grant pardons than Lincoln, and, with the war's end, many more were now interested in receiving this presidential favor. At the same time, Director O. O. Howard and the Freedmen's Bureau tried to prevent the small amount of confiscated property under their control from being returned to former rebels. During summer of 1865 Howard tried to devise a system that would protect the freedmen whose title to the land was hardly secure. By September, however, Johnson ran out of patience and ordered Howard and the bureau to begin returning lands to those pardoned who were both eager to regain their property and turn the freedmen into laborers. The speed at which various bureaus in the former Confederate states returned land to pardoned rebels varied, but by early 1866 the process was well under way, even though some officials remained reluctant to accede to the president's demand. Although some Republicans such as Thaddeus Stevens remained committed to land for the freedmen, by 1867 most of the party had abandoned that dream. Neither did the black leaders elected to the various state conventions support the idea of confiscation. Nonetheless, many freedmen still hoped for the promised "forty acres and a mule."

From 1861 on opponents had claimed both the principle of confiscation and the methods were unconstitutional. It was, therefore, a considerable irony that the Supreme Court consistently supported the laws that had provoked so much disagreement and accomplished so little. The Court, in fact, often suggested that Congress could have been much more aggressive in pursuing confiscation during the war. On the issue of jurisdiction, the Court broadly interpreted the acts so that all manner of property, on land or sea, could be confiscated. In doing so, the Court said the laws' intent to confiscate the property owned by rebels or used to aid the rebellion must be appreciated even if their language was imprecise or sloppy. The Court also upheld the use of in rem proceedings when rebels were unable to appear and offer testimony in their own behalf. If they were able to appear, however, the Court said, they must be heard. Confiscation's critics had predicted it would be impossible to seize intangible property such as stocks, bonds, or mortgages, but the Court found that, however inadequate the procedures in the second act were for such seizures, they were sufficient. As well, the Court generally gave the benefit of the doubt to district attorneys and marshals in their handling of the seizures.

Most significantly, the Court upheld the constitutionality of the confiscation acts. Only on the issue of duration of forfeiture did the Court disappoint those who had supported vigorous and permanent confiscation. In *Miller v. United States*, the most important confiscation case, the Court found that Congress had the power to confiscate the property of those in rebellion against the Union. The sections of the act involving confiscation, the Court said, were meant to end the rebellion, not to punish individuals for their behavior, and that was within Congress's power. Nor did this power, said the Court, rest upon the law of nations. Instead, the right to confiscate was a belligerent right of war, be it civil or foreign, found in the Constitution. The Court's majority also suggested that Congress could have confiscated even more property from a wider range of people had it wished to do so. In its consideration of the joint resolution, the Court said Congress clearly meant to limit the duration of forfeiture. According to the resolution, the Court said, only a right to the property could be conveyed to the purchaser; the fee itself, which devolved to the offender's heirs upon his death, could not be conveyed. Although the Court also got involved in a tangled and interesting analysis of where the fee resided during the life of the offender, its essential conclusion about duration remained, emphasizing the critical importance of the joint resolution to confiscation. The Republicans' refusal to agree to permanent forfeiture in 1862 or later meant that no matter how Lincoln chose to implement the law, confiscation would play no part in the Reconstruction or help freedmen obtain land.

Appendix

The First Confiscation Act, August 6, 1861

CHAP. LX—*An Act to confiscate Property used for Insurrectionary Purposes.*

Be it enacted by the Senate and House of Representatives of the United States of America in Congress assembled, That if, during the present or any future insurrection against the Government of the United States, after the President of the United States shall have declared, by proclamation, that the laws of the United States are opposed, and the execution thereof obstructed, by combinations too powerful to be suppressed by the ordinary course of judicial proceedings, or by the power vested in the marshals by law, any person or persons, his, her, or their agent, attorney, or employé, shall purchase or acquire, sell or give, any property of whatsoever kind or description, with intent to use or employ thc same, or suffer the same to be used or employed, in aiding, abetting, or promoting such insurrection or resistance to the laws, or any person or persons engaged therein; or if any person or persons, being the owner or owners of any such property, shall knowingly use or employ, or consent to the use or employment of the same as aforesaid, all such property is hereby declared to be lawful subject of prize and capture wherever found; and it shall be the duty of the President of the United States to cause the same to be seized, confiscated, and condemned.

Sec. 2. *And be it further enacted*, That such prizes and capture shall be condemned in the district and circuit court of the United States having jurisdiction of the amount, or in admiralty in any district in which the same may be seized, or into which they may be taken and proceedings first instituted.

Sec. 3. *And be it further enacted*, That the Attorney-General, or any district attorney of the United States in which said property may at the time be, may institute the proceedings of condemnation, and in such case they shall be wholly for the benefit of the United States; or any person may file an information with such attorney, in which case the proceedings shall be for the use of such informer and the United States in equal parts.

Sec. 4. *And be it further enacted*, That whenever hereafter, during the present insurrection against the government of the United States, any person claimed

U.S. Statutes at Large 12:319.

to be held to labor or service under the law of any State, shall be required or permitted by the person to whom such labor or service is claimed to be due, or by the lawful agent of such person, to take up arms against the United States, or shall be required or permitted by the person to whom such labor or service is claimed to be due, or his lawful agent, to work or to be employed in or upon any fort, navy yard, dock, armory, ship, entrenchment, or in any military or naval service whatsoever, against the Government and lawful authority of the United States, then, and in every such case, the person to whom such labor or service is claimed to be due shall forfeit his claim to such labor, any law of the State or of the United States to the contrary notwithstanding. And whenever thereafter the person claiming such labor or service shall seek to enforce his claim, it shall be a full and sufficient answer to such claim that the person whose service or labor is claimed had been employed in hostile service against the Government of the United States, contrary to the provision of this act.

APPROVED, August 6, 1861

The Second Confiscation Act

Chap. CXCV.—*An Act to suppress Insurrection, to punish Treason and Rebellion, to seize and confiscate the Property of Rebels, and for other Purposes.*

Be it enacted by the Senate and House of Representatives of the United States of America in Congress assembled, That every person who shall hereafter commit the crime of treason against the United States, and shall be adjudged guilty thereof, shall suffer death, and all his slaves, if any, shall be declared and made free; or, at the discretion of the court, he shall be imprisoned for not less than five years and fined not less than ten thousand dollars, and all his slaves, if any, shall be declared and made free; said fine shall be levied and collected on any or all of the property, real and personal, excluding slaves, of which said person so convicted was the owner at the time of committing said crime, any sale or conveyance to the contrary notwithstanding.

Sec. 2. *And be it further enacted*, That if any person shall hereafter incite, set on foot, assist, or engage in any rebellion or insurrection against the authority of the United State, or the laws thereof, or shall give aid or comfort thereto, or shall engage in, or give aid and comfort to, any such existing rebellion or insurrection, and be convicted thereof, such person shall be punished by imprisonment for a period not exceeding ten years, or by a fine not exceeding ten thousand dollars, and by the liberation of his slaves, if any he have; or by both said punishments, at the discretion of the court.

U.S. Statutes at Large 12:589–92.

Sec. 3. *And be it further enacted*, That every person guilty of either of the offenses described in this act shall be forever incapable and disqualified to hold any office under the United States.

Sec. 4. *And be it further enacted*, That this act shall not be construed in any way to affect or alter the prosecution, conviction, or punishment of any person or persons guilty of treason against the United States before the passage of this act, unless such person is convicted under this act.

Sec. 5. *And be it further enacted*, That, to insure the speedy termination of the present rebellion, it shall be the duty of the President of the United States to cause the seizure of all the estate and property, money, stocks, credits, and effects of the persons hereinafter named in this section, and to apply and use the same and the proceeds thereof for the support of the army of the United States, that is to say:

First. Of any person hereafter acting as an officer of the army or navy of the rebels in arms against the government of the United States.

Secondly. Of any person hereafter acting as President, Vice-President, member of Congress, judge of any court, cabinet officer, foreign minister, commissioner or consul of the so-called confederate states of America.

Thirdly. Of any person acting as governor of a state, member of a convention or legislature, or judge of any court of the so-called confederate states of America.

Fourthly. Of any person who, having held an office of honor, trust, or profit in the United States, shall hereafter hold an office in the so-called confederate states of America.

Fifthly. Of any person hereafter holding any office or agency under the government of the so-called confederate states of America, or under any of the several states of said confederacy, or the laws thereof, whether such office or agency be national, state, or municipal in its name or character: *Provided*, That the persons, thirdly, fourthly, and fifthly above described shall have accepted their appointment or election since the date of the pretended ordinance of cecession of the state, or shall have taken an oath of allegiance to, or to support the constitution of the so-called confederate states.

Sixthly. Of any person who, owning property in any loyal State or Territory of the United States, or in the District of Columbia, shall hereafter assist and give aid and comfort to such rebellion; and all sales, transfers, or conveyances of any such property shall be null and void; and it shall be a sufficient bar to any suit brought by such person for the possession or the use of such property, or any of it, to allege and prove that he is one of the persons described in this section.

Sec. 6. *And be it further enacted,* That if any person within any State or Territory of the United States, other than those named as aforesaid, after the passage of this act, being engaged in armed rebellion against the government of the United States, or aiding or abetting such rebellion, shall not, within sixty days after public warning and proclamation duly given and made by the President of the United States, cease to aid, countenance, and abet such rebellion, and return to his allegiance to the United States, all the estate and property, moneys, stocks, and credits of such person shall be liable to seizure as aforesaid, and it shall be the duty of the President to seize and use them as aforesaid or the proceeds thereof. And all sales, transfers, or conveyances, of any such property after the expiration of the said sixty days from the date of such warning and proclamation shall be null and void; and it shall be a sufficient bar to any suit brought by such person for the possession or the use of such property, or any of it, to allege and prove that he is one of the persons described in this section.

Sec. 7. *And be it further enacted,* That to secure the condemnation and sale of any such property, after the same shall have been seized, so that it may be made available for the purpose aforesaid, proceedings in rem shall be instituted in the name of the United States in any district court thereof, or in any territorial court, or in the United States district court for the District of Columbia, within which the property above described, or any part thereof, may be found, or into which the same, if moveable, may first be brought, which proceedings shall conform as nearly as may be to proceedings in admiralty or revenue cases, and if said property, whether real or personal, shall be found to have belonged to a person engaged in rebellion, or who has given aid or comfort thereto, the same shall be condemned as enemies' property and become the property of the United States, and may be disposed of as the court shall decree and the proceeds thereof paid into the treasury of the United States for the purposes aforesaid.

Sec. 8. *And be it further enacted,* That the several courts aforesaid shall have power to make such orders, establish such forms of decree and sale, and direct such deeds and conveyances to be executed and delivered by the marshals thereof where real estate shall be the subject of sale, as shall fitly and efficiently effect the purposes of this act, and vest in the purchasers of such property good and valid titles thereto. And the said courts shall have the power to allow such fees and charges of their officers as shall be reasonable and proper in the premises.

Sec. 9. *And be it further enacted,* That all slaves of persons who shall hereafter be engaged in rebellion against the government of the United States, or who shall in any way give aid or comfort thereto, escaping from such persons and taking refuge within the lines of the army; and all slaves captured from such persons or deserted by them and coming under the control of the government of the United States; and all slaves of such persons found *on* [or] being within any place occupied by rebel forces and afterwards occupied by the forces of the

United States, shall be deemed captives of war, and shall be forever free of their servitude, and not again held as slaves.

Sec. 10. *Be it further enacted*, That no slave escaping into any State, Territory, or the District of Columbia, from any other State, shall be delivered up, or in any way impeded or hindered of his liberty, except for crime, or some offence against the laws, unless the person claiming said fugitive shall first make oath that the person to whom the labor or service of such fugitive is alleged to be due is his lawful owner, and has not borne arms against the United States in the present rebellion, nor in any way given aid and comfort thereto; and no person engaged in the military or naval service of the United States shall, under any pretence whatever, assume to decide on the validity of the claim of any person to the service or labor of any other person, or surrender up any such person to the claimant, on pain of being dismissed from service.

Sec. 11. *And be it further enacted*, That the President of the United States is authorized to employ as many persons African descent as he may deem necessary and proper for the suppression of this rebellion, and for this purpose he may organize and use them in such manner as he may judge best for the public welfare.

Sec. 12. *And be it further enacted*, That the President of the United States is hereby authorized to make provision for the transportation, colonization, and settlement, in some tropical country beyond the limits of the United States, of such persons of the African race, made free by the provisions of this act, as may be willing to emigrate, having first obtained the consent of the government of said country to their protection and settlement within the same, and all the rights and privileges of freemen.

Sec. 13. *And be it further enacted*, That the President is hereby authorized, at any time hereafter, by proclamation, to extend to persons who may have participated in the existing rebellion in any State or part thereof, pardon and amnesty, with such exceptions and at such time and on such conditions as he may deem expedient for the public welfare.

Sec. 14. *And be it further enacted*, That the courts of the United States shall have the full power to institute proceedings, make orders and decrees, issue process, and do all other things necessary to carry this act into effect.

APPROVED, July 17, 1862.

The Joint Resolution

[No. 63.] *Joint Resolution explanatory of "An Act to suppress Insurrection, to punish Treason and Rebellion, to seize and confiscate the Property of Rebels, and for other Purposes.*

U.S. Statutes at Large 12:627.

Resolved by the Senate and House of Representatives of the United Sates of America in Congress assembled, That the provisions of the third clause of the fifth section of "An act to suppress insurrection, to punish treason and rebellion, to seize and confiscate the property of rebels, and for other purposes," shall be so construed as not to apply to any act or acts done prior to the passage thereof; nor to include any member of a State legislature, or judge of any State court, who has not in accepting or entering upon his office, taken an oath to support the constitution of the so-called "Confederate States of America"; nor shall any punishment or proceedings under said act be so construed as to work forfeiture of the real estate of the offender beyond his natural life.

APPROVED, July 17, 1862.

Notes

1. The First Confiscation Act

1. Howe to Charles Sumner, April 16, 1861, ser. 2, Reel 4 (hereafter 2:4), Charles Sumner Papers, Lamont Library, Harvard University; Christopher N. Breiseth, "Lincoln and Frederick Douglass: Another Debate," *Journal of the Illinois State Historical Society* 68 (February 1975): 12.

2. Philip S. Paludan, *A "People's Contest": The Union and the Civil War 1861–1865*, 2nd ed. (Lawrence: University Press of Kansas, 1996), 6; James Moorhead, *American Apocalypse: Yankee Protestants and the Civil War 1860–1869* (New Haven, Conn.: Yale University Press, 1978), 97–98.

3. Duke Frederick, "The Second Confiscation Act: A Chapter of Civil War Politics," (Ph.D. diss., University of Chicago, 1966); James G. Randall, *The Confiscation of Property During the Civil War* (Indianapolis: Mutual Printing and Lithographing, 1913); James G. Randall, *Constitutional Problems Under Lincoln*, rev. ed. (Urbana: University of Illinois Press, 1964); Henry D. Shapiro, *Confiscation of Confederate Property in the North* (Ithaca, N.Y.: Cornell University Press, 1962).

4. See Herman Belz, *Abraham Lincoln, Constitutionalism, and Equal Rights* (New York: Fordham University Press, 1998), and Michael Les Benedict, "Equality and Expediency in the Reconstruction Era: A Review Essay," *Civil War History* 23 (December 1977): 322–35, for discussions of the problems surrounding the change from emancipation to equal rights.

5. Roy Basler et al., eds., *The Collected Works of Abraham Lincoln* (New Brunswick, N.J.: Rutgers University Press, 1954), 4:331–32; Phillip S. Paludan, *The Presidency of Abraham Lincoln* (Lawrence: University Press of Kansas, 1994), 70; Paludan, *A People's Contest*, 15–18; Burrus M. Carnahan, "Lincoln, Lieber and the Laws of War: The Origins of the Principle of Military Necessity," *American Journal of International Law* 92 (April 1998): 219–20.

6. K. K. Jones to Trumbull, April 25, 1861, Lyman Trumbull Papers, Library of Congress; J. D. Easton to Senator John Sherman, April 11, 1861, John Sherman Papers, Library of Congress; Mark Grimsley, *The Hard Hand of War: Union Military Policy Toward Southern Civilians 1861–1865* (New York: Cambridge University Press, 1996), 8–9; James M. McPherson, "The Ballot and Land for the Freedmen, 1861–1865," in *Reconstruction: An Anthology of Revisionist Writings*, ed. Kenneth M. Stampp and Leon F. Litwack (Baton Rouge: Louisiana State University Press, 1969), 142.

7. Everett to Virginia, May 17, 1861, Reel 18, Edward Everett Papers, Massachusetts Historical Society, Boston. Everett had been sympathetic to the problems of slavery in the Union earlier in his career. But following Sumter he became a staunch supporter of the North. See Ronald Reid, *Edward Everett: Unionist Orator* (Westport, Conn.: Greenwood Press, 1990).

8. Benjamin F. Butler, *Private and Official Correspondence of Gen. Benjamin F. Butler During the Period of the Civil War* (Norwood, Mass.: Plimpton Press, 1917), 1:104–8, 114, 116–17; U.S. War Department, *War of the Rebellion: A Compilation of the Official Records of the Union and Confederate Armies* (Washington, D.C.: U.S. Government Printing

Office, 1880–1901), ser. 1, vol. 2, 52–54, 648–52 (hereafter cited as *Official Records*); Howard P. Nash Jr., *Stormy Petrel: The Life and Times of General Benjamin F. Butler, 1818–1893* (Rutherford, N.J.: Fairleigh Dickinson University Press, 1969), 106–8; Louis S. Gerteis, "Salmon P. Chase, Radicalism, and the Politics of Emancipation, 1861–1864," *Journal of American History* 60 (June 1973): 45; Frank Freidel, *Francis Lieber: Nineteenth-Century Liberal* (Baton Rouge: Louisiana State University Press, 1947), 327; Murray M. Horowitz, "Ben Butler and the Negro: 'Miracles Are Occurring,'" *Louisiana History* 17 (Spring 1976): 167; Gilroy G. Clinton to Sumner, June 5, 1861, 1:22, Sumner Papers; Don E. Fehrenbacher, *The Dred Scott Case: Its Significance in American Law and Politics* (New York: Oxford University Press, 1978), 4–5. Butler did not use the word "contraband" in any of his communications over this event. [Edward L. Pierce], "The Contrabands at Fortress Monroe," *Atlantic Monthly* 8 (November 1861): 627, may have been the first to use the word "contraband."

9. Ira Berlin et al., eds., *Freedom: A Documentary History of Emancipation, 1861–1867*, ser. 1, vol. 1, *The Destruction of Slavery* (New York: Cambridge University Press 1985), 15; Ira Berlin et al., eds., *Freedom: A Documentary History of Emancipation, 1861–1867* ser. 1, vol. 2, *The Wartime Genesis of Free Labor: The Upper South* (New York: Cambridge University Press, 1993), 86–87; Louis S. Gerteis, *From Contraband to Freedom: Federal Policy Toward Southern Blacks, 1861–1865* (Westport, Conn.: Greenwood Press, 1973), 16–17.

10. Butler, *Correspondence*, 1:119; Peter J. Parish, *The American Civil War* (New York: Holmes and Meier, 1975), 234; *Official Records*, ser. 1, vol. 1, 47–48; ser. 2, vol. 1, 753 (quotation).

11. Basler et al., *Collected Works of Lincoln*, 4:437, 439; *Official Records*, ser. 2, vol. 1, 759.

12. James W. Hurst, *The Law of Treason in the United States* (Westport, Conn.: Greenwood Press, 1970), 81–84, 102–6; Forrest McDonald, *Novus Ordo Seclorum: The Intellectual Origins of the Constitution* (Lawrence: University Press of Kansas, 1985), 13, 20, 43, 91–93; Brooks D. Simpson, *The Reconstruction Presidents* (Lawrence: University Press of Kansas, 1998), 18. See chapter 2, note 3, for sources on confiscation in the Revolution.

13. Randall, *Constitutional Problems Under Lincoln*, 275; Randall, *Confiscation*, 8n; Shapiro, *Confiscation*, 4–5; Berlin et al., *Destruction of Slavery*, 332; *Congressional Globe*, 37 Congress, 1 Session, Appendix 5, Salmon P. Chase, "Report of the Secretary of the Treasury," July 14, 1861 (hereafter cited as *Cong. Globe*, 37:1); ibid., vol. 31, pp. 11, 23, 78; Arthur C. Cole, "President Lincoln and the Illinois Radical Republicans," *Mississippi Valley Historical Review* 4 (March 1918): 423.

14. *Cong. Globe*, 37:1, vol. 31, pp. 120, 218; Ralph J. Roske, *His Own Counsel: The Life and Times of Lyman Trumbull* (Reno: University of Nevada Press, 1979), 74–76 (the most recent biography of Trumbull); Shapiro, *Confiscation*, 7n; Patricia A. Lucie, *Freedom and Federalism: Congress and Courts, 1861–1866* (New York: Garland, 1986), 24–28. Lucie supports Randall's view that the first act, like the second act, was vindictive. It is hard to see how these measures to attack slavery and cripple the Confederacy can be viewed as vindictive, however.

15. *Cong. Globe*, 37:1, vol. 31, 219, 431, 434; Shapiro, *Confiscation*, 6–7; James Doolittle, "A Statesman's Letters of the Civil War Period," *Journal of Illinois State Historical Society* 2 (July 1909): 45. Democrats and border state Republicans opposed it in the House. In the Senate, Edgar Cowan (Penn.) was the only Republican to oppose it, while James McDougall (Cal.) was the only Democrat to support it. B. F. Pershing, "Senator Edgar A. Cowan 1861–1867," *Pennsylvania Historical Magazine* 4 (October 1921): 224–33; John Hope Franklin, *The Emancipation Proclamation* (Garden City, N.Y.: Anchor Books, 1965), 17; Leonard P. Curry, *Blueprint for Modern America: Nonmilitary Legislation of the First Civil War Congress* (Nashville: Vanderbilt University Press, 1968), 75–77. See *U.S. Statutes at Large*, 12:319, for the first act and the appendix.

16. *Cong. Globe*, 37:1, vol. 31, 219, 434. Republican Orville Browning of Illinois voted for the first act. He subsequently became a vocal critic of the second act. Theodore C. Pease and James G. Randall, eds., *The Diary of Orville Hickman Browning* (Springfield: Illinois State Historical Library, 1925), 1:493n.

17. *Cong. Globe*, 37:1, vol. 31, 411–12, 414–15; James A. Woodburn, "The Attitude of Thaddeus Stevens Toward the Conduct of the Civil War," *American Historical Review* 12 (April 1907): 569–70. See Hans L. Trefousse, *Thaddeus Stevens: Nineteenth Century Egalitarian* (Chapel Hill: University of North Carolina Press, 1997), 111–12, for the most recent biography of Stevens.

18. *Cong. Globe*, 37:1, vol. 31, 413; Henry J. Raymond, *The Life and Public Services of Abraham Lincoln, Together with his State Papers* (New York: Derby & Miller, 1865), 201. See James M. McPherson, *Battle Cry of Freedom: The Civil War Era* (New York: Oxford University Press, 1988), 348–50, for reaction to Bull Run.

19. *Cong. Globe*, 37:1, vol. 31, 413. Edward Everett agreed; he believed that to call it a war acknowledged "the wretched and suicidal logic of 'Secession.'" Everett to Sir Henry Holland, July 21, 1861, Reel 32, Everett Papers.

20. *Cong. Globe*, 37:1, vol. 31, 411–12; Curry, *Blueprint for Modern America*, 75–78.

21. Heather Cox Richardson, *The Greatest Nation of the Earth: Republican Economic Policies during the Civil War* (Cambridge, Mass.: Harvard University Press, 1997), 213–14; Charles Eliot Norton, "The Advantages of Defeat," *Atlantic Monthly* 8 (September 1861): 360; George F. Williams to Sumner and Richard Henry Dana Jr., to Sumner, both on July 29, 1861, 1:23, Sumner Papers; Herman Belz, "Protection of Personal Liberty in Republican Emancipation Legislation of 1862," *Journal of Southern History* 42 (August 1976): 387–89; Patricia M. L. Lucie, "Confiscation: Constitutional Crossroads," *Civil War History* 23 (December 1977): 321–23; *U.S. Statutes at Large*, 12:319.

22. Bullard to Cameron, August 26, 1861, Roll 39, John A. Andrew Papers, Massachusetts Historical Society, Boston; *Official Records*, ser. 2, vol. 2, 1368–69 (Aug. 8, 1861), ser. 4, vol. 1, 586–92 (Aug. 30, 1861); Trumbull to Senator James R. Doolittle, August 31, 1861, in Frederick, "The Second Confiscation Act," 85–86; Robert M. York, *George B. Cheever, Religious and Social Reformer, 1807–1890* (Orono: University Press of Maine, 1955), 187. See Brian R. Dirck, "Posterity's First Blush: Civil Liberties, Property Rights, and Property Confiscation in the Confederacy," *Civil War History* 48 (September 2002): 237–56; Richard F. Bensel, *Yankee Leviathan: The Origins of Central State Authority in America, 1859–1877* (Cambridge: Cambridge University Press, 1990), 157; and Edward McPherson, *The Political History of the United States During the Great Rebellion* (New York: Appleton & Co., 1864), 203–4, for the Confederate legislation.

23. William Reddick to Trumbull, July 25, 1861, Sherman to Trumbull, July 30, 1861, John B. Wood to Trumbull, August 26, 1861, Anonymous to Trumbull, July 18, 1861, Trumbull Papers; John Jay to Sumner, July 28, 1861, 2:23, Sumner Papers; Samuel Clark to Sherman, July 30, 1861, Sherman Papers; J. H. Jordan to William Pitt Fessenden, William Pitt Fessenden Papers, Library of Congress; Marble to Wade, August 19, 1861, Benjamin F. Wade Papers, Library of Congress.

24. Sumner to Phillips, Aug. 3, 1861, 2:75, Sumner Papers; James M. McPherson, *The Struggle for Equality: Abolitionists and the Negro in the Civil War and Reconstruction* (Princeton, N.J.: Princeton University Press, 1964, 72 (Higginson quotation). See George M. Fredrickson, *The Black Image in the White Mind: The Debate on Afro-American Character and Destiny, 1817–1914* (New York: Harper & Row, 1971); V. Jacque Voegeli, *Free But Not Equal: The Midwest and the Negro During the Civil War* (Chicago: University of Chicago Press, 1967); Paludan, *A People's Contest*; Forrest G. Wood, *Black Scare: The Racist Response to Emancipation and Reconstruction* (Berkeley: University of California Press, 1968); and C. Vann Woodward, "Seeds of Failure in Racial Race Policy," in *Ameri-*

can Counterpoint: Slavery and Racism in the North South Dialogue (Boston: Little Brown, 1971), 163–83, for racism in the North.

25. *Official Records*, ser. 1, vol. 3, 466–67. See Andrew Rolle, *John Charles Frémont: Character as Destiny* (Norman: University of Oklahoma Press, 1963), 204–7; Allan Nevins, *Frémont: Pathmaker of the West* (New York: Longman's, Green, 1955), 497–500; Elbert B. Smith, *Francis Preston Blair* (New York: Free Press, 1980), 294–97; James M. McPherson, "From Limited to Total War: Missouri and the Nation, 1861–1865," *Gateway Heritage* 12 (Spring 1992): 4–19; and William E. Parrish, *Frank Blair: Lincoln's Conservative* (Columbia: University of Missouri Press, 1998), 116–20, for the background.

26. William E. Parrish, *The Turbulent Partnership: Missouri for the Union, 1861–1865* (Columbia: University of Missouri Press, 1963), 61; Pease and Randall, *Diary of Orville Browning*, 1:502–3; Smith, *Blair*, 298; William Dusinberre, *Civil War Issues in Philadelphia, 1856–1865* (Philadelphia: University of Pennsylvania Press, 1965), 131; J. R. Fry to Sumner, October 8, 1861, 1:23, Sumner Papers; Wendy Hammond Venet, *Neither Ballots nor Bullets: Women Abolitionists and the Civil War* (Charlottesville: University of Virginia Press, 1991), 76 (Howe quotation); Nevins, *Frémont*, 504–5; McPherson, *Struggle for Equality*, 72–73 (Garrison quotation); Henry G. Pearson, *The Life and Times of John Andrew: Governor of Massachusetts, 1861–1862* (Boston: Houghton Mifflin, 1904), 1:249; Speed to Chase, September 2, 1861, Davis to Chase, September 3, 1861, in John Niven, ed., *The Salmon P. Chase Papers* (Kent, Ohio: Kent State University Press, 1996), 3:92–95; Victor Howard, *Black Liberation in Kentucky: Emancipation and Freedom, 1862–1884* (Lexington: University Press of Kentucky, 1983), 6–7; Wilson Porter Shortridge, "Kentucky Neutrality in 1861," *Mississippi Valley Historical Review* 9 (March 1923): 295–301.

27. Lincoln to Frémont, September 2, 1861, Basler et al., *Collected Works of Lincoln*, 4:504; Frémont to Lincoln, September 8, 1861, *Official Records*, ser. 1, vol. 3, 469–70; Smith, *Blair*, 300–301.

28. Lincoln to Frémont, September 11, 1861, Lincoln to Mrs. John C. Frémont, September 12, 1861, Basler et al., *Collected Works of Lincoln*, 4:517–19; Herman Belz, "Abraham Lincoln and American Constitutionalism," *Review of Politics* 50 (Spring 1988): 186–87; Michael F. Holt, "Abraham Lincoln and the Politics of Union," in *Abraham Lincoln and the American Political Tradition*, ed. John L. Thomas (Amherst: University of Massachusetts Press, 1986), 112–13; Nicholas Parrillo, "Lincoln's Calvinist Transformation: Emancipation and War," *Civil War History* 46 (September 2000): 240; Eugene H. Berwanger, "Lincoln's Constitutional Dilemma: Emancipation and Black Suffrage," *Papers of the Abraham Lincoln Association* 5 (1983): 28.

29. David W. Blight, *Frederick Douglass' Civil War: Keeping Faith in Jubilee* (Baton Rouge: Louisiana State University Press, 1989), 151; Sumner to Phillips, September 17, 1861, 2:75, Sumner to Lieber, September 7, 1861, Moncure Conway to Sumner, September 17, 1861, Daniel R. Goodloe to Sumner, September 19, 1861, James Chestney to Sumner, October 1, 1861, 1:64, Sumner Papers; William E. Danbliday to Chandler, September 16, 1861, Wade to Chandler, September 23, 1861, Wade to Chandler, October 8, 1862, Zachariah Chandler Papers, Library of Congress; McPherson, *Struggle for Equality*, 72; Victor B. Howard, *Religion and the Radical Republican Movement, 1860–1870* (Lexington: University Press of Kentucky, 1990), 12–13. Abolitionist George Cheever, pastor of the Church of the Puritans in New York City, urged Congress to reconstruct the South following Lincoln's dismissal of Frémont. York, *George B. Cheever*, 190.

30. E. Merton Coulter, *The Civil War and Readjustment in Kentucky* (Chapel Hill: University of North Carolina Press, 1926), 112–13; Howard, *Black Liberation*, 7; Berlin et al., *Destruction of Slavery*, 17, 397–98; Medill to Chase, September 15, 1861, Niven, *Chase Papers*, 3:97–98; Lincoln to Browning, September 22, 1861, Basler et al., *Collected Works of Lincoln*, 4:531–33; George Sinkler, *The Racial Attitudes of American Presidents from Lincoln to Theodore Roosevelt* (Garden City, N.Y.: Doubleday, 1971), 54.

31. Michael Les Benedict, "The Constitution of the Lincoln Presidency and the Republican Era," in *The Constitution and the American Presidency*, ed. Martin L. Fausold and Alan Shank (Albany: State University of New York Press, 1991), 57–58; James M. McPherson, "Who Freed the Slaves?" in *Drawn with the Sword*, ed. James M. McPherson (New York: Oxford University Press, 1996), 193–94, 201–2.

32. Paludan, *The Presidency*, 87–88; McPherson, *Struggle for Equality*, 73–74; Trumbull to Lincoln, October 1, 1861, Reel 26, Robert Todd Lincoln Papers, Library of Congress; James G. Randall, *Lincoln the President: From Springfield to Gettysburg* (New York: Dodd, Mead, 1945), 2–25; David W. Blight, "Frederick Douglas and the American Apocalypse," *Civil War History* 31 (December 1985): 317n; Parrish, *Turbulent Partnership*, 72–75; William B. Hesseltine, *Lincoln and the War Governors* (New York: Knopf, 1948), 230; Norman L. Peterson, *Freedom and Franchise: The Political Career of B. Gratz Brown* (Columbia: University of Missouri Press, 1965), 108; Smith, *Blair*, 303–4; Chase to Richard Smith, November 11, 1861, Niven, *Chase Papers*, 3:107–8; John Niven, *Salmon P. Chase: A Biography* (New York: Oxford University Press, 1995), 281. John Formby, *The American Civil War* (New York: Charles Scribner's, 1910), 146–47, claimed that Lincoln did not enforce the first act because the North was not strong enough. This ignores the property liable to confiscation in the North.

33. Cameron to Butler, August 8, 1861, Butler, *Correspondence*, 1:201–3; *Official Records*, ser. 2, vol. 1, 761–62, 764–65, 770–71, 773–74; Berlin et al., *Destruction of Slavery*, 62–64; Barbara Jeanne Fields, *Slavery and Freedom on the Middle Ground: Maryland During the Nineteenth Century* (New Haven, Conn.: Yale University Press, 1985), 108.

34. Grimsley, *The Hard Hand of War*, 54–55; Susie M. Ames, "Federal Policy Toward the Eastern Shore of Virginia in 1861," *Virginia Magazine of History and Biography* 69 (October 1961): 432–59; *Official Records*, ser. 2, vol. 2, 139–40, ser. 1, vol. 5, 428–32, 641–42.

35. Grimsley, *The Hard Hand of War*, 62–63; Berlin et al., *Destruction of Slavery*, 64, 469; *Official Records*, ser. 1, vol. 4, 302, 337, ser. 2, vol. 1, 774, 776–77; Howard, *Black Liberation*, 8; Coulter, *The Civil War and Readjustment*, 156–57; Stephen D. Engle, "Don Carlos Buell: Military Philosophy and Command Problems in the West," *Civil War History* 42 (June 1995): 94; Bruce Tap, *Over Lincoln's Shoulder: The Committee on the Conduct of the War* (Lawrence: University Press of Kansas, 1998), 19; Brooks D. Simpson, "'The Doom of Slavery': Ulysses S. Grant, War Aims, and Emancipation, 1861–1863," *Civil War History* 36 (March 1990): 39–41.

36. See Ira Berlin et al., eds., *Slaves No More: Three Essays on Emancipation and the Civil War* (New York: Cambridge University Press, 1992), 21–30; Ira Berlin, "Who Freed the Slaves? Emancipation and Its Meaning," in *Union and Emancipation: Essays on Politics and Race in the Civil War Era*, ed. David W. Blight and Brooks D. Simpson (Kent, Ohio: Kent State University Press, 1997), 108–14; Berlin et al., *Destruction of Slavery*, 63–64, for how slaves' entry into Union lines pushed the debate about emancipation forward. See McPherson, "Who Freed the Slaves?", for a counter to the thesis that slaves deserve most credit for ending slavery.

37. *Official Records*, ser. 1, vol. 6, 186–88, 192, 200, 205; Berlin et al., *Destruction of Slavery*, 20, 104–5; Berlin et al., *Slaves No More*, 27; Berlin et al., *Wartime Genesis: Upper South*, 368–69; David H. Donald, *Charles Sumner and the Rights of Man* (New York: Da Capo, 1996), 48.

38. Marvin R. Cain, *Lincoln's Attorney General: Edward Bates of Missouri* (Columbia: University of Missouri Press, 1965), 154–56; Paludan, *The Presidency*, 42; Shapiro, *Confiscation*, 17–20. David Donald characterized Bates as "extremely" conservative. See David Donald, "Devils Facing Zionwards," in *Grant, Lee, Lincoln and the Radicals*, ed. Grady McWhiney (Evanston, Ill.: Northwestern University Press, 1964), 81.

39. Basler et al., *Collected Works of Lincoln*, 6:45–46. See Paul Wallace Gates, "Southern Investments in Northern Lands Before the Civil War," *Journal of Southern History* 5 (May 1939): 155–85, for Northern property owned by Southerners, some of whom did not support the Confederacy. Most of the property was in Illinois, Wisconsin, Iowa, and Minnesota. No confiscation occurred in these states during the war. Bates does not mention the first act in his diary. See Howard K. Beale, ed., *The Diary of Edward Bates 1859–1866* (New York: Da Capo, 1971 [1933]).

40. Coffey to Benegah Deacon, August 29, 1861, Coffee to R.F. Paine, September 19, 1861, Attorney General Letterbooks, B-4, 125, 144, Attorney General Papers, Record Group 60, National Archives, Washington, D.C. (hereafter cited as Attorney General Letterbooks); *U.S. Statutes at Large*, 12:319; Shapiro, *Confiscation*, 17–20.

41. Coffey to Willey, September 12, 1861, Coffey to George A. Vourse, September 17, 1861, Coffey to E. M. Norton, September 12, 1861, Attorney General Letterbooks, B-4: 137, 143–44; Willey to Bates, September 1, 1861, Letters Received, Connecticut, Box 1, Attorney General Papers, Record Group 60, National Archives, Washington, D.C. (hereafter cited as Letters Received); Vourse to Bates, September 10, 1861, ibid., Minnesota, Box 1, Norton to Bates, September 5, 1861, ibid., Virginia, Box 1.

42. Bates to Seward, September 23, 1861, Bates to Hiram Willey, October 7, 1861, Attorney General Letterbooks, B-4: 149, 173–74; Cain, *Bates*, 157–59.

43. Coffey to Robert Crozier, December 3, 1861, Coffey to Benjamin H. Smith, December 12, 1861, Attorney General Letterbooks, B-4: 236, 237; Crozier to Bates, December 4, 1861, Kansas, Box 1, Smith to Bates, December 2, 1861, Virginia, Box 1, Letters Received.

44. Bates to Smith, May 7, 1862, Attorney General Letterbooks B-5: 86–87. See similar advice from Bates to James O. Broadhead, April 10, 1862, and Bates to William M. Addison, April 17, 1862, *Official Records*, ser. 2, vol. 1, 275; ser. 2, vol. 2, 285–86.

45. Shapiro, *Confiscation*, 22–26; Edward G. Everett, "Contraband and Rebel Sympathizers in Pennsylvania in 1861," *Western Pennsylvania Historical Magazine* 41 (Spring 1958): 31.

46. *Senate Executive Documents*, 40 Congress, 2 session, no. 58, ser. 1317, 2–7. Shapiro, *Confiscation*, and Randall, *Confiscation*, have not discovered any appreciable amount of property confiscated under the first act, either.

47. Cain, *Bates*, 160–61; *Official Records*, ser. 1, vol. 2, 182–83; Beale, *Diary of Edward Bates*, 207–11.

48. See *Official Records*, ser. 3, vol. 1, 698–708, for Cameron's altered report; see McPherson, *Political History of the United States*, for the original version, which New York newspapers published in early January 1862. Berlin et al., *Destruction of Slavery*, 20–21; Erwin S. Bradley, *Simon Cameron: Lincoln's Secretary of War* (Philadelphia: University of Pennsylvania Press, 1966), 202–5; Coulter, *The Civil War and Readjustment*, 156; Niven, *Chase*, 282–84; McPherson, *Battle Cry of Freedom*, 357–58. Lincoln removed Cameron from the Cabinet in early 1862 and appointed him ambassador to Russia.

49. Birney to Wade, November 1, 1861, Wade Papers; Brownson to Sumner, October 23, 1861, Kendrick to Sumner, October 5, 1861, Hart to Sumner, October 1, 1861, 1: 23; Schleiden to Sumner, November 3, 1861, 2:75, Sumner Papers; W. H. Henderson to Trumbull, November 20, 1861, Trumbull Papers; Parish to Sherman, November 5, 1861, Sherman Papers.

50. Everett to Joshua Bates, November 11, 1862, Everett to Sir Henry Holland, Nov. 9, 1861, Reel 32, Everett Papers.

51. Dalzel to Sherman, October 4, 1861, Winters to Sherman, October 10, 1861, Sherman Papers; Catlin to Sumner, October 4, 1861, 1:23, Sumner to Martin F. Tupper, November 11, 1861, 2:75, Sumner Papers; Grimes to Trumbull, October 24, 1861, Trumbull Papers; Trefousse, *Stevens*, 116; Stevens to Gerrit Smith, December 14, 1861, Thad-

deus Stevens Papers, Library of Congress; J. E. Field to Representative Henry L. Dawes, December 1, 1861, in Herman Belz, *Reconstructing the Union: Theory and Policy During the Civil War* (Ithaca, N.Y.: Cornell University Press, 1969), 43n.

52. "Annual Message to Congress," Basler et al., *Collected Works of Lincoln*, 4:35–53; Morgan D. Dowd, "Lincoln, the Rule of Law and Crisis Government: A Study of His Constitutional Law Theories," *University of Detroit Law Journal* 39 (June 1962): 644. See Gabor S. Boritt, "The Voyage of the Colony of Linconia: The Sixteenth President, Black Colonization, and the Defense Mechanism of Avoidance," *The Historian* 37 (August 1975): 619–32; Stephen B. Oates, "'Our Man of Redemption': Abraham Lincoln and the Emancipation of the Slaves," *Presidential Studies* 9 (Winter 1979): 15–25; Otto H. Olsen, "Abraham Lincoln as Revolutionary," *Civil War History* 24 (September 1978): 213–24; Jason H. Silverman, "'In Isles Beyond the Main': Abraham Lincoln's Philosophy on Black Colonization," *Lincoln Herald* 80 (Fall 1978): 115–22; Michael Vorenberg, "Abraham Lincoln and the Politics of Black Colonization," *Journal of the Abraham Lincoln Association* 14, no. 2 (1993): 23–45; Arthur Zilversmit, "Lincoln and the Problem of Race: A Decade of Interpretation," *Papers of the Abraham Lincoln Association* 2 (1980): 22–45; and James D. Bilotta, *Race and the Rise of the Republican Party, 1848–1865* (New York: Peter Lang, 1992), 449–55, for discussions of Lincoln on race and colonization.

53. Everett to Lincoln, December 12, 1861, Reel 32, Everett Papers.

54. See Frederick, "Second Confiscation Act," 87–91, 99–101, 103–6, for a discussion of newspapers and confiscation from late 1861 into the spring of 1862.

55. See Hans L. Trefousse, "Owen Lovejoy and Abraham Lincoln During the Civil War," *Journal of the Abraham Lincoln Association* 22 (Winter 2001): 16–32, for the argument that Lincoln and the radicals were not that far apart on crucial issues.

2. The Second Confiscation Act: The Act and Its Opponents

1. Lawrence to George Lunt, November 9, 1861, in Edith Ellen Ware, *Political Opinion in Massachusetts During the Civil War and Reconstruction* (New York: Longmans, Green, 1916), 94; Nicholas B. Wainwright, ed., *A Philadelphia Perspective: The Diary Sidney George Fisher Covering the Years 1834–1871* (Philadelphia: Historical Society of Pennsylvania, 1967), 410; Howe to Grace Howe, December 31, 1861, in David Donald, *Charles Sumner and the Rights of Man* (New York: Da Capo, 1996), 60–61; James M. McPherson, "Abolitionists and Negro Opposition to Colonization During the Civil War," *Phylon* 26, no. 4 (1965): 393; Allan G. Bogue, *The Congressmen's Civil War* (Cambridge: Cambridge University Press, 1989), 123; Robert D. Ilisevich, *Galusha A. Grow: The People's Candidate* (Pittsburgh: University of Pittsburgh, 1988), 207.

2. See Duke Frederick, "The Second Confiscation Act: A Chapter of Civil War Politics" (Ph.D. dissertation, University of Chicago, 1966), and Leonard P. Curry, *Blueprint for Modern America: Nonmilitary Legislation of the First Civil War Congress* (Nashville: Vanderbilt University Press, 1968), chapter 4, for descriptions of the act's legislative history; Herman Belz, *Reconstructing the Union: Theory and Policy During the Civil War* (Ithaca, N.Y.: Cornell University Press, 1969), for discussion of Congress during the war; Allen G. Guelzo, *Lincoln's Emancipation Proclamation: The End of Slavery in America* (New York: Simon & Schuster, 2004), for the most recent analysis of Lincoln's plans for ending slavery; and Allen Bogue, *The Earnest Men: Republicans of the Civil War* (Ithaca, N.Y.: Cornell University Press, 1981), 119–35, 307–11, 332–35, for voting analysis on the second act.

3. Wallace Brown, *The Good Americans: Loyalists of the American Revolution* (New York: Morrow, 1969), 127–30; Claude H. Van Tyne, *The Loyalists in the American Revolution* (Gloucester, Mass.: Peter Smith, 1959 [1902]), 240–41, 277–78, 280, 286, 295, 335–41; Harry B. Yopse, *The Disposition of Loyalist Estates in the Southern District of the State of New York* (New York: Columbia University Press, 1939); Isaac S. Harrell, *Loyalism in*

Virginia: Chapters in the Economic History of the Revolution (New York: AMS Press, 1965 [1926]), 86, 88–90, 94–96, 98, 100; Robert O. DeMond, *The Loyalists in North Carolina During the Revolution* (Hamden, Conn.: Archon Books, 1964 [1940]); Robert S. Lambert, *South Carolina Loyalists in the American Revolution* (Columbia: University of South Carolina Press, 1987), 235–39, 240, 286, 288, 291–93; Philip A. Crowl, *Maryland During and After the Revolution: A Political and Economic Study* (Baltimore: Johns Hopkins University Press, 1943), 41–42, 48–51, 54; Richard B. Morris, "Class Struggle and the American Revolution," *William and Mary Quarterly* 3rd ser., vol. 19 (January 1962): 3–29; Robert S. Lambert, "The Confiscation of Loyalist Property in Georgia, 1782–1786," *William and Mary Quarterly* 3rd ser., vol. 20 (January 1963): 80–94; Richard D. Brown, "The Confiscation and Disposition of Loyalists' Estates in Suffolk County, Massachusetts," *William and Mary Quarterly* 3rd ser., vol. 21 (October 1964): 534–50; Anne M. Ousterhout, "Pennsylvania Land Confiscations During the Revolution," *Pennsylvania Magazine of History and Biography* 102 (July 1978): 328–43; Ruth M. Keesey, "Loyalism in Bergen County, New Jersey," *William and Mary Quarterly* 3rd ser., vol. 18 (October 1961): 558–71; Catherine S. Crary, "Forfeited Loyalist Lands in the Western District of New York—Albany and Tryon Counties," *New York History* 35 (July 1954): 239–58; Dennis P. Ryan, "Landholding, Opportunity, and Mobility in Revolutionary New Jersey," *William and Mary Quarterly* 3rd ser., vol. 36 (October 1979): 571–92; Beatrice G. Reubens, "Pre-Emptive Rights in the Disposition of a Confiscated Estate: Philipsburgh Manor, New York," *William and Mary Quarterly* 3rd ser., vol. 22 (July 1965): 435–56; Emory G. Evans, "Private Indebtedness and the Revolution in Virginia, 1776 to 1796," *William and Mary Quarterly* 3rd ser., vol. 28 (July 1971): 347–74; Staughton Lynd, *Anti-Federalism in Dutchess County, New York: A Study of Democracy and Class Conflict in the Revolutionary Era* (Chicago: Loyola University Press, 1962), 63–67, 71–75; Staughton Lynd, "Who Should Rule at Home? Dutchess County, New York in the Revolution," *William and Mary Quarterly* 3rd ser., vol. 18 (July 1961): 330–59; Henry J. Young, "Treason and Its Punishment in Revolutionary Pennsylvania," *Pennsylvania Magazine of History and Biography* 90 (July 1966): 287–313; William H. Fisher III, "Ideology, Religion, and the Constitutional Protection of Private Property: 1760–1860," *Emory Law Journal* 39 (Winter 1990): 102, 126–27.

4. *Congressional Globe*, 37th Congress, 2 Session, 18–19 (hereafter *Cong. Globe*, 37:2). Trumbull's bill was more inclusive than other confiscation bills introduced. See ibid., 49–50, 176, 334, for the other bills. Guelzo, *Lincoln's Emancipation Proclamation*, 64–65; Mark M. Krug, *Lyman Trumbull: Conservative Radical* (New York: A. S. Barnes, 1965), 200–201; Ralph J. Roske, *In His Own Counsel: The Life and Times of Lyman Trumbull* (Reno: University of Nevada Press, 1979), 82–83.

5. The two Democrats on the committee were Lazarus Powell of Kentucky and James Bayard of Delaware, both opposed to confiscation.

6. Wendell H. Stephenson, *Publications of the Kansas State Historical Society Embracing the Political Career of James H. Lane* (Topeka: Kansas State University Press, 1930), 124; Bingham to Joshua Giddings, December 19, 1861, quoted in Hans L. Trefousse, *The Radical Republicans: Lincoln's Vanguard for Racial Justice* (New York: Knopf, 1969), 217; *New York Times*, December 8, 1861, and R. H. Gillet to Caleb Cushing, December 5, 1861, in Curry, *Blueprint for Modern America*, 78, Frederick, "Second Confiscation Act," 87–91, 99–106; Arthur C. Cole, "President Lincoln and the Illinois Radical Republicans," *Mississippi Valley Historical Review* 4 (March 1918): 420, 424; Bruce Tap, *Over Lincoln's Shoulder: The Committee on the Conduct of the War* (Lawrence: University Press of Kansas, 1998), 38–39; Howe to Grace Howe, December 13, 1861, in Allan G. Bogue, "Historians and Radical Republicans: A Meaning for Today," *Journal of American History* 70 (June 1983): 7; James G. Blaine, *Twenty Years of Congress: From Lincoln to Garfield* (Nor-

wich, Conn.: Henry Bill Publishing, 1884), 1:373–74; Ware, *Political Opinion in Massachusetts*, 96.

7. Henderson to Trumbull, November 20, 1861, Lord to Trumbull, December 5, 1861, Linegan to Trumbull, December 7, 1861, Allaire to Trumbull, December 10, 1861, Strong to Trumbull, December 13, 1861, Lyman Trumbull Papers, Library of Congress. There were many letters applauding Trumbull and Congress for taking action. Charles Sumner also received numerous letters, many from public figures, urging Congress to attack slavery. See the Charles Sumner Papers, ser. 2, Reel 24 (hereafter 2:24), Lamont Library, Harvard University. In February 1862 the Maine State Senate passed a resolution, twenty-four to four, in favor of confiscating and arming the slaves of rebels if it became a military necessity. See Frank Moore, *The Rebellion Record* (New York: G. P. Putnam, 1862), 4: 26.

8. *Cong. Globe*, 37:2, 334, 942–43 (Feb. 25, 1862); Bogue, *Earnest Men*, 98, 132–33, 220; Patricia A. Lucie; *Freedom and Federalism: Congress and the Courts, 1861–1866* (New York: Garland, 1986), 31.

9. *Cong. Globe*, 37:2, 942–44 (Feb. 25, 1862); Bogue, *Earnest Men*, 220–21; Harold Hyman and William Wiecek, *Equal Justice Under Law: Constitutional Development, 1832–1872* (New York: Harper & Row, 1982), 251–52; Lucie, *Freedom and Federalism*, 32–35; Patricia M. L. Lucie, "Confiscation: Constitutional Crossroads," *Civil War History* 23 (December 1977): 309, 311–12.

10. Jean Baker, "A Loyal Opposition: Northern Democrats in the Thirty-Seventh Congress," *Civil War History* 25 (June 1979): 139–55; Jean Baker, *Affairs of Party: The Political Culture of Northern Democrats in the Mid-Nineteenth Century* (Ithaca, N.Y.: Cornell University Press, 1983), 152; Phillip S. Paludan, *"A People's Contest": The Union and the Civil War, 1861–1865* (New York: Harper & Row, 1988), 90–92; Earl J. Hess, *Liberty, Virtue, and Progress: Northerners and Their War for the Union* (New York: Fordham University Press, 1997), 82, 86, 88; Joel H. Silbey, *A Respectable Minority: The Democratic Party in the Civil War Era, 1860–1868* (New York: Norton, 1977), 30–83; *Cong. Globe*, 37:2, pt. 4, Appendix, 122 (Allen, April 24, 1862), 151 (Holman, May 23, 1862); pt. 2, 1136 (Browning, March 10, 1862); Lucie, "Confiscation," 308. See Gerald Ham, ed., "The Mind of a Copperhead: Letters of John J. Davis on the Secession Crisis and Statehood Politics in West Virginia 1860–1862," *West Virginia History* 24 (January 1963): 93–109, for the attitudes of someone opposed to secession, confiscation, and abolition. Davis was the father of the Democratic presidential nominee in 1924, John W. Davis.

11. *Cong. Globe*, 37:2, pt. 4, 2898, 2900 (Saulsbury, June 24, 1862); pt. 2, 1573–74 (Henderson, April 8, 1862). See Richard O. Curry, "Congressional Democrats: 1861–1863," *Civil War History* 12 (September 1966): 213–29; Richard O. Curry, "The Civil War and Reconstruction, 1861–1877: A Critical Overview of Recent Trends and Interpretations," *Civil War History* 24 (September 1974): 215–38, for appraisals of Democrats and Republicans on the central issues of the Civil War.

12. *Cong. Globe*, 37:2, pt. 4, 2962 (Cowan, June 27, 1862); pt. 2, 1809 (Collamer, April 24, 1862), 1876–77 (Wright, April 30, 1862), 1791 (Dunn, April 23, 1862).

13. Ibid., 1137 (Browning, March 10, 1862); pt. 4, Appendix, 221 (Thomas, May 24, 1862); pt. 2, 1051 (Cowan, March 4, 1862), 1791 (Dunn, April 23, 1862); *Memphis Argus*, January 22, 1862, in Moore, *The Rebellion Record*, 4:15.

14. *Atlanta Confederacy*, March 20, 1862, in Moore, *The Rebellion Record*, 4:100; *Cong. Globe*, 37:2, pt. 4, Appendix, 272–73 (Law, May 26, 1862); pt. 2, 1561 (Trumbull, April 7, 1862), 1803 (Crittenden, April 23, 1862).

15. Ibid., 1917–18 (Cowan, May 2, 1862), 1880 (Cowan, April 30, 1862).

16. Ibid., pt. 4, 2924 (Dixon, June 25, 1862); pt. 4, Appendix, 234 (Killinger, May 23, 1862), 164 (Grider, May 22, 1862).

17. Ibid., 187–88 (Harding, May 24, 1862); pt. 2, 1895–96 (Wilson, May 1, 1862); pt. 4, 2896–97 (Saulsbury, June 24, 1862).

18. Ibid., pt. 4, Appendix, 271 (Law, May 26, 1862); James McPherson, *Battle Cry of Freedom: The Civil War Era* (New York: Oxford University Press, 1988), 312; Henry Steele Commager, ed., *Documents of American History*, 7th ed. (New York: Appleton-Century-Crofts, 1963), 1:395–96 (Crittenden–Johnson Resolutions); Belz, *Reconstructing the Union*, 24–28.

19. *Cong. Globe*, 37:2, pt. 4, Appendix, 107 (Powell, April 16, 1862), 155 (Mallory, May 21, 1862), 121 (Allen, April 24, 1862); pt. 2, 1903 (Davis, May 1, 1862). Representative Aaron Harding, Kentucky Unionist, made a similar plea to the House at the beginning of the confiscation debates. Ibid., pt. 4, Appendix, 30 (December 17, 1861).

20. Ibid., 120 (Allen, May 24, 1862), 240 (Nugent, May 24, 1862); pt. 3, 1923 (Saulsbury, May 2, 1862); see Robert Abzug, "The Copperheads: Historical Approaches to Civil War Dissent in the Midwest," *Indiana Magazine of History* 66 (March 1970): 40–55, for a discussion of this issue. See James D. Bilotta, *Race and the Rise of the Republican Party, 1848–1865* (New York: Peter Lang, 1992), for a study of Republican attitudes toward blacks before the war and their hope that freed slaves would remain in the South after the war.

21. *Cong. Globe*, 37:2, pt. 2, 1817 (Lovejoy, April 24, 1862). Lovejoy felt the emancipated slaves should be left alone. If given the opportunity, he said, they would take care of themselves. He believed it would be the slaveholders who would struggle after abolition, without slaves to support them.

22. See Guelzo, *Lincoln's Emancipation Proclamation*, 139–43; G. S. Boritt, "The Voyage of the Colony of Linconia: The Sixteenth President, Black Colonization, and the Defense Mechanism of Avoidance," *The Historian* 37 (August 1975): 619–32; Stephen B. Oates, "'The Man of Our Redemption': Abraham Lincoln and the Emancipation of the Slaves," *Presidential Studies* 9 (Winter 1979): 15–25; Otto H. Olsen, "Abraham Lincoln as Revolutionary," *Civil War History* 24 (September 1978): 213–24; Jason H. Silverman, "'In Isles Beyond the Main': Abraham Lincoln's Philosophy of Black Colonization," *Lincoln Herald* 80 (Fall 1978): 115–22; Michael Vorenberg, "Abraham Lincoln and the Politics of Black Colonization," *Journal of the Abraham Lincoln Association* 14, no. 2 (1993): 23–45; Arthur Zilversmit, "Lincoln and the Problem of Race: A Decade of Interpretation," *Papers of the Abraham Lincoln Association* 2 (1980): 22–45; McPherson, "Abolitionists and Negro Opposition to Colonization During the Civil War," 391–99; Bilotta, *Race and the Rise of the Republican Party*, 449–52, for discussions of Lincoln and colonization.

23. *Cong. Globe*, 37:2, pt. 4, Appendix, 156 (Mallory, May 21, 1862); pt. 4, 2923 (Browning, June 25, 1862), 2997 (Pomeroy, June 28, 1862); pt. 1, 945 (Pomeroy, February 25, 1862).

24. Ibid., pt. 2, 1158 (Carlile, March 11, 1862), 1602 (Willey, April 10, 1862); pt. 4, Appendix, 173 (Blair, May 23, 1862). See Edward L. Ayers, *The Promise of the New South: Life After Reconstruction* (New York: Oxford University Press, 1992); Joel Williamson, *The Crucible of Race: Black-White Relations in the American South Since Emancipation* (New York: Oxford University Press, 1984); and Philip Dray, *At the Hands of Persons Unknown: The Lynching of Black America* (New York: Modern Library, 2003), for discussions of how southern whites treated blacks after Reconstruction.

25. Kenneth M. Stampp, *Indiana Politics During the Civil War* (Bloomington: Indiana University Press, 1978 [1949]), 145; Lex Renda, *Running on the Record: Civil War–Era Politics in New Hampshire* (Charlottesville: University Press of Virginia, 1997), 102, 105, 107; Jerome Mushkat, *The Reconstruction of the New York Democracy, 1861–1874* (Rutherford, N.J.: Fairleigh Dickinson University Press, 1981), 26–29; Arnold M. Shankman, *The Pennsylvania Antiwar Movement, 1861–1865* (Rutherford, N.J.: Fairleigh Dickinson Uni-

versity Press, 1980), 83–86; Wainwright, ed., *Diary of Sidney George Fisher*, 415; Kenneth B. Shover, "Maverick at Bay: Ben Wade's Senate Re-election Campaign, 1862–1863," *Civil War History* 12 (March 1966): 28; Everett to Prince Napoleon, February 18, 1862, Everett to Sir John Coleridge, March 1, 1863, Reel 32, Edward Everett Papers, Massachusetts Historical Society, Boston.

26. *Cong. Globe*, 37:2, pt. 4, 2961 (Cowan, June 27, 1862); pt. 2, 1759 (Davis, April 22, 1862), 140 (Doolittle, May 2, 1862), 219 (Thomas, May 24, 1862); Maurice G. Baxter, *Orville H. Browning: Lincoln's Friend and Critic* (Bloomington: Indiana University Press, 1957), 137–39; James G. Randall, *The Confiscation of Property During the Civil War* (Indianapolis: Mutual Printing and Lithographing, 1913), 16–18, complains that the legislators were often confused about the principles of international law as they applied to military or judicial seizure. He also believed other scholars and even jurists shared this confusion. This view, while defensible, also derives from Randall's distaste for confiscation.

27. See Belz, *Reconstructing the Union* and *Abraham Lincoln, Constitutionalism, and Equal Rights* (New York: Fordham University Press, 1998), for discussions of this issue.

28. *Cong. Globe*, 37: 2, pt. 4, Appendix, 168 (Babbit, May 22, 1862); pt. 3, 2299 (S. Blair, May 22, 1862).

29. Ibid., pt. 4, 2925 (Dixon., June 25, 1862); pt. 4, Appendix, 260 (Wickliffe, May 26, 1862); pt. 2, 1573–74 (Henderson, April 8, 1862).

30. Silbey, *A Respectable Minority*, 50–51.

3. The Second Act: Divided Republican Support and Flawed Result

1. Michael Les Benedict, "Laissez-Faire and Liberty: A Re-Evaluation of the Meaning and Origins of Laissez-Faire Constitutionalism," *Law and History Review* 3 (Fall 1985): 325. See also Benedict, *A Compromise in Principle: Congressional Republicans and Reconstruction, 1863–1869* (New York: Norton, 1974); Benedict, "Preserving the Constitution: The Conservative Basis of Radical Reconstruction," *Journal of American History* 23 (June 1974): 65–90; Herman Belz, "The New Orthodoxy in Reconstruction Historiography," *Reviews in American History* 1 (March 1973): 106–12; Herman Belz, *Emancipation and Equal Rights in the Civil War Era* (New York: Norton, 1978); Richard O. Curry, "The Civil War and Reconstruction, 1861–1877: A Critical Overview of Recent Trends and Interpretations," *Civil War History* 24 (September 1974): 215–38; and Hans L. Trefousse, "Owen Lovejoy and Abraham Lincoln During the Civil War," *Journal of the Abraham Lincoln Association* 22 (Winter 2001): 16–32, for reassessments of the radicals' power and radicalism. For a more generous view of the Republicans, see Robert J. Kaczorowski, "Revolutionary Constitutionalism in the Era of the Civil War and Reconstruction," *New York University Law Review* 61 (October 1986): 863–940. See Robert F. Horowitz, *The Great Impeacher: A Political Biography of James M. Ashley* (New York: Brooklyn College Press, 1979); Patrick A. Riddleberger, *George Washington Julian, Radical Republican: A Study in Nineteenth-Century Politics and Reform* (Bloomington: Indiana Historical Bureau, 1966); and Hans L. Trefousse, *Benjamin F. Wade: Radical Republican from Ohio* (New York: Twayne, 1963), for biographies of Ashley, Julian, and Wade.

2. See Orestes Brownson to Sumner, December 2, 1861, ser. 1, Reel 23 (hereafter 1:23), Charles Sumner Papers, Lamont Library, Harvard University; William Lloyd Garrison to Sumner, December 20, 1861, Charles W. Slack to Sumner, December 27, 1861, Johnson H. Jordon to Sumner, January 14, 1862, Frederick S. Cabot to Sumner, February 10, 1862, 1:2, Sumner Papers; George Banell to Trumbull, December 23, 1861, John Russell to Trumbull, December 31, 1861, W. F. Fyfe to Trumbull, January 5, 1862, Lyman Trumbull Papers, Library of Congress, for a representative sample of letters in support of Congress's power to act. *Congressional Globe*, 37 Congress, 2 Session, volume 32, part 3, 2193 (Sumner, May 19, 1982); pt. 2, 1559, 1560 (emphasis in the original), 1561–62 (Trumbull, April 7, 1862). (Hereafter *Cong. Globe*, 37:2.)

3. Allan Bogue, *The Earnest Men: Republicans of the Civil War* (Ithaca, N.Y.: Cornell University Press, 1981), 220–21, argues that Browning, Cowan, Doolittle, and Foster were moderates. Glenn Linden, "'Radicals' and Economic Polices: The Senate, 1861–1873," *Journal of Southern History* 32 (May 1966): 192–93, believes they were either "Non-Radical" or "Unaligned." I believe on the issue of confiscation, however, they were among the conservatives in the Republican Party.

4. *Cong. Globe*, 37:2, pt. 2, 1559, 1561–62 (Trumbull, April 7, 1862); Patricia A. Lucie, *Freedom and Federalism: Congress and Courts 1861–1866* (New York: Garland Publishing, 1986), 34–35. See John Alvis, "The Slavery Provisions of the U.S. Constitution: Means for Emancipation," *Political Science Reviewer* 17 (Fall 1987): 240–65, for a discussion of how Congress could have extinguished slavery.

5. *Cong. Globe*, 37:2, pt. 3, 2325 (Sedgwick, May 23, 1862); pt. 4, 2929 (Wade, June 25, 1862); pt. 3, 2193, 2189 (Sumner, May 19, 1862), 2234 (Eliot, May 20, 186, emphasis in the original); David Donald, *Charles Sumner and the Rights of Man* (New York: Da Capo, 1996), 60–67; see Herman Belz, *Reconstructing the Union: Theory and Policy During the Civil War* (Ithaca, N.Y.: Cornell University Press, 1969), 10–13, 56, 64, 69–70, for discussions of state suicide and territorialization. Professor Joel Parker of Harvard sought to refute Sumner's thesis on territorialization in "Constitutional Law," *North American Review* 94 (April 1862): 435–63.

6. *Cong. Globe*, 37:2, pt. 2, 1813 (Sherman, April 23, 1862), 1819 (Conkling, April 24, 1862), 1768–69 (Walton, April 22, 1862), 1767 (Porter, April 22, 1862); pt. 4, Appendix, 181 (Loomis, May 23, 1862), (Clements, May 24, 1862; he was a Unionist); pt. 4, 2961 (Trumbull, June 27, 1862); James G. Randall, *The Confiscation of Property During the Civil War* (Indianapolis: Mutual Printing and Lithographing, 1913), 17–18; Bogue, *Earnest Men*, 224.

7. *Cong. Globe*, 37:2, pt. 4, Appendix, 233–34 (Killinger, May 23, 1862), 117 (Cutler, April 23, 1862); pt. 2, 1895–96 (Wilson, May 1, 1862), 1816 (Lovejoy, April 24, 1862); Charles A. Jellison, *Fessenden of Maine: Civil War Senator* (Syracuse, N.Y.: Syracuse University Press, 1962), 143–44; William Salter, *The Life of James W. Grimes* (New York: D. Appleton, 1876), 183, 187, 191.

8. Sumner to Phillips, December 8, 1861, 2:75, Sumner Papers; *Cong. Globe*, 37:2, pt. 2, 1077 (Morrill, March 5, 1862); pt. 4, 2996 (Wilmot, June 28, 1862); pt. 4, Appendix, 194–95 (Ely, May 26, 1862), 177 (Sargent, May 23, 1862); pt. 3, 2196 (Sumner, May 19, 1862); pt. 2, 1077 (Morrill, March 5, 1862; emphasis in the original); Lucie, *Freedom and Federalism*, 34. See Kenneth S. Greenberg, "The Civil War and the Redistribution of Land: Adams County, Mississippi, 1860–1870," *Agricultural History* 52 (April 1978): 292–307; A. Jane Townes, "The Effect of Emancipation on Large Landholdings, Nelson and Goochland Counties, Virginia," *Journal of Southern History* 45 (August 1979): 403–12; Jonathan M. Wiener, "Planter Persistence and Social Change: Alabama, 1850–1870," *Journal of Interdisciplinary History* 6 (Autumn 1976): 235–60; Jonathan Wiener, "Class Structure and Economic Development in the American South, 1865–1955," *American Historical Review* 84 (October 1979): 970–92; and Steven Hahn, *The Roots of Southern Populism: Yeoman Farmers and the Transformation of the Georgia Upcountry, 1850–1890* (New York: Oxford University Press, 1983), for the argument that the planter class survived the Civil War and Reconstruction.

9. Leonard P. Curry, *Blueprint for Modern America: Nonmilitary Legislation of the First Civil War Congress* (Nashville: Vanderbilt University Press, 1968), 80–83; Duke Frederick, "The Second Confiscation Act: A Chapter of Civil War Politics" (Ph.D. dissertation, University of Chicago, 1966), 98–116.

10. *The Palmyra* 12 Wheaton 1 (1827). The case involved the seizure of the *Palmyra*, a Spanish brig, taken for trial to Charleston, South Carolina, in 1822.

11. Ibid., 14–15.

12. See Patricia M. L. Lucie, "Confiscation: Constitutional Crossroads," *Civil War History* 23 (December 1977): 311–15, for a discussion of in rem proceedings. As Lucie notes, even Attorney General Edward Bates needed to ask the advice of his subordinates about admiralty and revenue procedures.

13. *Cong. Globe*, 37:2, pt. 3, 2234 (Eliot, May 20, 1862), 2357 (Eliot, May 26, 1862); pt. 4, Appendix, 167 (Babbit, May 22, 1862); pt. 2, 2239 (Noell, May 20, 1862); pt. 1, 942–43 (Trumbull, February 25, 1862). Noell was the only Democrat to support broad confiscation on the floor; he opposed emancipation through confiscation, however. Glenn M. Linden, "'Radicals' and Economic Policies: The House of Representatives, 1861–1873," *Civil War History* 13 (March 1967): 58–59, does not identify him as a radical.

14. See chapters 10 and 11 for discussions of *Miller v. United States* 268 (1870), in which the Supreme Court upheld the use of in rem proceedings. In the same year, however, the Court said in *McVeigh v. United States* 78 U.S. 268 (1870), that a rebel who appeared to defend himself must be heard. See Lucie, "Confiscation," 312n. William Whiting, solicitor of the War Department during the Civil War and a supporter of confiscation, later argued that due process had no place in war. William Whiting, *War Under the Constitution of the United States: Military Arrests, Reconstruction and Military Government* (Boston: Lee & Shephard, 1871), 49.

15. *Cong. Globe*, 37:2, pt. 4, 2962, (Cowan June 27, 1862); pt. 2, 1808–9 (Collamer, April 24, 1862); Bogue, *Earnest Men*, 224–25; Allan Nevins, *War Becomes Revolution, 1862–1863* (New York: Charles Scribner, 1960), 203; Lucie, "Confiscation," 312–13.

16. *Cong. Globe*, 37:2, pt. 2, 1558, 1959, 1813 (Trumbull, April 7, May 6, April 24, 1862), 1875 (Wilmot, April 30, 1862); pt. 3, 2234 (Eliot, May 20, 1862), 2238 (Noell, May 20, 1862); Lucie, *Freedom and Federalism*, 31, 33, 37–38. As Lucie observes, supporters of confiscation wanted in rem proceedings for landed property but not slaves. To describe slaves as property agreed with the *Dred Scott* decision. See Lucie, "Confiscation," 313.

17. *Cong. Globe*, 37:2, pt. 3, 2238 (Noell, May 20, 1862). See Henry D. Shapiro, *Confiscation of Confederate Property in the North* (Ithaca, N.Y.: Cornell University Press, 1962), 3n. Shapiro distinguishes between forfeiture, which usually involved internal or external commerce, and confiscation, which traditionally related to the exercise of sovereign power over person or property, not the violation of a specific law.

18. *Cong. Globe*, 37:2, pt. 3, 2234 (Eliot, May 20, 1862); pt. 4, Appendix, 220 (Thomas, May 24, 1862); pt. 4, 2962 (Cowan, June 27, 1862). Not all enthusiasts of confiscation were worried that much about the Constitution; see Donald, *Sumner*, 62–63. Thaddeus Stevens was also less anchored to the Constitution than others; see Hans L. Trefousse, *Thaddeus Stevens: Nineteen-Century Egalitarian* (Chapel Hill: University of North Carolina Press, 1997).

19. Everett to Rev. Dr. Parker, March 19, 1862, Reel 32, Edward Everett Papers, Massachusetts Historical Society, Boston; *Cong. Globe*, 37:2, pt. 3, 2299–3000 (Blair, May 22, 1862); pt. 2, 1719 (Howard, April 18, 1862); Theodore C. Pease and James G. Randall, eds., *The Diary of Orville Hickman Browning* (Springfield: Illinois State Historical Library, 1925), 1:533n, W. G. Snethen to Sumner, April 24, 1862, 1:25, Sumner Papers; William A. Dunning, *Essays on the Civil War and Reconstruction and Related Topics* (New York: Macmillan, 1904), 34; Lucie, *Freedom and Federalism*, 34.

20. Russell to Trumbull, December 17, 1861 (emphasis by Russell), Clay to Trumbull, December 17, 1861, Stanton to Trumbull, January 18, 1862 (emphasis by Stanton), Trumbull Papers; Hamilton to Sherman, December 26, 1861, Sherman Papers; Potts to Wade, January 3, 1862, Benjamin Wade Papers, Library of Congress; Thomas O'Reilly to Sumner, December 5, 1861, 1:24, Sumner Papers. O'Reilly wrote from St. Louis to complain about the absence of Republican generals. Many wrote Sherman about the recruiting problems that would develop if the government did not fight more aggressively. James A. Padgett, "Some Letters of George Stanton Denison, 1854–1866: Observations of a Yan-

kee on Conditions in Louisiana and Texas," *Louisiana Historical Quarterly* 23 (October 1940): 1186. See Arnold M. Shankman, *The Pennsylvania Antiwar Movement, 1861–1865* (Rutherford, N.J.: Fairleigh Dickinson University Press, 1980), 83–86, and Charles M. Knapp, *New Jersey Politics During the Period of the Civil War and Reconstruction* (Geneva, N.Y.: W. F. Humphrey, 1924), 72–73, for examples of concern among Democrats over abolition.

21. Smith to Wade, March 2, 1862 (emphasis by Smith), Root to Wade, May 5, 1862, Wade Papers; Watson to Trumbull, March 11, 1862, Trumbull Papers. See Eric Foner, *Reconstruction: America's Unfinished Revolution, 1863–1877* (New York: Harper & Row, 1988), for the most thorough discussion of this issue; and Foner, "Thaddeus Stevens, Confiscation, and Reconstruction," in *The Hofstadter Aegis: A Memorial*, ed. Eric McKitrick and Stanley Elkins (New York: Knopf, 1974), 153–83. See Herman Belz, "A New Orthodoxy," *Reviews in American History* 1 (March 1973): 106–12, for the argument that distributing confiscated land after the Civil War had little support and may not have worked even if tried. See William C. Harris, *With Charity for All: Lincoln and the Restoration of the Union* (Lexington: University Press of Kentucky, 1997), for the best evaluation of Lincoln and Reconstruction.

22. Lewis Tappan to Sumner, January 16, 1862, George S. Boutwell to Sumner, February 11, 1862, Charles Carroll to Sumner, February 23, 1863, 1:24, Dana to Sumner, April 7, 1862, 1:25, Sumner Papers; Anonymous to Trumbull, April 11, 1862, Trumbull Papers; the letter was written on the stationary of the Agency of the Illinois Mutual Fire Insurance Company. Elias Lee to Stevens, March 19, 1862, Thaddeus Stevens Papers, Library of Congress. Lee was Stevens's cousin; Boutwell was a Massachusetts politician. Sam Gaither to Wade, February 27, 1862; N. H. Brewley to Wade, May 1, 1862, W. G. Smith to Wade, March 1862, Wade Papers; J. D. Easton to Sherman, April 11, 1861, John Sherman Papers, Library of Congress.

23. Stevens to Salmon P. Chase, August 25, 1862, Stevens Papers. See chapter 2, note 23, for recent works on colonization.

24. Garrison to Sumner, December 20, 1861, 1:24, Brownson to Sumner, April 11, 1862, 1:25, Sumner Papers; D. E. Clay [?] to Trumbull, December 17, 1861, Boston to Trumbull, December 23, 1861, Thomas Lippincott to Trumbull, January 28, 1862, Trumbull Papers. See Richard K. Fleishman, "The Devil's Advocate: A Defense of Lincoln's Attitude Toward the Negro, 1837–1863," *Lincoln Herald* 81 (Fall 1979): 172–86, for a perceptive argument about understanding the antislavery North in their context, not ours, and Allen C. Guelzo, *Lincoln's Emancipation Proclamation: The End of Slavery in America* (New York: Simon & Schuster, 2004), 139–44, for Lincoln's view on race and colonization. See James D. Bilotta, *Race and the Rise of the Republican Party, 1848–1865* (New York: Peter Lang, 1992), 447–63, for a discussion of the Republicans' views on race during the war.

25. *Cong. Globe*, 37:2, pt. 1, 944, 946 (Trumbull, Ten Eyck, February 25, 1862); pt. 3, 2301 (Blair, May 22, 1862); pt. 4, Appendix, 117 (Cutler, April 23, 1862); Curry, *Blueprint for Modern America*, 79.

26. Jay to Sumner, January 4, 1862, William Powell et al., to Sumner, January 17, 1862, 1:24, Sumner Papers; Peter Grignon et al., to Trumbull, January 27, 1862 (quotation), Trumbull Papers; Stanton to Horace Binney, February 16, 1862, Edwin M. Stanton Papers, Library of Congress. See Willie Lee Rose, *Rehearsal for Reconstruction: The Port Royal Experiment* (Indianapolis: Bobbs-Merrill, 1964) and Akiko Ochiai, "The Port Royal Experiment Revisited: Northern Visions of Reconstruction and the Land Question," *New England Quarterly* 74 (March 2001): 94–117, for how one theater of the war handled freed slaves. See Stanton to Gen. Rufus Saxton, June 16, 1862, Stanton Papers, for general guidelines on what to do with freed slaves and Joseph Henry Allen, "Africans

in America, and Their New Guardians," *Christian Examiner* 72 (July 1862), for the view that freed slaves should work the land in the South as tenants, not owners.

27. Lieber to Sumner, December 19, 1861, 2: 75, Jordan to Sumner, January 14, 1862, 1:24, Sumner Papers; Donald, *Sumner*, 54. Sumner introduced his state suicide thesis on February 11, 1862 in Congress and wrote about the subject more than a year later. See Charles Sumner, "Our Domestic Relations; Or How to Treat the Rebel States," *Atlantic Monthly* 13 (October 1863): 507–29; Medill to Trumbull, July 4, 1862 (emphasis by Medill), Jordan to Trumbull, December 28, 1861, Jordan to Trumbull, February 20, 1862, Trumbull Papers; G. S. Rynard [?] to Wade, June 27, 1862, Wade Papers; Jordan to Sherman, December 22, 1861, Jordan to Sherman, January 1, 1862, Sherman Papers; Joel Parker, "Constitutional Law," *North American Review* 94 (April 1862): 435–63; Edward L. Gambill, *Conservative Ordeal: Northern Democrats and Reconstruction, 1865–1868* (Ames: Iowa State University Press, 1981), 10–15; Jean H. Baker, *Affairs of Party: The Political Culture of Northern Democrats in the Mid-Nineteenth Century* (Ithaca, N.Y.: Cornell University Press, 1983), 323–45.

28. Frederick, "Second Confiscation Act," 136–50, 171–76; Lucie, *Freedom and Federalism*, 37–39; Bogue, *Earnest Men*, 227–34; *Detroit Daily Advertiser*, March 12, 26, 1862 in Curry, *Blueprint for Modern America*, 80–89; *Cong. Globe*, 37:2, pt. 3, 1991 (Trumbull, May 7, 1862); Ralph J. Roske, *His Own Counsel: The Life and Times of Lyman Trumbull* (Reno: University of Nevada Press, 1979), 83–88. See *Cong. Globe*, 37:2, pt. 3, 2878–79 (June 23, 1862), for the text of the bill.

29. Frederick, "Second Confiscation Act," 174; Lucie, *Freedom and Federalism*, 38–39; Lucie, "Confiscation," 310–11, 311n; *Cong. Globe*, 37:2, pt. 3, 2165–66, 2172 (Trumbull, May 16, 1861); Curry, *Blueprint for Modern America*, 84–85; Roske, *Trumbull*, 85–86. Robert Toombs was secretary of state for the Confederacy before he resigned and became an officer in the Confederate army.

30. Frederick, "Second Confiscation Act," 176–82; Curry, *Blueprint for Modern America*, 86–90; Lucie, *Freedom and Federalism*, 39–41; Heather C. Richardson, *The Greatest Nation of the Earth: Republican Economic Policies During the Civil War* (Cambridge: Harvard University Press, 1997), 221–25; *Cong. Globe*, 37:2, pt. 2, 1767, 1770; pt. 3, 2361–63 (for texts of House bills and votes).

31. *Cong. Globe*, 37:2, pt. 4, 3006 (Chandler, June 28, 1862), 3106–7, 3166, 3184–85; William C. Harris, *Public Life of Zachariah Chandler 1851–1875* (Lansing: Michigan Historical Commission, 1917), 62. Trumbull voted for the bill, according to his most recent biographer, because it "was better than no legislation at all." Roske, *Trumbull*, 87. Herman Belz, *A New Birth of Freedom: The Republican Party and Negro Rights, 1861–1866* (Westport, Conn.: Greenwood Press, 1976), 9–12; Curry, *Blueprint for Modern America*, 92–95; Frederick, "Second Confiscation Act," 183–94; Lucie, *Freedom and Federalism*, 41–45; Lucie, "Confiscation," 318.

32. *Cong. Globe*, 37:2, 3267–68 for House vote on July 11, 1862 and 3274–76 for Senate vote on July 12, 1862; pt. 4, Appendix, 412–13, for the full text of the final bill. *New York Herald*, July 14, 1862, in Curry, *Blueprint for Modern America*, 92–95; Trumbull to Mrs. Trumbull, July 13, 1862, as quoted in Frederick, "Second Confiscation Act," 198; David Lindsey, *Americans in Conflict: The Civil War and Reconstruction* (Boston: Houghton Mifflin, 1974), 130. See Lucie, *Freedom and Federalism*, 40–44, for the second act's confusion over how to emancipate slaves. Sumner to Bright, August 5, 1862, in James Ford Rhodes, *History of the United States* (Port Washington, N.Y.: Kennikat Press, 1967 [1899]), 4:62; Edward L. Pierce, ed., *Memoirs and Letters of Charles Sumner* (Boston: Roberts Bros., 1893), 4:76.

33. Roy Basler et al., eds., *The Collected Works of Abraham Lincoln* (New Brunswick, N.J.: Rutgers University Press, 1953), 5:144–46 (Message), 169 (Greeley), 192 (Message); Guelzo, *Lincoln's Emancipation Proclamation*, 92–94; Phillip Paludan, *The Presidency of*

Abraham Lincoln (Lawrence: University Press of Kansas, 1994), 125–29; Barbara Jeanne Fields, *Slavery and Freedom on the Middle Ground: Maryland During the Nineteenth Century* (New Haven, Conn.: Yale University Press, 1985), 110–11.

34. Edward A. Miller, Jr., *Lincoln's Abolitionist General: The Biography of David Hunter* (Columbia: University of South Carolina Press, 1997), 96–104; U.S. War Department, *War of the Rebellion: A Compilation of the Official Records of the Union and Confederate Armies* (Washington, D.C.: U.S. Government Printing Office, 1880–1901), ser. 1, vol. 14, 333 (April 13, 1862), ser. 3, vol. 2, 42–43 (May 9, 1862); Ira Berlin et al., eds., *Freedom: A Documentary History of Emancipation, 1861–1867*, ser. 2, *The Black Military Experience* (New York: Cambridge University Press, 1982), 38–39; A. S. Bundy to Wade, May 20, 1862, Wade Papers; John Murray Forbes to Sumner, May 16, 1862, George S. Boutwell to Sumner, May 19, 1862, 1:25, Sumner Papers; Sumner to Wendell Phillips, May 22, 1862, in Beverly Wilson Palmer, ed., *The Selected Letters of Charles Sumner* (Boston: Northeastern University Press, 1990), 1:113; David Donald, "Devils Facing Zionwards," in *Grant, Lee, Lincoln and the Radicals*, ed. Grady McWhiney (Evanston, Ill.: Northwestern University Press, 1964), 75.

35. Basler et al., *Collected Works of Lincoln*, 5:222–23; Michael Burlingame, ed., *At Lincoln's Side: John Hay's Civil War Correspondence and Selected Writings* (Carbondale: Southern Illinois University Press, 2000), 22; Paludan, *The Presidency*, 130–31; Guelzo, *Lincoln's Emancipation Proclamation*, 103–4; Chase to Maj. Gen. David Hunter, May 20, 1862, Chase to Greeley, May 21, 1862, in John Niven, ed., *The Salmon P. Chase Papers* (Kent, Ohio: Kent State University Press, 1996), 3:202–3.

36. Basler et al., *Collected Works of Lincoln*, 5:317–19 (emphasis in the original); William K. Klingaman, *Abraham Lincoln and the Road to Emancipation, 1861–1865* (New York: Viking Press, 2001), 149–50.

37. *U.S. Statutes at Large*, 12: 589–92 (Second Confiscation Act), 627 (Joint Resolution); see the appendix for both the second act and the joint resolution; Pease and Randall, *Diary of Browning*, 1:560; Francis Fessenden, *The Life and Public Services of William Pitt Fessenden* (Boston: Houghton Mifflin, 1907), 1:272–75; Jellison, *Fessenden*, 146–47; Curry, *Blueprint for Modern America*, 95–98; Frederick, "Second Confiscation Act," 207–18; *Cong. Globe*, 37:2, pt. 4, 3370 (Maynard, July 5, 1862). The resolution was not read and there is no text of it in the *Journal of the House* for that day. Maynard was a Massachusetts-born Unionist who supported confiscation.

38. *Cong. Globe*, 37:2, pt. 4, 3380 (Clark, July 16, 1862), 3383 (Trumbull, July 16, 1862); Whiting, *War Powers Under the Constitution*, 122–23. William A. Dunning, no friend of the second act, correctly observed in 1904 that the resolution adopted by Congress was an effort to "reconcile the act with the prohibition against" attainder in the Constitution. But the resolution was wrong since "the forfeiture contemplated by the act was in no sense the result of an attainder of treason. Attainder of treason does not result from a proceeding *in rem*, but from a conviction in a criminal proceeding *in personam*." See Dunning, *Essays on the Civil War and Reconstruction*, 32–33.

39. Roske, *Trumbull*, 89, Nevins, *The War for the Union*, 2:145–46; *Cong. Globe*, 37:2, pt. 4, 3374–75, 3383, 3400; Frederick, "Second Confiscation Act," 219–23; Curry, *Blueprint for Modern America*, 96–98; Klingaman, *Abraham Lincoln*, 151. Republican Senators opposed to the Joint Resolution were Trumbull, Grimes and Harlan of Iowa, King of New York, Lane of Indiana, Wilkinson of Minnesota, and Wilmot of Pennsylvania. Sumner said he would vote for the joint resolution since it did not cripple the emancipation provisions of the bill, the most important of the measure. *Cong. Globe*, 37:2, pt. 4, 3382 (Sumner, July 16, 1862).

40. Basler et al., *Collected Works of Lincoln*, 5:328–31; Pease and Randall, *Browning Diary*, 1: 558; Guelzo, *Lincoln's Proclamation of Emancipation*, 114–15.

4. Enforcement of the Second Act: Lincoln and Bates

1. Patricia A. Lucie, *Freedom and Federalism: Congress and the Courts, 1861–1866* (New York: Garland, 1986), 14, 47–48. See Earl Maltz, "Reconstruction Without Revolution: Republican Civil Rights Theory in the Era of the Fourteenth Amendment," *Houston Law Review* 24 (March 1987): 239–40, for a discussion about the lack of enforcement provisions in various measures during and after the Civil War.

2. Philip Paludan, *The Presidency of Abraham Lincoln* (Lawrence: University Press of Kansas, 1994), 146–47; David Herbert Donald, *Lincoln* (New York: Simon & Schuster, 1995), 364–65; Allen C. Guelzo, *Lincoln's Emancipation Proclamation: The End of Slavery in America* (New York: Simon & Schuster, 2004), 115–17; Roy Basler et al., eds., *The Collected Works of Abraham Lincoln* (New Brunswick, N.J.: Rutgers University Press, 1953), 5:336–37 (Emancipation Proclamation—First Draft), 338 (memorandum on Recruiting Negroes), 341 (Proclamation of the Act to Suppress Insurrection); Stanton notes in the Cabinet, July 22, 1862, Executive Order, July 22, 1862, Edwin M. Stanton Papers, Library of Congress. See William K. Klingaman, *Abraham Lincoln and the road to Emancipation, 1861–1865* (New York: Viking Press, 2001), 153, 164, for requests to Lincoln to enforce the emancipation provisions of the second act.

3. Basler et al., *Collected Works of Lincoln*, 5:371–75; Guelzo, *Lincoln's Emancipation Proclamation*, 142–44; James M. McPherson, "Abolitionists and Negro Opposition to Colonization During the Civil War," *Phylon* 26, no. 4 (1965): 394–95; Jason Silverman, "'In Isles Beyond the Main': Abraham Lincoln's Philosophy on Black Colonization," *Lincoln Herald* 80 (Fall 1978): 115–22; Michael Vorenberg, "Abraham Lincoln and the Politics of Black Colonization," *Journal of the Abraham Lincoln Association* 14 (Summer 1993): 23–45; Don E. Fehrenbacher, "Only His Stepchildren: Lincoln and the Negro," *Civil War History* 20 (December 1974): 293–310; Paul J. Scheip, "Lincoln and the Chiriqui Colonization Project," *Journal of Negro History* 38 (October 1952): 418–53; Charles H. Wesley, "Lincoln's Plan for Colonizing the Emancipated Negroes," *Journal of Negro History* 4 (January 1919): 7–21; James D. Bilotta, *Race and the Rise of the Republican Party, 1848–1865* (New York: Peter Lang, 1992), 452–54.

4. Mark Grimsley, *The Hard Hand of War: Union Military Policy Toward Southern Civilians, 1861–1865* (New York: Cambridge University Press, 1995), 67–69; Daniel E. Sutherland, "Abraham Lincoln, John Pope, and the Origins of Total War," *Journal of Military History* 56 (October 1992): 567–86; Donald, *Lincoln*, 364; James G. Randall, "Some Legal Aspects of the Confiscation Acts of the Civil War," *American Historical Review* 18 (October 1912): 81; James G. Randall, *Constitutional Problems Under Lincoln*, rev. ed. (Urbana: University of Illinois Press, 1964), 279n; Stephen Sears, *George B. McClellan: The Young Napoleon* (New York: Ticknor and Fields, 1988), 226–29; McClellan to Lincoln, July 7, 1862, in Stephen Spears, ed., *The Civil War Papers of George B. McClellan: Selected Correspondence, 1860–1865* (New York: Ticknor and Fields, 1989), 344–45; Joel Silbey, *A Respectable Minority: The Democratic Party in the Civil War Era, 1860–1868* (New York: Norton, 1977), 49–51; John Sherman to William Sherman, August 24, 1862, in Rachel Sherman Thorndike, ed., *The Sherman Letters: Correspondence Between General Sherman and Senator Sherman from 1837 to 1891* (New York: Da Capo Press, 1969 [1894]), 157–58; Guelzo, *Lincoln's Emancipation Proclamation*, 104–7. McClellan's advice came in the famous Harrison's Landing Letter. See Eric T. Dean, Jr., "Rethinking the Civil War: Beyond 'Revolutions,' 'Reconstructions,' and "New Social History,'" *Southern Historian* 15 (Spring 1994): 28–50, for a caution against accepting the total war thesis and the role of antislavery generals in the North's victory.

5. Lucie, *Freedom and Federalism*, 6, 14; Joseph Logsdon, *Horace White: Nineteenth Century Liberal* (Westport, Conn.: Greenwood Press, 1971), 89; Wallace D. Farnham, "'The Weakened Spring of Government': A Study in Nineteenth-Century American

History," *American Historical Review* 68 (April 1963): 662–80; Daniel J. Elazar, "Civil War and the Preservation of American Federalism," *Publius* 1 (Fall 1971): 39–58; Paludan, *The Presidency*, 108–9; Harold M. Hyman and William M. Wiecek, *Equal Justice Under Law: Constitutional Development 1835–1875* (New York: Harper & Row, 1982), 266–67; Harold M. Hyman, *A More Perfect Union: The Impact of the Civil War and Reconstruction on the Constitution* (New York: Knopf, 1973), 178–81; William B. Scott, *In Pursuit of Happiness: American Conceptions of Property from the Seventeenth to the Twentieth Century* (Bloomington: Indiana University Press, 1977); David R. Wrone, "Abraham Lincoln's Idea of Property," *Science and Society* 33, no. 1 (1969): 54–70; Steven Joseph Ross, "Freed Soil, Freed Labor, Freed Men: John Eaton and the Davis Bend Experiment," *Journal of Southern History* 44 (May 1978): 214–16; Morton J. Horowitz, *The Transformation of American Law, 1780–1860* (Cambridge, Mass.: Harvard University Press, 1977); Gaines M. Foster, "The Limitations of Federal Health Care for Freedmen, 1862–1868," *Journal of Southern History* 48 (August 1982): 349–72; Herman Belz, *Abraham Lincoln, Constitutionalism, and Equal Rights in the Civil War Era* (New York: Fordham University Press, 1998), 111–12.

6. Paludan, *The Presidency*, 146; Lucie, *Freedom and Federalism*, 39, 44; Patricia M. Lucie, "Confiscation: Constitutional Crossroads," *Civil War History* 23 (December 1977): 312–20; Guelzo, *Lincoln's Emancipation Proclamation*, 112–14; Hyman and Wiecek, *Equal Justice Under Law*, 251–53; Randall, *Constitutional Problems Under Lincoln*, 357–63; *U.S. Statutes at Large*, 12: 589–92. According to supporters of confiscation, the attainder clause applied to the first four sections of the second act, not to sections five through eight; see chapter 3. See Robert J. Plowman, "An Untapped Source: Civil War Prize Case Files," *Prologue* 21 (Fall 1989): 197–204; Virginia Jean Lass, "'Sleepless Sentinels': The North Atlantic Blockade Squadron, 1862–1864," *Civil War History* 31 (March 1985): 24–38; Stuart L. Bernarth, *Squall Across the Atlantic: American Civil War Prize Cases and Diplomacy* (Berkeley: University of California Press, 1970), for prize cases.

7. Lucie, "Confiscation," 307–9; Herman Belz, *Emancipation and Equal Rights: Politics and Constitutionalism in the Civil War Era* (New York: Norton, 1978), 33–38.

8. Marvin R. Cain, *Lincoln's Attorney General: Edward Bates of Missouri* (Columbia: University of Missouri Press, 1965), 196–97, 212–14, 285–86; Gideon Welles, ed., *Diary of Gideon Welles: Secretary of the Navy Under Lincoln and Johnson* (Boston: Houghton Mifflin, 1911), 1:152.

9. Henry Steele Commager, ed., *Documents of American History*, 7th ed. (New York: Appleton-Century-Crofts, 1963), 1:415–17; Glyndon Van Deusen, *Horace Greeley: Nineteenth Century Crusader* (Philadelphia: University of Pennsylvania Press, 1953), 285–87.

10. Basler et al., *Collected Works of Lincoln*, 5:388–89 (emphasis in the original); Guelzo, *Lincoln's Emancipation Proclamation*, 132–36; Paludan, *The Presidency*, 150; Hans L. Trefousse, "Owen Lovejoy and Abraham Lincoln During the Civil War," *Journal of the Abraham Lincoln Association* 22 (Winter 2001): 27–28.

11. Basler et al., *Collected Works of Lincoln*, 5:419–25 (emphasis in the original); Guelzo, *Lincoln's Emancipation Proclamation*, 151; Paludan, *The Presidency*, 151–52; Donald, *Lincoln*, 366–67, 374; Nicholas Parrillo, "Lincoln's Calvinist Transformation: Emancipation and War," *Civil War History* 46 (September 2000): 242–44.

12. Basler et al., *Collected Works of Lincoln*, 5:433–36; Guelzo, *Lincoln's Emancipation Proclamation*, 152–56.

13. David Donald, *Charles Sumner and the Rights of Man* (New York: Da Capo, 1996), 81; John Hope Franklin, *The Emancipation Proclamation* (Garden City, N.Y.: Anchor Books, 1963), 55–66; James M. McPherson, *The Negro's Civil War: How American Negroes Felt and Acted During the War for the Union* (New York: Pantheon Books, 1965), 49; Guelzo, *Lincoln's Emancipation Proclamation*, 157–60; Paludan, *The Presidency*, 155–57; Eugene H. Berwanger, "Lincoln's Constitutional Dilemma: Emancipation and

Black Suffrage," *Papers of the Abraham Lincoln Association* 5 (1983): 25–38; Michael F. Holt, "Abraham Lincoln and the Politics of Union," in *Abraham Lincoln and the American Political Tradition*, ed. Michael F. Holt (Amherst: University of Massachusetts Press, 1986), 129–30.

14. Everett to Chase, August 14, 1862, Everett to William Everett, September 29, 1862 (emphasis in the original), Reel 32, Edward Everett Papers, Massachusetts Historical Society, Boston; Theodore C. Pease and James G. Randall, eds., *The Diary of Orville Hickman Browning* (Springfield: Illinois State Historical Library, 1925), 1:587–88; Dana to Sally, October 1, 1862 (emphasis in the original), Richard Henry Dana Jr. Papers, Massachusetts Historical Society, Boston; H. B. Whiting to Thomas H. Seymour, September 29, 1862, Thomas H. Seymour Papers, Connecticut Historical Society, Hartford; Berwanger, "Lincoln's Dilemma," 33–34; Edith E. Ware, *Political Opinion in Massachusetts During the Civil War and Reconstruction* (New York: Longmans, Green, 1916), 102–5. Seymour, a Democrat and former governor of Connecticut, was well known for his opposition to the war.

15. Donald, *Sumner*, 44, 68–69; [Joel Parker], "The Character of the Rebellion, and the Conduct of the War," *North American Review* 95 (October 1862): 500–33; Ware, *Political Opinion in Massachusetts*, 114.

16. Randall, *Constitutional Problems Under Lincoln*, 357–63; Willie Lee Rose, *Rehearsal for Reconstruction: The Port Royal Experiment* (Indianapolis: Bobbs-Merrill, 1964), 186–87, 195–96; Lucie, *Freedom and Federalism*, 36, 40–44.

17. See Herman Belz, "The New Orthodoxy in Reconstruction Historiography," *Reviews in American History* 1 (March 1973): 106–12, for the argument that the radicals failed to secure permanent confiscation and that even if confiscation had occurred it might not have helped blacks very much in any case.

18. William W. Freehling, *The South vs. The South: How Anti-Confederate Southerners Shaped the Course of the Civil War* (New York: Oxford University Press, 2001), 105; Jordan to Chase, October 20, 1862, in Henry D. Shapiro, *Confiscation of Confederate Property in the North* (Ithaca, N.Y.: Cornell University Press, 1962), 46; Herman Belz, *Reconstructing the Union: Union and Policy During the Civil War* (Ithaca, N.Y.: Cornell University Press, 1969), 105–10; Basler et al., *Collected Works of Lincoln*, 5:496; Howard K. Beale, ed., *The Diary of Edward Bates 1859–1866* (New York: Da Capo, 1971 [1933]), 266–67; Cain, *Bates*, 200–201.

19. Basler et al., *Collected Works of Lincoln*, 5:496; Cain, *Bates*, 203. The military's role in confiscation is discussed more fully in chapters 5 and 6.

20. Coffey to Richard H. Dana, E. Delafield Smith, George A. Vourse and William Rice, December 1, 1862, Attorney General Letterbooks, B-5: 262–64, Attorney General Papers, Record Group 60, National Archives (hereafter cited as Attorney General Letterbooks); Lucie, *Freedom and Federalism*, 47–48.

21. Bates to U.S. District Attorneys and Marshals, January 8, 1862, Attorney General Letterbooks, B-5: 340–41; Cain, *Bates*, 203–4. Bates had told Grow that seizures could not be based on rumors or newspapers reports. Bates to Grow, January 14, 1863, ibid., 203.

22. Shapiro, *Confiscation*, 43; Attorney General Letterbooks, B-5: 341; Coffey to A. S. Goodwin, April 23, 1863, Coffey to Ransom Crippen, July 22, 1863, Bates to William Edwards, September 22, 1863, C:121, 214, 267; Lawrence Weldon to Bates, March 11, 1863, Letters Received, Illinois, Box 2, Attorney General Papers, Record Group 60, National Archives (hereafter cited as Letters Received).

23. William Grover to Bates, November 6, 1863, Missouri, Box 1, ibid.; Bates to Grover, November 11, 1863, Coffey to Rufus Waples, February 11, 1864, Bates to Stanton, April 19, 1864, Attorney General Letterbooks, C:314, 8–9, 520–21; Bates to Lawrence Weldon, March 17, 1863, B-5: 406 (quotation). Weldon was a district attorney in Illinois.

24. Larned to Bates, April 17, 1863, Letters Received, Illinois, Box 2; Coffey to Flamen Ball, February 4, 1863, Attorney General Letterbooks, B-5:360; Allen Thorndike Rice, ed., *Reminiscences of Abraham Lincoln by Distinguished Men of His Time*, 6th ed. (New York: North American Review, 1888), 238–39.

25. Chase to Gen. Ormsby M. Mitchell, October 4, 1862, in John Niven, ed., *The Salmon P. Chase Papers* (Kent, Ohio: Kent State University Press, 1996), 3:289; Bates to E. Delafield Smith, January 10, 1863, Coffey to Wingate Hays, January 22, 1863, Bates to George Ives, January 2, 1863, Attorney General Letterbooks, B-5: 312, 345, 313; Bates to Joshua Tevis, October 2, 1863, Bates to Edwin M. Stanton, April 16, 1863, Coffey to E. L. Carrington, July 24, 1863, Coffey to John Trimble, July 6, 1863, C: 278, 112–13, 216, 202; George Ives to Bates, December 30, 1863, Letters Received, Massachusetts, Box 1; Wingate Hays to Bates, December 31, 1862, Rhode Island, Box 1; Chase to Bates, July 1863, Treasury Department, Box 10; Ira Berlin et al., eds., *Freedom: A Documentary History of Emancipation, 1861–1867*, ser. 1, vol. 2, *Wartime Genesis of Free Labor: The Upper South* (New York: Cambridge University Press, 1993), 35.

26. Hooker to Bates, November 14, 1862, Letters Received, Connecticut, Box 1, H. G. Banta to Bates, June 17, 1863, Kentucky, Box 1, Lewis Johnson to Bates, December 5, 1863, Illinois, Box 2; J. Hubley Ashton to Benjamin H. Smith, November 8, 1864, Ashton to Luciens Chandler, November 18, 1864, Ashton to Levi Hooker, November 18, 1864, Coffey to H. G. Banta, June 23, 1863, Coffey to Stanton, July 24, 1863, Bates to Seward, May 25, 1864, Ashton to Theodore Edwards, May 14, 1864, Bates to Lewis Johnson, December 19, 1863, Attorney General Letterbooks, C: 718, 195, 218, 573, 559, 342.

27. Paul Wallace Gates, "Southern Investments in Northern Lands Before the Civil War," *Journal of Southern History* 5 (February 1939): 155–85; Bates to Close, September 13, 1863, Bates to John Underwood, October 9, November 12, 1863, Attorney General Letterbooks, C: 260–61, 317–18; Close to Bates, September 18, 1863, Underwood to Bates, November 5, 1863, Letters Received, Virginia, Box 1.

28. See *Pelham v. Rose* 9 Wall. 103 (1869), *Miller v. United States* 11 Wall. 268 (1870), *Tyler v. Defrees* 11 Wall. 331 (1870), *The Confiscation Cases* 20 Wall. 92 (1873), and other cases involving seizure discussed in chapter 10.

29. Bates to Horace Harrison, January 15, 1864, Bates to Underwood, December 8, 1863, Bates to Underwood, April 26, 1864, Bates to Benjamin H. Smith, April 1864, Attorney General Letterbooks, C: 368–70, 329, 345–56; Smith to Bates, May 16, 1864, Letters Received, Virginia, Box 1.

30. See *Brown v. Kennedy* 15 Wall. 591 (1872), for a case involving mortgages that had been seized and the Supreme Court's approval. The case is discussed in chapter 10.

31. Bates to District Attorneys, January 8, 1863, Attorney General Letterbooks, B-5: 341, Bates to Moss, October 2, 1863, Bates to Browne, April 20, 1863, C: 275, 119–20; Moss to Bates, September 25, 1863, Letters Received, Minnesota, Box 1; *Miller v. United States* 11 Wall. 268 (1870).

32. See Shapiro, *Confiscation*, 48–51, on which this paragraph is based.

33. See chapter 10 and *United States v. One Thousand Seven Hundred and Fifty-Six Shares* 27 Fed. Cas. 335.

34. Ball to Bates, July 3, 1864, Letters Received, Ohio, Box 1, Grover to Jordan, June 15, 1864, Grover to Bates, August 2, 1864, Missouri, Box 1; Bates to Ball, August 28, 1864, Bates to Grover, August 23, 1864, Attorney General Letterbooks, C: 242, 661–62. Secretary Chase brought Albert Jenkins's property to Bates's attention, Chase to Bates, December 30, 1862, Letters Received, Treasury Department, Box 9. Jenkins's property, when sold, brought only $1,753 to the government. There is no record that the property Grover mentioned ever sold at public auction; see *Senate Executive Documents*, 40 Congress, 2nd session, no. 58, serial 1317.

35. Bates to Stanton, April 19, 1864, Coffey to Edward L. Bradford, July 17, 1863, Coffey to E. Delafield Smith, March 19, 1864, Bates to A. L. Keasby, May 27, 1863, Attorney General Letterbooks, C: 520–21, 309, 463, 158; Stanton to Bates, May 25, 1863, Letters Received, War Department, Box 5, A. L. Keasby to Bates, June 1, 1863, New Jersey, Box 1.

36. Bates to Lackey, January 19, 1863, in U. S. Department of War, *The War of the Rebellion: A Compilation of the Official Records of the Union and Confederate Armies* (Washington, D.C.: U.S. Government Printing Office, 1880–1901), ser. 2, vol. 5, 190–91.

37. Alexander to Bates, May 30, June 10, 15, 1865, Letters Received, Texas, Box. 1, Ballard to Bates, October 25, 1862, Kentucky, Box 1; Arny to Theodore Wheaton, September 27, 1862, Arny to Seward, September 29, 1862, Department of State, Box 5. See Edward D. Tittman, "Exploitation of Treason," *New Mexico Historical Review* 4 (April 1929): 129–45, for a review of the confiscation cases in New Mexico, most of which were lost for lack of witnesses to the alleged treason or evidence of the participation in the rebellion.

38. Ashton to Bell, July 22, 1864, Bates to Tevis, January 7, 1864, Coffey to Dart, December 6, 1864, Coffey to William E. Prince, February 15, 1864, Attorney General Letterbooks, C: 635, 261, 401, 420–21; Ball to Bates, July 8, 1864, Letters Received, Ohio, Box 1, Tevis to Bates, September 22, 1864, Kentucky, Box 1, Prince to Bates, January 28, 1864, Maryland, Box 2, Dart to Bates, February 11, 1864, New York, Box 4.

39. The final totals for confiscation appeared in a report to the Treasury Department in December 1867. The total proceeds for confiscation were only $129,680, a sum that James G. Randall calls "insignificant." See Randall, *Confiscation*, 15. For a table of the confiscation figures by state, see Randall, *Constitutional Problems Under Lincoln*, 288.

5. Early Military Confiscation

1. Half the money realized from confiscation came from New Orleans while under the authority of Gen. Butler and Gen. Nathanial Banks. See James G. Randall, *Constitutional Problems Under Lincoln*, rev. ed. (Urbana: University of Illinois Press, 1964), 288, for the figures realized from confiscation.

2. See chapter 1.

3. McClellan to Col. J. B. Steedman, May 26, 1861, McClellan to Union Men of Western Virginia, McClellan to Robert S. Garnett, July 15, 1861, U.S. War Department, *War of the Rebellion: A Compilation of the Official Records of the Union and Confederate Armies* (Washington, D.C.: U.S. Government Printing Office, 1880–1901), ser. 1, vol. 2, 48–49, 753, 252 (hereafter cited as *Official Records*); House Resolution, July 9, 1861, vol. 2, 759.

4. Dix to Simon Cameron, August 8, 1861, *Official Records*, ser. 2, vol. 1, 763; Dix to George McClellan, August 21, 1861, 764–65; Deed of Manumission, September 12, 1861, 769–70; Dix to Col. H. E. Paine, November 4, 1861, 775; McClellan to Brig. Gen. D. C. Buell, November 7, 1861, 776; William T. Sherman to Brig. Gen. McCook, November 8, 1861, 777; Ira Berlin et al., eds., *Slaves No More: Three Essays on Emancipation and the Civil War* (New York: Cambridge University Press, 1992), 25–26; Ira Berlin et al., eds., *Freedom: A Documentary History of Emancipation, 1861–1867*, ser. 1, vol. 1, *The Destruction of Slavery* (New York: Cambridge University Press, 1985), 17–21.

5. Mark Grimsley, *The Hard Hand of War: Union Military Policy Toward Southern Civilians 1861–1865* (New York: Cambridge University Press, 1995), 13–17, 54–66; Hawkins to People of North Carolina, September 1, 1861, *Official Records*, ser. 1, vol. 4, 658–59; Scott to Sherman, October 14, 1861, vol. 6, 176–77; Sherman to Adjutant-General, November 15, 1861, 188; McClellan to Buell, November 12, 1861, vol. 4, 355; General Orders No. 3, November 20, 1861, vol. 8, 370; Dix to Lincoln, November 15, 1861, vol. 5, 431; Dix to Colonel H. E. Paine, November 4, 1861, 641–42; Dix to Brig. Gen. H. H. Lockwood, November 11, 1861, 424–25; Dix to Lockwood, November 28, 1861, ser. 2, vol. 2, 157–58; Brooks D. Simpson, "'The Doom of Slavery': Ulysses S. Grant, War Aims, and Emancipation, 1861–1863," *Civil War History* 36 (March 1990): 39–41; Mary Berry, *Mili-*

tary Necessity and Civil Rights Policy: Black Citizenship and the Constitution (Port Washington, N.Y.: Kennikat Press, 1977), 38; Ira Berlin et al., eds., *Freedom: A Documentary History of Emancipation, 1861–1867*, ser. 1, vol. 2, *The Wartime Genesis of Free Labor: The Upper South* (New York: Cambridge University Press, 1993), 626–27. See chapter 1 for Dix and the first act.

6. Stephen V. Ash, *Middle Tennessee Society Transformed, 1860–1870: War and Peace in the Upper South* (Baton Rouge: Louisiana State University Press, 1988), 107; Foote to Inhabitants of Clarkesville, February 20, 1862, *Official Records*, ser. 1, vol. 7, 423; General Orders No. 13a, February 26, 1862, 669–70; Buell to the Board on Property, March 19, 1862, vol. 10, pt. 2, 47–48; Morgan to Edwin M. Stanton, June 27, 1862, vol. 16, pt. 1, 1009–10; see *U.S. Statutes at Large*, 12:319, for the first act; Grimsley, *The Hard Hand of War*, 63–64; Peter Maslowski, *Treason Must Be Made Odious: Military Occupation and Wartime Reconstruction in Nashville, Tennessee, 1862–65* (Millwood, N.Y.: KTO Press, 1978), 56–57, 67; Simpson, "The Doom of Slavery," 42. See Stephen D. Engle, "Don Carlos Buell: Military Philosophy and Command Problems in the West," *Civil War History* 42 (June 1995): 89–115, for Buell's conservative military methods.

7. General Orders 26, March 13, 1862, *Official Records*, ser. 1, vol. 5, 747; Rosecrans to Edwin M. Stanton, April 19, 1862, vol. 12, pt. 3, 92; Assistant Adjutant-General S. Williams to Gens. Smith, Couch, Casey, Keyes, Hentzelman, Hooker and Kearney, May 10, 1862, vol. 11, pt. 3, 161; General Orders No. 122, May 11, 1862, 165–66; General Orders No. 18, June 3, 1862, vol. 12, pt. 1, 54; McClellan to Hill Carter, July 11, 1862, vol. 11, pt. 3, 316. The same pattern was also evident in other parts of the South. See ibid., vol. 6, 126, 244–45 (Florida), 238 (Georgia), vol. 16, pt. 2, 155–56 (Alabama), vol. 8, 562–63, 577–78 (Arkansas), vol. 7, 551 (Missouri, from U. S. Grant); Lieut. T. H. Stevens to Commander P. Drayton, April 13, 1862, in Berlin et al., *Destruction of Slavery*, 120–21 (Florida).

8. See chapter 4 for Hunter's proclamation and Lincoln's reaction, and *Official Records*, ser. 3, vol. 2, 42–43.

9. Berlin et al., *Destruction of Slavery*, 25, Grimsley, *The Hard Hand of War*, 98–99; Ruth A. Gallagher, "Samuel Ryan Curtis," *Iowa Journal of History and Politics* 25 (July 1927): 339–48; Earl J. Hess, "Confiscation and the Northern War Effort: The Army of the Southwest at Helena," *Arkansas Historical Quarterly* 44 (Spring 1985): 56–59; Carl H. Moneyhon, "The Impact of the Civil War in Arkansas: The Mississippi River Plantation Counties," *Arkansas Historical Quarterly* 51 (Summer 1992): 108; Carl H. Moneyhon, "From Free Slave to Free Labor: The Federal Plantation Experiment in Arkansas," in *Civil War Arkansas: Beyond Battles and Leaders*, ed. Anne Bailey and Daniel Sutherland (Fayetteville: University of Arkansas Press, 2000), 178 (slave quotation); Halleck to Curtis, March 23, 1862, *Official Records*, ser. 1, vol. 8, 636–37; Curtis to Halleck, July 31, 1862, vol. 13, 524–25.

10. Proclamation of Butler, May 1, 1862, in Benjamin F. Butler, *Private and Official Correspondence of Gen. Benjamin F. Butler During the Period of the Civil War* (Norwood, Mass.: Plimpton Press, 1917), 1:434; Butler to Edwin M. Stanton, May 25, 1862, *Official Records*, ser. 1, vol. 15, 439–42; Howard Palmer Johnson, "New Orleans Under General Butler," *Louisiana Historical Quarterly* 24 (January–October 1941): 517–19; Thomas E. Dabney, "The Butler Regime in Louisiana," *Louisiana Historical Quarterly* 27 (April 1944): 499; Berlin et al., *Destruction of Slavery*, 192–93; Chester G. Hearn, *When the Devil Came Down to Dixie: Ben Butler in New Orleans* (Baton Rouge: Louisiana State University Press, 1997), 204–5; Peter C. Ripley, *Slaves and Freedmen in Civil War Louisiana* (Baton Rouge: Louisiana State University Press, 1976), 25–35; William F. Messner, *Freedmen and the Ideology of Free Labor: Louisiana, 1862–1865* (Lafayette: Center for Louisiana Studies, University of Southwestern Louisiana, 1978), 1–7; Peyton McCrary, *Abraham Lincoln and Reconstruction: The Louisiana Experiment* (Princeton, N.J.: Princeton University Press, 1978), 76–77.

11. Butler to Phelps, May 10, 1862, *Official Records*, ser. 1, vol. 15, 443; Butler to Phelps, May 23, 1862, 443–44; General Orders No. 32, May 27, 1862, 445; Captain Edward Page to Butler, May 27, 1862, 446–47; Captain P. Haggerty to Phelps, May 28, 1862, 446–47; Frank H. Peck to Phelps, June 15, 1862, 491; Phelps to Captain R. S. David, June 16, 1862, 486–90; Butler to Stanton, June 18, 1862, 485–86; General Orders No. 27, March 21, 1862, ser. 3, vol. 1, 937–38 (March 13 act of Congress); Johnson, "New Orleans Under Butler," 518–21; James Parton, *General Butler in New Orleans: History of the Administration of the Department of the Gulf* (New York: Mason Bros., 1864), 495–516; Hearn, *Butler in New Orleans*, 205–7; Messner, *Freedmen and the Ideology of Free Labor*, 9–13; McCrary, *The Louisiana Experiment*, 83–85; Murray M. Horowitz, "Ben Butler and the Negro: 'Miracles Are Occurring,'" *Louisiana History* 17 (Spring 1976): 173–76.

12. Stanton to Butler, July 29, 1862, *Official Records*, ser. 1, vol. 15, 515–16; Stanton to Butler, July 3, 1862, ser. 3, vol. 2, 200; Lincoln to Reverdy Johnson, July 26, 1862, Lincoln to Cuthbert Bullitt, July 28, 1862, in Roy Basler et al., eds., *The Collected Works of Abraham Lincoln* (New Brunswick, N.J.: Rutgers University Press, 1953), 5:342–43, 344–46; Theodore C. Pease and James G. Randall, eds., *The Diary of Orville Hickman Browning* (Springfield: Illinois State Historical Library, 1925), 1:564; Allen C. Guelzo, *Lincoln's Emancipation Proclamation: The End of Slavery in America* (New York: Simon & Schuster, 2004), 126; William C. Harris, *With Charity for All: Lincoln and the Restoration of the Union* (Lexington: University Press of Kentucky, 1997), 72–76.

13. Brig. Gen. Daniel Ruggles to Gen. Van Dorn, July 22, 1862, *Official Records*, ser. 1, vol. 15, 785; Phelps to Captain R. S. Davis, July 30, 1862, 534–35; Johnson, "New Orleans Under Butler," 522; Hearn, *Butler in New Orleans*, 207–8; Messner, *Freedmen and the Ideology of Free Labor*, 13–17; Howard C. Westwood, "Benjamin Butler's Enlistment of Black Troops in New Orleans in 1862," *Louisiana History* 26 (Winter 1985): 5–22; Chase to Butler, June 24, July 31, 1862, in J. W. Schuckers, *The Life and Public Services of Salmon Portland Chase* (New York: Appleton & Co., 1874), 376–78.

14. See *U.S. Statutes at Large*, 12: 589, for the provisions of the second act.

15. Basler et al., *Collected Works of Lincoln*, 5:338 (Memorandum on Recruiting Negroes), 341 (Proclamation of the Act to Suppress Insurrection); Burrus M. Carnahan, "Lincoln, Lieber and the Laws of War: The Origins and Limits of the Principle of Military Necessity," *American Journal of International Law* 92 (April 1998): 219–20; Messner, *Freedmen and the Ideology of Free Labor*, 17–18.

16. See *Mechanics' and Traders' Bank v. Union Bank* 89 U.S. 276 (1874), for a case involving Butler's creation of a court that supported his decision to suspend Confederate currency. The Supreme Court, with Justice Field dissenting, upheld Butler's right to establish the court.

17. See *Confiscation Cases* 20 Wall. 92 (1873), *Claims of Marcuard et al.* 20 Wall. 114 (1873), and *Brugere v. Slidell, Heath v. Slidell* 154 U.S. 598 (1893), for cases involving Slidell's property.

18. Barnes A. Lathrop, "The Lafourche District in 1861–1862: A Problem in Local Defense," *Louisiana History* 1 (Spring 1960): 126; General Orders No. 29, May 16, 1862, *Official Records*, ser. 1, vol. 15, 426; General Orders No. 30, May 19, 1862, 437–38; General Orders No. 41, June 10, 1862, 483–84; Butler to Stanton, June 27, 1862, 500; Adjutant General's Office to Butler, June 23, 1862, 493; General Orders No. 46, June 26, 1862, Butler, *Correspondence*, 2:3; Dabney, "Butler Regime," 515.

19. Hearn, *Butler in New Orleans*, 164–66; Butler, *Correspondence*, 1:574–75; Butler to Stanton, June 17, 1862, *Official Records*, ser. 3, vol. 2, 153–54; Juan Callejon et al. to Butler, June 1862, 154–56; Butler to Cte. Mejan et al., June 16, 1862, 157–59; Stanton to Butler, June 29, 1862, ser. 1, vol. 15, 515–16; Butler to Seward, September 19, 1862, ser. 3, vol. 2, 571–73; Bernard C. Steiner, *Life of Reverdy Johnson* (New York: Russell & Russell, 1970 [1914]), 58–59; Thomas W. Helis, "Of Generals and Jurists: The Judicial System of New

Orleans Under Union Occupation, May 1862–April 1865," *Louisiana History* 29 (Spring 1988): 152.

20. See Chase to Butler, October 29, 1862, in John Niven, ed., *The Salmon P. Chase Papers* (Kent, Ohio: Kent State University Press, 1996), 3:307–8, for the secretary's frank estimate of the corruption underway by the Butler brothers.

21. Hearn, *Butler in New Orleans*, 180–87, 195–96. Hearn estimates that Butler arrived in New Orleans worth no more than $150,000 and his brother with far less. By 1868, Butler alone was worth $3 million. James G. Hollandsworth Jr., *Pretense of Glory: The Life of General Nathaniel P. Banks* (Baton Rouge: Louisiana State University Press, 1998), 158, estimates that Andrew Butler left over $200,000 to his brother upon his death in 1868. Gen. Neal Dow, of Maine temperance fame, also enriched himself through the second act while in the Gulf region. In addition, Dow was the plaintiff in a case before the Supreme Court involving his right to act in Louisiana under the laws of war. See Frank L. Byrne, "'A Terrible Machine': General Neal Dow's Military Government on the Gulf Coast," *Civil War History* 12 (March 1966): 5–22; *Dow v. Johnson* 100 U.S. 158 (1879); John D. Winters, *The Civil War in Louisiana* (Baton Rouge: Louisiana State University Press, 1963), 140–41; Ludwell H. Johnson, "Contraband Trade during the Last Year of the Civil War," *Mississippi Valley Historical Review* 49 (March 1963): 641, 644.

22. Hearn, *Butler in New Orleans*, 180–87; Parton, *General Butler in New Orleans*, 468–74; Dabney, "Butler Regime," 515; John R. Ficklen, *History of Reconstruction in Louisiana (Through 1868)* (Baltimore: Johns Hopkins University Press, 1910), 37–40; General Orders No. 71, September 13, 1862, General Orders No. 73, September 18, 1862, General Orders No. 76, September 24, 1862, General Orders No. 82, October 17, 1862, *Official Records*, ser. 1, vol. 15, 571–73, 575–76, 581.

23. Barnes F. Lathrop, "The Lafourche District In 1862: Invasion," *Louisiana History* 2 (Spring 1961): 176, 182, 186–89; R. Dana Russell, *The Pughs of Bayou Lafourche* (Austin, Tex.: Plain View Press, 1985), 56–58, 61, 65–67; Hearn, *Butler in New Orleans*, 192–93; General Orders No. 91, November 9, 1862, *Official Records*, ser. 1, vol. 15, 592–94; see 594–95 for the agreement on black labor for the plantations in Saint Bernard and Plaquemines made by the Union and planters. This agreement was to apply to the District of Lafourche, too. Butler to Stanton, November 14, 1862, ibid., 592; William F. Messner, "Black Violence and White Response: Louisiana, 1862," *Journal of Southern History* 41 (February 1975): 27–32; McCrary, *The Louisiana Experiment*, 91.

24. Butler, *Correspondence*, 2:426, 4:32–33; Gerald M. Capers, *Occupied City: New Orleans Under the Federals, 1862–1865* (Lexington: University of Kentucky Press, 1965); Parton, *General Butler in New Orleans*, 483–84; Johnson, "New Orleans Under Butler," 501–2; Dabney, "The Butler Regime," 515.

25. Randall, *Constitutional Problems Under Lincoln*, 288, notes that $67,972.18 of the total realized from confiscation came from Louisiana, which was more than triple what came to the Treasury from New York, which produced the second largest amount. One can only guess how much might have been made from confiscation in Louisiana had the Butler brothers not done so well for themselves.

26. McClellan to H. W. Halleck, August 1, 1862, *Official Records*, ser. 1, vol. 2, 345–46; General Orders No. 154, August 9, 1862, 362–64; Sherman to Captain Fitch, August 7, 1862, vol. 17, pt. 2, 156–57; General Orders No. 67, August 8, 1862, 158–59; General Orders No. 107, vol. 40, pt. 2, August 15, 1862, 466–67; Samuel J. Kirkwood to Halleck, August 5, 1862, in Ira Berlin et al., eds., *Free At Last: A Documentary History of Slavery, Freedom and the Civil War* (New York: New Press, 1992), 67–68.

27. Stanton to Schofield, September 5, 1862, *Official Records*, ser. 1, vol. 13, 614; General Orders No. 19, September 11, 1862, 624–25; General Orders No. 34, September 17, 1862, vol. 50, 125–26; see Tittman, "The Exploitation of Treason," 128–45, for an explanation of why the efforts at confiscation in the New Mexico territory failed for lack of evidence.

28. Halleck to Grant, August 2, 1862, *Official Records*, ser. 1, vol. 17, pt. 2, 150; W. L. Elliott to Morgan, August 6, 1862, 154–55; John W. Brinsfield, "The Military Ethics of General William T. Sherman: A Reassessment," in *The Parameters of War. Military History from the Journal of the U.S. Army War College*, ed. Lloyd J. Matthews and Dale E. Brown (Washington, D.C.: Pergamon-Brassey's, 1987), 95; General Orders No. 13, July 25, 1862, *Official Records*, ser. 1, vol. 12, pt. 3, 509; General Orders No. 19, August 14, 1862, 573; Col. George D. Ruggles to Maj. Gen. Franz Sigel, August 16, 1862, 577; Grimsley, *The Hard Hand of War*, 85–87; Daniel E. Sutherland, "Abraham Lincoln, John Pope, and the Origins of Total War," *Journal of Military History* 65 (October 1992): 582–86; Bruce Tap, *Over Lincoln's Shoulder: The Committee on the Conduct of the War* (Lawrence: University Press of Kansas, 1998), 128–29; Simpson, "The Doom of Slavery," 46–47.

29. General Orders No. 154, August 9, 1862, *Official Records*, ser. 1, vol. 2, pt. 3, 363; Dix to Brig. Gen. O. S. Ferry, September 7, 1862, vol. 18, 386; General Orders 159, October 1, 1862, vol. 19, 376.

30. Wayne K. Durrill, *War of Another Kind: A Southern Community in the Great Rebellion* (New York: Oxford University Press, 1990), 121 (quotation), 122, 128, 131–34; Hess, "Confiscation and the Northern War Effort," 56–66; Moneyhon, "The Impact of the Civil War in Arkansas," 108, 110; Kim Allen Scott, "The Preacher, the Lawyer, and the Spoils of War," in *Civil War Arkansas: Beyond Battles and Leaders*, ed. Anne J. Bailey and Daniel E. Sutherland (Fayetteville: University of Arkansas Press, 2000), 106–9; David W. Adams, "Illinois Soldiers and the Emancipation Proclamation," *Journal of the Illinois Historical Association* 67 (September 1974): 408, 411–12, 416; Adelaide Gill, "Frederick Steele," *Palimpsest* 11 (April 1930): 151–59.

31. John Cimprich, *Slavery's End in Tennessee, 1861–1865* (University: University of Alabama Press, 1985), 34–41; John Cimprich, "Slavery's End in East Tennessee," *East Tennessee Historical Society's Publications* 52–53 (1981–82): 79–80; Ash, *Middle Tennessee Society Transformed*, 106–7, 111–13; Maslowski, *Treason Must Be Made Odious*, 66–69; Paul Horton, "Submitting to the 'Shadow of Slavery': The Secession Crisis and Civil War in Alabama's Lawrence County," *Civil War History* 44 (June 1998): 124n, 126 (quotation); Noel C. Fisher, "'Prepare Them for My Coming': General William T. Sherman, Total War and Pacification of West Tennessee," *Tennessee Historical Quarterly* 51 (Summer 1992): 75–85; Bobby L. Lovett, "The Negro's Civil War in Tennessee, 1861–1865," *Journal of Negro History* 61 (January 1976): 37–39; John Eaton, *Grant, Lincoln and the Freedmen: Reminiscences of the Civil War* (New York: Longmans, Green, 1907), 20; George R. Bentley, *A History of the Freedmen's Bureau* (Philadelphia: University of Pennsylvania Press, 1955), 21.

32. Berry, *Military Necessity and Civil Rights Policy*; Ripley, *Slaves and Freedmen*; Orders No. 44, June 18, 1862, *Official Records*, ser. 1, vol. 17, pt. 2, 15; Sherman to Captain Fitch, August 7, 1862, 157; Orders No. 67, August 8, 1862, 159; Fisher, "'Prepare Them for My Coming,'" 81–82.

6. Rules of War and Later Military Confiscation

1. James Turner Johnson, *Just War Tradition and the Restraint of War: A Moral and Historical Inquiry* (Princeton, N.J.: Princeton University Press, 1981), 292–95; Frank Freidel, "General Orders 100 and Military Government," *Mississippi Valley Historical Review* 32 (March 1946): 542–43; Freidel, *Francis Lieber: Nineteenth Century Liberal* (Baton Rouge: Louisiana State University Press, 1947), 324.

2. Henry W. Halleck, *International Law, or, Rules Regulating the Intercourse of State in Peace and War*, 3rd ed. (London, 1893 [1861]), 60–69; Freidel, "General Orders," 544; David Herbert Donald, *Charles Sumner and the Rights of Man* (New York: Da Capo, 1996), 12–13; Freidel, *Lieber*, 320, 327; Quincy Wright, "The American Civil War (1861–65)," in *The International Law of Civil War*, ed. Richard Faulk (Baltimore: Johns Hop-

kins University Press, 1971): 60; Frank Freidel, "Francis Lieber, Charles Sumner, and Slavery," *Journal of Southern History* 9 (February 1943): 75–93. Halleck also began a correspondence with Attorney General Bates in 1861 on the treatment of prisoners.

3. Lieber to Sumner, September 14, 1861, ser. 2, Reel 75 (hereafter 2:75), Charles Sumner Papers, Lamont Library, Harvard University; Freidel, *Lieber*, 322–29; Freidel, "General Orders," 549; James F. Childress, "Francis Lieber's Interpretation of the Laws of War: General Orders 100 in the Context of His Life and Thought," *American Journal of Jurisprudence* 21 (1976): 34; Brainerd Dyer, "Francis Lieber and the American Civil War," *Huntington Library Quarterly* 2 (July 1939): 450–55; Burrus M. Carnahan, "Lincoln, Lieber and the Laws of War: The Origins and Limits of the Principle of Military Necessity," *American Journal of International Law* 92 (April 1998): 215; Richard S. Hartigan, *Lieber's Code and the Laws of War* (Chicago: Precedent, 1983), 13, 74. See Reverend L. Bacon, "Reply to Professor [Joel] Parker, *The New Englander* 22 (April 1863): 191–258, in which Bacon argued that the rebels could claim no rights under the Constitution. He said only the laws of war and nations could protect them from whatever the military thought was necessary.

4. General Orders 100 was entitled "General Orders, no. 100: Instructions for the Government of Armies of the United States in the Field," U.S. War Department, *The War of the Rebellion: A Compilation of Official Records of the Union and Confederate Armies* (Washington, D.C.: U.S. Government Printing Office, 1880–1901), ser. 3, vol. 3, 148–64 (hereafter cited as *Official Records*); Dorris A. Graber, *The Development of the Law of Belligerent Occupation, 1863–1914* (New York: Columbia University Press, 1949), 192–94 (Lieber quotation); Phillip Paludan, *A Covenant with Death: The Constitution, Law, and Equality in the Civil War Era* (Urbana: University of Illinois Press, 1975), 96–97.

5. Michael Les Benedict, "The Constitution of the Lincoln Presidency and the Republican Era," in *The Constitution and the American Presidency*, ed. Martin L. Fausold and Alan Shank (Albany: State University of New York Press, 1991): 55, 58; Allen C. Guelzo, *Lincoln's Emancipation Proclamation: The End of Slavery in America* (New York: Simon & Schuster, 2004), 197–202; Lieber to Sumner, December 16, 1861 (emphasis in the original), 2:75, Sumner Papers; Paludan, *A Covenant with Death*, 94–97; Theodor Meron, "Francis Lieber's Code and Principles of Humanity," *Columbia Journal of Transnational Law* 36:1–2 (1997): 269–81; "Instructions for the Government," *Official Records*, ser. 3, vol. 3, 152–53; Freidel, "General Orders," 553, suggests Union military officers gave little notice to the orders.

6. See James M. McPherson, "Who Freed the Slaves?" in *Drawn with the Sword: Reflections on the Civil War*, ed. James M. McPherson (New York: Oxford University Press, 1996), 192–207; Ira Berlin, "Who Freed the Slaves? Emancipation and Its Meaning," in *Union and Emancipation: Essays on Politics and Race in the Civil War Era*, ed. David W. Blight and Brooks D. Simpson (Kent, Ohio: Kent State University Press, 1997), 105–21; Mark E. Neely Jr., "Lincoln and the Theory of Self-Emancipation," in *The Continuing Civil War: Essays in Honor of the Civil War Round Table of Chicago*, ed. John Y. Simon and Barbara Hughett (Dayton, Ohio: Morningside, 1992), 45–59; Guelzo, *Lincoln's Emancipation Proclamation*, 8–9, for the debate on who deserves credit for emancipation.

7. Peyton McCrary, *Abraham Lincoln and Reconstruction: The Experiment in Louisiana* (Princeton, N.J.: Princeton University Press, 1978), 108; Halleck to Banks, November 9, 1862, *Official Records*, ser. 1, vol. 15, 590–91; General Orders 111, December 17, 1862, 610; James G. Hollandsworth Jr., *Pretense of Glory: The Life of General Nathaniel P. Banks* (Baton Rouge: Louisiana State University Press, 1998), 88–97; Fred H. Harrington, *Fighting Politician: Major General N. P. Banks* (Westport, Conn.: Greenwood Publishers, 1970 [1948]), 92–95.

8. See *The Grapeshot* 9 Wall. 129 (1869), for the Supreme Court's unanimous ruling, written by Chief Justice Salmon Chase, that Lincoln's creation of the Provisional Court of Louisiana was constitutional.

9. Charles A. Peabody, "United States Provisional Court for the State of Louisiana, 1862–1865," *Annual Report of the American Historical Association for 1892* (Washington, D.C.: 1893): 204; Thomas W. Helis, "Of Generals and Jurists: The Judicial System of New Orleans Under Union Occupation, May 1862–June 1865," *Louisiana History* 29 (Spring 1988): 153–55; A. H. Carpenter, "Military Government of Southern Territory, 1861–1865," *Annual Report of the American Historical Association of 1900* (Washington, D.C.: American Historical Association, 1901): 485–86.

10. Helis, "Of Generals and Jurists," 155–58; Harrington, *Fighting Politician*, 102; Peabody, "Provisional Court," 205–6; Banks to S. B. Holabird, March 27, 1862, *Official Records*, ser. 1, vol. 15, 694–95; Halleck to Banks, April 18, 1863, 702; William C. Harris, *With Charity for All: Lincoln and the Restoration of the Union* (Lexington: University Press of Kentucky, 1997), 115; *New Orleans Delta*, June 25, 1863, Edward H. Durell Papers, New York Historical Society, New York City. Like many Union officials in New Orleans, Durell was from the East. A graduate of Harvard Law School, he came to the city in 1836. In 1863 he believed that support for abolition was "making converts" in the region. Durell to "My very dear Sisters," January 16, 1863, ibid. Durell was the judge in a number of confiscation cases. See *Confiscation Cases* 7 Wall. 454 (1868); *Day v. McCou* 18 Wall. 156 (1873); and *Semmes v. United States* 91 U.S. 21 (1875). He resigned in 1874 as proceedings for his impeachment began. See Allen Johnson and Dumas Malone, eds., *Dictionary of American Biography* (New York: Charles Scribner's Sons, 1930), 5:545–46; Charles Fairman, *The History of the Supreme Court of the United States*, vol. 6: *Reconstruction and Reunion, 1864–88* (New York: Macmillan, 1971), 793, 814, 821n, 837.

11. Waples was involved in a number of confiscation cases, some of which are discussed in chapters 10 and 11. He was the district attorney in *Armstrong's Foundry* 6 Wall. 766 (1866); *St. Louis Foundry* 6 Wall. 770 (1867); *Confiscation Cases* 7 Wall. 454 (1868); and *Day v. McCou* 18 Wall. 156 (1873). He was a litigant in *Ex Parte Waples* 154 U.S. 579 (1871); *Conrad v. Waples* 96 U.S. 279 (1877); *Waples v. Hays* 108 U.S. 6 (1882); and *Waples v. United States* 110 U.S. 630 (1883). See Fairman, *Reconstruction and Reunion*, 792, 812–13, 813n, 817, 823. After the war Waples wrote *A Treatise on Proceedings in Rem* (Chicago: Callaghan & Co., 1882).

12. Helis, "Of Generals and Jurists," 158–59; Harrington, *Fighting Politician*, 102; Stone to Banks, November 12, 1862, Stone to Durell, November 12, 1863, Stone to Rufus Waples, November 12, 1863, Stone to Banks, November 15, 1863, Stone to Adjutant-General of the Army, November 19, 1862, *Official Records*, ser. 1, vol. 26, pt. 1, 793–95, 800–802, 807–9. See *Mechanics' and Traders' Bank v. Union Bank* 22 Wall. 276 (1874); *United States v. Diekelman* 92 U.S. 520 (1875); *Dow v. Johnson* 100 U.S. 158 (1879), for three others cases about the Louisiana occupation that reached the Supreme Court.

13. In addition to their work as a District Attorney and Marshal, Waples and Graham also bought confiscated property in New Orleans. See *Conrad v. Waples* 96 U.S. 279 (1877) and *Waples v. Hayes* 108 U.S. 6 (1882), for cases where Waples bought property that had been confiscated. See *Ex Parte Graham* 10 Wall. 541 (1870), for the case involving property purchased by Graham. John Niven, ed., *The Salmon Chase Papers* (Kent, Ohio: Kent State University Press, 1993), 1:376n; Fairman, *Reconstruction and Reunion*, 813n.

14. See Harrington, *Fighting Politician*, 92–108; McCrary, *Experiment in Louisiana*, 120–21, 133; William F. Messner, *Freedmen and the Ideology of Free Labor 1862–1865* (Lafayette: University of Southwestern Louisiana, 1978), 89–107; Harris, *With Charity for All*, 112–20; Hollandsworth, *Nathaniel P. Banks*, 157–71, for assessments of Banks's problems; Banks to Colonel S. B. Holabird, March 27, 1863, *Official Records*, ser. 1, vol. 15, 694–95; Banks to Col. E. G. Beckwish, March 31, 1863, 697–98; Banks to Halleck, May 4,

1863, 309–10; George S. Denison to Chase, January 8, 1863, Chase to Denison, March 3, 1863, Denison to Chase, March 29, 31, 1863, in Niven, *Chase Papers*, 3:361, 393, 404, 415.

15. Banks to Lincoln, February 2, 1864, *Official Records*, ser. 3, vol. 4, 68–70; Maj. Gen. R. Taylor to Brig. Gen. W. R. Boggs, January 11, 1864, ser. 1, vol. 34, pt. 2, 852–53; [E. Kirby Smith] to R. Taylor, January 24, 1864, 911; Taylor to Boggs, February 16, 1864, 971–72; Taylor to Boggs, February 21, 1864, 977–78; Hollandsworth, *Nathaniel P. Banks*, 160–61.

16. In March 1861 Campbell had corresponded with Jefferson Davis about Secretary of State Seward's apparent wish to evacuate Fort Sumter, and in January 1865 Campbell was one of three men Davis chose to meet with Lincoln about possible terms of peace. See chapter 9 for this meeting. William J. Cooper Jr., *Jefferson Davis, American* (New York: Vintage Books, 2000), 363, 549.

17. Lamon to Bates, December 18, 1862, Dosten to Lt. Murphy, December 18, 1862, Dosten to Bates, December 18, 1862, Martindale to Bates, December 20, 1862, Letters Received, District of Columbia, Box 3, Record Group 60, Attorney General Papers, National Archives, (hereafter cited as Letters Received); Bates to Martindale, December 19, 1862, Attorney General Letterbooks, B-5: 271, 273, Record Group 60, Attorney General Papers, National Archives (hereafter cited as Attorney General Letterbooks); Marvin R. Cain, *Lincoln's Attorney General: Edward Bates of Missouri* (Columbia: University of Missouri Press, 1965), 201–2.

18. Martindale to Bates, December 20, 1862, Letters Received, District of Columbia, Box 3; Bates to Dosten, December 22, 1862, Bates to Martindale, December 26, 1862, Bates to Carrington, December 27, 1862 (emphasis by Bates), Attorney General Letterbooks, B-5, 281, 283; the entire correspondence can be found in *House Executive Documents* 37 Congress, 3 session, no. 44, serial 1161.

19. Carrington to Bates, January 10, 1863, Letters Received, District of Columbia, Box 3. Carrington's proposed amendments were enclosed in his letter. *McVeigh v. United States* 11 Wall. 259 (1870) involved whether or not rebels within the Confederacy had a right to be heard if their property was confiscated and is discussed in chapter ten.

20. *House Executive Documents*, 37 Congress, 3 Session, no. 44, serial 1161; Stanton sent his letter to the House on January 23, 1863. Stanton's biographers give no evidence that he worked in other ways to expand the scope of the confiscation acts. See Benjamin P. Thomas and Harold M. Hyman, *Stanton: The Life and Times of Lincoln's Secretary of War* (New York: Knopf, 1962).

21. Bates to Stanton, January 31, 1863, Bates to E.R. Glascock, February 27, 1863, Attorney General Letterbooks, B-5: 337–38; Stanton to Rosecrans, February 27, 1863, *Official Records*, ser. 3, vol. 3, 57–58.

22. Rosecrans to Stanton, March 7, 1863, ibid., ser. 3, vol. 3, 59–60; Brig. E. Canby to Bates, March 13, 1863, Letters Received, War Department, Box 5; John Cimprich, *Slavery's End in Tennessee, 1861–1865* (University: University of Alabama Press, 1985), 37–38; see Mark Grimsley, *The Hard Hand of War: Union Military Policy Toward Southern Civilians, 1861–1865* (New York: Cambridge University Press, 1995), 100–102, and Walter T. Durham, *Nashville: The Occupied City: The First Seventeen Months—February 16, 1862, to June 30, 1863* (Nashville: Tennessee Historical Society, 1985), 236, 246–48, 258–60, for slightly different assessments of Rosecrans's handling of civilians in and around Nashville at the time.

23. Cain, *Bates*, 288, 292; [John A. Bolles, Dix's Aide-de-Camp] to Captain C. B. Wilder, March 28, 1863, *Official Records*, ser. 1, vol. 18, 570–71.

24. Noel C. Fisher, *War at Every Door: Partisan Politics and Guerilla Violence in East Tennessee, 1860–1869* (Chapel Hill: University of North Carolina Press, 1997), 135–41.

25. Harris, *With Charity for All*, 102–3; Naglee to Gen. John G. Foster, August 12, 1863, *Official Records*, ser. 1, vol. 29, pt. 2, 36; Special Orders No. 1, August 12, 1862, 37; Foster to Stanton, August 16, 1863, 54–58.

26. See General Orders No. 10, January 16, 1864, ibid., ser. 1, vol. 33, 549–51, for Butler's directives on the seizure of property for military purposes; Howard K. Beale, ed., *The Diary of Edward Bates 1859–1865* (New York: Da Capo, 1971 [1933]), 350; Butts to Bates, March 19, 1864, in *Private and Official Correspondence of Gen. Benjamin F. Butler During the Period of the Civil War*, ed. Benjamin Butler (Norwood, Mass: Plimpton Press, 1917), 4:18; Bates to Stanton, March 21, 1864, Attorney General Letterbooks, C: 489; Cain, *Bates*, 292–94; Roy P. Basler et al., eds., *The Collected Works of Abraham Lincoln* (New Brunswick, N.J.: Rutgers University Press, 1953), 6:371, 7:292.

27. Beale, *Diary of Edward Bates*, 350, 358–59; Wild to Butler, March 30, 1864, Butler to Stanton, April 4, 1864, in *Correspondence*, 4:16–21; Bates to Stanton, April 7, 1864, Attorney General Letterbooks, C: 503.

28. General Orders No. 30, April 26, 1864, *Official Records*, ser. 1, vol. 33, 989–90; General Orders No. 33, May 1, 1864, vol. 37, pt. 1, 638–39; Bates to Wallace, May 25, 1863, ser. 3, vol. 4, 407–8. After the war Wallace served as the governor of the Territory of New Mexico (1878–81) and minister to Turkey (1881–88). He also wrote *Ben-Hur* (1880).

29. Bates to Wallace, May 25, 1863, *Official Records*, ser. 3, vol. 4, 407–8; Cain, *Bates*, 294–95; Patricia A. Lucie, *Freedom and Federalism: Congress and Courts 1861–1866* (New York: Garland, 1986), 50.

30. Wallace to Bates, May 30, 1864, *Official Records*, ser. 3, vol. 4, 413–15.

31. Beale, *Diary of Edward Bates*, 376–77.

32. Stanton to Wallace, June 14, 1864, *Official Records*, ser. 3, vol. 4, 431; Wallace to Stanton, June 14, 1864, 432; J. Sherman to W. T. Sherman, March 20, 1863, in *The Sherman Letters: Correspondence Between General Sherman and Senator Sherman from 1837 to 1891*, ed. Rachel Sherman Thorndike (New York: Da Capo, 1969 [1894]), 194–95; Beale, *Diary of Edward Bates*, 379.

33. Brig. Gen. James H. Carleton to Judge John S. Watts, Dec. 9, 1864, *Official Records*, ser. 1, vol. 41, pt. 4, 816.

7. The Treasury's Part in Confiscation

1. See John Niven, *Salmon P. Chase: A Biography* (New York: Oxford University Press, 1995), for the best evaluation of Chase.

2. Chase to Adams, September 5, 1861, Chase to Jesse Stubbs, November 1, 1861, in John Niven, ed., *The Salmon P. Chase Papers* (Kent, Ohio: Kent State University Press, 1996) 3:95–97; Niven, *Chase*, 279–81; Louis S. Gerteis, "Salmon P. Chase, Radicalism, and the Politics of Emancipation, 1861–1864," *Journal of American History* 60 (June 1973): 42–43.

3. Willie Lee Rose, *Rehearsal for Reconstruction: The Port Royal Experiment* (Indianapolis: Bobbs-Merrill, 1964), 17–62; Roy P. Basler et al., eds., *The Collected Works of Abraham Lincoln* (New Brunswick, N.J.: Rutgers University Press, 1953), 5:48; Chase to Pierce, February 19, 1862; Curtis to Chase, February 24, 1862, in Niven, *Chase Papers*, 3:136–37, 140–41; Niven, *Chase*, 324; John G. Sproat, *"The Best Men": Liberal Reformers in the Gilded Age* (New York: Oxford University Press, 1968), 15, 17; David Donald, ed., *Inside Lincoln's Cabinet: The Civil War Diaries of Salmon P. Chase* (New York: Longmans, Green, 1954), 69. Pierce had been the author of the report on Gen. Benjamin Butler's use of freed slaves as laborers in the spring of 1861 and probably coined the word "contraband." See chapter 1.

4. Rose, *Rehearsal for Reconstruction*, 17–19, 152–53; Akiko Ochiai, "The Port Royal Experiment Revisited: Northern Visions of Reconstruction and the Land Question," *New England Quarterly* 74 (March 2001): 94–117; Philip Shaw Paludan, "*'A People's Contest': The Union and Civil War, 1861–1865*, 2nd ed. (Lawrence: University of Kansas Press, 1996), 203–4; Pierce to Chase, January 1, 1862, Chase to Pierce, February 19, 1862, in

Niven, *Chase Papers*, 3:117, 136–37; Niven, *Chase*, 323; Stanton to Saxton, April 29, 1862, Edwin Stanton Papers, Library of Congress.

5. Chase to Greeley, May 21, 1862, Chase to Halstead, May 24, 1862, Chase to Butler, June 24, 1862, in Niven, *Chase Papers*, 3:202–3, 204–5, 218–19; Niven, *Chase*, 303. Chase also reported to Butler that he had heard the general was engaging "in mercantile speculations" and had already "made considerable shipments north on private account."

6. Niven, *Chase*, 303–4; Gideon Welles, *Diary of Gideon Welles: Secretary of the Navy Under Lincoln and Johnson* (Boston: Houghton Mifflin, 1911), 1:70–71; Chase to Richard C. Parsons, July 20, 1862, Chase to Butler, July 31, 1862, in Niven, *Chase Papers*, 3:229–31, 235–37; Gerteis, "Salmon P. Chase," 47–49; Stanton notes, Tuesday, July 22, Stanton Papers.

7. Akiko Ochiai argues there were some on the Sea Islands like Rufus Saxton who believed that blacks had the right to acquire the land they had worked, by preemption, and become yeoman farmers in the South. Ochiai calls these men "preemptionists" and contrasts them with those like Edward Philbrick, a Boston businessman, who believed freedmen should be laborers first. Ochiai calls them "anti-preemptionists" and says they presumed freed slaves were not equal to the whites. William Gannett, the son of a minister, and others occupied the middle ground. See Ochiai, "Port Royal Experiment Revisited," 94–117.

8. V. Jacque Veogeli, *Free But Not Equal: The Midwest and the Negro during the Civil War* (Chicago: University of Chicago Press, 1967), 22–25; Chase to Butler, July 31, 1862, in Niven, *Chase Papers*, 3: 235–37; Niven, *Chase*, 326; Peter C. Ripley, *Slaves and Freedom in Civil War Louisiana* (Baton Rouge: Louisiana State University Press, 1976), 34–35; William F. Messner, *Freedmen and the Ideology of Free Labor: Louisiana 1862–1865* (Lafayette: University of Southwestern Louisiana, 1978), 67; George Bentley, *A History of the Freedmen's Bureau* (Philadelphia: University of Pennsylvania Press, 1955), 20; Heather Cox Richardson, *The Greatest Nation of the Earth: Republican Economic Policies During the Civil War* (Cambridge: Harvard University Press, 1997), 218–26; see Eric Foner, *Free Soil, Free Labor, Free Men: The Ideology of the Republican Party before the Civil War* (New York: Oxford University Press, 1970), for a discussion of the free labor ideology before 1860.

9. *U.S. Statutes at Large*, 12:422–26. See James G. Randall, *Constitutional Problems Under Lincoln*, rev. ed. (Urbana: University of Illinois Press, 1964), 317–23, for a discussion of the Direct Tax Act. Property was sold on the Sea Islands under the Direct Tax Act, most of which white businessmen bought. See Ochiai, "Port Royal Experiment Revisited," 97–101.

10. *U.S. Statutes at Large*, 12: 820–21. See James G. Randall, "Captured and Abandoned Property during the Civil War," *American Historical Review* 19 (October 1913): 65–79, for a discussion of this act. Randall considered both the tax act and the captured and abandoned property acts others forms of confiscation visited upon the South.

11. James M. McPherson, *Battle Cry of Freedom: The Civil War Era* (New York: Oxford University Press, 1988), 620–25; E. Merton Coulter, "Commercial Intercourse with the Confederacy in the Mississippi Valley, 1861–1865," *Mississippi Valley Historical Review* 5 (March 1919): 377–95; Ludwell H. Johnson, "Contraband Trade during the Last Year of the Civil War," *Mississippi Valley Historical Review* 49 (March 1963): 635–36; J. W. Schuckers, *The Life and Public Services of Salmon Portland Chase* (New York: Appleton & Co., 1874), 324–25.

12. Treasury Department Circular, July 3, 1863, Letters of the Special Agencies, Letters of the General Agent, Box 355, Treasury Department Papers, Record Group 366, National Archives; Chase to William Mellen, June 15, 1863, in Niven, *Chase Papers*, 4: 65–66, 55; Randall, "Captured and Abandoned Property During the Civil War," 65–79; *U.S. Statutes at Large*, 12:820; William E. Birkhimer, *Military Government and Maritime*

Law, 3rd ed. (Kansas City, Mo.: Franklin Hudson, 1914), 186–87; Rose, *Rehearsal for Reconstruction*, 202. A study written in 1950 argued that most treasury agents were honest, despite the widespread impression at the time that many were corrupt. See Brooks D. Simpson, Leroy P. Graf, and John Muldowny, eds., *Advice After Appomattox: Letters to Andrew Johnson, 1865–1866* (Knoxville: University of Tennessee Press, 1987), 52n.

13. Treasury Department Circular, July 3, 1863, Letters of the Special Agencies, Letters of the General Agent, Box 355, Treasury Department Papers.

14. See Paludan, *A People's Contest*, 206–8, and Leon P. Litwack, *Been in the Storm So Long: The Aftermath of Slavery* (New York: Vintage Books, 1980), 133–34, for descriptions of contraband camps, where freed slaves were housed and put to work under military supervision.

15. Chase to Mellen, December 17, 27, 1863, in Niven, *Chase Papers*, 4:221, 227–29; Niven, *Chase*, 354; Frederick J. Blue, *Salmon P. Chase: A Life in Politics* (Kent, Ohio: Kent State University Press, 1987), 200–201.

16. J. W. Harrington to William Orme, November 17, 1864; Orme to J. F. Richardson, March 3, 1865, Letters of the Special Agencies, Second Special Agency, Letters Received by the Asst. Special Agent, Box 157; Chase to Benjamin F. Flanders, April 13, 1864, ibid., Third Special Agency, Letters Received by Supervising Special Agent Flanders, Box 224, Treasury Department Papers; William P. Mellen to M. C. Bledsoe, October 25, 1864, Thomas J. Durant Papers, New York State Historical Society, New York City.

17. George Denison to L. B. Morey, November 13, 1865, Letters of the Special Agencies, Fourth Special Agency, Box 296; Steward Goodrell to Orme, April 14, May 10, 1865, ibid., Second Special Agency, Letters Received by Supervising Special Agent, Box 50; Orme to Goodrell, May 17, 1865, ibid., Second Special Agency, Letters Received by Assistant Special Agent, Box 157; Hugh McCulloch to J. R. Dillon, October 20, 1865, ibid., First Special Agency, Letters Received by Dillon, Box 27, Treasury Department Papers; Reynolds to Chase, January 1, 1862, Chase to Mellen, October 1, 1862, Chase to Galusha Grow, February 18, 1863, in Niven, *Chase Papers*, 3:116–67, 288–89, 385–87; Niven, *Chase*, 323; George Winston Smith, "Carpetbag Imperialism in Florida, 1862–1868," *Florida Historical Quarterly* 27 (October 1948): 107–8, 118.

18. Carl H. Moneyhon, *The Impact of the Civil War and Reconstruction on Arkansas* (Baton Rouge: Louisiana University Press, 1994), 149; Michael Wayne, *The Reshaping of the Plantation Society: The Natchez District, 1860–80* (Urbana: University of Illinois Press, 1990), 31, 33; Halleck to Chase, March 8, 1862, U.S. War Department, *War of the Rebellion: A Compilation of the Official Records of the Union and Confederate Armies* (Washington, D.C.: U.S. Government Printing Office, 1880–1901), ser. 1, vol. 10, pt. 2, 19 (hereafter cited as *Official Records*); Chase to Mellen, July 4, 1863, vol. 24, pt. 3, 468; Chase to Grant, July 21, 1863, 538; Porter to Maj. Gen. William T. Sherman, October 29, 1863, vol. 31, pt. 1, 780–83; Grant to Chase, September 26, 1863, ser. 3, vol. 3, 841–42; Mellen to Grant, October 25, 1863, 922–23; Lorenzo Thomas to Stanton, February 20, 1864, vol. 4, 124; Lincoln to Thomas, February 23, 1864, 143; Thomas to Sherman, March 30, 1864, 210–11; Thomas to Colonel E. D. Townsend, April 19, 1864, 235–36.

19. Schoefield to Brig. Gen. I. N. Palmer, May 16, 1865, ibid., ser. 1, vol. 47, pt. 3, 513; Grant to Canby, February 15, 1865, vol. 49, pt. 1, 723; General Orders No. 51, May 25, 1865, vol. 49, pt. 2, 908; Brig. Gen. John B. Sanborn to Major O. P. Newberry, February 12, 1864, vol. 34, pt. 2, 312; Circular No. 3, April 29, 1864, vol. 32, pt. 3, 537–40; Coulter, "Commercial Intercourse with the Confederacy," 391.

20. Rosecrans to Gen. Montgomery C. Meigs, July 24, 1863 (telegram); Meigs to Chase, July 25, 1863; Meigs to Rosecrans, July 25, 1863; J. W. Harrington to William G. Brownlow, August 4, 1863; Brownlow to William P. Mellen, August 25, 1863, Letters of the Special Agencies, Letters of the General Agent, Box 360, Treasury Department Papers.

21. Frank J. White to Gen. Benjamin Butler, September 30, 1864, Letters of the Special Agencies, Seventh Special Agency, Box 316; Charles Fuller to D. G. Barnitz, July 11, 1864; Brownlow to Mellen, September 17, 1864, ibid., Letters of the General Agent, Box 362, Treasury Department Papers; J. A. Garfield to Maj. Gen. McCook, July 9, 1863, *Official Records*, ser. 1, vol. 23, pt. 2, 524; E. Merton Coulter, *William G. Brownlow: Fighting Parson of the Southern Highlands* (Knoxville: University of Tennessee Press, 1971 [1937]), 246, 251, 253–55, 261, 288–92. Brownlow was elected governor of Tennessee in early 1865.

22. William Polk to George Denison, December 26, 1865, Letters of the Special Agencies, Fourth Special Agency, Box 296; C. W. Montross to William Orme, May 15, 1865, ibid., Second Special Agency, Box 51; H. R. Riddle to H. A. Risley, May 10, 1864, ibid., Seventh Special Agency, Box 318; Montross to J. H. Tomeny, February 20, 1865, ibid., Second Special Agency, Box 109; W. N. Yeatmen to Mellen, December 21, 1863, ibid., Letters of the General Agent, Box 360; Simonds to Tomeny, August 4, 1864, ibid., Second Special Agency, Box 110, Treasury Department Papers.

23. E. L. Parkhurst to Risley, May 8, 1866; Benjamin Price to Risley, February 3, 1865, Letters of the Special Agencies, Seventh Special Agency, Box 317; N. O Stoddard to Mellen [?], January 31, March 28, 1865, ibid., Letters of the General Agent, Box 363; B. F. Tuttle to Orme, January 26, 1865, ibid., Second Special Agency, Box 52, Treasury Department Papers.

24. See Peyton McCary, *Abraham Lincoln and Reconstruction: The Louisiana Experiment* (Princeton, N.J.: Princeton University Press, 1978); Joseph G. Tregle Jr., "Thomas J. Durant, Utopian Socialism, and the Failure of Presidential Reconstruction in Louisiana," *Journal of Southern History* 45 (November 1979): 485–512; Lawanda Cox, *Lincoln and Black Freedom: A Study of Presidential Leadership* (Columbia: University of South Carolina Press, 1981); Ted Tunnell, *Crucible of Reconstruction: War, Radicalism and Race in Louisiana, 1862–1877* (Baton Rouge: Louisiana State University Press, 1984); Ripley, *Slaves and Freedmen*, 52–67; William C. Harris, *With Charity For All: Lincoln and the Restoration of the Union* (Lexington: University of Kentucky Press, 1997); and James G. Hollandsworth, *Pretense of Glory: The Life of General Nathaniel P. Banks* (Baton Rouge: Louisiana State University Press, 1998), for assessments of the politics in the state during the Civil War.

25. Waples left New Orleans at the start of the war; he returned in May 1863. He remained district attorney for just over a year. Charles Fairman, *The History of the Supreme Court of the United States*, vol. 6, *Reconstruction and Reunion, 1864–88* (New York: Macmillan, 1971), 813n. See chapter 6, note 13, for the cases involving property bought by Waples and Marshal Graham.

26. For information on Flanders and Waples, see Niven, *Chase Papers*, 1:376n, 505n; 3:223, 262n; Flanders to Chase, April 30, 1863, Chase to Benjamin R. Plumly, May 23, 1863; ibid., 4:19, 21n, 38–39n; Basler et al., *Collected Works of Lincoln*, 6:223–24n; Fred H. Harrington, *Fighting Politician: Major General N. P. Banks* (Westport, Conn.: Greenwood Press, 1970 [1948]), 101; Eric Foner, *Reconstruction: America's Unfinished Revolution 1863–1877* (New York: Harper & Row, 1988), 46; Fairman, *Reconstruction and Reunion*, 812–13n; Howard K. Beale, ed., *The Diary of Edward Bates 1859–1866* (New York: Da Capo, 1971 [1933]), 382; Rufus Waples to Bates, May 23, 1863, Letters Received, Louisiana, Box 2, Attorney General Papers, Record Group 60, National Archives (hereafter cited as Letters Received).

27. After the Civil War, Durant appeared before the Supreme Court in a number of confiscation cases, in some of which he represented Waples. See *St. Louis Foundry* 6 Wallace 770 (1867); *Confiscation Cases* 7 Wall. 454 (1868); *The Grapeshot* 9 Wall. 129 (1869); *Ex Parte Graham* 10 Wall. 541 (1870); *Ex Parte Waples* 154 U.S. 579 (1871); *Wallach et al. v Van Riswick* 92 U.S. 202 (1875); *Conrad v. Waples* 96 U.S. 279 (1877); *Burbank v. Conrad* 96 U.S. 291 (1877); *Burbank v. Semmes* 99 U.S. 138 (1878); and *Dow v. Johnson*

100 U.S. 158 (1879). See Tunnell, *Crucible for Reconstruction*, 26–30, for Durant's background and politics.

28. I have followed Tunnell, *Crucible of Reconstruction*, 26–56, and Harris, *With Charity for All*, 170–96, in their interpretations of the complicated political factions in New Orleans. Flanders to Chase, December 4, 1863, Niven, *Chase Papers*, 4: 209; see the letters from Denison to Chase, ibid., 3:223, 322–24, 360, 404–5, 416, 418, 4:23–24, 85–87, 100, 137, 269–70, 318; Amos E. Simpson and Vaughan Baker, "Michael Hahn: Steady Patriot," *Louisiana History* 13 (Summer 1972): 229–52; Ripley, *Slaves and Freedmen*, 55–57, 63–65; Thomas J. Durant to W. R. Hish[?], February 5, 1864; microfilm entitled "New Orleans," Durant Papers. Lincoln appointed Edward Durell, a member of the Banks faction, a judge for the United States Circuit Court. John S. Whitaker was judge of the Second District Court in New Orleans. *New Orleans True Delta*, February 25, 1864, Edward H. Durell Papers, New York Historical Society, New York City.

29. Chase to Stanton, May 28, 1863 *Official Records*, ser. 3, vol. 3, 229–30; Waples to Flanders, September 25, 1863 (AM), Letters of the Special Agencies, Third Special Agency, Box 225, Treasury Department Papers; Beale, ed., *Diary of Edward Bates*, 382; Denison to Chase, September 12, 1863, Niven, *Chase Papers*, 4:137.

30. Waples to Flanders, September 25, 1863 (PM), Letters of the Special Agencies, Third Special Agency, Box 225, Treasury Department Papers; Ripley, *Slaves and Freedmen*, 53–55; Harrington, *Fighting Politician*, 101, argues that Waples was in Durant's faction with Flanders. Tregle, "Thomas J. Durant," and Tunnell, *Crucible of Reconstruction*, argue that Harrington's analysis is too simple. After the war Waples's adherence to certain procedures received several rebukes. Attorney General Henry Stanbery, in the government brief for *Armstrong's Foundry*, observed: "The proceedings had upon this information appear to have been conducted with most uncommendable conformity to that very peculiar system of procedure and practice which seems to prevail" in New Orleans confiscation cases. Stanbery said the record was only intelligible to those "versed in the mongrel methods" that were used there in such cases. See *Armstrong's Foundry* 6 Wallace 766 (1867) and Fairman, *Reconstruction and Reunion*, 792. Notwithstanding Stanbery's criticism, Waples later wrote a large volume on in rem proceedings. It is the most detailed examination of both the confiscation acts and the joint resolution before the courts. See Rufus Waples, *Treatise on Proceedings in Rem* (Chicago: Callaghan & Co., 1882).

31. L. E. Chittenden to Bates, October 15, 1863, Letters Received, Treasury Department, Box 5; Bates to Chittenden, October 17, 1863, Attorney General Letterbooks, C: 289–90, Attorney General Papers, Record Group 60, National Archives. In *The Confiscation Cases*, 6 Fed. Cas. 270 (1872), Supreme Court Justice Bradley, acting as a circuit justice, said this about the "insufficiency of the information" presented by Waples in the trial record of the confiscation case: "It is one of the most remarkable specimens of loose pleading and uncertain statement that I remember ever to have seen."

32. Harris, *With Charity for All*, 171–73, explains the confusing rivalries in Louisiana at the time. Niven, *Chase Papers*, 4:39n; Denison to Chase, January 29, 1863[4], 268; petition of Lillenburger, November 18, 1863; petition of Waples, November 13, 1863, order of Durell, November 13, 1863, Letters of the Special Agencies, Third Special Agency, Box 295, Treasury Department Papers; Basler et al., *Collected Works of Lincoln*, 4:371, 373n;

33. Waples to Flanders, December 17, 1863, Letters of the Special Agencies, Third Special Agency, Box 225, Treasury Department Papers; Waples to Bates, December 17, 1863, Letters Received, Louisiana, Box 2.

34. Waples to Bates, December 17, 1863, Letters Received, Louisiana, Box 2.

35. Waples to Flanders, December 21, 1863; Waples to Flanders, December 15, 1864; Waples to Flanders January 13, 25, 28, April 3, May 13, 1865, Letters of the Special Agencies, Third Special Agency, Box 225, Treasury Department Papers.

36. Lincoln to Banks, February 16, 1864, Banks to Lincoln, March 26, 1864, in Basler et al., *Collected Works of Lincoln*, 7:186, 186–87n; Harris, *With Charity for All*, 174–79; Chase to Flanders, April 13, 1864 (emphasis by Chase), Letters of the Special Agencies, Third Special Agency, Box 227, Treasury Department Papers. It is noteworthy that Hahn won the election, with 6,183 votes, while Fellows was second with 2,996 and Flanders third with 2,944.

37. Cuthebert Bullit to Bates, September 21, 1864, Letters Received, Louisiana, Box 2; John Levering to Flanders, March 19, 1865; Alfred Snow to Flanders, March 21, 1865, Letters to the Special Agencies, Third Special Agency, Box 227; William Orme to Flanders, April 5, 1865, ibid., Box 224, Treasury Department Papers. By September 1865 Chase heard there was much dissatisfaction over Flanders's work. In early 1865 Lincoln replaced Waples as District Attorney with Charles Peabody, who formerly had been judge of the provisional court. Chase to Dennison, September 20, 1864, in Niven, *Chase Papers*, 4:433, 434n.

38. See *Senate Executive Documents*, 40th Congress, 2 session, no. 58, serial 1317, for the totals of confiscated property by states. Waples to Bates, January 21, May 24, June 7[?], June 10, 1864, Letters Received, Louisiana, Box 2; Waples to Bates, February 20, 1865, ibid., Box 3.

8. The Politics of Confiscation

1. See Bruce Tap, *Over Lincoln's Shoulder: The Committee on the Conduct of the War* (Lawrence: University of Kansas Press, 1998), for that committee and William C. Harris, *With Charity for All: Lincoln and the Restoration of the Union* (Lexington: University Press of Kentucky, 1997) for the best discussion of Lincoln's Reconstruction policy. The one inquiry about confiscation occurred in January 1863 when Congress inquired about the second act's enforcement in Washington. Bates sarcastically replied that the rumors of much confiscable property in the District of Columbia were unfounded. Bates to Galusha Grow, January 14, 1863, Attorney General Letterbooks, B-5:316–19, Attorney General Papers, National Archives (hereafter cited as Attorney General Letterbooks); *House Executive Documents*, 37th Congress, 3 session, no. 32, serial 1161.

2. Philip Shaw Paludan, *The Presidency of Abraham Lincoln* (Lawrence: University Press of Kansas, 1994), 155–57; Allan C. Guelzo, *Abraham Lincoln: Redeemer President* (Grand Rapids, Mich.: William B. Eerdmans, 1999), 342–43; Allan C. Guelzo, *Lincoln's Emancipation Proclamation: The End of Slavery in America* (New York: Simon & Schuster, 2004), 157–60; Roland C. McConnell, "From Preliminary to Final Emancipation Proclamation The First Hundred Days," *Journal of Negro History* 48 (October 1963): 260–67; Mark M. Krug, "The Republican Party and the Emancipation Proclamation," *Journal of Negro History* 48 (April 1963): 106–7; Lex Renda, *Running on the Record: Civil War–Era Politics in New Hampshire* (Charlottesville: University Press of Virginia, 1997), 111–12; Edith Ellen Ware, *Political Opinion in Massachusetts During the Civil War and Reconstruction* (New York: Longmans, Green, 1916), 102; Jerome Mushkat, *The Reconstruction of the New York Democracy, 1861–1874* (Rutherford, N.J.: Fairleigh Dickinson University Press, 1981), 33–35; Phyllis F. Field, *The Politics of Race in New York: The Struggle for Black Suffrage in the Civil War Era* (Ithaca, N.Y.: Cornell University Press, 1982), 150–52; V. William Gillette, *Jersey Blue: Civil War Politics in New Jersey 1854–1865* (New Brunswick, N.J.: Rutgers University Press, 1995), 197–98; V. Jacque Voegeli, *Free But Not Equal: The Midwest and the Negro During the Civil War* (Chicago: University of Chicago Press, 1967), 53–55; L. E. Ellis, "The *Chicago Times* During the Civil War," *Illinois State Historical Society Transactions for the Year 1932* 39 (1933): 144–46; Emma Lou Thornbrough, "The Race Issue in Indiana Politics During the Civil War," *Indiana Magazine of History* 47 (June 1951): 178; Michael Les Benedict, "The Constitution of the Lincoln Presidency and the Republican Era," in *The Constitution and the American Presidency*,

ed. Martin L. Fausold and Alan Shank (Albany: State University of New York Press, 1991), 57–58; Frank L. Klement, "Midwestern Opposition to Lincoln's Emancipation Policy," *Journal of Negro History* 49 (July 1964): 169–83.

3. Charles R. Williams, ed., *Diary and Letters of Rutherford Birchard Hayes* (Columbus: Ohio State Archeological and Historical Society, 1922), 2:361; Reid Mitchell, *Civil War Soldiers* (New York: Penguin Books, 1988), 126–28; Bell I. Wiley, *The Life of Billy Yank: The Common Soldier in the Union* (Indianapolis: Bobbs-Merrill, 1951), 40–42; David W. Adams, "Illinois Soldiers and the Emancipation Proclamation," *Journal of Illinois Historical Association* 67 (September 1974): 407–21; James M. McPherson, *What They Fought For, 1861–1865* (Baton Rouge: Louisiana State University Press, 1994), 56–66; James M. McPherson, *Battle Cry of Freedom: The Civil War Era* (New York: Oxford University Press, 1988), 558–60; Joseph A. Frank, *With Ballot and Bayonet: The Political Socialization of American Civil War Soldiers* (Athens: University of Georgia Press, 1998), 69–70; John Beatty, *Memoirs of a Volunteer 1861–1863* (New York: Norton, 1946 [1879]), 118–22.

4. See chapter 4 for a discussion of Parker's essay in a slightly different context.

5. Joel Parker, "The Character of the Rebellion and the Conduct of the War," *North American Review* 95 (October 1862): 500–33. See Benjamin R. Curtis, *Executive Power* (Cambridge, Mass.: H. O. Houghton, 1862), for an argument similar to Parker's against the September 22 proclamation. Curtis did not discuss the second act, however. See a reply to Parker by Reverend Leonard Bacon, "Reply to Professor Parker," *The New Englander* 22 (April 1863): 191–258, which supported Lincoln's proclamation on the basis of military necessity. Guelzo, *Lincoln's Emancipation Proclamation*, 190–93.

6. Elias H. Derby, "Resources of the South," *Atlantic Monthly* 10 (October 1862): 502–10. Frederick Douglass offered much the same analysis a month later; he suggested that freed slaves should be colonized on abandoned lands in Florida. Philip S. Foner, ed., *The Life and Writings of Frederick Douglass* (New York: International Publishers, 1952), 3:41; Philip Shaw Paludan, *"A People's Contest": The Union and Civil War 1861–1865*, 2nd ed. (Lawrence: University of Kansas Press, 1996), 98–100.

7. Paludan, *The Presidency*, 156–57; Paludan, *A People's Contest*, 100–102; McPherson, *Battle Cry of Freedom*, 560–62; Guelzo, *Lincoln's Emancipation Proclamation*, 166–68; Lex Renda, "'A White Man's State in New England': Race, Party, and Suffrage in Civil War Connecticut," in *An Uncommon Time: The Civil War and the Northern Home Front*, ed. Paul A. Cimbala and Randall M. Miller (New York: Fordham University Press, 2002), 259; Patience Essah, *A House Divided: Slavery and Emancipation in Delaware, 1638–1865* (Charlottesville: University Press of Virginia, 1996), 174–76; James A. Woodburn, "Party Politics in Indiana During the Civil War," *Annual Report of the American Historical Association for the Year 1902* (Washington, D.C.: U.S. Government Printing Office, 1903), 1:246–47; Winfred A. Harbison, "The Elections of 1862 as A Vote of Want of Confidence in President Lincoln," *Michigan Academy of Science, Arts and Letters* 14 (1930): 503; Arnold Shankman, "Francis W. Hughes and the 1862 Pennsylvania Election," *Pennsylvania Magazine of History and Biography* 95 (July 1971): 385; Voegeli, *Free But Not Equal*, 52–63; Gillette, *Civil War Politics in New Jersey*, 202–3; Bruce Tap, "Race, Rhetoric, and Emancipation: The Election of 1862 in Illinois," *Civil War History* 39 (January 1993): 101–2, 105–7, 112, 121; William C. Harris, "Andrew Johnson's First 'Swing Around the Circle': His Northern Campaign of 1863," *Civil War History* 5 (June 1989): 154–55.

8. William D. Mallam, "Lincoln and the Conservatives," *Journal of Southern History* 38 (February 1962): 31–45; Field, *The Politics of Race*, 152–53; William Salter, *The Life of James W. Grimes* (New York: Appleton & Co., 1876), 218; Robert D. Ilisevich, *Galusha A. Grow: The People's Candidate* (Pittsburgh: University of Pittsburgh, 1988), 206–10, 214–17; Susan G. Hall, *Appalachian Ohio and the Civil War, 1862–1863* (Jefferson, N.C.:

McFarland, 2000), 59–71, 106–7; Erving E. Beauregard, *Bingham of the Hills: Politician and Diplomat Extraordinary* (New York: Peter Lang, 1989), 64, 67–70.

9. Arthur Larsen, ed., *Crusader and Feminist: Letters of Jane Grey Swisshelm, 1858–1865* (St. Paul: Minnesota Historical Society, 1934), 170–71; James M. McPherson, *The Struggle for Equality: Abolitionists and the Negro in the Civil War and Reconstruction* (Princeton, N.J.: Princeton University Press, 1964), 246–49; David Herbert Donald, *Charles Sumner and the Rights of Man* (New York: Da Capo, 1996), 119; Patrick W. Riddleberger, "George W. Julian: Abolitionist Land Reformer," *Agricultural History* 29 (July 1955): 109; David Lindsey, *Americans in Conflict: The Civil War and Reconstruction* (Boston: Houghton Mifflin, 1974), 159.

10. Willie Lee Rose, *Rehearsal for Reconstruction: The Port Royal Experiment* (Indianapolis: Bobbs-Merrill, 1964), 213–16; Akiko Ochiai, "The Port Royal Experiment Revisited: Northern Visions of Reconstruction and the Land Question," *New England Quarterly* 74 (March 2001): 94–117; Julie Saville, *The Work of Reconstruction: From Slave Labor to Wage Laborer in South Carolina, 1860–1870* (New York: Cambridge University Press, 1994), 40–41; McPherson, *Struggle for Equality*, 249–52; Lindsey, *Americans in Conflict*, 159; James G. Randall, *The Confiscation of Property During the Civil War* (Indianapolis: Mutual Printing and Lithographing, 1913), 7.

11. Joel H. Silbey, *A Respectable Minority: The Democratic Party in the Civil War Era, 1860–1868* (New York: Norton, 1977), 111–12, 116–18, 146–48; Paludan, *The Presidency*, 226–28; McPherson, *Battle Cry of Freedom*, 594–600, 684–86; Renda, *Running on the Record*, 115–17; James Harvey Young, "Anna Elizabeth Dickinson and the Civil War: For and Against Lincoln," *Mississippi Valley Historical Society* 31 (June 1994): 65–67; William C. Harris, "Conservative Unionists and the Presidential Election of 1864," *Civil War History* 38 (December 1992): 303–4; Harris, "Andrew Johnson's First 'Swing Around the Circle,'" 153–71; Kenneth A. Deitreich, "Edward G. Roddy and the Anti-War Movement in Civil War Pennsylvania," *Pennsylvania History* 66 (Summer 1999): 369–70; Kenneth H. Wheeler, "Local Autonomy and Civil War Draft Resistance: Holmes County, Ohio," *Civil War History* 45 (June 1999): 147–59; Frank L. Klement, *Wisconsin in the Civil War: The Home Front and the Battle Front, 1861–1865* (Madison: State Historical Society of Wisconsin, 1997), 77–79; Eric McKitrick, "Party Politics and the Union and Confederate War Efforts," in *The American Party Systems: Stages of Political Development*, ed. William N. Chambers and Walter D. Burnham (New York: Oxford University Press, 1967), 139–41.

12. Harris, *With Charity for All*, 97–99, 130; Roy P. Basler et al., eds., *The Collected Works of Abraham Lincoln* (New Brunswick, N.J.: Rutgers University Press, 1953) 6:428–29; Guelzo, *Lincoln's Emancipation Proclamation*, 198–99; Herman Belz, *Reconstructing the Union: Theory and Policy During the Civil War* (Ithaca, N.Y.: Cornell University Press, 1969), 155–66.

13. Basler et al., *Collected Works of Lincoln*, 7:53–56, 8:152; Harris, *With Charity for All*, 131–32; Belz, *Reconstructing the Union*, 155–64; Jonathan T. Dorris, *Pardon and Amnesty Under Lincoln and Johnson: The Restoration of the Confederates to Their Rights and Privileges, 1861–1898* (Westport, Conn.: Greenwood Press, 1977 [1953]), 67–68.

14. See Harris, *With Charity for All*, and the pages devoted to New Orleans, Tennessee, Virginia, and North Carolina as of December 1863.

15. Harris, *With Charity for All*, 132–33; Basler et al., *Collected Works of Lincoln*, 7:53–56; Brooks D. Simpson, *The Reconstruction Presidents* (Lawrence: University Press of Kansas, 1998), 21, 39. See Ted Tunnell, *Crucible of Reconstruction: War, Radicalism and Race in Louisiana, 1862–1877* (Baton Rouge: Louisiana State University Press, 1984) and James G. Hollandsworth Jr., *Pretense of Glory: The Life of General Nathaniel P. Banks* (Baton Rouge: Louisiana State University Press, 1998) for discussions of Louisiana and Banks.

16. Harris, *With Charity for All*, 134–37. See chapter 3 for a discussion of the joint resolution.

17. *House Journal*, 38 Congress, 1 session, serial 1179, 21, 43, 94, 102, 112; *Congressional Globe*, 38 Congress, 1 session, 184–85 (Wilson, January 13, 1864). Hereafter cited as *Cong. Globe*, 38:1.

18. *Cong. Globe*, 38:1, 184, (January 13, 1864).

19. Samuel S. Cox, *Union-Disunion-Reunion: Three Decades of Federal Legislation* (Providence, R.I.: Reid, 1886), 249; *Cong. Globe*, 38:1, 301; 409 (Andrew Rogers, Dem.-N.J., January 21, 1864); 185 (Charles Edgerton, Dem.-Wisc., January 28, 1864); 404–5 (Kernan, January 13, 1864); 188 (Garfield, January 27, 1864); 267–68 (Godlove Orth, Rep.-Ind., January 13, 1864); 265 (George S. Boutwell, Rep.-Mass., January 19, 1864); 317 (George Bliss, Dem.-Ohio, January 19, 1864); 214, 375 (Stevens, January 19, 22, 1864); 266 (Davis, January 14, 1864); 392 (Smithers, January 27, 1864). The 83–74 vote occurred on February 5, 1864. Five of the six Republicans against came from the border states, ibid., 519.

20. Harris, *With Charity for All*, 134–45, 298; Donald, Sumner, 178–89; *Cong. Globe*, 38:1, 317 (Stevens, January 22, 1864); Belz, *Reconstructing the Union*, 132n; Herman Belz, *Abraham Lincoln, Constitutionalism, and Equal Rights in the Civil War Era* (New York: Fordham University Press, 1998), 39. Belz refers to Whiting as "Lincoln's legal advisor in the War Department." The Senate Judiciary Committee consisted of Republicans Lyman Trumbull, Lafayette Foster (Conn.), John Ten Eyck (N. J.), Ira Harris (N.Y.), and Jacob Howard (Michigan). The Democrats were James Bayard (Del.) and Lazarus Powell (Kentucky). Only Harris, Trumbull and Howard had supported the second act. *Cong. Globe*, 38:1, 693 (February 17, 1864).

21. Marvin R. Cain, *Lincoln's Attorney General: Edward Bates of Missouri* (Columbia: University of Missouri Press, 1965), 285–87; *New York Times*, February 22, 1864; Harris, *With Charity for All*, 149.

22. *New York Times*, February 22, 1864; Bates to Lackey, January 19, 1863 (emphasis by Bates), in Patricia A. Lucie, *Freedom and Federalism: Congress and the Courts 1861–1866* (New York: Garland, 1986), 48.

23. *New York Times*, February 22, 1864; Harris, *With Charity for All*, 148.

24. Sorrells to Johnson, June 23, 1864, in *The Papers of Andrew Johnson*, ed. Leroy P. Graf and Ralph W. Haskins (Knoxville: University of Tennessee Press, 1983), 6:753–54; Woodruff to friend, March 3, 1864, in Harris, *With Charity for All*, 149.

25. *New York Times*, Feb. 22, 1864; Henry D. Shapiro, *Confiscation of Confederate Property in the North* (Ithaca, N.Y.: Cornell University Press, 1962), 52–53; Cain, *Bates*, 287–90.

26. Basler et al., *Collected Works of Lincoln*, 8:269–70, "Proclamation About Amnesty," March 26, 1864; Joshua Tevis to Bates, March 11, 1864, Letters Received, Kentucky, Box 1; William Grover to Bates, March 30, 1864, Missouri, Box 1; L. Weldon to Bates, April 15, 1864, Illinois, Box 1, Attorney General Papers, Record Group 60, National Archives (hereafter cited as Letters Received).

27. Shapiro, *Confiscation*, 52.

28. In November 1863 Judge John C. Underwood of the United States District Court for the eastern district of Virginia had ruled the joint resolution did not prevent forfeiture beyond the life of the rebel whose property had been confiscated. See chapter 11 for this decision.

29. Robert F. Horowitz, "Land to the Freedmen: A Vision of Reconstruction," *Ohio History* 86 (Summer 1977): 197–98; *Cong. Globe*, 38:2, 688–94, (Eliot, February 9, 1864), 1186–87 (Julian, March 18, 1864).

30. *Cong. Globe*, 38:1, 874, February 29, 1864; 1186–87 (Julian, March 18, 1864); 2253, May 12, 1864, for passage of Julian's bill by House; 3116, June 21, 1864, for Senate's rejec-

tion of Julian's bill; George W. Julian, *Political Recollections 1840 to 1872* (New York: Negro Universities Press, 1970 [1884]), 238, 245; Riddleberger, "George W. Julian," 109–10; Harris, *With Charity for All*, 298; Belz, *Reconstructing the Union*, 132–33; McPherson, *Struggle for Equality*, 255–56; Paludan, *The Presidency*, 271–72; Allen Thorndike Rice, ed., *Reminiscences of Abraham Lincoln by Distinguished Men of His Time* (New York: North American Review, 1888), 59; William Whiting, *War Powers Under the Constitution of the United States, Military Arrests, Reconstruction, and Military Government*, 43rd ed. (Boston: Lee & Shepard, 1871), 470–78.

31. Belz, Abraham Lincoln, Constitutionalism, 121, 135–36n; Harris, *With Charity for All*, 111–12; William Wiecek, *The Guarantee Clause of the U.S. Constitution* (Ithaca, N.Y.: Cornell University Press, 1972), 178; Philip A. Paludan, *A Covenant with Death: The Constitution, Law, and Equality in the Civil War Era* (Urbana: University of Illinois Press, 1975), 42; McPherson, *Struggle for Equality*, 248; Gideon Welles, *Diary of Gideon Welles: Secretary of the Navy Under Lincoln and Johnson* (Boston: Houghton Mifflin, 1911), 1:381, 400, 408; Edward L. Pierce, ed., *Memoir and Letters of Charles Sumner* (Boston: Roberts Brothers, 1893), 4:143; Whiting, *War Powers Under the Constitution*, 409. In this edition to his work Whiting also claimed that Lincoln had been persuaded to change his position on the joint resolution of 1862 but Whiting offered no evidence to support the assertion.

32. William Whiting, *The War Powers of the President and the Legislative Powers of Congress in Relation to Rebellion, Treason and Slavery*, 3rd ed. (Boston: John L. Shorey, 1862), 95–128; *U.S. Statutes at Large*, 12:589–92.

33. *Cong. Globe*, 38:1, 3327. The vote on Trumbull's amendment was on June 28, seven days after the Senate rejected Julian's bill on June 21. Julian said he saw Lincoln on July 2. Ralph J. Roske, *His Own Counsel: The Life and Times of Lyman Trumbull* (Reno: University of Nevada Press, 1979), 104–5; Julian, *Recollections*, 245; Herman Belz, "The Freedmen's Bureau Act of 1865 and the Principle of No Discrimination According to Color," *Civil War History* 21 (September 1975): 198–99; Donald, *Sumner*, 174–78; Harris, *With Charity for All*, 186–87; Robert Dale Owen, Samuel Gridley Howe, and James McKaye, "Office of American Freedmen's Inquiry Commission [Preliminary Report]," June 30, 1863; "Final Report of the American Freedmen's Inquire Commission to the Secretary of War," May 15, 1864, *The War of the Rebellion: A Compilation of Official Records of the Union and Confederate Armies* (Washington, D.C.: U.S. Government Printing Office, 1880–1901), ser. 3, vol. 3, 430–54; vol. 4, 289–382. In 1864 James McKaye also published *The Mastership and Its Fruits: The Emancipated Slave Face to Face with His Old Master* (New York: Loyal Publication Society, 1864), 18, 28–29, 35–38, in which he argued that freed slaves needed education, protection from former masters and land. James D. Bilotta, *Race and the Rise of the Republican Party, 1848–1865* (New York: Peter Lang, 1992), 460–61; Robert F. Horowitz, *The Great Impeacher: A Political Biography of James M. Ashley* (New York: Brooklyn College Press, 1979), 92–93. See the appendix for the joint resolution of July 1862.

34. Belz, "The Freedmen's Bureau Act," 202–7, 213–14n; *Cong. Globe*, 38:2, 563; LaWanda Cox, "The Promise of Land for the Freedmen," *Mississippi Valley Historical Review* 45 (December 1958): 415–18; Donald, *Sumner*, 194–95; Heather Cox Richardson, *The Greatest Nation of the Earth: Republican Economic Policies During the Civil War* (Cambridge, Mass.: Harvard University Press, 1997), 230–40. The conference committee consisted of Kelley, Eliot and Warren P. Noble (Dem.-Ohio) from the House and Jacob Howard (Rep.-Mich.), Sumner and Charles Buckalew (Dem.-Pa.) from the Senate. All four Republicans had supported confiscation in 1962.

35. See Belz, "The Freedmen's Bureau," 198–214, for an analysis of the politics involved in the bill and Richardson, *The Greatest Nation*, 230–40, for the free labor emphasis of the Republicans.

36. Belz, "The Freedmen's Bureau," 209–15; H.R. No. 51, *Cong. Globe*, 38:2, 1182 (February 28, 1865); Cox, "The Promise," 418–40. The second conference committee consisted of Schenck, George Boutwell (Rep.-Mass.) and James Rollins (Rep.-Mo.) from the House and Henry Wilson (Rep.-Mass), James Harlan (Rep.-Iowa), and Waitman Willey (Union-Va.). James M. McPherson claims Whiting used his influence to have a land provision included in the final Freedmen's Bureau bill. See James M. McPherson, "The Ballot and Land for Freedmen, 1861–1865," in *Reconstruction: An Anthology of Revisionist Writings*, ed. Kenneth M. Stampp and Leon F. Litwack (Baton Rouge: Louisiana University Press, 1969), 152. McPherson offers no notes to support his claim.

37. See Horowitz, "Land to the Freedmen," 197–98; Cox, "The Promise," 432–35; Lindsey, *Americans in Conflict*, 160–61; McPherson, *Struggle for Equality*, 256–57.

38. Harris, *With Charity for All*, 275; Richardson, *Greatest Nation of the Earth*, 230–40. See Guelzo, *Lincoln's Emancipation Proclamation*, 236–37, who believes "the problem of land" began with Andrew Johnson and not, as I argue, with the Republicans themselves in 1864, if not earlier.

9. Andrew Johnson and the End of Confiscation

1. Speed to Crawford Hill, January 11, 1865, Attorney General Letterbooks, E: 358, Attorney General Papers, Record Group 60, National Archives (hereafter cited as Attorney General Letterbooks). Lincoln had asked Judge Advocate Joseph Holt to replace Bates, who had resigned after the 1864 election. Holt declined but recommended Speed who was from Kentucky and the brother of Lincoln's closest prewar friend. The Speed family had owned slaves. David Herbert Donald, *Lincoln* (New York: Simon & Schuster, 1996), 590.

2. Alexander H. Stephens, *A Constitutional View of the Late War Between the States: Its Causes, Character, Conduct and Results* (Philadelphia: n.p., 1870), 2:617; William C. Harris, *With Charity for All: Lincoln and the Restoration of the Union* (Lexington: University Press of Kentucky, 1997), 238–39, 250; Roy P. Basler et al., eds., *The Collected Works of Abraham Lincoln* (New Brunswick, N.J.: Rutgers University Press, 1953), 7:386–87.

3. Hans L. Trefousse, *The Radical Republicans: Lincoln's Vanguard for Racial Justice* (New York: Knopf, 1969), 146, 312; Hans L. Trefousse, *Andrew Johnson: A Biography* (New York: Norton, 1989), 144, 155, 164–69, 172, 183, 191–92; Harris, *With Charity for All*, 47–48; Leroy P. Graf and Ralph W. Haskins, eds., *Andrew Johnson Papers* (Knoxville: University of Tennessee, 1979, 1983, 1986), 5:liii, 381, 383, 538; 6:726; 7:613; Brooks D. Simpson, Leroy P. Graf, and John Muldowny, eds., *Advice After Appomattox: Letters to Andrew Johnson, 1865–1866* (Knoxville: University of Tennessee Press, 1987), xxiii; Eric Foner, *Reconstruction: America's Unfinished Revolution 1863–1877* (New York: Harper & Row, 1988), 43–44; David W. Bowen, *Andrew Johnson and the Negro* (Knoxville: University of Tennessee Press, 1989), 86–88, 93–96, 114–15; Peter Maslowski, "From Reconciliation to Reconstruction: Lincoln, Johnson, and Tennessee, Part II," *Tennessee Historical Quarterly* 42 (1983): 343; Ira Berlin et al., eds., *Freedom: A Documentary History of Emancipation, 1861–1867*, ser. 1, vol. 2, *The Wartime Genesis of Free Labor: The Upper South* (Cambridge: Cambridge University Press, 1993), 373; Brooks D. Simpson, *The Reconstruction Presidents* (Lawrence: University Press of Kansas, 1998), 71; William C. Harris, "Andrew Johnson's First 'Swing Around the Circle': His Northern Campaign of 1863," *Civil War History* 35 (June 1989): 153–71.

4. Harris, *With Charity for All*, 242–43, 254–55; Harris, "Andrew Johnson's First 'Swing Around the Circle,'" 170; Trefousse, *Johnson*, 138; see Donald, *Lincoln*, 352, 373, 399, 423, 424–25, 436, for examples of the criticism directed at Lincoln.

5. Trefousse, *Johnson*, 175, 188, 192, 226–28.

6. Hubley Ashton to District Attorneys of Missouri, Kentucky and Tennessee, April 22, 1865; Speed to District Attorneys of Missouri, Kentucky, and Tennessee, April 29,

1865, Attorney General Letterbooks, D: 268–69, 280; Grover to Ashton, April 25, 1865, Letters Received, Missouri, Box 1, Attorney General Papers, Record Group 60, National Archives (hereafter cited as Letters Received); James G. Randall, *Constitutional Problems Under Lincoln*, rev. ed. (Urbana: University of Illinois Press, 1964), 329–30.

7. Speed to Chandler, May 13, 1865, Attorney General Letterbooks, D: 311–15; E: 181; Randall, *Constitutional Problems Under Lincoln*, 329–30; James D. Richardson, ed., *Messages and Papers of the Presidents* (Washington, D.C.: U.S. Government Printing Office, 1896–1903), 6:314, 322, 324–25, 328, 330, 338.

8. Trefousse, *Johnson*, 215–16; Richardson, ed., *Messages and Papers of the Presidents*, 6:311–12; Simpson, *Reconstruction Presidents*, 73–74;

9. Ashton to District Attorneys in Missouri, Kentucky, and Tennessee, June 13, 1865, Ashton to Bradford, June 13, 1865, Attorney General Letterbooks, E: 63, 61.

10. The one exception followed a request from Provisional Governor William Marvin of Florida to suspend a sale of confiscated property in Jacksonville. Marvin believed the Treasury officials involved were corrupt. See William W. Davis, *The Civil War and Reconstruction in Florida* (New York: Longmans, Green, 1913), 250, 357, 427n; Ashton to Nathaniel Usher, July 27, 1865; Ashton to Marvin, July 27, 1865; Ashton to Maj. Gen. Gillmore, July 27, 1865, Attorney General Letterbooks, E: 116, 131, 133–34.

11. Hays to Edward Horton, September 8, 1865, Letters Received, Treasury Department, Box 10; Ashton to Hays, September 14, 1865; Stewart to Pike, July 9, 1865, Attorney General Letterbooks, E: 206, 94. Other examples of such instructions can be found in the months of June and August, too.

12. A close examination of the Andrew Johnson Papers on microfilm failed to uncover one instance where Johnson wrote Speed about confiscation. Yet it was doubtless under Johnson's instructions that Speed changed his office policy from that pursued by Lincoln. See the Andrew Johnson Papers, Microfilm, Ser. B, vol. 2, real 43, Letters Sent, Butler Library, Columbia University, New York City.

13. *Congressional Globe*, 39 Congress, 1 session, 2536, May 19, 1866 (hereafter cited as *Cong. Globe*, 39:1). Foner, *Reconstruction*, 190–91, and Trefousse, *Johnson*, 227, confirm that Johnson was very liberal with pardons.

14. See James G. Randall, "Captured and Abandoned Property During the Civil War," *American Historical Review* 19 (October 1913): 66–72, still the authority on this issue. James M. McPherson, *The Negro's Civil War: How American Negroes Felt and Acted during the War for the Union* (New York: Pantheon Books, 1965), 293–97; Willie Lee Rose, *Rehearsal for Reconstruction: The Port Royal Experiment* (Indianapolis: Bobbs-Merrill, 1964), 276–85; Akiko Ochiai, "The Port Royal Experiment Revisited: Northern Visions of Reconstruction and the Land Question," *New England Quarterly* 74 (March 2001): 94–117; Paul A. Cimbala, "The Freedmen's Bureau, the Freedmen, and Sherman's Grant in Reconstruction Georgia, 1865–1867," *Journal of Southern History* 55 (November 1989): 597–632.

15. Edmund L. Drago, "How Sherman's March Through Georgia Affected the Slaves," *Georgia Historical Quarterly* 57 (Fall 1973): 363; Paul D. Escott, "The Context of Freedom: Georgia Slaves During the Civil War," *Georgia Historical Quarterly* 58 (Spring 1974): 84; Claude D. Oubre, *Forty Acres and a Mule: The Freedmen's Bureau and Black Ownership of Land* (Baton Rouge: Louisiana State University Press, 1978), 18–19; Howard C. Westwood, "Sherman Marched—And Proclaimed 'Land for the Landless,'" *South Carolina Historical Magazine* 85 (January 1984): 33–50; Benjamin P. Thomas and Harold M. Hyman, *Stanton: The Life and Times of Lincoln's Secretary of War* (New York: Knopf, 1962), 234–35, 342–45; William T. Sherman, *Memoirs of Gen. W. T. Sherman* (New York: Charles L. Webster, 1891), 2:242–52; William Dusinberre, *Them Dark Days: Slavery in the American Rice Swamps* (New York: Oxford University Press, 1996), 375, 526–27; "Minutes of an interview between colored ministers and church officers at Savannah with

Secretary of War and Major-General Sherman," January 12, 1865, U.S. War Department, *The War of the Rebellion: A Compilation of the Official Records of the Union and Confederate Armies* (Washington, D.C.: U.S. Government Printing Office, 1880–1901), ser. 1, vol. 47, pt. 2, 37–41; McPherson, *The Negro's Civil War*, 300.

16. Dusinberre, *Them Dark Days*, 375, 526–27; Russell Duncan, *Freedom's Shore: Tunis Campbell and the Georgia Freedmen* (Athens: University of Georgia Press, 1986), 18–19; Noel C. Fisher, "'Prepare Them for My Coming': General William T. Sherman, Total War, and Pacification in West Tennessee," *Tennessee Historical Quarterly* 51 (Summer 1992): 78–85; Carol K. Blesor, *The Promised Land: The History of the Southern Carolina Land Concession, 1869–1890* (Columbia: University of South Carolina Press, 1969), 8–9 (Sherman quotation); Rose, *Rehearsal for Reconstruction*, 322–28; Oubre, *Forty Acres and a Mule*, 18–19; Joel Williamson, *After Slavery: The Negro in South Carolina During Reconstruction, 1861–1877* (Chapel Hill: University of North Carolina Press, 1965), 59–61.

17. *U.S. Statutes at Large*, 13:507–9. See Paul S. Peirce, *The Freedmen's Bureau: A Chapter in the History of Reconstruction* (Iowa City: University of Iowa, 1904); George R. Bentley, *A History of the Freedmen's Bureau* (Philadelphia: University of Pennsylvania Press, 1955); John A. Carpenter, *The Sword and the Olive Branch: Oliver Otis Howard* (Pittsburgh: University of Pittsburgh Press, 1964); William S. McFeely, *Yankee Stepfather: General O. O. Howard and the Freedmen* (New Haven, Conn.: Yale University Press, 1968); Donald G. Nieman, *To Set the Law in Motion: The Freedmen's Bureau and the Legal Rights of Blacks, 1865–1868* (Millwood, N.Y.: KTO Press, 1979); and Paul A. Cimbala and Randall M. Miller, eds., *The Freedmen's Bureau and Reconstruction* (New York: Fordham University Press, 1999), for major works on the Freedmen's Bureau.

18. For the free labor discussion, see Eric Foner, *Politics and Ideology in the Age of the Civil War* (New York; Oxford University Press, 1980), 97–105; William Cohen, "Black Immobility and Free Labor: The Freedmen's Bureau and the Relocation of Black Labor, 1865–1868," *Civil War History* 30 (September 1984), 222–25; Heather Cox Richardson, *The Greatest Nation of the Earth: Republican Economic Policies During the Civil War* (Cambridge, Mass.: Harvard University Press, 1997), 230–40; and Heather Cox Richardson, *The Death of Reconstruction: Race, Labor, and Politics in the Post Civil War North, 1865–1901* (Cambridge, Mass.: Harvard University Press, 2001), 34–35, 46–47, 60–67; see Nieman, *To Set The Law in Motion*, 46, for the acres held by the Freedmen's Bureau.

19. Bentley, *Freedmen's Bureau*, 92 (Howard quotation); McFeely, *Yankee Stepfather*, 95–98; Rose, *Rehearsal for Reconstruction*, 329; Oliver Otis Howard, *Autobiography of Oliver Otis Howard* (New York: Baker and Taylor, 1907), 2:221.

20. McFeely, *Yankee Stepfather*, 98–100; Nieman, *To Set the Law in Motion*, 47–48; Speed to Stanton, June 22, 1865, Opinions of the Attorney General, P: 185–88 (Speed's emphasis), Attorney General Papers, Record Group 60, National Archives; Randall, "Captured and Abandoned Property," 72–73. The Captured and Abandoned Property Act of 1863 required Treasury officials to seize the property and send it North, assuming it was portable, like cotton, or hold land in the South. No judicial process occurred under the act, unlike the requirements under the Second Confiscation Act. See *U.S. Statutes at Large*, 12:820–21.

21. Carpenter, Sword and Olive Branch, 107; McFeely, *Yankee Stepfather*, 100–103; Nieman, *To Set the Law in Motion*, 49–50 (both Howard quotations); Bentley, *Freedmen's Bureau*, 92–93; Martin Abbott, *The Freedmen's Bureau in South Carolina, 1865–1872* (Chapel Hill: University of North Carolina Press, 1967), 54; Foner, *Reconstruction*, 158–59; Cimbala, "Freedmen and Sherman's Grant," 599–600; Duncan, *Freedom's Shore*, 28; Howard to B. F. Perry, July 29, 1865, Oliver Otis Howard Papers, Bowdoin College, Brunswick, Maine.

22. *House Executive Documents*, 39 Congress, 1 session, no. 11, serial 1255 (Circular No. 13; Howard quotation); McFeely, *Yankee Stepfather*, 103–6; Bentley, *Freedmen's Bureau*, 92–93; Nieman, *To Set the Law in Motion*, 50–51.

23. McFeely, *Yankee Stepfather*, 104, 106, 111–14 (Fowler quotation); Bentley, *Freedmen's Bureau*, 92–93; Carpenter, *Sword and Olive Branch*, 108; Nieman, *To Set the Law in Motion*, 51; *House Executive Documents*, 39 Congress, 1 session, no. 99, serial 1263, 12–13 (Johnson quotation); James Fullerton to Howard, August 18, 1865, Howard Papers.

24. McFeely, *Yankee Stepfather*, 114–18, 127–28; Nieman, *To Set the Law in Motion*, 51–52 (Fullerton quotation); Paul A. Cimbala, "A Black Colony in Dougherty County: The Freedmen's Bureau and the Failure of Reconstruction in Southwest Georgia," *Journal of Southwest Georgia History* 4 (Fall 1986): 74 (Wild quotation and his emphasis); John C. Rodrique, "The Freedmen's Bureau and Wage Labor in the Louisiana Sugar Regime," in Cimbala and Miller, *The Freedmen's Bureau*, 201.

25. McFeely, *Yankee Stepfather*, 129–31; Nieman, *To Set the Law in Motion*, 52; Carpenter, *Sword and Olive Branch*, 108–9; Howard, *Autobiography*, 2: 234–36; Bentley, *Freedmen's Bureau*, 95–96; Howard to his wife, September 2, 9 (quotation), 1865, Howard Papers; *House Executive Documents*, 39 Congress, 1 session, no. 11, serial 1255.

26. Speed to William Grover, September 20, 1865, Attorney General Letterbooks, E: 220; Richardson, ed., *Messages and Papers of the Presidents*, 6:349; Howard to his wife, September 13, 1865, Howard Papers; Nieman, *To Set the Law in Motion*, 52–53.

27. McFeely, *Yankee Stepfather*, 136–39; Bentley, *Freedmen's Bureau*, 98 (Johnson quotation); Howard to Wilson, November 25, 1865, Howard Papers; Williamson, *After Slavery*, 79–82; Abbott, *Freedmen's Bureau*, 56–57; Cimbala, "Freedmen and Sherman's Grant," 608–13; Foner, *Reconstruction*, 159–61;

28. Peirce, *Freedmen's Bureau*, 23, for the figures; Speed to John K. Goodloe, November 27, 1865; Speed to Nathaniel Usher, December 9, 1865, Attorney General Letterbooks, E: 323, 336; Nieman, *To Set the Law in Motion*, 53–55.

29. James Marten, "'What is to become of the Negro?': White Reaction to Emancipation in Texas," *Mid-America* 73 (April–July 1991): 133; James Smallwood, "Charles Culver, A Reconstruction Agent in Texas: The Work of Local Freedmen's Bureau Agents and the Black Community," *Civil War History* 27 (December 1981): 351; James Smallwood, *Time of Hope, Time of Despair: Black Texans During Reconstruction* (Port Washington, N.Y.: Kennikat Press, 1981), 36–38; Elizabeth Bethel, "The Freedmen's Bureau in Alabama," *Journal of Southern History* 14 (February 1948): 56–57, 62; LaWanda Cox, "James F. McGogy and the Freedmen's Bureau in Alabama," in *Freedom, Racism and Reconstruction*, ed. Donald G. Nieman (Athens: University of Georgia Press, 1997), 184–97; Kenneth B. White, "Wager Swayne: Racist or Realist?," *Alabama Review* 31 (April 1978): 101–7; John B. Myers, "Reaction and Adjustment: The Struggle of Alabama Freedmen in Post-Bellum Alabama, 1865–1867," *Alabama Historical Quarterly* 32 (Spring–Summer 1970): 15; John B. Myers, "The Freedmen and the Labor Supply: The Economic Adjustments in Post-Bellum Alabama, 1865–1867," *Alabama Historical Quarterly* 32 (Fall–Winter 1970): 158, 162; Foner, *Reconstruction*, 143, 162; Nieman, *To Set the Law in Motion*, 39–40, 44; Oubre, *Forty Acres and a Mule*, 45; Kenneth S. Greenberg, "The Civil War and the Redistribution of Land: Adams County, Mississippi, 1860–1870," *Agricultural History* 52 (April 1978): 292–307; Janet Sharp Hermann, *The Pursuit of a Dream* (New York: Vintage Books, 1983), 64–65.

30. Randy Finley, *From Slavery to Uncertain Freedom: The Freedmen's Bureau in Arkansas, 1865–1869* (Fayetteville: University of Arkansas Press, 1996), 76–78; Carl H. Moneyhon, *The Impact of the Civil War and Reconstruction on Arkansas* (Baton Rouge: Louisiana State University Press, 1994), 210–13; Oubre, *Forty Acres and a Mule*, 36–39.

31. See note 10 above. Davis, *The Civil War and Reconstruction in Florida*, 357–59, 381; Jerrell H. Shoftner, "Andrew Johnson and the Fernandina Unionists," *Prologue* 10 (Winter 1978): 211–15; George R. Bentley, "The Political Activity of the Freedmen's Bureau in Florida," *Florida Historical Quarterly* 28 (1949–50): 29–30.

32. Robert F. Engs, *Freedom's First Generation: Black Hampton, Virginia, 1861–1890* (Philadelphia: University of Pennsylvania Press, 1979), 99–109; Allen E. Richardson, "Architects of a Benevolent Empire: The Relationship Between the American Missionary Association and the Freedmen's Bureau in Virginia, 1865–1872," in Cimbala and Miller, *Freedmen's Bureau*, 131–32; Foner, *Reconstruction*, 105, 158, 162.

33. McFeely, *Yankee Stepfather*, 166–76; Peter Ripley, *Slaves and Freedmen in Civil War Louisiana* (Baton Rouge: Louisiana State University Press, 1976), 194–95; Howard A. White, *The Freedmen's Bureau in Louisiana* (Baton Rouge: Louisiana State University Press, 1970), 46–58 (Conway quotation); Howard to Conway, December 29, 1865, May 25, 1866, Howard Papers; Foner, *Reconstruction*, 158, 162; Ted Tunnell, "Free Negroes and the Freedmen: Black Politics in New Orleans During the Civil War," *Southern Studies* 9 (Spring 1980): 23–24.

34. McFeely, *Yankee Stepfather*, 220–23, 225–27; Foner, *Reconstruction*, 159–64; Abbott, *Freedmen's Bureau*, 56–57; Williamson, *After Slavery*, 79–83; Robert R. Singleton, "James C. Beecher and the Freedmen's Bureau," *Mississippi Quarterly* 53 (Winter 1999–2000): 8–10,16–19, 30–32; James D. Schmidt, "'A Full-Fledged Government of Men': Freedmen's Labor Policy in South Carolina, 1865–1868," in Cimbala and Miller, *Freedmen's Bureau*, 224–47; Oubre, *Forty Acres and a Mule*, 49–61, 51 (Saxton quotation).

35. Oubre, *Forty Acres and a Mule*, 60–61; Paul A. Cimbala, *Under The Guardianship of the Nation: The Freedmen's Bureau and the Reconstruction of Georgia* (Athens: University of Georgia Press, 1997), 166–80; Paul Cimbala, "The 'Talisman Power': Davis Tillson, the Freedmen's Bureau, and Free Labor in Reconstruction Georgia," *Civil War History* 28 (June 1982): 154, 157–58; Cimbala, "A Black Colony in Dougherty County," 74–80; Cimbala, "Freedmen and Sherman's Grant," 597–609, 611–19; Cimbala, "On the Front Line of Freedom: Freedmen's Bureau Officers and Agents in Reconstruction Georgia, 1865–1868," *Georgia Historical Quarterly* 76 (Fall 1992): 578, 580n, 581; Tillson to Howard, February 21, 1866, Howard Papers; Duncan, *Freedom's Shore*, 26–32; Foner, *Reconstruction*, 159–64.

36. Eric Foner, "Thaddeus Stevens, Confiscation, and Reconstruction," in *The Hofstadter Aegis: A Memorial*, ed. Eric McKitrick and Stanley Elkins (New York: Knopf, 1974), 154–83; Trumbull to Howard, February 21, 1866, Howard Papers; James A. Woodburn, *The Life of Thaddeus Stevens* (Indianapolis: Bobbs-Merrill, 1913), 521–28; Lydia Maria Child to Sarah Shaw, September 7, 1866, in *Lydia Maria Child: Selected Letters, 1817–1880*, ed. Milton Meltzer and Patricia G. Holland (Amherst: University of Massachusetts Press, 1982), 463; Walter L. Fleming, ed., *Documentary History of Reconstruction* (New York: Peter Smith, 1950), 1:149, 151; Foner, *Reconstruction*, 242–46; McFeely, *Yankee Stepfather*, 211–35; Michael L. Lanza, "'One of the Most Appreciated Labors of the Bureau': The Freedmen's Bureau and the Southern Homestead Act," in Cimbala and Miller, *Freedmen's Bureau*, 67–92; Gerald David Jaynes, *Branches Without Roots: The Genesis of the Black Working Class in the American South* (New York: Oxford University Press, 1986), 6–7, 10–11; Ralph J. Roske, *His Own Counsel: The Life and Times of Lyman Trumbull* (Reno: University of Nevada Press, 1979), 121–23.

37. Foner, *Politics and Ideology*, 106–7; Leon F. Litwack, *Been in the Storm So Long: The Aftermath of Slavery* (New York: Vintage Books, 1979), 392, 398–408; Patricia A. Turner, *I Heard It Through the Grapevine: Rumor in African-American Culture* (Berkeley: University of California Press, 1993), 42; McPherson, *The Negro's Civil War*, 293–94, 298; Julie Saville, *The Work of Reconstruction: From Slave to Wage Laborer in South Carolina, 1860–1870* (New York: Cambridge University Press, 1994), 18, 20, 78–79, 86, 190; Jonathan M. Wiener, *Social Origins of the New South: Alabama, 1860–1885* (Baton Rouge: Louisiana State University Press, 1978), 43; Foner, *Reconstruction*, 160–61, 164–68; Jaynes, *Branches Without Roots*, 73, 114–15, 158–59, 295; Richardson, *Death of Reconstruction*, 55, 61; Fleming, *Documentary History of Reconstruction*, 1:356; August Meier, *Negro Thought*

in America, 1880–1915: Racial Ideologies in the Age of Booker T. Washington (Ann Arbor: University of Michigan Press, 1963), 5, 11.

38. Edward F. Sweat, "Francis L. Cardoza [*sic*]—Profile of Integrity in Reconstruction Politics," *Journal of Negro History* 46 (October 1961): 217–32; R. H. Woody, "Jonathan Jasper Wright, Associate Justice of the Supreme Court of South Carolina, 1870–1877," *Journal of Negro History* 18 (April 1933): 114–31; William C. Harris, "James Lynch: Black Leader in Southern Reconstruction," *The Historian* 34 (November 1971): 40–61; David C. Rankin, "The Origins of Black Leadership in New Orleans During Reconstruction," *Journal of Southern History* 40 (August 1974), 217–40; Euline W. Brock, "Thomas W. Cardozo: Fallible Reconstruction Leader," *Journal of Southern History* 47 (May 1981): 183–206; Richard L. Hume, "Negro Delegates to the State Constitutional Conventions of 1867–69," in *Southern Black Leaders of the Reconstruction Era*, ed. Howard N. Rabinowitz (Urbana: University of Illinois Press, 1982), 129–53; Richard L. Hume, "Membership of the Florida Constitutional Convention of 1868: A Case Study of Republican Factionalism in the Reconstruction South," *Florida Historical Quarterly* 51 (July 1972): 8–9, 11; Richard L. Hume, "The Membership of the Virginia Constitutional Convention of 1867–1868: A Study of the Beginnings of Congressional Reconstruction of the Upper South," *Virginia Magazine of History and Biography* 86 (October 1978): 463, 469, 472, 477; Richard L. Hume, "The Arkansas Constitutional Convention of 1868: A Case Study in the Politics of Reconstruction," *Journal of Southern History* 39 (May 1973): 186, 191: Joseph P. Reidy, "Aaron A. Bradley: Voice of Black Labor in the Georgia Lowcountry," in Rabinowitz, *Southern Black Leaders*, 281–308; Howard N. Rabinowitz, "Holland Thompson and Black Participation in Montgomery, Alabama," in Rabinowitz, *Southern Black Leaders*, 249–80; Michael W. Fitzgerald, *The Union League Movement in the Deep South: Politics and Agricultural Change During Reconstruction* (Baton Rouge: Louisiana State University Press, 1989), 125, Richardson, *Death of Reconstruction*, 52–53, 63, 66; Joe M. Richardson, "Jonathan C. Gibbs: Florida's Only Negro Cabinet Member," *Florida Historical Quarterly* 42 (April 1964): 364–65; Okon Edet Uya, *From Slavery to Public Service: Robert Smalls, 1839–1915* (New York: Oxford University Press, 1971), 47–50.

39. Michael Les Benedict, "The Rout of Radicalism: Republicans and the Elections of 1867," *Civil War History* 18 (December 1972): 334–44; Fitzgerald, *The Union League Movement*, 14–15, 28, 113, 117–23; Michael W. Fitzgerald, "Radical Republicanism and the White Yeomanry During Alabama Reconstruction," *Journal of Southern History* 54 (November 1988): 571; Richardson, *Death of Reconstruction*, 65–66.

40. Child to Lucy Osgood, April 13, 1865, in *Lydia Maria Child: Selected Letters*, 451–52; Speed to Bennett Pike, June 15, 1866, Attorney General Letterbooks, F: 66.

41. See Ronald E. Butchart, *Northern Schools, Southern Blacks, and Reconstruction: Freedmen's Education, 1862–1875* (Westport, Conn.: Greenwood Press, 1980), 70–73, 177–79, 197–205, for the argument that most whites interested in helping blacks after the war came to see education as a panacea and could not accept confiscation. Butchart believes confiscation violated their bourgeois attitudes toward private property. Kenneth White, "Wager Swayne," 93, 101, came to a similar conclusion in his study of the Freedmen's Bureau in Alabama.

10. Confiscation and the Courts: Jurisdiction and Procedures

1. In this chapter and chapter 11 the Court refers to the Supreme Court. Allen C. Guelzo claimed near the end of his authoritative monograph on the Emancipation Proclamation: "standing firmly to block the goal of land distribution was the Supreme Court, fully as determined to preserve prewar property rights in land (if no longer in slaves) as President Johnson." He then cites *Ex parte Milligan* (1866) and *Ex parte McCardle* (1867) as examples of the Court's "chipping away at the war power's doctrine." I agree with

the latter assertion but, as the next two chapters try to show, do not believe the Court took a position against the idea of land distribution after the war.

2. In the late 1600s the English introduced admiralty courts in the American colonies. Colonists often opposed them because they did not employ juries to determine the facts in cases of property seized. See Alfred H. Kelly, Winfred A. Harbison, and Herman Belz, *The American Constitution and Its Origins and Development*, 6th ed. (New York: Norton, 1983), 42. In article III, section 2, the Constitution says the "judicial Power shall extend . . . to all Cases of admiralty and maritime Jurisdiction." The Judiciary Act of 1789 provided that district courts should allow a jury trial in seizure cases whenever possible. *U.S. Statutes at Large*, 1:77; James G. Randall, *Constitutional Problems Under Lincoln*, rev. ed. (Urbana: University of Illinois Press, 1964), 285n.

3. *United States v. Republican Banner Officers* 27 Fed. Cas. 781 (1863); *American Annual Cyclopaedia and Register of Important Events of the Year 1863* (New York: Appleton & Co., 1868), 222.

4. *United States v. Republican Banner*, 782–83.

5. *Mrs. Alexander's Cotton* 2 Wall. 404 (1864); Quincy Wright, "The American Civil War (1861–1865)," in *The International Law of Civil War*, ed. Richard Falk (Baltimore: Johns Hopkins University Press, 1971), 56; Charles Fairman, *The History of the Supreme Court of the United States*, vol. 6: *Reconstruction and Reunion, 1864–88* (New York: Macmillan, 1971), 38–39.

6. *Prize Cases* 2 Black 687 (1862); Harold M. Hyman and William M. Wiecek, *Equal Justice Under Law: Constitutional Development 1863–1875* (New York: Oxford University Press, 1982), 263–65; Randall, *Constitutional Problems Under Lincoln*, 71–72.

7. *Mrs. Alexander's Cotton*, 417–22.

8. *Union Insurance Company v. United States* 6 Wall. 759 (1868); Fairman, *Reconstruction and Reunion*, 791.

9. *Union Insurance Company*, 763–64 (italics in the original); Rufus Waples, *A Treatise on Proceedings in Rem* (Chicago: Callaghan & Co., 1882), 435–36.

10. See *Armstrong's Foundry* 6 Wall. 766 (1867); *St. Louis Street Foundry* 6 Wall. 770 (1876); and *United States v. Hart* 6 Wall. 770 (1867), the last of which involved the second act.

11. Cases that involved admiralty or maritime jurisdiction went to the Supreme Court on appeal. This brought the entire matter before the Supreme Court. A writ of error, by contrast, brought particular issues, or errors, before the court to be adjudicated. See Fairman, *Reconstruction and Reunion*, 839n.

12. *Union Insurance v. United States*, 765.

13. *United States v. Athens* 24 Fed. Cas. 878 (April 1868).

14. Randall, *Constitutional Problems*, 285n; *U.S. Statutes at Large*, 1:76–77.

15. *Semple v. United States* 21 Fed. Cas. 1072 (May 1868).

16. Ibid., 173. The plaintiffs in *Semple* also claimed the second act was unconstitutional. But Chase brushed aside this point by noting that no similar objection had been raised in *Union Insurance Company* or other cases involving confiscation heard by the Supreme Court in 1867. In 1863 the Kentucky Court of Appeals ruled the second act unconstitutional but the Supreme Court made no mention of the case thereafter. See *Norris v. Doniphan* 4 Met. (Ky.) 385 (1863). *Brown v. United States* 4 Fed. Cas. (1868), a case in Kansas, followed *Semple* and *Athens Armory*.

17. *Morris's Cotton* 8 Wall. 507 (1869)

18. Ibid., 510–12. For other cases involving jurisdictional questions under the first and second acts, but not affecting their purpose, see *Confiscation Cases* 7 Wall. 454 (1869); *Knoefel v. Williams* 30 Indiana 1 (1868); *Garnett v. United States* 11 Wall. 256 (1870); and *Pasteur v. Lewis and Lynd* 39 Louisiana Annual 5 (1887). District Attorney Rufus Waples had represented the government in the *Confiscation Cases*. Judge Edward H. Durell,

appointed by President Lincoln as judge for the eastern district of Louisiana in 1863, ruled against the government in the nine *Confiscation Cases*. See Fairman, *Reconstruction and Reunion*, 816–19, for the *Confiscation Cases*, and Allen Johnson and Dumas Malone, eds., *Dictionary of American History* (New York: Charles Scribner's Sons, 1930), 5:545, for Durell's background.

19. *Ex Parte Graham* 10 Wall. 541 (1870). Justice Swayne's son was an agent for the Freedmen's Bureau in Alabama. See Kenneth B. White, "Wager Swayne: Racist or Realist?" *Alabama Review* 31 (April 1978): 92–109.

20. As noted in chapter 7, James Graham was a marshal in New Orleans. L. Madison Gray was a lawyer and wrote *The Constitutionality and Legality of Confiscations in Fee, Under the Act of July 17, 1862* (New Orleans: n.p., 1870). Day was also a litigant in *Day v. McCou* 18 Wall. 156 (1873), discussed in chapter 11. Thomas J. Durant represented Graham and Day in *Ex Parte Graham*. Durant was a prominent New Orleans lawyer and Republican politician.

21. *Ex Parte Graham*, 542–43; *U.S. Statutes at Large*, 1: 80–81.

22. *United States v. One Thousand Seven Hundred and Fifty-Six Shares* 27 Fed. Cas. 335 (1864). The Supreme Court docketed this case in October 1865, *United States v. LeRoy M. Wiley*, but counsel accepted the circuit court's decision and it was never reported along with other cases. Fairman, *Reconstruction and Reunion*, 789–91; Randall, *Constitutional Problems Under Lincoln*, 310–12; *American Annual Cyclopaedia and Register of Important Events of the Year 1863*, 220.

23. *United States v. One Thousand Seven Hundred and Fifty-Six Shares of Capital Stock* 27 Fed. Cas. 337 (1865).

24. *McVeigh v. United States* 11 Wall. 259 (1871); Fairman, *Reconstruction and Reunion*, 799; James G. Randall, *The Confiscation of Property During the Civil War* (Indianapolis: Mutual Printing and Lithographing, 1913), 22–23; Patricia A. Lucie, *Freedom and Federalism: Congress and Courts 1861–1866* (New York: Garland, 1986), 49.

25. *McVeigh v. United States*, 266; Waples, *Proceedings in Rem*, 425, 467; Fairman, *Reconstruction and Reunion*, 823–24. Marshall John Underwood, as instructed by Judge John C. Underwood, perhaps a relative, sold McVeigh's property to the highest bidder, who appears to have been Mrs. Maria J. Underwood, the judge's wife. For Judge Underwood's background, see Patricia Hickin, "John C. Underwood and the Antislavery Movement in Virginia, 1847–1860," *Virginia Magazine of History and Biography* 73 (April 1965): 156–68.

26. *McVeigh v. United States*, 264–66. The question of whether the second act confiscated property that was guilty, as Ackerman claimed, or the property of those who were guilty of supporting the Confederacy, as McVeigh's counsel argued, was a complicated issue and directly related to the question of duration. Chapter 11 discusses the issue in more detail.

27. *McVeigh v. United States*, 266–67.

28. *Gregory v. McVeigh* 23 Wall. 294 (1974); Fairman, *Reconstruction and Reunion*, 824–27, explains the complicated details of the judge and Mrs. Underwood and the claims to the property in the three cases.

29. *Gregory v. McVeigh*, 298–307; Fairman, *Reconstruction and Reunion*, 826n. Waite's opinion did not discuss the second act.

30. *Windsor v. McVeigh* 93 U.S. 274 (1876).

31. Ibid., 282–84; Fairman, *Reconstruction and Reunion*, 827–28. Field's opinion in *Windsor* was often cited thereafter to courts that exceeded their authority. A later case, *Avril v. Alexandria Water Company* 2 Fed. Cas. 254 (1877), also involved a fraudulent sale of McVeigh's property, shares in a water company. The circuit court ruled in the company's favor, since it had continually denied the validity of the sale and had maintained

that Avril had known upon receipt of the shares that the company claimed they had been wrongly confiscated from McVeigh.

32. *Chapman v. Phoenix National Bank* 85 New York 437 (1881).

33. See *Chapman v. Phoenix National Bank*, 449, for the cases cited by Judge Earl.

34. *Miller v. United States* 11 Wall. 268 (1871); Waples, *Proceedings in Rem*, 357, 468.

35. Ibid., 274–79; Fairman, *Reconstruction and Reunion*, 804.

36. *Miller v. United States*, 296–98.

37. Ibid., Field, 314–28, Davis, 328–31. Justice Clifford concurred with Field and objected to the majority's constitutional argument, discussed in the next chapter. Davis only dissented on seizure. Fairman, *Reconstruction and Reunion*, 805–6, supported Davis's argument on seizure.

38. Although James G. Randall thought the *Miller* decision wrong on constitutional grounds, he offered no criticism of the majority views on seizure and jurisdiction. See Randall, *Constitutional Problems Under Lincoln*, 283–84, 312–15.

39. *Alexandria v. Fairfax* 95 U.S. 774 (1877).

40. *Phoenix Bank v. Risley* 111 U.S. 125 (1884).

41. *Pelham v. Rose* 9 Wall. 103 (1870).

42. *Pelham v. Way* 15 Wall. 196 1872).

43. *Tyler v. Defrees* 11 Wall. 331 (1870); Fairman, *Reconstruction and Reunion*, 808–11; Waples, *Proceedings in Rem*, 357, 474. L. Madison Day represented Defrees before the Court. In *Cooper v. Reynolds* 10 Wall. 308 (1870), which did not involve confiscation, the Court had already said it would ignore procedural errors involving in rem proceedings and grant jurisdiction. Miller quoted *Cooper* at some length in his majority opinion in *Tyler*. Field dissented in *Cooper*. He claimed the state court in Tennessee never acquired jurisdiction but he did not elaborate.

44. *Tyler v. Defrees*, 344–49.

45. In *Bragg v. Lorio* 4 Fed. Cas. 2 (1871) and *Griswold v. Connolly* 11 Fed. Cas. 59 (1871), the Circuit Court of Louisiana followed *Tyler v. Defrees* and ignored procedural errors in how the seizure of property had been accomplished.

46. *Tyler v. Defrees*, 350–56.

47. *Brown v. Kennedy* 15 Wall. 591 (1872); Fairman, *Reconstruction and Reunion*, 838–39; Waples, *Proceedings in Rem*, 477. Justice Field dissented in *Brown*, without an opinion, perhaps because he had already dissented at length in *Miller* and *Tyler v. Defrees*. Charles Fairman agreed that "certainly Brown did not have justice on his side" in the majority's decision.

48. Brown did receive sympathy from the court in *Brown v. Hiatts* 15 Wall. 117 (1872), heard and decided in the same term as *Brown v. Kennedy*. Benajah and Martha Ann Hiatt had borrowed $2,400 from Brown in 1860 and secured the loan with mortgages on some of their property and that of two others. During the war Benajah Hiatt persuaded a district attorney to confiscate the debt owed Brown, save the Hiatts' portion, which he falsely alleged had been paid off. Justice Field, for a unanimous Court, ruled in Brown's favor since, among other things, Hiatt had "concocted a scheme to defraud" Brown. See *Brown v. Hiatt* 4 Fed. 384 (1970) and Fairman, *Reconstruction and Reunion*, 838–39, for more on the case.

49. *The Confiscation Cases* 20 Wall. 92 (1874); Fairman, *Reconstruction and Reunion*, 816–19.

50. *The Confiscation Cases* 6 Fed. Cas. 270 (1870). The property of Charles M. Conrad and Francis H. Hatch were also involved but the decisions discussed the various aspects of the seizure of Slidell's property.

51. Waples later defended himself against Bradley's criticism by saying "the allegations of the libel [written by Waples] had not been in accord with the hypothesis that the act of 1862 authorized personal prosecution against the owners of enemy property,

or proceedings equivalent thereto." He then observed with some satisfaction that because "there were alternate allegations, allowable in informations *in rem*, forbidden in criminal indictments, the decree was reversed" by Supreme Court. See Waples, *Proceedings in Rem*, 484.

52. *The Confiscation Cases*, 104–13 (1874).

53. Ibid., 113–14 (italics in the original). Both had also dissented from *Miller*. Justice Davis dissented but without an opinion in *The Confiscation Cases*.

11. Confiscation and the Courts: Constitutionality and Duration

1. *Miller v. United States* 11 Wall. 268 (1870). Justices Nathan Clifford and Stephen J. Field dissented over the majority's views on the constitutionality of the confiscation acts. Justice David Davis dissented over the issue of seizure. In 1863 the Court of Appeals of Kentucky had ruled the second act to be unconstitutional but there is no discussion of this decision in the federal courts. The Kentucky court said the act was unconstitutional because it confiscated the property of citizens without due process of law, which Miller argued in his appeal to the Supreme Court in *Miller v. United States*. See *Norris v. Doniphan* 1863 WL 2582 (Ky.) and Thomas M. Cooley, *A Treatise on the Constitutional Limitations Which Rest Upon the Legislative Powers of the United States of the American Union*, 2nd ed. (Boston: Little, Brown, 1871), 278n.

2. *The Prize Cases* 2 Black 635 (1863). The cases involved four vessels, the brig *Amy Warwick*, the schooners *Crenshaw* and *Brilliante*, and the barque *Hiawatha*, that ran the blockade, ordered by President Lincoln, of southern ports. Harold M. Hyman and William M. Wiecek, *Equal Justice Under Law: Constitutional Development 1835–1875* (New York: Harper & Row, 1982), 263–65.

3. *Miller v. United States*, 292–308; Charles Fairman, *The History of the Supreme Court of the United States*, vol. 6, *Reconstruction and Reunion, 1864–1868* (New York: Macmillan, 1971), 800–807.

4. *Miller v. United States*, 308–14.

5. Rufus Waples, *A Treatise on Proceedings in Rem* (Chicago: Callaghan & Co., 1882), 357, 446, 452n, 456n.

6. James G. Randall, *Constitutional Problems Under Lincoln*, rev. ed. (Urbana: University of Illinois Press, 1964), 295–306. Randall's arguments relied heavily upon his first work on the subject, *The Confiscation of Property During the Civil War* (Indianapolis: Mutual Printing and Lithographing, 1913), 16–18.

7. *Ware v. Hilton* 3 Dallas 199 (1796). Justice Samuel Chase said in *Ware* that all nations at war were authorized "by the general and strict law of nations, to seize and confiscate all moveable property of its enemy (of any kind or nature whatsoever) wherever found, whether within its territory or not." Ibid., 226. Randall, *Constitutional Problems Under Lincoln*, 300.

8. *Brown v. United States* 8 Cranch 110 (1814). Marshal's majority opinion said that "war gives to the sovereign full right to take the persons and confiscate the property of the enemy wherever found" and that "the power of confiscating enemy property is in the legislature." Ibid., 122, 129.

9. *Miller v. United States*, 305.

10. Ibid., 307.

11. Ibid., 313.

12. Ibid., 314–28. Justice Clifford joined in Field's dissent. Justice David Davis also dissented, but not over the constitutionality of the confiscation acts. See Fairman, *Reconstruction and Reunion*, 805–6, for support of Davis's dissent. Randall applauded Field's dissent in *Miller* and quoted the justice's dissent in *Tyler v. Defrees*, for specific praise. See *Tyler v. Defrees* 11 Wall. 331 (1870) and Randall, *Constitutional Problems Under Lincoln*, 314–15.

13. Field said criminal legislation like the second act should be "subject to all the limitations prescribed by the Constitution for the protection of the citizen against hasty and indiscriminate accusation, and which insure to him, when accused, a speedy and public trial by a jury of his peers." *Miller v. United States*, 815; Fairman, *Reconstruction and Reunion*, 801–2.

14. *U.S. Statutes at Large*, 12:591; *Miller v. United States*, 319. See the appendix for the second act.

15. *Miller v. United States*, 321–23.

16. Randall, *Constitutional Problems Under Lincoln*, 308.

17. Fairman, *Reconstruction and Reunion*, 801n.

18. William Whiting, *The War Powers of the President and the Legislative Powers of Congress in Relation to Rebellion, Treason and Slavery*, 4th ed. (Boston: John L. Shorey, 1863), 114; L. Madison Day, *The Constitutionality and Legality of Confiscations in Fee* (New Orleans: n.p., 1870), 77–82; Waples, *Proceedings in Rem*, 456–61.

19. *The American Annual Cyclopaedia and Register of Important Events of the Year 1863*, vol. 3 (New York: Appleton & Co., 1868), 221; Randall, *Constitutional Problems Under Lincoln*, 286n; Fairman, *Reconstruction and Reunion*, 797; William Whiting, *War Powers under the Constitution of the United States. Military Arrests, Reconstruction, and Military Government* (Boston: Lee & Shepard, 1871), 111n; Edward McPherson, *The Political History of the United States of America During the Great Rebellion* (New York: Appleton & Co., 1864), 206. Attorney General Edward Bates recorded Underwood's ruling in his diary on November 19, 1863 without comment. See Howard K. Beale, ed., *The Diary of Edward Bates, 1859–1866* (New York: Da Capo, 1971 [1933]), 316. Underwood, reversed by the Court in *McVeigh v. United States*, was originally from New York, had helped organize an antislavery organization in Virginia before the Civil War, and was a Republican. For his background, see Patricia Hicken, "John C. Underwood and the Anti-Slavery Movement in Virginia, 1847–1860," *Virginia Magazine of History and Biography* 73 (April 1965): 156–68.

20. *Bigelow v. Forrest* 9 Wall. 339 (1869).

21. *Bigelow v. Forrest*, 339–45 (italics in Bigelow's argument); Fairman, *Reconstruction and Reunion*, 797. Forrest's property was in Virginia, but the case did not come before Underwood's court.

22. *Bigelow v. Forrest*, 347–53; Fairman, *Reconstruction and Reunion*, 798; Waples, *Proceedings in Rem*, 462–63, 472, 498, 517–18. As L. Madison Day observed, Senator Daniel Clarke [*sic*], Republican of New Hampshire, noted in July 1862 when the joint resolution had been proposed that it was "to meet what I believe to be the objection of the President." Lincoln was concerned about attainder of treason, which had no relation to the provisions in the act involving confiscation. See *Congressional Globe*, 37 Congress, 2 session, pt, 4, 3380; Day, *Constitutionality and Legality of Confiscations*, 79–81.

23. The court also dismissed Bigelow's claim that Douglass Forrest, the heir and a Confederate military officer, could not sue because he too was liable under the second act. Strong said Douglass Forrest had no interest in the land when it was forfeited and it had not been confiscated for anything he had done. *Bigelow v. Forrest*, 345, 352.

24. *Day v. Micou* 18 Wall. 156 (1873); Waples, *Proceedings in Rem*, 477–78, 480–81. Judge Durell, on a motion by District Attorney Waples, had ruled that when real estate had been condemned, the marshal would insure that all mortgages were cancelled. See Fairman, *Reconstruction and Reunion*, 814–15.

25. Day's loss in the lower courts may have prompted him to write his work on the constitutionality of the confiscation acts, which came out three years before the Court decided *Day v. Micou*.

26. Day remained unconvinced and asked for redress from Congress for years thereafter. Fairman, *Reconstruction and Reunion*, 816, 816n. Strong also ruled in *Claims of*

Marcuard et al. 20 Wall. 114 (1873) that those who owned liens against the properties of John Slidell, another high Confederate official, had no right to any of the proceeds from their sale after confiscation.

27. *Wallach et al. v. Van Riswick* 92 U.S. 202 (1875); Waples, *Proceedings in Rem*, 453–54, 494–97, 530–32.

28. *Wallach et al. v. Van Riswick*, 202–6; Fairman, *Reconstruction and Reunion*, 848–49. Albert Pike, a former Confederate army general, represented Wallach, while Thomas J. Durant, a Unionist from New Orleans by way of New York, represented Van Riswick. Like Waples and Durell, Durant was involved in numerous confiscation cases and the complicated politics of New Orleans. See chapters 6 and 7 for more on these men.

29. *Wallach et al. v. Van Riswick*, 207–14.

30. Randall, *Confiscation*, 26–27. Randall, by contrast, thought the *Wallach* decision a "categorical and positive declaration of law" and lamented the Court's retreat from its position over the next five years.

31. *Wallach et al. v. Van Riswick*, 212.

32. *Pike v. Wassell* 94 U.S. 711; Fairman, *Reconstruction and Reunion*, 850; Waples, *Proceedings in Rem*, 503–5.

33. *Pike v. Wassell*, 714–15.

34. *French v. Wade* 102 U.S. 132 (1880); Waples, *Proceedings in Rem*, 512–13

35. *Avegno v. Schmidt* 113 U.S. 293 (1884).

36. *Shields v. Schiff* 124 U.S. 351 (1887).

37. Ibid., 358; Randall, *Confiscation*, 27. Although *Avegno* and *Shields* grew out of the confiscation of property under the second act, the cases principally involved the interpretation of a Louisiana mortgage law.

38. *Illinois Central Railroad Company v. Bosworth* 133 U.S. 92 (1889).

39. *Illinois Central Railroad Company v. Bosworth*, 99–103; Fairman, *Reconstruction and Reunion*, 850–53; Randall, *Confiscation*, 27.

40. *Jenkins v. Collard* 145 U.S. 546 (1891); Randall, *Confiscation*, 27–28.

41. *United States v. Dunnington* 146 U.S. 338 (1892). Justice Brown had been a deputy marshal in Michigan in the confiscation case that led to *Miller v. United States*. See Fairman, *Reconstruction and Reunion*, 852.

42. *United States v. Dunnington*, 349.

43. *Kirk v. Lynd* 106 U.S. 315 (1882). The first act generated few cases of note, other than the important ones involving proceedings, such as *Union Insurance Co. v. United States* and *Armstrong's Foundry*, discussed in chapter 10, and pardon cases, discussed below. For cases that involved the rights of informers, see *Francis v. United States* 5 Wall. 338 (1866); *Confiscation Cases* 7 Wall. 454 (1868); and *Titus v. United States* 20 Wall. 475 (1874). For other cases involving the first act, see *United States v. William Arthur* 28 Fed. Cas. 624 (1861); *United States v. Tract of Land* 28 Fed. Cas. 203 (1871); *United States v. One Thousand Five Hundred Bales of Cotton*, 27 Fed. Cas. 325 (1872); *United States, Lyon v. Huckabee* 16 Wallace 414 (1872); and *Whitfield v. United States* 92 U.S. 165 (1875).

44. The property in *Kirk v. Lynd* was a cotton press in New Orleans owned by R. M. Pasteur. See *Pasteur v. Lewis*, 39 Louisiana Annual 5 (1887), for a further effort by Pasteur's heirs, also unsuccessful, to retrieve their father's confiscated property.

45. On a less significant matter, the Supreme Court held that the second act's prohibition against the sales or transfers of confiscable property applied only to such transactions after the act's passage and only those that threatened the national authority or the rights of loyal citizens. Justice Field wrote all three opinions and argued that the second act was not meant to prevent all sales or transfers of property between citizens of the Confederacy. See *Corbett v. Nutt* 10 Wall. 464 (1870), *Conrad v. Waples* 96 U.S. 279 (1877), and *Burbank v. Conrad* 96 U.S. 291 (1877).

46. The Supreme Court ruled on one case involving pardon and confiscation before the war ended, but it was not important in relation to later cases. In *Mrs. Alexander's Cotton* 2 Wall. 404 (1864), the Court held a pardon invalid when the pardoned rebel voluntarily resumed her residence within Confederate military lines.

47. *Congressional Globe*, 39:2, vol. 37, pt. 1, p. 4, December 3, 1866 (hereafter cited as *Cong. Globe*, 39:2). The vote was 112 to 29, with mostly Democrats opposed. For the comments in the spring of 1866, see ibid., 39:1, vol. 36, pt. 3, 2463, 2532, 2536. Hans L. Trefousse, *Andrew Johnson: A Biography* (New York: Norton, 1989), 216–17, 227.

48. See *Cong. Globe*, 39:2, vol. 37, pt. 1, 8 (December 4, 1866, for Howard); 144, 268–69 (December 17, 1866 and January 4, 14, 1867 for Johnson); 9, 15 (quote), and 144 (December 4, 5, 17, 1866, for Trumbull). See 227 for the Senate vote. It was 27 to 7, with only two Republicans, James Dixon of Connecticut and James Doolittle of Wisconsin, opposed. Jonathan T. Dorris, *Pardon and Amnesty under Lincoln and Johnson: The Restoration of the Confederates to Their Rights and Privileges, 1861–1868* (Westport, N.Y.: Greenwood Press, 1977 [1953]), 322–29. Reverdy Johnson was one of the lawyers for A. H. Garland in *Ex parte Garland,* 4 Wall. 333 (1866). The Court ruled that Garland's pardon was full and restored him to all his previous rights and privileges. According to Justice Field, a full pardon "blots out the existence of the guilt, so that in the eye of the law the offender is as innocent as if he had never committed the offense." Ibid., 380. See Hyman and Wiecek, *Equal Justice Under Law*, 373–81, for a discussion of *Garland.*

49. In *Klein v. United States* 13 Wall. 128 (1871), the Supreme Court ruled that Congress's repeal of section thirteen did not affect the president's power of pardon. The repeal "was after the close of the war, when the [second] act had ceased to be important as an expression of the legislative disposition to carry into effect the clemency of the Executive," said Chief Justice Chase. He also said Congress could not limit the effect of the president's pardon, nor exclude any group from its benefits. *Klein* involved pardons under the Captured and Abandoned Property Act of 1863. Dorris, *Pardon and Amnesty*, 406.

50. *Armstrong's Foundry* 6 Wall. 766 (1867); Randall, *Constitutional Problems Under Lincoln*, 333–35, also found the Court's reasoning in *Armstrong* odd.

51. *Armstrong's Foundry*, 769; see Fairman, *Reconstruction and Reunion*, 791–92, for Stanbery's remarks.

52. *Semmes v. United States* 91 U.S. 21 (1875).

53. Randall, *Confiscation*, 46n; Fairman, *Reconstruction and Reunion*, 821n; Dorris, *Pardon and Amnesty*, 415. Semmes later sought to recover another piece of property but lost again in *Burbank v. Semmes* 99 U.S. 138 (1878).

54. *Osborn v. United States* 91 U.S. 474 (1875).

55. *Brown v. United States* 4 Fed. Cas. 435 (1868). Miller said that pardons would normally restore rights to confiscated property unless the proceeds of the sale were not put into the hands of another party, such as the U.S. Treasury. On the other hand, in 1871 a federal circuit court in Louisiana ruled that Braxton Bragg, a Confederate general, could not have his plantation returned after receiving a pardon in 1868 because the title of the property had been vested in the United States before that date. See *Bragg v. Lorio et al.* 4 Fed. Cas. 2 (1871); Dorris, *Pardon and Amnesty*, 414.

56. *Osborn v. United States*, 478; Dorris, *Pardon and Amnesty*, 416–17; Fairman, *Reconstruction and Reunion*, 832–36. The Kansas District Court deposited proceeds from confiscation cases, including those from Brown, in a bank account and then used these funds to defray expenses. Suspicions of dishonesty were leveled at Judge Mark W. Delahay, a Lincoln appointee, and various court officials.

57. *Knote v. United States* 95 U.S. 149 (1877).

58. *Knote v. United States*, 153–54; Fairman, *Reconstruction and Reunion*, 846–47; Dorris, *Pardon and Amnesty*, 417.

59. *Illinois Central Railroad v. Bosworth* 133 U.S. 92 (1889). See above in this chapter for a discussion of *Illinois Central* and the fee.

60. *Illinois Central Railroad v. Bosworth*, 106.

61. *Jenkins v. Collard* 145 U.S. 54 (1891). See above in this chapter for a discussion of *Jenkins* and *United States v. Dunnington* 16 U.S. 338 (1892), both of which reaffirmed *Bosworth*.

62. *Jenkins v. Collard*, 560.

Selected Bibliography

Primary Sources

Manuscripts

John A. Andrew Papers, Massachusetts Historical Society, Boston

Attorney General Papers, Record Group 60, National Archives, Washington, D.C.

Zachariah Chandler Papers, Library of Congress, Washington, D.C.

Thomas J. Durant Papers, New York Historical Society, New York City

Edward H. Durell Papers, New York Historical Society, New York City

Edward Everett Papers, Massachusetts Historical Society, Boston

William Pitt Fessenden Papers, Library of Congress, Washington, D.C.

Oliver Otis Howard Papers, Bowdoin College, Brunswick, Maine

Thomas H. Seymour Papers, Connecticut Historical Society, Hartford

John Sherman Papers, Library of Congress, Washington, D.C.

Edwin M. Stanton Papers, Library of Congress, Washington, D.C.

Thaddeus Stevens Papers, Library of Congress, Washington, D.C.

Charles Sumner Papers, Houghton Library, Harvard University, Cambridge, Mass.

Treasury Department Papers, Record Group 366, National Archives, Washington, D.C.

Lyman Trumbull Papers, Library of Congress, Washington, D.C.

Benjamin F. Wade Papers, Library of Congress, Washington, D.C.

Public Documents

Congressional Record, 1861–1868

The War of the Rebellion: A Compilation of the Official Records of the Union and Confederate Armies. 128 vols. Washington, D.C.: U.S. Government Printing Office, 1880–1901.

Statutes at Large, Treaties, and Proclamations of the United States of America. 17 vols. Boston: Little, Brown, 1850–1873.

United States Federal Cases

United States Reports

Pamphlets, Books, Articles

Allen, Joseph Henry. "Africans in America and Their New Guardians." *The Christian Examiner* 72 (July 1862): 96–133.

American Annual Cyclopaedia and Register of Important Events of the Year 1863. New York: Appleton & Co., 1868.

Bacon, Rev. L. "Reply to Professor Parker." *The New Englander* 22 (April 1863): 191–258.

Bushnell, Rev. Horace. "The Doctrine of Loyalty." *The New Englander* 22 (July 1863): 560–581.

Church, William C. "The Policy of Confiscation." *The Galaxy* 3 (January–April 1867): 28–35.

Cooley, Thomas M. *A Treatise on the Constitutional Limitations Which Rest Upon the Legislative Powers of the United States of the American Union.* 2nd ed. Boston: Little Brown, 1871.

Cox, Samuel S. *Union-Disunion-Reunion: Three Decades of Federal Legislation, 1855–1885.* Providence, R.I.: Reid, 1886.

Curtis, Benjamin R. *Executive Power.* Cambridge, Mass.: H. O. Houghton, 1862.

Davis, Woodbury. "Political Problems and Conditions of Peace." *Atlantic Monthly* 13 (August 1863): 252–259.

Day, L. Madison. *The Constitutionality and Legality of Confiscations in Fee, Under Act of July, 1862.* New Orleans: n.p., 1870.

Derby, Elias H. "Resources of the South." *Atlantic Monthly* 10 (October 1862): 502–510.

Farrar, Timothy. "Adequacy of the Constitution." *The New Englander* 21 (January 1862): 51–73.

———. "Congress and the Territories." *The New Englander* 21 (April 1862): 194–205.

Fisher, Sidney George. *The Trial of the Constitution.* Philadelphia: Lippincott, 1862.

Grosvenor, William M. "The Law of Conquest and the True Basis of Reconstruction." *The New Englander* 24 (January 1865): 111–131.

———. "The Rights of the Nation, and the Duty of Congress." *The New Englander* 24 (October 1865): 755–777.

Hale, E. E. "Northern Invasions." *Atlantic Monthly* 13 (February 1864): 245–250.

———. "How to Use Victory." *Atlantic Monthly* 13 (June 1864): 763–768.

Halleck, Henry W. *International Law, or, Rules Regulating the Intercourse of States in Peace and War.* 3rd ed. London: n.p., 1893.

Lieber, Francis. *Slavery Plantations, and the Yeomanry.* New York: Loyal Publication Society, 1863.

McKaye, James. *The Mastership and Its Fruits: The Emancipated Slave Face to Face with His Old Master*. New York: Loyal Publication Society, 1864.
McPherson, Edward. *The Political History of the United States of America During the Great Rebellion*. New York: Appleton & Co., 1864.
Moore, Frank. *Rebellion Record*. 10 vols. New York: G. P. Putnam, 1862.
Norton, Charles Eliot. "The Advantages of Defeat." *Atlantic Monthly* 8 (September 1861): 360–365.
Owen, Robert Dale, James McKaye, and Samuel G. Howe. "Office of American Freedmen's Inquiry Commission (Preliminary Report)." *Official Records*, ser. III, 3 (June 30, 1863): 430–454.
———. "Final Report of the American Freedmen's Inquiry Commission to the Secretary of War." *Official Records*, ser. III, 4 (May 15, 1864): 289–382.
[Parker, Joel]. "Loyalty." *North American Review* 94 (January 1862): 153–174.
———. "Constitutional Law." *North American Review* 95 (April 1862): 435–463.
———. "The Character of the Rebellion, and the Conduct of the War." *North American Review* 95 (October 1862): 500–533.
———. "The Trial of the Constitution." *North American Review* 97 (October 1863): 338–372.
Parton, James. *General Butler in New Orleans: History of the Administration of the Gulf in the Year 1862*. New York: Mason Bros., 1864.
———. *Revolution and Reconstruction*. New York: Hurd & Houghton, 1866.
Peabody, Charles A. "United States Provisional Court for the State of Louisiana, 1862–1865." *Annual Report of the American Historical Association for 1892* (Washington, D.C.: 1893): 199–210.
Pierce, Edward L. "Contrabands at Fortress Monroe." *Atlantic Monthly* 8 (November 1861): 626–640.
Sumner, Charles. "Our Domestic Relations; Or, How to Treat the Rebel States." *Atlantic Monthly* 13 (October 1863): 507–529.
Waples, Rufus. *A Treatise on Proceedings in Rem*. Chicago: Callaghan, 1882.
Whiting, William. *The War Powers of the President and the Legislative Powers of Congress in relation to Rebellion, Treason and Slavery*. 4th ed. Boston: John L. Shorey, 1863.
———. *War Powers under the Constitution of the United States: Military Arrests, Reconstruction, and Military Government*. Boston: Lee & Shepherd, 1871)

Memoirs, Diaries, Reminiscences, Collected Writings

Basler, Roy P., et al., eds. *The Collected Works of Abraham Lincoln*. 9 vols. New Brunswick, N.J.: Rutgers University Press, 1953.
Beale, Howard K., ed. *The Diary of Edward Bates, 1859–1866*. New York: Da Capo, 1971 (1933).

Beatty, John. *Memoirs of a Volunteer 1861–1863*. Ed. Harvey S. Ford. New York: Norton, 1946 (1879).

Blaine, James G. *Twenty Years of Congress: From Lincoln to Garfield*. 2 vols. Norwich, Conn.: Henry Bill, 1884.

Butler, Benjamin F. *Private and Official Correspondence of Gen. Benjamin F. Butler During the Period of the Civil War*. 5 vols. Norwood, Mass.: Plimpton Press, 1917.

Donald, David H., ed. *Inside Lincoln's Cabinet: The Civil War Diaries of Salmon P. Chase*. New York: Longmans, Green, 1954.

Doolittle, James. "A Statesman's Letters of the Civil War Period." *Journal of the Illinois State Historical Society* 2 (July 1909): 43–50.

Fleming, Walter L., ed. *Documentary History of Reconstruction*. 2 vols. New York: Peter Smith, 1950.

Foner, Philip S., ed. *The Life and Writings of Frederick Douglass*, vol. 4, *Reconstruction and After*. New York: International, 1955.

Freidel, Frank, ed. *Union Pamphlets of the Civil War, 1861–1865*. 2 vols. Cambridge, Mass.: Harvard University Press, 1967.

Graf, Leroy P., and Ralph W. Haskins, eds. *Papers of Andrew Johnson*. 16 vols. Knoxville: University of Tennessee Press, 1967– .

Howard, Oliver Otis. *Autobiography of Oliver Otis Howard*. 2 vols. New York: Baker & Taylor, 1907.

Julian, George W. *Political Recollections, 1840 to 1872*. New York: Negro Universities Press, 1970 (1884).

Meltzer, Milton, and Patricia G. Holland, eds. *Lydia Maria Child: Selected Letters, 1817–1880*. Amherst: University of Massachusetts Press, 1982.

Nevins, Allan, and Milton H. Thomas, eds. *The Diary of George Templeton Strong*. 3 vols. New York: Macmillan, 1952.

Niven, John, ed. *The Salmon P. Chase Papers*. 5 vols. Kent, Ohio: Kent State University Press, 1993–1997.

Padgett, James A. "Some Letters of George Stanton Dennison, 1854–1866: Observations of a Yankee on Conditions in Louisiana and Texas." *Louisiana Historical Quarterly* 23 (October 1940): 1132–1240.

Palmer, Beverly Wilson, ed. *The Selected Letters of Charles Sumner*. 2 vols. Boston: Northeastern University Press, 1990.

———, ed. *The Selected Papers of Thaddeus Stevens*. 2 vols. Pittsburgh: University of Pittsburgh Press, 1997.

Pease, Theodore C., and James G. Randall, eds. *The Diary of Orville Hickman Browning*. 2 vols. Springfield: Illinois State Historical Library, 1925.

Pierce, Edward L., ed. *Memoir and Letters of Charles Sumner*. 4 vols. Boston: Robert Bros., 1893.

Rice, Allen Thorndike. *Reminiscences of Abraham Lincoln by Distinguished Men of His Time.* 6th ed. New York: North American Review, 1885.
Sears, Stephen W., ed. *The Civil War Papers of George B. McClellan: Selected Correspondence, 1860–1865.* New York: Ticknor & Fields, 1989.
Simpson, Brooks D., Leroy P. Graf, and John Muldowny, eds. *Advice After Appomattox: Letters of Andrew Johnson, 1865–1866.* Knoxville: University of Tennessee Press, 1987.
Thorndike, Rachel Sherman, ed. *The Sherman Letters: Correspondence Between General Sherman and Senator Sherman from 1837 to 1891.* New York: Da Capo, 1969 (1894).
Wainwright, Nicholas B., ed. *A Philadelphia Perspective: The Diary of Sidney George Fisher Covering the Years 1834–1871.* Philadelphia: Historical Society of Pennsylvania, 1967.
Welles, Gideon. *Diary of Gideon Welles: Secretary of the Navy Under Lincoln and Johnson.* 3 vols. Boston: Houghton Mifflin, 1911.
Williams, Charles R., ed. *Diary and Letters of Rutherford Birchard Hayes.* 5 vols. Columbus: Ohio Archeological and Historical Society, 1922.

Secondary Works

Books

Abbott, Martin. *The Freedmen's Bureau in South Carolina, 1865–1872.* Chapel Hill: University of North Carolina Press, 1967.
Abbott, Richard H. *The Republican Party and the South, 1855–1877: The First Southern Strategy.* Chapel Hill: University of North Carolina Press, 1986.
Ash, Stephen V. *Middle Tennessee Society Transformed, 1860–1870: War and Peace In the Upper South.* Baton Rouge: Louisiana State University Press, 1987.
———. *When the Yankees Came Home: Conflict and Chaos in the Occupied South, 1861–1865.* Chapel Hill: University of North Carolina Press, 1995.
Bailey, Ann J., and Daniel E. Sutherland, eds. *Civil War Arkansas: Beyond Battles and Leaders.* Fayetteville: University of Arkansas Press, 2000.
Baker, Jean. *Affairs of Party: The Political Culture of Northern Democrats in the Mid-nineteenth Century.* Ithaca, N.Y.: Cornell University Press, 1983. Reprinted New York: Fordham University Press, 1998.
———. *The Politics of Continuity: Maryland Political Parties, 1858–1870.* Baltimore: Johns Hopkins University Press, 1973.
Beauregard, Erving E. *Bingham of the Hills: Politician and Diplomat Extraordinary.* New York: Peter Lang, 1989.

Belz, Herman. *Abraham Lincoln, Constitutionalism, and Equal Rights in the Civil War Era*. New York: Fordham University Press, 1998.

———. *Emancipation and Equal Rights: Politics and Constitutionalism in the Civil War Era*. New York: Norton, 1978.

———. *A New Birth of Freedom: The Republican Party and Negro Rights, 1861–1866*. Westport, Conn.: Greenwood Press, 1976. Reprinted New York: Fordham University Press, 2000.

———. *Reconstructing the Union: Theory and Policy during the Civil War*. Ithaca, N.Y.: Cornell University Press, 1969.

Benedict, Michael Les. *A Compromise of Principle: Congressional Republicans and Reconstruction, 1863–1869*. New York: Norton, 1974.

Bentley, George R. *A History of the Freedmen's Bureau*. Philadelphia: University of Pennsylvania Press, 1955.

Berlin, Ira, et al. *Slaves No More: Three Essays on Emancipation and Civil War*. New York: Cambridge University Press, 1992.

———, ed. *Free at Last: A Documentary History of Slavery, Freedom and Civil War*. New York: Free Press, 1992.

———, et al. *Freedom: A Documentary History of Emancipation 1861–1867*, ser. 1, vol. 1, *The Destruction of Slavery*. New York: Cambridge University Press, 1985.

———, et al. *Freedom: A Documentary History of Emancipation 1861–1867*, ser. 1, vol. 2, *The Wartime Genesis of Free Labor: The Upper South*. New York: Cambridge University Press, 1993.

———, et al. *Freedom: A Documentary History of Emancipation 1861–1867*, ser. 1, vol. 3, *The Wartime Genesis of Free Labor: The Lower South*. New York: Cambridge University Press, 1990.

———, et al. *Freedom: A Documentary History of Emancipation 1861–1867*, ser. 2, *The Black Military Experience*. New York: Cambridge University Press, 1982.

Berry, Mary. *Military Necessity and Civil Rights Policy: Black Citizenship and the Constitution, 1861–1868*. Port Washington, N.Y.: Kennikat Press, 1977.

Bilotta, James D. *Race and the Rise of the Republican Party, 1848–1865*. New York: Peter Lang, 1992.

Birkhimer, William E. *Military Government and Martial Law*. 3rd ed. Kansas City, Mo.: Franklin Hudson, 1914.

Blight, David W., and Brooks D. Simpson, eds. *Union and Emancipation: Essays on Politics and Race in the Civil War Era*. Kent, Ohio: Kent State University Press, 1977.

Bogue, Allan G. *The Congressman's Civil War*. New York: Cambridge University Press, 1989.

———. *The Earnest Men: Republicans of the Civil War Senate.* Ithaca, N.Y.: Cornell University Press, 1981.

Boritt, Gabor S. *Lincoln and the Economics of the American Dream.* Memphis: Memphis State University Press, 1978.

Bowen, David W. *Andrew Johnson and the Negro.* Knoxville: University of Tennessee Press, 1989.

Butchart, Ronald E. *Northern Schools, Southern Blacks, and Reconstruction: Freedmen's Education, 1862–1875.* Westport, Conn.: Greenwood Press, 1980.

Cain, Marvin R. *Lincoln's Attorney General: Edward Bates of Missouri.* Columbia: University of Missouri Press, 1965.

Carpenter, John A. *The Sword and the Olive Branch: Oliver Otis Howard.* Pittsburgh: University of Pittsburgh Press, 1964.

Cimbala, Paul A. *Under the Guardianship of the Nation: The Freedmen's Bureau and the Reconstruction of Georgia.* Athens: University of Georgia Press, 1997.

Cimbala, Paul A., and Randall M. Miller, eds. *The Freedmen's Bureau and Reconstruction.* New York: Fordham University Press, 1999.

Cimprich, John. *Slavery's End in Tennessee, 1861–1865.* University: University of Alabama Press, 1985.

Cohen, William. *At Freedom's Edge: Black Mobility and the Southern White Quest for Racial Control, 1861–1915.* Baton Rouge: Louisiana State University Press, 1991.

Cooper, William J. Jr. *Jefferson Davis, American.* New York: Vintage Books, 2000.

Coulter, E. Merton. *The Civil War and Readjustment in Kentucky.* Chapel Hill: University of North Carolina Press, 1926.

———. *William G. Brownlow: Fighting Parson of the Southern Highlands.* Knoxville: University of Tennessee Press, 1971 (1937).

Cox, LaWanda. *Lincoln and Black Freedom: A Study of Presidential Leadership.* Columbia: University of South Carolina Press, 1981.

Curry, Leonard P. *Blueprint of Modern America: Non-military Legislation of the First Civil War Congress.* Nashville: Vanderbilt University Press, 1968.

Davis, William W. *The Civil War and Reconstruction in Florida.* New York: Longmans, Green, 1913.

Donald, David H. *Charles Sumner and the Rights of Man.* New York: Da Capo, 1996.

———. *Lincoln.* New York: Simon & Schuster, 1995.

Dorris, Jonathan T. *Pardon and Amnesty Under Lincoln and Johnson: The Restoration of the Confederates to Their Rights and Privileges, 1861–1898.* Westport, Conn.: Greenwood Press, 1977 (1953).

Drago, Edmund L. *Black Politicians and Reconstruction in Georgia: A Splendid Failure*. Baton Rouge: Louisiana State University Press, 1982.

DuBois, W. E. B. *Black Reconstruction*. Millwood, N.Y.: Kraus-Thomson, 1963 (1935).

Duncan, Russell. *Freedom's Shore: Tunis Campbell and the Georgia Freedmen*. Athens: University of Georgia Press, 1986.

Dunning, William A. *Essays on the Civil War and Reconstruction and Related Topics*. New York: Macmillan, 1904.

Dusinberre, William. *Civil War Issues in Philadelphia, 1856–1865*. Philadelphia: University of Pennsylvania Press, 1965.

Engs, Robert F. *Freedom's First Generation: Black Hampton, Virginia, 1861–1890*. Philadelphia: University of Pennsylvania Press, 1979. Reprinted New York: Fordham University Press, 2004.

Fairman, Charles. *The History of the Supreme Court of the United States*, vol. 6, *Reconstruction and Reunion, 1864–88*. New York: Macmillan, 1971.

Fehrenbacher, Don E. *The Dred Scott Case: Its Significance in American Law and Politics*. New York: Oxford University Press, 1978.

Field, Phyllis F. *The Politics of Race in New York: The Struggle for Black Equality in the Civil War Era*. Ithaca, N.Y.: Cornell University Press, 1982.

Finley, Randy. *From Slavery to Uncertain Freedom: The Freemen's Bureau in Arkansas, 1865–1869*. Fayetteville: University of Arkansas Press, 1996.

Fisher, Noel C. *War at Every Door: Partisan Politics and Guerrilla Violence in East Tennessee, 1860–1869*. Chapel Hill: University of North Carolina Press, 1997.

Foner, Eric. *Reconstruction: America's Unfinished Revolution, 1863–1877*. New York: Harper & Row, 1988.

Freidel, Frank. *Francis Lieber: Nineteenth Century Liberal*. Baton Rouge: Louisiana State University Press, 1947.

Gathings, James A. *International Law and American Treatment of Alien Enemy Property*. Washington, D.C.: Council on Public Affairs, 1940.

Gerteis, Louis S. *From Contraband to Freedman: Federal Policy Toward Southern Blacks, 1861–1865*. Westport, Conn.: Greenwood Press, 1973.

Graber, Dorris A. *The Development of the Law of Belligerent Occupation, 1863–1914*. New York: Columbia University Press, 1949.

Grimsley, Mark. *The Hard Hand of War: Union Military Policy Toward Southern Civilians, 1861–1865*. New York: Cambridge University Press, 1995.

Guelzo, Allen G. *Lincoln's Emancipation Proclamation: The End of Slavery in America*. New York: Simon & Schuster, 2004.

Harris, William C. *With Charity for All: Lincoln and the Restoration of the Union*. Lexington: University of Kentucky Press, 1997.

Hearn, Chester G. *When the Devil Came Down to Dixie: Ben Butler in New Orleans*. Baton Rouge: Louisiana State University Press, 1997.

Hess, Earl J. *Liberty, Virtue, and Progress: Northerners and Their War for the Union*. 2nd ed. New York: Fordham University Press, 1997.

Hollandsworth, James G. Jr. *Pretense of Glory: The Life of Nathaniel P. Banks*. Baton Rouge: Louisiana State University Press, 1998.

Horowitz, Robert F. *The Great Impeacher: A Political Biography of James M. Ashley*. New York: Brooklyn College Press, 1979.

Howard, Victor B. *Religion and the Radical Republican Movement, 1860–1870*. Lexington: University of Kentucky Press, 1990.

Hyman, Harold M. *A More Perfect Union: The Impact of the Civil War and Reconstruction on the Constitution*. New York: Knopf, 1973.

Hyman, Harold M., and William M. Wiecek. *Equal Justice Under Law: Constitutional Development 1835–1875*. New York: Harper & Row, 1982.

Jellison, Charles A. *Fessenden of Maine: Civil War Senator*. Syracuse, N.Y.: Syracuse University Press, 1962.

Johnson, James Turner. *Just War Tradition and the Restraint of War: A Moral and Historical Inquiry*. Princeton, N.J.: Princeton University Press, 1981.

Lingaman, William K. *Abraham Lincoln and the Road to Emancipation, 1861–1865*. New York: Viking Press, 2001.

Lucie, Patricia Allan. *Freedom and Federalism: Congress and Courts, 1862–1866*. New York: Garland, 1986.

Magdol, Edward. *A Right to the Land: Essays on the Freedmen's Community*. Westport, Conn.: Greenwood Press, 1977.

McCrary, Peyton. *Abraham Lincoln and Reconstruction: The Louisiana Experiment*. Princeton, N.J.: Princeton University Press, 1978.

McFeely, William S. *Yankee Stepfather: General O. O. Howard and the Freedmen*. New York: Norton, 1970.

McPherson, James M. *Battle Cry of Freedom: The Civil War Era*. New York: Oxford University Press, 1988.

———. *The Negro's Civil War: How American Negroes Felt and Acted During the War for the Union*. New York: Pantheon Books, 1965.

———. *Ordeal By Fire: The Civil War and Reconstruction*. 2nd ed. New York: McGraw Hill, 1992.

———. *The Struggle for Equality: Abolitionists and the Negro in the Civil War and Reconstruction*. Princeton, N.J.: Princeton University Press, 1964.

———. *What They Fought For, 1861–1865*. Baton Rouge: Louisiana State University Press, 1994.

Messner, William F. *Freedom and the Ideology of Free Labor: Louisiana, 1862–1865*. Lafayette: University of Southwestern Louisiana, 1978.

Moneyhon, Carl H. *The Impact of the Civil War and Reconstruction on Arkansas: Persistence in the Midst of Ruin.* Baton Rouge: Louisiana State University Press, 1994.

Nieman, Donald G. *To Set the Law in Motion: The Freedmen's Bureau and the Legal Rights of Blacks, 1865–1868.* Millwood, N.Y.: KTO Press, 1979.

Niven, John. *Salmon P. Chase: A Biography.* New York: Oxford University Press, 1995.

Oubre, Claude F. *Forty Acres and a Mule: The Freedmen's Bureau and Black Land Ownership.* Baton Rouge: Louisiana State University Press, 1978.

Paludan, Phillip S. *A Covenant with Death: The Constitution, Law, and Equality in the Civil War Era.* Urbana: University of Illinois Press, 1975.

———. *"A People's Contest": The Union and the Civil War, 1861–1865.* 2nd ed. New York: Harper & Row, 1996.

———. *The Presidency of Abraham Lincoln.* Lawrence: University Press of Kansas, 1994.

Parrish, William E. *Frank Blair: Lincoln's Conservative.* Columbia: University of Missouri Press, 1998.

Peirce, Paul S. *The Freedmen's Bureau: A Chapter in the History of Reconstruction.* Iowa City: University of Iowa, 1904.

Rabinowitz, Howard N., ed. *Southern Black Leaders of the Reconstruction Era.* Urbana: University of Illinois Press, 1982.

Randall, James G. *The Confiscation of Property During the Civil War.* Indianapolis: Mutual Printing and Lithographing, 1913.

———. *Constitutional Problems Under Lincoln.* Rev. ed. Urbana: University of Illinois Press, 1964.

Reid, Ronald. *Edward Everett: Unionist Orator.* Westport, Conn.: Greenwood Press, 1990.

Renda, Lex. *Running on the Record: Civil War Era Politics in New Hampshire.* Charlottesville: University Press of Virginia, 1997.

Richardson, Heather Cox. *The Death of Reconstruction: Race, Labor, and Politics in the Post Civil War North, 1865–1901.* Cambridge, Mass.: Harvard University Press, 2001.

———. *The Greatest Nation of the Earth: Republican Economic Policies During the Civil War.* Cambridge, Mass.: Harvard University Press, 1997.

Ripley, C. Peter. *Slaves and Freedmen in Civil War Louisiana.* Baton Rouge: Louisiana State University Press, 1976.

Rose, Willie Lee. *Rehearsal for Reconstruction: The Port Royal Experiment.* New York: Vintage Books, 1967.

Roske, Ralph J. *His Own Counsel: The Life and Times of Lyman Trumbull.* Reno: University of Nevada Press, 1979.

Saville, Julie. *The Work of Reconstruction: From Slave to Wage Laborer in South Carolina, 1860–1870*. New York: Cambridge University Press, 1994.

Shankman, Arnold M. *The Pennsylvania Antiwar Movement, 1861–1865*. Rutherford, N.J.: Fairleigh Dickinson University Press, 1980.

Shapiro, Henry D. *Confiscation of Confederate Property in the North*. Ithaca, N.Y.: Cornell University Press, 1962.

Silbey, Joel H. *A Respectable Minority: The Democratic Party in the Civil War Era, 1860–1868*. New York: Norton, 1977.

Simpson, Brooks D. *The Reconstruction Presidents*. Lawrence: University Press of Kansas, 1998.

Tap, Bruce. *Over Lincoln's Shoulder: The Committee on the Conduct of the War*. Lawrence: University Press of Kansas, 1998.

Thomas, Benjamin P., and Harold M. Hyman, *Stanton: The Life and Times of Lincoln's Secretary of War*. New York: Knopf, 1962.

Trefousse, Hans L. *Andrew Johnson: A Biography*. New York: Norton, 1989.

———. *Thaddeus Stevens: Nineteenth Century Egalitarian*. Chapel Hill: University of North Carolina Press, 1997.

Tunnell, Ted. *Crucible of Reconstruction: War, Radicalism and Race in Louisiana, 1862–1877*. Baton Rouge: Louisiana State University Press, 1984.

Voegeli, V. Jacque. *Free But Not Equal: The Midwest and the Negro During the Civil War*. Chicago: University of Chicago Press, 1967.

Ware, Edith Ellen. *Political Opinion in Massachusetts During Civil War and Reconstruction*. New York: Longmans, Green, 1916.

Articles and Dissertations

Abbott, Martin. "Free Land, Free Labor, and the Freedmen's Bureau." *Agricultural History* 30 (October 1956): 150–156.

Abzug, Robert H. "The Copperheads: Historical Approaches to Civil War Dissent in the Midwest." *Indiana Magazine of History* 60 (March 1970): 40–55.

Adams, David W. "Illinois Soldiers and the Emancipation Proclamation." *Journal of the Illinois Historical Association* 67 (September 1974): 407–421.

Ahern, Joseph J. "Prize Rules: Civil War Prize Procedure in the Philadelphia Prize Court, 1861–1865." *The American Neptune* 58 (Fall 1998): 342–352.

Ahern, Wilbert H. "Laissez Faire vs. Equal Rights: Liberal Republicans and the Limits to Reconstruction." *Phylon* 40 (March 1979): 52–65.

Alvis, John. "The Slavery Provisions of the U.S. Constitution: Means for Emancipation." *Political Science Reviewer* 17 (Fall 1987): 240–265.

Ames, Susie M. "Federal Policy Toward the Eastern Shore of Virginia in 1861." *Virginia Magazine of History and Biography* 69 (October 1961): 432–459.

Armstrong, Thomas F. "From Task Labor to Free Labor: The Transition Along Georgia's Rice Coast, 1820–1880." *Georgia Historical Quarterly* 64 (Winter 1980): 432–447.

Baker, Jean H. "A Loyal Opposition: Northern Democrats in the Thirty-Seventh Congress." *Civil War History* 25 (June 1979): 139–155.

Barnhart, John D. "The Impact of the Civil War on Indiana." *Indiana Magazine of History* 57 (September 1961): 185–224.

Beck, Warren A. "Lincoln and Negro Colonization in Central America." *Abraham Lincoln Quarterly* 6 (September 1950): 162–183.

Belz, Herman. "Abraham Lincoln and American Constitutionalism." *Review of Politics* 50 (Spring 1988): 169–197.

———. "The Freedmen's Bureau Act of 1865 and the Principle of No Discrimination to Color." *Civil War History* 21 (September 1975): 197–217.

———. "The New Orthodoxy in Reconstruction Historiography." *Reviews of American History* 1 (March 1973): 106–113.

———. "The Protection of Personal Liberty in Republican Emancipation Legislation in 1862." *Journal of Southern History* 42 (August 1976): 383–400.

Benedict, Michael Les. "The Constitution of the Lincoln Presidency and the Republican Era." In Martin Fausold and Alan Shank, eds., *The Constitution and the American Presidency* (Albany: State University of New York Press, 1991), 45–61.

———. "Equality and Expediency in the Reconstruction Era: A Review Essay." *Civil War History* 23 (December 1977): 322–335.

———. "Laissez-Faire and Liberty: A Re-Evaluation of the Meaning and Origins of Laissez-Faire Constitutionalism." *Law and History Review* 3 (Fall 1985): 293–331.

———. "Preserving the Constitution: The Conservative Basis of Radical Reconstruction." *Journal of American History* 61 (June 1974): 65–90.

———. "The Rout of Radicalism: Republicans and the Election of 1867." *Civil War History* 18 (December 1972): 334–344.

Bentley, George R. "The Political Activity of the Freedmen's Bureau in Florida." *Florida Historical Quarterly* 28 (1949–50): 28–37.

Berlin, Ira. "Emancipation and Its Meaning in American Life." *Reconstruction* 2, no. 3 (1994): 41–44.

———. "Who Freed the Slaves? Emancipation and Its Meaning," in David W. Blight and Brooks D. Simpson, eds., *Union and Emancipation: Essays on Politics and Race in the Civil War Era* (Kent, Ohio: Kent State University Press, 1977), 105–125.

Berlin, Ira, et al. "'To Canvass the Nation': The War for Union Becomes a War for Freedom," *Prologue* 20 (Winter 1988): 227–47.

Berwanger, Eugene H. "Lincoln's Constitutional Dilemma: Emancipation and Black Suffrage." *Papers of Abraham Lincoln Association* 5 (1983): 25–38.

Bethel, Elizabeth. "The Freedmen's Bureau in Alabama." *Journal of Southern History* 14 (February 1948): 49–92.

Blight, David W. "Frederick Douglass and the American Apocalypse." *Civil War History* 31 (December 1985): 309–328.

Bogue, Allan G. "Bloc and Party in the United States Senate, 1861–1863." *Civil War History* 13 (September 1967): 221–241.

———. "Historians and Radical Republicans: A Meaning for Today." *Journal of American History* 70 (June 1983): 7–34.

———. "The Radical Voting Dimension in the U. S. Senate During the Civil War." *Journal of Interdisciplinary History* 3 (Winter 1973): 449–474.

Bonekemper, Edward H. "Negro Ownership of Real Property in Hampton and Elizabeth City County, Virginia, 1860–1870." *Journal of Negro History* 55 (July 1970): 165–181.

Boritt, Gabor S. "The Voyage of the Colony Linconia: The Sixteenth President, Black Colonization, and the Defense Mechanism of Avoidance." *The Historian* 37 (August 1975): 619–632.

Bowen, David W. "Andrew Johnson and the Negro." *East Tennessee Historical Society Publications* 40 (1968): 28–49.

Boyd, Willis D. "Negro Colonization in the Reconstruction Era, 1865–1870." *Georgia Historical Quarterly* 20 (December 1956): 360–382.

Bright, Thomas R. "Yankee in Arms: The Civil War Era as a Personal Experience." *Civil War History* 19 (September 1973): 197–218.

Brinsfield, John W. "The Military Ethics of General William T. Sherman: A Reassessment." In Lloyd J. Matthews and Dale E. Brown, eds., *Parameters of War: Military History from the Journal of the U.S. Army War College* (Washington, D.C.: Pergamon-Brassey, 1997), 87–103.

Brock, Euline W. "Thomas W. Cardozo: Fallible Black Reconstruction Leader." *Journal of Southern History* 47 (May 1981): 183–206.

Byrne, Frank L. "'A Terrible Machine': General Neal Dow's Military Government on the Gulf Coast." *Civil War History* 12 (March 1966): 5–22.

Campbell, James B. "East Tennessee During the Federal Occupation, 1863–1865." *East Tennessee Historical Society Publications* 19 (1947): 64–80.

Carnahan, Burrus M. "Lincoln, Lieber and the Laws of War: The Origins and Limits of the Principle of Military Necessity." *American Journal of International Law* 92 (April 1998): 213–231.

Carpenter, A. H. "Military Government of Southern Territory, 1861–1865." *Annual Report of the American Historical Association of 1900* (Washington, D.C., 1901): 465–498.

Castel, Albert. "Civil War Kansas and the Negro." *Journal of Negro History* 51 (April 1966): 125–138.

Childress, James F. "Francis Lieber's Interpretation of the Laws of War: General Orders No. 100 in the Context of His Life and Thought." *The American Journal of Jurisprudence* 21 (1976): 34–70.

Cimbala, Paul A. "A Black Colony in Dougherty County: The Freedmen's Bureau and the Failure of Reconstruction in Southwest Georgia." *Journal of Southwest Georgia History* 4 (Fall 1986): 72–89.

———. "The Freedmen's Bureau, the Freedmen, and Sherman's Grant in Reconstruction Georgia, 1865–1867." *Journal of Southern History* 55 (November 1989): 597–632.

———. "On the Front Line of Freedom: Freedmen's Bureau Officers and Agents in Reconstruction Georgia, 1865–1868." *Georgia Historical Quarterly* 76 (Fall 1992): 577–611.

———. "The Talisman Power': Davis Tillson, the Freedmen's Bureau, and Free Labor in Reconstruction Georgia, 1865–1866." *Civil War History* 28 (June 1982): 153–171.

Cimprich, John. "Military Governor Johnson and Tennessee Blacks, 1862–65." *Tennessee Historical Quarterly* 34 (1980): 459–470.

Clarke, Robert L. "Northern Plans for the Economic Invasion of Florida, 1862–1865." *Florida Historical Quarterly* 28 (April 1950): 262–270.

Cohen, William. "Black Immobility and Free Labor: The Freedmen's Bureau and the Relocation of Black Labor, 1865–1868." *Civil War History* 30 (September 1984): 221–234.

Connor, William P. "Reconstruction Rebels: The *New Orleans Tribune* in Post-War Louisiana." *Louisiana History* 21 (Spring 1980): 159–181.

Coulter, E. Merton. "Commercial Intercourse with the Confederacy in the Mississippi Valley, 1861–1865." *Mississippi Valley Historical Review* 5 (March 1919): 377–395.

———. "Tunis G. Campbell, Negro Reconstructionist in Georgia." *Georgia Historical Quarterly* 51 (December 1967): 401–424.

Cox, LaWanda. "Lincoln and Black Freedom." In Gabor S. Boritt, ed., *The Historian's Lincoln: Pseudo-History, Psychohistory and History* (Urbana: University of Illinois Press, 1988), 175–208.

———. "The Promise of Land for the Freedmen," *Mississippi Historical Review* 45 (December 1958): 413–40.

Cox, LaWanda, and John H. Cox. "Andrew Johnson and His Ghost Writers: An Analysis of the Freedmen's Bureau and Civil Rights Veto Messages." *Mississippi Valley Historical Review* 48 (December 1961): 460–479.

———. "Negro Suffrage and Republican Politics: The Problem of Motivation in Reconstruction Historiography." *Journal of Southern History* 33 (August 1967): 303–330.

Curry, Leonard P. "Congressional Democrats: 1861–1863." *Civil War History* 12 (September 1966): 213–239.

Curry, Richard O. "The Abolitionists and Reconstruction: A Critical Appraisal." *Journal of Southern History* 34 (November 1968): 427–445.

———. "The Civil War and Reconstruction, 1861–1877: A Critical Review of Recent Trends and Interpretations." *Civil War History* 24 (September 1974): 215–238.

———. "The Union As It Was: A Critique of Recent Interpretations of the 'Copperheads.'" *Civil War History* 13 (March 1967): 25–39.

Dean, Eric T. Jr. "Rethinking the Civil War: Beyond 'Revolution,' 'Reconstructions,' And the 'New Social History.'" *Southern Historian* 15 (Spring 1994): 28–50.

Dirck, Brian R. "Posterity's Blush: Civil Liberties, Property Rights, and Property Confiscation in the Confederacy." *Civil War History* 48 (September 2002): 237–256.

Donald, David. "Devils Facing Zionwards." In Grady McWhiney, ed., *Grant, Lee, Lincoln and the Radicals* (Evanston, Ill.: Northwestern University Press, 1964), 72–91.

Dowd, Morgan D. "Lincoln, the Rule of Law and Crisis Government: A Study of His Constitutional Law Theories." *University of Detroit Law Journal* 39 (June 1962): 633–649.

Drago, Edmund L. "How Sherman's March Through Georgia Affected the Slaves." *Georgia Historical Quarterly* 57 (Fall 1973): 361–375.

Dyer, Brainerd. "Francis Lieber and the American Civil War." *Huntington Library Quarterly* 2 (July 1939): 449–465.

Elazar, Daniel J. "Civil War and the Preservation of American Federalism." *Publius* 1 (Fall 1971): 39–58.

Ellis, L. E. "The *Chicago Times* During the Civil War." *Illinois State Historical Society Transactions for the Year 1932* 39 (1933): 135–181.

Farnham, Wallace D. "'The Weakened Spring of Government': A Study in Nineteenth- Century American History." *American Historical Review* 68 (April 1963): 662–680.

Fisher, Noel C. "'Prepare Them for My Coming': General William T. Sherman, Total War, and Pacification in West Tennessee." *Tennessee Historical Quarterly* 51 (Summer 1992): 75–85.

Fleischman, Richard K. "The Devil's Advocate: A Defense of Lincoln's Attitude Toward the Negro, 1837–1863." *Lincoln Herald* 81 (Fall 1979): 172–186.

Fleming, Walter L. "Forty Acres and a Mule." *North American Review* 182 (1906): 721–737.

Foner, Eric. "Reconstruction and the Crisis of Free Labor." In Eric Foner, ed., *Politics and Ideology in the Age of the Civil War* (New York: Oxford University Press, 1980), 97–127.

———. "Thaddeus Stevens, Confiscation, and Reconstruction." In Eric McKitrick and Stanley Elkins, eds., *The Hofstadter Aegis: A Memorial* (New York: Knopf, 1974), 154–183.

Frederick, Duke. "The Second Confiscation Act: A Chapter of Civil War Politics." Ph.D. diss. University of Chicago, 1966.

Freidel, Frank. "General Orders 100 and Military Government." *Mississippi Valley Historical Review* 32 (March 1946): 541–556.

Gerteis, Louis S. "Salmon P. Chase, Radicalism, and the Politics of Emancipation, 1861–1864." *Journal of American History* 60 (June 1973): 42–62.

Gottlieb, Manuel. "The Land Question in Georgia During Reconstruction." *Science and Society* 3 (Summer 1939): 356–388.

Greenberg, Kenneth S. "The Civil War and the Redistribution of Land: Adams County, Mississippi, 1860–1870." *Agricultural History* 52 (April 1978): 292–307.

Harris, William C. "Andrew Johnson's First 'Swing Around the Circle': His Northern Campaign of 1863." *Civil War History* 35 (June 1989): 153–171.

Helis, Thomas W. "Of Generals and Jurists: The Judicial System of New Orleans Under Union Occupation, May 1862–April 1865." *Louisiana History* 29 (Spring 1988): 143–162.

Hess, Earl J. "Confiscation and the Northern War Effort: The Army of the Southwest at Helena." *Arkansas Historical Quarterly* 44 (Spring 1985): 56–75.

Hoffnagle, Warren. "The Southern Homestead Act: Its Origins and Operation." *The Historian* 32 (August 1970): 612–629.

Holt, Michael F. "Abraham Lincoln and the Politics of Union." In John L. Thomas, ed., *Abraham Lincoln and the American Political Tradition* (Amherst: University of Massachusetts Press, 1986), 111–141.

Horowitz, Murray M. "Ben Butler and the Negro: 'Miracles Are Occurring.'" *Louisiana History* 17 (Spring 1976): 159–186.

Horowitz, Robert F. "Land to the Freedmen: A Vision of Reconstruction." *Ohio History* 86 (Summer 1977): 189–199.

Hume, Richard L. "Negro Delegates to the State Constitutional Conventions." In Howard N. Rabinowitz, ed. *Southern Black Leaders of the Reconstruction Era* (Urbana: University of Illinois Press, 1982), 129–153.

Johnson, Howard Palmer. "New Orleans Under General Butler." *Louisiana Historical Quarterly* 24 (January–October 1941): 434–536.

Johnson, Ludwell H. "Contraband Trade During the Last Year of the Civil War." *Mississippi Valley Historical Review* 49 (March 1963): 635–652.

Kaczorowski, Robert J. "Revolutionary Constitutionalism in the Era of the Civil War and Reconstruction." *New York University Law Review* 61 (October 1986): 863–940.

———. "To Begin the Nation Anew: Congress, Citizenship, and Civil Rights After the Civil War." *American Historical Review* 92 (February 1987): 45–68.

Klement, Frank L. "Midwestern Opposition to Lincoln's Emancipation Policy." *Journal Negro History* 49 (July 1964): 169–183.

Lanza, Michael L. "'One of the Most Appreciated Labors of the Bureau': The Freedmen's Bureau and the Southern Homestead Act." In Paul A. Cimbala and Randall M. Miller, eds., *The Freedmen's Bureau and Reconstruction* (New York: Fordham University Press, 1999), 67–92.

Lucie, Patricia M. "Confiscation: Constitutional Crossroads." *Civil War History* 23 (December 1977): 307–321.

Maltz, Earl. "Reconstruction Without Revolution: Republican Civil Rights Theory in the Era of the Fourteenth Amendment." *Houston Law Review* 24 (March 1987): 221–279.

McCrary, Peyton. "The Party of Revolution: Republican Ideas About Politics and Social Change, 1862–1867." *Civil War History* 30 (December 1984): 330–350.

McKitrick, Eric L. "Party Politics and the Union and Confederate War Efforts." In William N. Chambers and Walter D. Burnham, eds., *The American Party Systems: States of Political Development* (New York: Oxford University Press, 1967), 117–151.

McPherson, James M. "The Ballot and Land for the Freedmen, 1861–1865." In Kenneth M. Stampp and Leon F. Litwack, eds., *Reconstruction: An Anthology of Revisionist Writings* (Baton Rouge: Louisiana State University Press, 1969), 139–158.

———. "From Limited to Total War: Missouri and the Nation, 1861–1865." *Gateway Heritage* 12 (Spring 1992): 4–19.

———. "Who Freed the Slaves?" In James M. McPherson, ed., *Drawn with the Sword* (New York: Oxford University Press, 1996), 192–207.

Moneyhon, Carl H. "The Impact of the Civil War in Arkansas: The Mississippi River Plantation Counties." *Arkansas Historical Quarterly* 51 (Summer 1992): 105–118.

Neely, Mark E. Jr. "Lincoln and the Theory of Self-Emancipation." In John Y. Simon and Barbara Hughett, eds., *The Continuing Civil War: Essays in Honor of the Civil War Round Table in Chicago* (Dayton, Ohio: Morningside, 1992), 45–59.

Oates, Stephen B. "'The Man of Our Redemption': Abraham Lincoln and the Emancipation of the Slaves." *Presidential Studies* 9 (Winter 1979): 15–25.

Ochiai, Akiko. "The Port Royal Experiment Revisited: Northern Visions of Reconstruction and the Land Question." *New England Quarterly* 74 (March 2001): 94–117.

Parrillo, Nicholas. "Lincoln's Calvinist Transformation: Emancipation and War." *Civil War History* 46 (September 2000): 227–253.

Pickens, Donald K. "The Republican Synthesis and Thaddeus Stevens." *Civil War History* 31 (March 1985): 57–73.

Planck, George R. "Abraham Lincoln and Black Colonization: Theory and Practice." *Lincoln Herald* 72 (Summer 1970): 61–77.

Pope, Christie F. "Southern Homesteads for Negroes." *Agricultural History* 44 (April 1970): 201–212.

Powell, Lawrence N. "The American Land Company and Agency: John A. Andrew and the Northernization of the South." *Civil War History* 21 (December 1975): 293–308.

Randall, James G. "Captured and Abandoned Property During the Civil War." *American Historical Review* 19 (October 1913): 65–79.

———. "Some Legal Aspects of the Confiscation Acts of the Civil War." *American Historical Review* 18 (October 1912): 79–96.

Riddleberger, Patrick W. "George W. Julian: Abolitionist Land Reformer." *Agricultural History* 29 (July 1955): 108–115.

———. "The Radicals' Abandonment of the Negro During Reconstruction." *Journal of Negro History* 45 (April 1960): 88–102.

Rosenberg, John S. "Toward a New Civil War Revisionism." *The American Scholar* 38 (Spring 1969): 250–272.

Ross, Steven Joseph. "Freed Soil, Freed Labor, Freed Men: John Easton and the Davis Bend Experiment." *Journal of Southern History* 44 (May 1978): 213–232.

Shoftner, Jerrell H. "Andrew Johnson and the Fernandina Unionists." *Prologue* 10 (Winter 1978): 211–223.

Shover, Kenneth B. "Maverick at Bay: Ben Wade's Senate Re-election Campaign, 1862–1863." *Civil War History* 12 (March 1966): 23–42.

Silverman, Jason H. "'In Isles Beyond the Main': Abraham Lincoln's Philosophy on Black Colonization." *Lincoln Herald* 80 (Fall 1978): 15–22.

Simpson, Brooks D. "'The Doom of Slavery': Ulysses S. Grant, War Aims, and Emancipation, 1861–1863." *Civil War History* 36 (March 1990): 36–56.

Smith, George Winston. "Carpetbag Imperialism in Florida 1862–1868." *Florida Historical Quarterly* 27 (October 1948–January 1949): 99–130, 260–299.

Sutherland, Daniel E. "Abraham Lincoln, John Pope, and the Origins of Total War." *Journal of Military History* 56 (October 1992): 567–586.

Syrett, John. "The Confiscation Acts: Efforts at Reconstruction During the Civil War." Ph.D. diss., University of Wisconsin, 1971.

———. "The Confiscation Acts: The North Strikes Back." In Paul A. Cimbala and Randall M. Miller, eds., *An Uncommon Time: The Civil War on the Northern Home Front* (New York: Fordham University Press, 2002), 280–325.

Tap, Bruce. "Race, Rhetoric, and Emancipation: The Election of 1862 in Illinois." *Civil War History* 39 (June 1993): 101–125.

Thornbrough, Emma Lou. "The Race Issue in Indiana Politics During the Civil War." *Indiana Magazine of History* 47 (June 1951): 169–190.

Trefousse, Hans L. "Owen Lovejoy and Abraham Lincoln During the Civil War." *Journal of the Abraham Lincoln Association* 22 (Winter 2001): 16–32.

Tregle, Joseph H. "Thomas J. Durant, Utopian Socialism, and the Failure of Presidential Reconstruction." *Journal of Southern History* 45 (November 1979): 485–512.

Tunnell, Ted. "Free Negroes and the Freedmen: Black Politics in New Orleans During the Civil War." *Southern Studies* 19 (Spring 1980): 5–28.

Vorenberg, Michael. "Abraham Lincoln and the Politics of Colonization." *Journal of the Abraham Lincoln Association* 14 (Summer 1993): 23–45.

Westwood, Howard C. "Sherman Marched—And Proclaimed 'Land for the Landless.'" *South Carolina Historical Magazine* 85 (January 1984): 33–50.

White, Kenneth B. "Wager Swayne: Racist or Realist?" *Alabama Review* 31 (April 1978): 92–109.

Woodward, C. Vann. "Seeds of Failure in Radical Race Policy." In *American Counterpoint: Slavery and Racism in the North-South Dialogue* (Boston: Little, Brown, 1971), 163–183.

Index